France 1814-1919 Th
A Liberal Democratic ety

John B Wolf

FRANCE: *1814-1919*

The Rise of a Liberal-Democratic Society

BY JOHN B. WOLF

HARPER TORCHBOOKS
The University Library
Harper & Row, Publishers, Inc
New York, Evanston, and London

values that western European men had developed in the preceding century. As I wrote the preface to the first edition, it was abundantly clear that the story of France since the fall of Napoleon could best be explained in terms of the emergence of liberal-democratic institutions, but only the last sentence in Chapter XIV gave any indication of the fact that the story that I had written should terminate in 1919.[1] This volume is a study of the development of the complex of laws, institutions, customs, and ideas associated with the liberal-democratic compromise, which was, in effect, the adjustment of the forces released by the French revolution in the society and civilization of France that was already ancient in 1789 The history of France since 1919, however, should be told in other terms Charles Péguy understood on the eve of 1914 that the France of his youth was on the verge of a new series of crises, but he could never have foreseen the terrible problems that his France was to face in the years following his death at the front.

Post-Versailles French civilization has had several ingredients that were either missing or only partly matured in the nineteenth century. The most important, of course, was the war of 1914-1918, so destructive of institutions and values It had dislocated markets and economic relationships, had assaulted men's spirits, confronted their mystiques, and finally compulsively taught the specious lesson of totalitarian organization as the panacea for social crisis. There was hardly a level of human activity left undisturbed, and the millions of young Frenchmen dead or maimed physically or spiritually made it evident that the problems would not easily be solved. Another factor that had not been so important earlier was the new industrial system that followed the war. France had not moved as fast as her neighbors in the direction of industrial reorganization. This problem is explored in Chapter XIII in which we see how traditional economic forms and political policies combined with problems of raw materials to put heavy brakes on the adoption of "modern" industrial technology. The

[1] This edition does, in fact, do this, since we have omitted the last chapter of the original book

World Fair in Paris at the turn of the century caused some French observers to question the future, but it wasn't until after the War of 1914–1918 that the plight of French economy became drastic The war taught Americans, Germans, Japanese, and others to apply scientific and technological knowledge, on a scale heretofore unheard of, to the problems of producing and distributing goods. The gap between the French economy and that of the other technologically advanced countries become tragically apparent André Siegfried gloomily reflected the problem when he asked whether a society of peasants, artisans, and petty manufacturers could hope to survive in the modern world

Thus in the France of 1919 three facts were most apparent. The first was that the war had claimed the flower of the adult male population, and therefore the nation was destined to be controlled by older men. The second was that large sections of France were in desolation from war damage, and that the reconstruction of these lands and installations would be a tremendous work, and the third that France, unlike her neighbors, had not greatly expanded her industrial capacity during the war, for her most important industrial provinces had been under enemy control. To solve these problems, and give the nation a will to drive ahead in spite of the catastrophe, would have required great creative political imagination, but the nation re-elected the very men who had been the leaders of opinion and politics before 1914. These men may have had creative ideas before 1914, but after 1919 they appeared more and more in the roles of frightened elderly men anxious to re-establish a "normalcy" that could not be recovered

In that first decade after 1919 France did reconstruct the devastated areas, but with little imagination or understanding of the fact that the reconstruction should have looked to the future rather than to a rebuilding of the past The first of the three great problems could not be resolved and that of industrial expansion was not When the depression overwhelmed the nation in 1930–1931, these facts became painfully evident. France was dangerously confronted with the great political crisis of the post-Versailles world. in its most brutal form that crisis demanded the destruction of the pluralistic European society and the substitution of totalitarian control over the vital life of the community For the entire decade preceding the Second War of the twentieth century, fascist and communist totalitarian parties vied with each other to create disorder, and the regime of the liberal-democratic republic seemed to be living on borrowed time As the disaster of 1940 demonstrated, the paralyses of the national will reflected the political and economic disorder in the country[2]

There has been a spate of accounts attempting to explain the twenty years between the two wars, and it is perhaps inevitable that most of them take the disaster of 1940 as the lodestar for their analyses. Unquestionably the problem of the historian is to explain that defeat, but it may well be that future discussions of the history of those twenty years will shift some of the emphasis to an analysis of the forces that permitted the French nation to hold at bay the totalitarian threats to its pluralistic democracy, in other words, to the one positive achievement of the period, as well as to the failures that obviously helped to bring on the disaster. It seems to me that this unexplored problem may have as important implications as any. Clearly such an analysis must assume that the post-Versailles France was no longer fundamentally concerned with the great problems of the nineteenth century except in that the compromises made between the France of the dynastic kings and the France of Mirabeau, Robespierre, the Directory and the Empire were themselves under attack from forces foreign to French traditions. French politicians during these post-1919 years marked time, they refused to face up either to the problems of the new industrial society, or those that came with the shift from a European to a global balance of power Somehow, however, French society managed to withstand both fascist and communist totalitarianism until after decisions on the battlefields (1939–1945) gave a new generation a chance

[2] See my essay in E M Earle, *Modern France*, 1951

to grapple with the great questions of the twentieth century. If this is a correct assessment, the War of 1914–1918 marked the end of one era and the opening of another. It was the end of the period when the French nation could hope to control its own destiny as well as of the period when the political life of the nation was primarily concerned with adjustment of the several political traditions in its own national history It opened a period in which French politics required new insights into France's role in Europe and the world, new understandings of the economy that the machine civilization was building, and a new vision of the national "image" The history of the years since Versailles may someday be told as the story of the successes and failures of the pluralistic liberal-democracy to meet the post-1918 world When that story is written, the problem that concerns this book—that is, the emergence of French liberal-democratic society—must be of fundamental importance to its narrative.

There is, of course, no real dissociation between the European world of the nineteenth century and that of the twentieth, obviously the history of man is a continuous web, an organic emanation out of the past, but the historian is interested in defining the characteristic forms of this process Like the biologist who can study the horse without reference to its origins, but whose understanding of the life process would be quite incomplete if he did not project the horse back to Eohippus and beyond, or the astronomer who can study both the stars and the galaxies, but whose understanding of these phenomena would be limited if he did not attempt to project their evolution into past eons, so the historian can best study the present and the past by critical analyses of the insights that the one affords to the other. Thus by identifying the problem of the nineteenth century as essentially different from the ones confronted by twentieth-century men, we do not dissociate the two societies any more than the biologist dissociates Eohippus from the winner of the Kentucky Derby. However, while the historian's analysis shares with the biologist's the effort to describe and delineate the form of the process of development, it is essentially different in that the historian presents material that may and should be used as the basis for critical and moral judgments about man's institutions and value systems The geneticist may do something about the breeding of horses as a result of his studies, but he does not make a moral value-judgment about the processes that are at work, whereas the historian must recognize that the critical judgments men make about their past, the understandings that they share about that past, the interpretations that they accept of that past also become part of the value system that assumes a role in directing the human society of the present Thus the study of the nineteenth-century political compromises should help to form a basis for judgment about the value systems and institutions that twentieth-century men inherited from their fathers, and especially is this true at a time when new aggressive political dogmas, proclaimed by tight-lipped, serious men, are proposed as alternatives to the inherited institutions

The liberal-democratic system that came so brusquely under attack by totalitarian fascists and communists is not really a doctrine or a program of political action, it is rather a confluence of institutions, laws, customs, practices, and ideas often only half expressed, that had been hammered together by the compromises of a century Like the feudal societies, which the political institutions of Europe find at their very roots, there was no "standard pattern" for a liberal-democratic society, just as there were "feudal laws" rather than "a feudal law," there was a variety of European liberal-democratic political institutions, each conditioned by variations in the historical development of the particular nation. These differences, and the subsequent tensions inherent in their development, may well be the dynamo that has made the wonderful civilization of the West, but they also create frustratingly difficult problems for the historian, and set subtle traps for the moralist and the philosopher who must base their judgments on Europe's experience. Thus the liberal-democracy that fascist and communist orators and theoreticians berate so violently was not—and is not—an orderly body of teachings and institutions; rather it is a series of similar, yet diverse, socio-political complexes in which the important common ingredients are the recognition of the value of pluralistic decentralization of social, economic and political power, the acknowledgment of regularized procedures to normalize the processes of change, the acceptance of the notion that social goals are more or less subject to popular consent, and the recognition of the right of individuals to freedom from organized social controls in important areas of their lives. Lastly, it is a system that proclaims no ultimate goals for society beyond vague expressions about human happiness, and therefore any political decision can be reversed by lawful process whenever it becomes no longer viable or useful Unlike totalitarian societies, a *coup d'état* is not necessary to effect political change.

It requires very little knowledge of the history of Europe to understand that the English revolutions of the seventeenth century, Anglo-French thought of the eighteenth, and, most of all, the revolutionary epoch following 1789, provide the fundamental ingredients of this system. But the student must beware of any quick judgment, for the important fact that becomes clear from this study of nineteenth-century France is that French liberal-democracy is a complex of laws, institutions, customs, and patterns of behavior operating in the minds of men, in the institutional memories and the social consciousness of corporate groups, and in the rich variety of political, social, and economic organizations that comprise the pluralistic society of France The past of an ancient society, as well as the more recent revolutionary experience, is to be found embedded in the total system.

Since this book was first published I have become increasingly aware that it should contain a more direct statement of the underlying problems that confronted French political choices in the nineteenth century It has been assumed that one could subsume the problem by the simple statement that it was a question of reconciling the old and the new regimes: the France of the monarchy with the France of the Revolution. This is undoubtedly partially true, but it is too brusque and simple a statement The France of the Bourbons was not an uncomplicated, easily definable, monolithic society any more than the Revolution was a single, homogeneous solution for the problems of politics I do not find that I should alter the text of this study in which I have analyzed the interactions between economic and social forces and the emerging political compromises, but I am happy that the editors of the *Torchbook* series will allow me to add this preface to this third edition of the book so that I can make more explicit what seem to have been the underlying forces involved in the evolution of French liberal-democracy

The first thing which confronts the student of French political history, whether he is studying the problems of Louis XIV or Charles de Gaulle, is the fact that the French state began its life as a medieval kingdom that was at bottom simply a confederation of feudal principalities in which the centers of power were highly dispersed Ducal and baronial authorities and quasi-independent cities were only loosely united by the overlordship of the king In time war, marriage, and chance related to births and deaths changed the confederation into a federal monarchy in which the king exercised more or less direct authority over the entire kingdom, but in the process of acquiring that authority he had been forced to confirm the provincial and urban privileges of his subjects with the result that many variations that had started with the confederation were perpetuated in the federal constitution of the monarchy. In our time we talk about pluralistic society often forgetting that this pluralism is deeply rooted in the medieval structure in which every fief had its own characteristic laws, the church an array of special privileges and separate institutions as old as the monarchy itself, the towns, their own governments, the universities, merchant- and craft-corporations (guilds), each their own laws, customs, and statutes Historians, forgetting that this medieval culture is the seedbed for our modern civilization, have called it organized anarchy. This judgment can be only partially true, for we must also recognize that the rich variety of social, intellectual, economic, religious, and cultural institutions characteristic of the pluralisms of our civilization are the lineal heirs of that medieval tradition.

Strong kings from the time of Philippe Augustus onward tried to bring order out of this diversity, but in the process they often created new centers of dispersed power to take the place of those they suppressed The king's authority had to be exercised by men, and in an era when it was difficult to recruit and pay personnel, and perhaps even more difficult to supervise their behavior, the royal officials themselves became new centers of power that often escaped the royal authority. Venality in office came to allow them to own their positions as one might own a mill, so that they could not be removed without great difficulty; indeed, they could not even be "replaced" when they died because they had the right to pass on their offices by testament. This became true for the officers of the so-called Sovereign Courts that dispensed justice to the kingdom, regulated the feudal contracts between the king and his nobles, controlled the expenditure of monies, administered forests, estates and endowments, and even passed on the orthodoxy of printed books. These Courts, of which the Parliaments were the most important, pretended to be independent corporations with the right of judicial review over the acts of the king; they could be controlled when the king was strong, but a weak king or a regency government often had trouble with them. What was true for these Sovereign Courts was in a lesser degree also true for the governors of provinces and towns, some of whom managed to acquire hereditary rights to their posts, and for the officials of the town governments who were willing to subvert the ancient constitutions of their municipalities by purchasing office from the king Richelieu, Mazarin, and Louis XIV attempted to remedy this situation by the creation of new officials, the Intendants, who would be responsive to the orders of the king's council, but they were only partly successful The *Fronde,* in which both the venal officials and the feudal dignitaries cooperated in an attempt to undermine the royal authority, was defeated, but the history of

Parliament after 1652 demonstrates the fact that this institution remained a check on royal power—a check that at times could be slight because the king could browbeat or bribe his judges, but at other times was great, when the king's personal prestige failed to match the pretensions of his office In the eighteenth century even the tax farmers were in the process of making their positions independent of the king and quasi-hereditary in character by placing the central government deeply in their debt. The important thing about this is that French officials and judges learned that the acquisition of established positions could give security and power.

The Revolution of 1789 wiped out provincial and municipal privileges as well as the tenure of these venal officials, but neither the new demarcation of the departments, nor the creation of a new administrative and judicial system with non-venal officers could strike from the hearts and minds of French officialdom the idea that privilege could be established by place and position, and that time could make these privileges quasi-hereditary. Under Charles de Gaulle Frenchmen still strive to establish family positions and to maintain acquired rights with the same tenacity that the so-called Sovereign Courts formerly defended theirs. The idea of hereditary right to acquired position and place did not disappear with the proclamation of the Rights of Man and Citizen. Napoleon may have believed that every soldier carried the baton of a marshal in his knapsack, but in point of fact the high ranks in the French army today are crowded with sons and grandsons of officers, just as the important places in the administration are so often filled by men from "administrative families" It is amusing to note that this urge for established positions can even be found in the ranks of the legislators who formed the acts of the French Revolution: they became the "perpetuals": every legislative corps from the time of the Convention until the establishment of Louis XVIII's House of Peers found many of these men among their members, and they were not freely elected to these bodies; they passed laws assuring themselves membership!

Europe with other civilized peoples Throughout the nineteenth century, with the exception of the two decades when Louis Napoleon, who lived most of his life outside of France, was at the head of the French state, Frenchmen more or less resisted ideas of and economic contacts with their neighbors This does not mean, of course, that Frenchmen completely refused to associate with other peoples or to adopt the political and economic ideas of other peoples if they could be used to advantage. This isolationist tendency was strong enough, however, to influence the development of a French nationalism—with a love of *patrie*—resembling the peasant's tenacious love of his few acres and suspicion of everything beyond the frontiers of his village In other words, even though French culture and the ideas of French thinkers had become a substantial part of the cosmopolitan culture of Europe, the French themselves very often seemed provincial, with narrow horizons bounded by their own experiences and their own traditions. This accounts for the shock that the Parisian World Fair in 1899 gave to thoughtful Frenchmen when they began to perceive the growing gap between the French economy and that of her neighbors. This cultural isolation is deeply ingrained in French society and must be taken into account in any assessment of the underlying forces affecting the processes of political and economic development.

If we turn our attention to the arena of political debate in which the constitutional forms and practices that became the liberal-democratic Republic were discussed and ultimately decided, it is immediately clear that France owes much to her monarchical past. Indeed, whether France was to be a monarchy or a republic was not settled until the last decades of the nineteenth century But the important thing to remember is that the monarchical party was by no means united on a single program or by a common *mystique*. Some of the monarchists were deeply committed to the traditional belief in the "divine right" of kings and complete loyalty to the Bourbon dynasty Others supported monarchy simply because they believed it was the form of government best suited to maintain a natural, ascendant aristocracy. Still others supported the monarchy because it was the form that could best guarantee the maintenance of controls over society through the Roman Catholic Church. And finally there was a relatively large segment of the monarchist right that wished to create a limited, liberal monarchy similar to the one that was coming into being in England in the nineteenth century. Of all these groups, as they merged imperceptibly one with the other, only the first was completely, unalterably, and uncompromisingly opposed to the republican solution, though none of them wanted or would support a republic except on their own terms.

This fan of monarchical opinion is evidence of the fact that the remote as well as the recent past of the kingdom of France still lived in the hearts of men. Fourteenth-century French kings had urged their "divine right" to counter papal pretensions, and later as a weapon against their great feudal vassals. By the seventeenth century the Bourbon monarchy under Louis XIII and Louis XIV had succeeded in elevating the royal authority by annihilating many of the rights and political powers of the aristocracy. Bishop Bossuet crowned this work with a thoroughgoing doctrine of "divine right" drawn from Holy Scripture itself, while Louis XIV proclaimed it both in the memoirs written for his son and in his actions and decrees. No one listening to the Sun King can doubt the absolute sincerity of his belief in his "divine right", he was convinced not only that God placed him on the throne, but also that He would give him the wisdom with which to govern the realm. This royalism of a Louis XIV was, however, almost as distasteful to many monarchists as a republic would have been. In the sixteenth century first the Huguenots and then the Catholic League proclaimed the doctrine that the *entire social hierarchy* was the work of God, and hence that the aristocracy (and the urban patricians as well) also had "divine right." At the opening of the eighteenth century this idea was again taken up by men like Saint-Simon and Fénélon who wanted to re-establish the aristocracy in their "natural" positions of power. In the nineteenth century men with this aristocratic tradition were to call the work of Richelieu and Louis XIV "revolutionary," and to urge that France should go back to her true traditions—a society governed by its natural aristocratic hierarchies. Thus, long before the Revolution of 1789 divergent notions about the true constitution of the kingdom divided the supporters of monarchy. The *mystique* associated with these doctrines of "divine right" assumes that God made the world of men and things, that inequality and social hierarchies are everywhere in evidence so that they, too, must be His handiwork. The men who direct His state and His church, it was assumed, would naturally cooperate to carry out His intentions on earth as He regulated those in His heaven. In a rural society composed of landlords and illiterate peasants such a doctrine seemed to have much to recommend it to anyone not committed to the revolutionary ideal of equality. The relationships between lord and peasant were paternalistic, just as the king was the "father of his people," so the lord had paternal responsibility for those under him: both king and lord must accept the fact that they were finally to be judged by God for the way in which they carried out His will. To those who cynically see this as pure cant, we should hastily add that there were many landlords who, in their own way, freely accepted and executed their responsibilities, just as there were kings who lived up to theirs These men who insisted upon the notion of the divine origins of society regarded the equalitarian doctrines of the Revolution as heretical if not sacrilegious; they saw the men who proposed them as charlatans or demagogues who hoped to exploit the gullibility of the ignorant for their own purposes. These men completely agreed with de Maîstre when he insisted that one could not "make" a constitution for society other than the one it already had, and that the complexities of society were such that any change men might make in the structure would necessarily be for the worse. In other words, while not denying that there might be unfortunate aspects of the world, they did deny the possibility of doing anything about them without disastrous results

The third rightist party found its most important reason for supporting monarchical principles in the traditional relationship between throne and altar It relied upon the ancient constitution of the French kingdom in which the church and the state were inseparably bound together in a joint effort to control the lives and behavior of men. They also remembered the disorders that had occurred when the dispute over the Revolutionary Civil Constitution of the clergy led to an attempt to do without the church altogether. For these monarchists the authority of Rome was an absolute necessity, without it there could be no moral order in society. It is amusing to note that this point of view spread rapidly among the upper bourgeoisie when social revolutionary doctrines gained prominence during the later years of the July Monarchy In fact, when socialistic, sectarian dogmas offered the masses heaven on earth in return for a social revolution, many people, who had been anti-clerical if not even anti-religious, were willing to forget their conflicts with the church that might teach the masses the necessity of respecting the natural orders of society if they were ever to attain their true heaven in the next world.

Not all men who supported the ideal of monarchy, however, dipped their pens in ink made before the era of popular revolutions. In the eighteenth century a considerable body of Frenchmen, including the flower of the bourgeoisie and the more liberal of the nobility, attempted to understand the significance of the revolutionary history of the island across the Channel The English had beheaded one king, chased another from the throne, and finally installed a new dynasty that owed its authority to an act of the English Parliament rather than to God Frenchmen may never have completely understood what was happening in eighteenth-century England (nor did Englishmen, for that matter), but the example of England inspired their faith in a monarchy limited by constitutional laws. At the same time, the gradual emergence of the *mystiques* associated with liberalism (discussed below) and the proclamation of the doctrine of popular sovereignty by the revolution in America combined to prepare the way for belief in a liberal, limited monarchy. As a matter of fact, this was the first fruit of the Revolution of 1789, and men who hoped for stability in a monarchical solution severely blamed Louis XVI because his failure to become a true constitutional monarch opened the floodgates of disorder. Thus the liberal ideals of the Revolution were adopted in their own way by both monarchists and republicans. As we shall see, the "liberal" *mystiques* that develop as part of the Revolution are very much in conflict with the democratic ideals implicit in popular sovereignty, it was therefore not difficult for landlords and capitalists, willing to recognize each other as part of a new aristocracy, to appropriate to their own purposes the "Liberty" of the revolutionary era, always, of course, explaining liberty in the terms of traditional liberalism.

Clearly these doctrines on the right were not attuned to make a democratic appeal. The number of men with wealth and position in any society is necessarily small, but their influence is very great even in a society that accepts universal manhood suffrage, and especially great if the society is largely composed of rural villages and small towns The whole tribe of notaries, lawyers, bailiffs, tradesmen, managers, and clergymen living under the shadow, and often from the largess, of the chateau, finds it difficult to resist its influence The peasantry, whose ancestors for generations have been dependent in one way or another on the owners of the land, also find it hard not to listen to their counsels This pattern was true up to the middle, and to a lesser degree even to the end, of the nineteenth century Thus even though there was universal manhood suffrage, the party of Moral Order in 1849, the Bonapartists, and the Monarchists in 1871, had no trouble securing a majority of the votes. In this way, although the monarchical parties sympathized only to a small degree with many of the dominant ideals of the nineteenth century, they were to have a large voice in the debates that were to make up the bundle of compromises that we call the liberal-democratic Republic.

If the traditions associated with the old France of kings and noblemen did not speak up in the debates of the nineteenth century as a single voice, neither did the France inspired by the great Revolution. The slogan of "Liberty, Equality, Fraternity" which so warmed the emotions of men could be used equally well by orators with diverse views about their meaning. One of the ironies of the nineteenth-century political debate was the fact that the political ideals of the Revolution were in conflict among themselves as well as with the ideals of the earlier society. On the one extreme, men emphasized the value of individual liberty in contrast with the social controls that had been characteristic of previous régimes; for these men government should become a system of guarantees, of constitutional barriers, that would assure the individual against the tyranny of family, church, clan, guild, and even of the state. At the other extreme, men urged the importance of popular sovereignty and associated it with their own interpretation of the "general will" proposed by Rousseau; to them a government responsive to the "general will" would never hurt the people. Therefore, as long as an assembly was democratically elected, it could be trusted with the power to act in all areas of society. French liberal-democracy at the opening of the twentieth century was as much the result of the compromise effected between these two extremes as between the ideals of the Revolution and those of the earlier régime.

The cluster of ideas and programs of action that supported the notion of individual liberty has been grouped together under the term "liberalism," but it has nothing at all to do with the word as we use it in the mid-twentieth century. Traditional liberalism was a reaction to the oppressive social and political controls imposed at all levels of society upon the individual man. The eighteenth-century *philosophes* "discovered" that the individual was the important force in society, and they developed a doctrine to the effect that society could prosper only when the individual had the freedom to develop his personality, to discover and follow his interests, and to control his own life without interference. *Laissez-faire* was a slogan that could apply equally to economic, religious, or social controls. Where the old régime had insisted upon the paramount importance of the organic parts of society (family, clan, church, state, etc.) the liberals argued the importance of the individual man. In the early years of the nineteenth century, the English schools of philosophical radicals and classical economists gave a rigorous intellectual underpinning to these ideas.

The revolutionary slogans were easily applied to this traditional liberalism Equality came to mean that all men were to be equal before the tax collector, the bar of justice, and in the right to qualify for employment in the state Liberty meant that all were to be free from constraints that would hamper the development of personality or personal interests "Fraternity" then became a mystic ideal of nationality shared by all citizens. Under such an interpretation the state could be made into a court of justice where men could obtain equity, with a police system to ensure order and prevent crime, and a system of defense to protect the society from foreign aggression For the most part the individual would thereby be free to work out his own destiny in the rough and tumble of life. The liberals have been accused of assuming that life was like a race in which the referee ordered the rules and the conditions of the track, but victory was to the strong of wind and muscle who had the will to win. This was a revolutionary doctrine in 1789 and, indeed, in 1815, for it ran counter to everything that the paternalistic, monarchical societies of Europe had believed in.

The liberals were largely suspicious of the mass of men, and wished to assure themselves that the areas left to government would not fall into the hands of people unprepared to administer them Only those with the leisure and the education necessary for understanding public affairs, they argued, should be allowed to govern society Thus they became advocates of property and education requirements for both voters and elected office holders. These conditions did not in any way seem to be incompatible with equality as an ideal for the society As Guizot explained when his opponents demanded electoral reforms: the law applies equally to all, and so if you wish to vote "enrich yourselves, Messieurs, enrich yourselves!" This same attitude, when applied to the conditions of economic life, created another series of problems If, as they suggest, the individual must not be subject to the "tyranny" of groups in the society, and if there really are only individual interests and the interests of the state as a whole, then, for example, labor contracts must be made between individuals equal before the law, and not via the interference of "combinations" of any kind. This notion justified suppression of labor unions. By the mid-nineteenth century, in fact, cynics argued that the liberals were men who proposed that the rich as well as the poor should be allowed to sleep under bridges at night, if they wished to do so!

The other pole of the revolutionary firmament was occupied by men who accepted the implications of popular sovereignty and the Rousseauian ideal that government should execute the "general will" of the governed. In many of their writings and speeches these men referred to the "people" with something of the same reverence and general optimism that the eighteenth-century had used in connection with the "noble savage." The "people" they assumed could be disinterested, intelligent, and fair in their political judgments, they would always act correctly if they were given the right to do so. There were two basic propositions in the arguments of these democrats. First, they insisted that universal manhood suffrage was a cure-all for social and political ills, secondly, they saw no reason for limiting the spheres in which government should be allowed to act, since the people could be trusted not to hurt themselves. Not all of the democrats completely shared both of these beliefs, of course, but all of them were convinced that universal manhood suffrage was a panacea for society's ills.

While the democrats were not fearful of the people, the liberals shuddered when they heard men quote Rousseau to the effect that those who did not will the "general will" must be "forced to be free"! This could mean that the guarantees that liberals wished to erect protecting property, and minority opinion not shocking to men of property, might well be destroyed by democratic action. This problem was at the center of the arguments in both France and Germany in 1848, when liberals and democrats fell to quarreling with each other and prepared the way for the Party of Moral Order and Authority—with a capital "A."

The 1848 period, however, taught the liberals something about universal manhood suffrage When the Provisional Government of February granted the right to vote to all adult males, there was much speculation about the type of deputy that would be returned from such an electorate. To the surprise of almost everyone, the men elected were almost without exception from the same social class, that is wealthy, reasonably well-educated men; a high percentage of them were lawyers or notaries, but landlords, businessmen, and professional men were all represented. In other words, universal suffrage did not necessarily mean the election of the "wild men" who preached social revolutionary doctrines, although a few of these people were elected. This was the first time the liberals understood that it might be possible to maintain their ideal of a government that did not interfere with the "essential liberties of property and opinion" even though the vote was given to everyone. The problem really resolved itself into a question of the choice of candidates to stand for office and the election campaign that secured the majority of the votes Both of these are susceptible to the control of men of wealth

At the same time, the political ferment of the 1840's that bubbled over in 1848 also drove a wedge between the democrats. The June days particularly brought home to many men who believed in the efficacy of political democracy that it would be very important to prevent the social radicals from controlling society The petty bourgeois shopkeepers, the petty professional people, and the landowning peasants, excluded from the vote by their wealthier neighbors, wished to participate in political decisions so that their fiscal and other interests could be satisfied, but they were as fearful of the social revolutionary prophets of equalitarian utopias as their wealthier neighbors were. It was characteristic of French politics in the nineteenth century that each group on the left, upon achieving an established position, became conservative, and resisted the encroachments of the men further to the left Thus, we find that men who were radically and unalterably republican—insisting upon democratic suffrage because they feared the aristocratic assumptions of both monarchy and empire—were willing to accept many of the assumptions of the traditional liberals on their right in order to prevent the greater evils threatening them from their own left These men, who demanded universal suffrage and the Republic, were more willing to guarantee the freedom of press, assembly, and religious belief than the aristocratic liberals had been; they also were willing to allow working men the right to organize in unions and to strike for better wages; but they should be called political democrats, for they were not ready to create the "socialistic" state so feared by the people who had strongly objected to democratic suffrage.

When Thiers and his friends joined the republican camp in the early 1870's, the basis for the compromise between liberalism and democracy had already become apparent the liberals and the political democrats had cooperated in the suppression of the Commune of 1871 and they had proved that a democracy could be conservative A number of historians have severely criticized the men who directed the first four decades of the Third French Republic (1879–1914) as being uncreative and unimaginative in their politics, this criticism neglects the fact that these men were governing a nation still largely composed of villages and small towns with agriculture as the principal resource, and urban centers in which commerce and small manufacturing by artisans, rather than large-scale factory production, were the characteristic economic forms The liberal-democratic solution they achieved satisfied the needs of the politically conscious majority; they saw no reason for further "creative" political experiments

The doctrines of "social democracy" that so frightened the wealthy as well as the petty bourgeoisie were as native to French soil as the ideals of the great Revolution, but they were quite unable until very late in the nineteenth century to reach the people who might have been converted by them. When the eighteenth-century *philosophes* "discovered" that salvation had to be achieved in this world, sensitive men were confronted with the fact that the poor and the downtrodden, who heretofore had to expect their rewards in heaven, must now somehow be relieved of their burdens. The crusade against slavery, the concern for the insane and the criminal, the recognition of the problem of the poor, indeed, the very word "humanitarianism"—all this evidenced a concern for the mass of humanity absent in earlier periods. After 1820–1840, with the introduction of the "English system" of producing goods, mining coal, and transporting all manner of things by using machinery powered by steam engines, the problems of the poor became more pressing, for they were often terribly exploited by the new factories and utterly exposed to the periodic economic crises characteristic of the new system. While the Malthusians in France as well as in England insisted that the poor were the authors of their own misery because they continued to breed more of their number, and therefore that nothing could be done for them, other thinkers became convinced that radical reorganizations of society could solve the problems of poverty. A Saint-Simon, for example, could urge that the steam engine announced the era when man could cease the exploitation of man and exploit the earth for the benefit of all men.

In the late 1830's and the 1840's the words "socialism" and "communism" appeared in western languages largely from the pens of French thinkers. A fan of social radicalism, ranging from men who would do without the state completely to men who would give total power to the state, created a babble of voices that frightened men of wealth without providing any program of action that the social radicals could agree upon. Furthermore, these prophets of the new society could be heard and understood only by the traditionally conservative bourgeoisie and wealthy peasants, while the miserable landless workers and the urban proletariat were too illiterate to make contact with their ideas. In June 1848 and again in 1871 the Parisian poor were willing to die for programs they only half understood, but Paris, and especially the poor of Paris, was not France, so their deaths only consolidated the alliance between the political democrats and the traditional liberals.

Even after the Third Republic relaxed the laws to allow freedom of the press, assembly and association, the social radical doctrines found French society to be stony soil A petty bourgeois-peasant party arose calling itself "radical-socialist," but while it was "radically" republican, it was in no real way socialist A worker's party also appeared, associated with the Social Democratic International, but this party had little influence even after it had changed its avowed aims from social revolution to social reform As late as 1914 French society and the French economy had not yet reached the stage at which a social-democratic program of action was possible On the eve of the War of 1914–1918 the French were still fighting about the separation of church and state, a problem inherited from the heroic period of the Revolution rather than about problems deriving from the changes of new economic system that was destined to remake French society

This discussion is not intended to explain, but only to supplement the complex story that unfolds in this book. As I said in the opening of this new preface, the French society that emerged into the post-Versailles world was the result of the interaction of many complex forces deeply embedded in the pluralistic structure inherited from both the remote and the recent past; it was above all captive to patterns of behavior in political, economic, and social life that were a part of the total experience of the nation. In the text of this book I have tried to show how these forces acted through real human beings and social institutions, rather than as abstract ideas in conflict with one another Thus this preface is intended more as a "pointer" to light up problems, than as an explanation of the course of nineteenth-century French political evolution

JOHN B WOLF

Bone Lake, Wisconsin
July, 1962

PREFACE TO THE ORIGINAL EDITION

THIS book was written to fill the need for a compact, balanced history of French civilization and politics since the collapse of Napoleon's Empire. It is intended as a guide for the general reader and an introductory survey for the student of modern European history. It should serve both as a background in French history and as a starting place for a more intensive study of French civilization, and should properly be considered as a companion piece to the several excellent accounts of the Revolution and the Empire that are available to the English-reading public.

In preparing a one-volume history of a great nation like France, I have had to keep certain aspects of the problem in the forefront of my discussion, and it is only proper that the reader should have the approach explained. France since 1815 provides a classic example of the development of European liberal democracy in our times. The seeds of the revolutionary movement that destroyed the old régime on the European continent and placed the power and the benefits of modern civilization in the hands of the bourgeoisie, the landowning peasantry, and the intellectuals, were sown in France during the eighteenth century. It was not, however, until the late nineteenth or even the twentieth century that liberal democracy struck firm roots in French political soil. There were many factors—political, social, economic, and intellectual—interwoven into that movement, and I have attempted to bring them together in this history. Such an attempt, since it includes the whole matrix of a society, must necessarily fall short of this aim; I only hope that I shall not have missed the mark too far.

The reader will also soon perceive that a second theme runs through much of the book. While the bourgeoisie, landowning peasants, and intellectuals were establishing a system of society that gave them power, prestige, and wealth, the emerging classes of the urban and rural proletariat and the petty bourgeoisie also came to demand a share in the civilization. The degree to which those demands can be met without undermining the fundamental liberal structure of French society may well be one of the most important factors in determining the permanence of French liberal democracy. It should be obvious to any casual student of European history that the so-called liberal democratic system can last only as long as the compromise between nineteenth century liberalism and democracy can be continued effectively

With this in mind, I have given special attention to the crisis of 1848–51 At that time there was no compromise effected between the liberals and the democrats The June Days, the election of Louis Napoleon, and finally the *coup d'état* of 1851 blighted the hopes of the revolutionaries who had wished to give France free institutions No student who is at all familiar with the present problems of Europe can miss the parallel between the rise of Louis Napoleon and the rise of our modern dictators. Whether there is much or little to be learned from this parallel is, however, an open question

For the most part, the problems of foreign, colonial, and military affairs have not been extensively treated in this history. This is not because the author is unaware of their importance, but rather because any really adequate treatment would have extended the bounds of this book beyond the single volume. To describe the rôle of France in world affairs would require an exhaustive discussion of high politics that, obviously, has no place in this history Foreign, colonial, and military affairs appear in this study only as an indication of how they were affected by and, in turn, have influenced the internal problems of the nation.

When this book was being written, the author was, of course, unaware that its publication would coincide with one of the darkest days in French history. Broken and defeated by superior force France may be, but that does not becloud the fact that she has made great contributions to western culture in the past, nor does it preclude an important cultural role for the

French in the future The author hopes that his American readers will gain from these pages a clearer and more sympathetic understanding of the patterns of French civilization and a better picture of the problems that the French people have to face. The author is no propagandist, nor is he a blind Francophile, in his opinion the only intellectually honest approach to the problem of history is a detached and honest attempt to interpret the materials in as fair and unbiased a way as possible. His effort to reach such an interpretation, he sincerely hopes, will aid the readers of this book to achieve a better perspective, both of the problems that confront the French people, and of the forces that are at work in the Europe of today

The author is deeply indebted to a number of his colleagues and friends for advice, encouragement, and criticism. His teachers, Professor C C. Eckhardt of the University of Colorado, and Professor L D. Steefel of the University of Minnesota, very generously consented to read the whole manuscript. Professor F. B Artz of Oberlin College read the chapters dealing with the Restoration and the July Monarchies; Professor Lynn M. Case of Louisiana State University, the chapters dealing with the Second Republic and the Empire, and Professor J G. Heinberg, of the Political Science Department at the University of Missouri, the chapters on the Third Republic Professor Edward Ainsworth of the English department at the University of Missouri read the entire manuscript for stylistic comment Dean Carl Wittke, the general editor of the Prentice-Hall history publications, and the editorial department of Prentice-Hall have demonstrated the great importance of a publisher's editorial assistance in the final preparation of a manuscript. The writer's wife also most conscientiously followed all of the very best traditions by being critic and typist, and supplying both encouragement—and an index. The responsibility for any errors in fact or interpretation rests entirely upon the author

Columbia, Mo. J. B. W.
May 1, 1940

CHAPTER I

FRANCE AT THE END OF THE NAPOLEONIC WARS

HISTORY rarely records an episode more dramatic than the career of Napoleon. He appeared out of the tumult and confusion of the Revolution and foreign intervention; in a little more than a decade he had carried the banners of France from Madrid to Moscow and had created an empire which rivaled that of Rome His fall was as theatrical as his rise. The Spanish war, the Moscow campaign, and the battle of Leipzig followed in rapid succession, and the imperial structure cracked, swayed, and came down like a house of cards. In 1814 it only remained to be seen what the years of misery and glory had done to the France that had provided Napoleon with his thunder and energy. The allies, who had defeated the emperor, were still too surprised at their own audacity to take a serious invoice of the situation; the French were still too stunned by the unbelievable collapse of the Grand Army to begin an introspective examination. One thing alone was obvious. France, a country of almost thirty million souls, must find a place in the family of nations

Both the allies and the French knew that the France of 1814 was not the nation that Louis XVI had ruled in the eighteenth century The feudal foundations of the old régime were forever destroyed, and new institutions framed men's lives. The rigid, classic structure of Napoleon, superimposed on the freer architecture of revolutionary builders, stood in place of the ramshackle palace of the old monarchy. It should have been obvious to any observer that the new France could not return to her status before 1789 In the wagon train of the conquerors of Napoleon, however, there were men who wished to force France to forget her tumultuous, revolutionary past and to return to the patterns of the old régime These men were the émigrés; they had spent twenty-odd years in exile, always moving to keep ahead of the victorious march of the French armies. They had lost their lands, their wealth, and their king in the triumph of the slogan, Liberty, Equality, Fraternity. Their friends had been butchered, their church pillaged, their civilization uprooted and burned These were the men who came back to France anxious to efface the work which had been done in their absence

When these émigrés returned to Paris in the spring of 1814, however, they must have been agreeably surprised to find that the France through which they rode had not, apparently, been changed in their absence. The fields, the villages, even the great towns, looked much as they had when Louis XVI held court at Versailles It is not altogether surprising that these courtiers of the late king, who prided themselves on their inability to learn anything new or to forget anything old, should conclude that the twenty-odd years of their exile had been merely a bad dream, a horrible nightmare which was now over and could happily be forgotten The physical aspect of France was highly deceptive The Revolution and the Empire had left the landscape practically untouched Along the roads to Paris from the east or the south there was little to see which would explain the fundamental changes of the revolutionary age. Long rows of poplar trees waving peacefully over the road could hardly be expected to stir the imagination of men who saw everywhere the familiar routine of peasant life

In the East the peasants still practiced a system of agriculture that they had inherited from the Middle Ages. the open fields with cattle grazing on the stubble; the small villages with the parish church in the center; the three fields with the scattered holdings; the time-honored rotation of wheat, fallow, rye—all were as evident in the France of 1814 as they had been in the France of Louis XVI. In the South the agriculture handed down from Roman times seemed everywhere largely unchanged The walled vine, fruit, and olive orchards; the open fields of wheat, rye, clover, lucern; the fallow fields resting a year before they were expected to produce; the

ical, uniform legal system In 1806 the *Code de Procédure* put the practice in all of the courts of France on a uniform basis. In 1807 the commercial code regularized the law of commercial and industrial associations, bills of exchange, bankruptcies, and so forth, and gave France a body of commercial law well suited to her emerging bourgeois civilization The penal code of 1810, while it reintroduced some of the barbarous usages of the old régime which the revolutionary legislation had outlawed, gave France a uniform code for the entire country. Since these codes were as useful to the Bourbons as they had been to the emperor, they were retained after his exile.

THE Catholic Church of the old régime had monopolized the religious life of France. In addition, it was a wealthy landlord, the principal dispenser of charities, the foremost educator, and the only institution with traditions older than the monarchy itself. It is true that the king, through concordats with the pope, had acquired considerable authority over the Church; nevertheless, the power and influence that it had retained was considerable indeed The Revolution started with the confiscation of the Church property and the destruction of its privileges, and ended by the reconstitution of the Church, on a new basis, that made it definitely dependent upon the state. At the opening of the nineteenth century Napoleon made a concordat with the pope that was to fix the church organization for a century to come. With the ecclesiastical lands confiscated, the state undertook to support the priests and to provide places of worship. The number of French bishops was greatly reduced, and their dioceses were drawn to correspond exactly with the boundaries of France. The personnel of the clergy was placed under the control of the state, and the pope's only official contact with his bishops was through the government of France. Gone also was the monopoly of government favor, for Napoleon organized the Protestants and even the Jews under a similar arrangement.

Under the old régime the Church and the clergy had a virtual monopoly of education The educational institutions were not well co-ordinated, and the education that they offered was often poor and impractical, but it provided the Church with a powerful social agency for shaping men's minds The Revolution destroyed this monopoly, and Napoleon—again completing work begun in the earlier stages of the Revolution—gave France an educational system as orderly and completely centralized as the other imperial institutions. The sum total of all education in France, from the primary school to the University of Paris, was included in the Université de France The Grand Master of the Université de France controlled the entire educational system of the state. In this way Napoleon assured himself that his subjects would not absorb seditious doctrines The only infringement upon this system came from the *petits séminaires* which the emperor allowed to the Church to train its priests, but which often attracted other students because of their lower fees. In time the Church opened *grands séminaires* with the connivance of imperial functionaries who did not enforce the Université's monopoly. The instructors in these Church schools were often Jesuits who returned to France under the new name, "Fathers of the Faith" In 1815, then, there were two systems of education: the one official and powerful under the direction of the state, the other semicovert under the control of the clergy The great questions of control of education and of universal education were still to be fought out in the arena of French public life

IN NO other country in Europe had the social organization been so profoundly affected by the revolutionary movement as in France. France of the eighteenth century was strictly regimented by traditions. The social stratification of a clergy that prayed, a nobility that fought, and a third estate that labored had been maintained at least as a social fiction until the summer of 1789 But these social distinctions were based upon medieval society, and were feudal in their implications In the interval between the Middle Ages and the Revolution the dynamics of French society had done much to alter the basis upon which this system rested. The rise of the national state and the concentration of power in the hands of the king had deprived the nobility of most of its responsibilities, and robbed it of its vitality, but left it in possession of its privilege The great increase in wealth and the expanding economic organization had opened the way to the creation of an intelligent, prosperous new class, the bourgeoisie, which could not find a satisfying position in the feudal social organization The conquest of new knowledge and the progressive secularization of learning had broken the clergy's monopoly on the intellectual and spiritual life of man Broad vistas of a new social organization opened for men who wished to push aside the curtains of the future The old order had been assailed on all sides long before the mob stormed the Bastille on that fateful July day of 1789. The men who pushed over the façade of feudalism by revolution were merely completing the work that had been in the making since before the age of Richelieu.

The theory of feudal society was replaced by a new slogan. "Liberty, Equality, and Fraternity." Liberty meant freedom for the individual from the restraints of state and society; it guaranteed him the right to work out his own destiny without help or interference Equality destroyed distinctions based on blood or tradition, and assured all citizens of the impartiality of the tax collector, the law, the courts, and the administration It did not imply economic equality except in that each individual would stand before the same law. Fraternity carried a vaguer and more mystic connotation; it did not signify a communistic blood-brotherhood of man in which each is his brother's keeper, but rather it had the idea of nationality, of homogeneity, of popular democratic unity. It was this mystic gospel of fraternity that filled the ranks of the revolutionary armies and made Frenchmen of all classes acutely conscious of their common fatherland.

The twenty-five years of revolutionary and imperial government had made these ideals of the Revolution very real forces in French life and society. The common soldier knew that, as Napoleon declared, he might carry the baton of a marshal of France in his knapsack The struggling young lawyer knew that he could aspire to the very highest position in the administration or the judiciary Protestants and Jews knew that neither their race nor their religion could bar them from an important place in society. The peasant knew that he could prevent hunters from ruining his crops, and that the neighboring noble could no longer hold him to a feudal contract The masses knew that all must help to bear the taxes. Liberal legislation opened new prospects of economic advantages to the master craftsman and the merchant. The society created by the Revolution fell short of the ideals of the eighteenth-century philosophers, but it had gone far to rationalize the state and destroy the willfulness of the old temporal and spiritual feudal authorities.

THUS, the members of the old privileged class found their position in 1814 considerably less desirable than it had been under the old régime The guillotine, the migration, and the war had considerably reduced their numbers, revolutionary legislation had dried up many of the sources of their wealth; and they found by their side a new "privileged" class of men who depended upon wealth for position and aspired to usurp the former rôle of the nobility as leaders of French society. In prerevolutionary France the nobility had enjoyed many privileges and immunities: they paid no taxes; they owned, or had feudal claims on, a large part of the land of France, and they had a virtual monopoly of high positions in Church, army, and state. They enjoyed the favor of the king and there was always the possibility of obtaining a royal grant They could demand the homage and respect of both peasants and bourgeoisie, for their claims to position, based on the blood in their veins, were recognized by practically the entire population. The Revolution produced a new dogma: Equality. Privileges based on blood, tradition, and royal patent were destroyed. In the turmoil of the revolutionary and the Napoleonic era, ex-peasants became generals; unfrocked priests, diplomats and ministers of state; pettifogging lawyers, officials and peers. These new men based their claims to distinction on ability or wealth, and they stood ready to guard their gains in the name of equality. The members of the old nobility were not excluded from their time-honored professions, but they had to compete for them with men from the people.

Their economic status, too, had undergone a change for the worse. Many of the old nobility had lost both their property and their lives in the violent social shake-up. Likewise, all of the survivors found themselves poorer in 1815 than they had been in 1789. Their wealth had been based upon land, and the Revolution took much of it away from them. Contrary to a widespread misconception, however, the nobility and the Church did not own all the land of France even in 1789, although they did hold seignorial rights over most of it; that is to say, the nobility owned outright between twenty and forty per cent of the arable land in France, and had feudal claims on the peasants who held much of what remained. These claims, in some cases, had almost disappeared; in others, they had been very heavy, involving obligations to render personal service as well as money or goods. In some sections the obligations had retained the form of serfdom. The revolutionary legislation had destroyed all of the feudal claims at one blow, leaving the nobility in possession of only such lands as they owned outright. This legislation had been harder on the great nobles who had lived near the king, for the country gentry who did not run off to Versailles but stayed on their estates had long since consolidated their claims and were renting their lands to *métayers* or tenant farmers, even before the Revolution broke out.

Many of the old nobility, therefore, were in possession of their ancestral lands in 1815. A large number of them, especially in the West and Southwest, had never left France during the entire revolutionary period. Others had returned after 1799 to make peace with Napoleon—who never asked about a man's past if he could use him in the present—and in return for favors to him had recovered their estates Still others received their old lands with the return of the Bourbons when the king, to the discomfiture of the revolutionaries, returned all the unsold confiscated properties to their former owners But if the nobility still played a considerable rôle on the countryside, they had to share their position with men whose great-grandfathers had not fought for or against Henry of Navarre When the Church and other confiscated lands were being sold during the revolutionary era, many of the old estates were picked up by land speculators of one kind or another—ex-bailiffs of the nobility, ex-tax farmers, and ex-merchants, in 1814 these men insisted on sharing the power and influence that had formerly belonged to the nobility alone

The world outlook of this ex-privileged class also had experienced a change. It was the nobility of the old France that had patronized the Voltaires and Rousseaus, that had lionized Franklin, that had considered themselves children of the Age of Reason It was precisely this class that had produced Lafayette, Mirabeau, and other prominent figures of the early revolutionary era. The nobility had toyed lightly with reason and rationalism and had furnished an admiring audience for the men who were making intellectual dynamite for Robespierre. Their affection and respect for the Church had been corroded with the anticlericalism of the philosophers and the spectacle of their brothers in high ecclesiastical positions But the violence of the Revolution, the horror that the logical development of rationalism produced in their hearts, converted them. Rationalism went out of style, freethinking became bad taste As a class the nobility embraced Mother Church and vowed never to leave her comforting arms again They found spiritual solace and assurance in the doctrines of authority, which effaced all their erstwhile desire for discovering the truth through reason The Catholic Church conceived an orderly society, disciplined and regimented in social hierarchies, which offered a powerful weapon against the disciples of equalitarianism Along with Catholicism the nobility embraced the current literary fashion of romanticism, and lost themselves in a dream world of the Middle Ages in which gallant knights and beautiful ladies graciously ruled the countryside and fought evil in the form of Saracens, wicked men, and witches. This sham world in the fortress of romanticism saved them from contemplating their fate in the emerging capitalistic civilization of the new age.

THE very forces that had gone far to undermine the social position formerly enjoyed by the nobility were working to raise the bourgeoisie to new pinnacles of power Its members based their claims to leadership on ability and wealth. They had seen the sham of feudal régime, and when the occasion presented itself they proclaimed the new dogma of Equality: equality of opportunity, equality before the law. These men benefited most from the Revolution; it opened to them ways to wealth and power, and at the same time guaranteed to them legal and social recognition. In the society of the new order, wealth and ability rather than blood and traditions differentiated between men. The new favored class never thought of questioning the difference between the distinctions of this new society of wealth and those of the old society of blood, nor did they stop to analyze the possible implications of their equalitarianism.

The "equality" of the revolutionary bourgeoisie never was extended to cover more than political and social equality. The sacredness of private property was not only respected, but even reinforced through the legislation of the earlier revolutionary governments and finally by the great law codes of the Empire. The bourgeoisie, from the wealthy capitalists to the petty shopkeepers, stood firmly together to repel any suggestion of economic democracy. Theirs was the new world, a world raised on the property rights of the individual, a world in which wealth and ability alone gave promise of social recognition

Naturally, there were great differences of wealth within the ranks of the bourgeoisie At the top stood a small group of rich capitalists, land speculators, bankers, great merchants, landlords, and entrepreneurs Their homes, their mode of life set a standard of living with which even the wealthiest of the old nobility found it hard to keep pace. Indeed, under the Empire and even subsequently, marriage alliances between the children of these men of the new era and the sons and daughters of the old nobility were not uncommon, for only thus could many of the titled nobles keep above water Napoleon had been a great matchmaker to consolidate the upper crust of French society, and after his exile the custom continued Below these men of great wealth, the bourgeoisie ranged themselves from families who owned both a town and a country house to men who could hardly afford to keep a domestic servant, and who probably would leave only a scanty legacy to their children. But the doctrine of equality meant that the lowest could rise to the top rank of society, even though in actual practice only a few did so

The wealth of the French bourgeoisie was the result of hard work, thrift, crafty dealings, and speculation; the class had been in process of formation for several hundred years, and its accumulated wealth finally had brought power It was recruited from the urban craftsmen and wealthy peasants who had branched out into merchants, bankers, entrepreneurs, industrialists, and professional men The wealth was largely invested in urban and rural real estate or government bonds, there were few large industrial or commercial ventures, and the French bourgeoisie were definitely timid about lending their money for speculation The introduction of the steam engine and the modern factory system did not create the "captain of industry" until after 1830.

Naturally, many of the upper bourgeoisie were men of affairs, bankers, wholesale merchants, and manufacturers, who were interested in expanding their fortunes in every way, but the majority were people of scant means that did a small but safe business Their chief ambition was to save enough money to enable them to retire and live on their incomes The sons of the wealthy bourgeoisie usually entered the professional classes, or joined the army of functionaries, business, unless it were wholesale, was not considered a satisfactory profession for the sons of retired businessmen. Government place-hunting became one of the penchants of the class A government position carried with it not only a degree of respectability but also a safe, secure income Under the old régime these government posts could be purchased for money; after 1814, they became part of the spoils in the game of politics.

The French bourgeoisie of 1814 still carried the virus of rationalism which they had caught from Voltaire and the philosophers of the eighteenth century. The hold of the Church on the middle-class Frenchman had been weakening for over a century. The privileges which the Church had enjoyed during the old régime and the obvious monopoly of high Church positions of the nobility had long been a sore spot for which the anticlericalism of the eighteenth-century philosophers provided a balm After 1814 their naturally anticlerical bias was strengthened by the alliance between the churchmen and the old nobility which made them tremble for the fate of their Revolution Most of the bourgeoisie were too conservative to break their connections with religion; they still went through the forms of Catholicism while they molded their lives without too much advice from their spiritual mentors When they saw the union between altar and reaction established, they did not hesitate to raise hands against their priests and bishops. The women, however, if they were educated at all, received their education from the Church, and, educated or not, they tended to cling to the spiritual consolations of religion; thus the seeds of Catholicism remained embedded in the class. Later in the century, when the wealthy bourgeoisie discovered that a radicalism had developed which was as dangerous to their wealth as the Revolution had been to the privileges of the old nobility, Catholicism again regained its place with men of wealth, for the Church has always been a powerful institution for social control

In politics and economics the bourgeoisie were largely converted to the twin dogmas of the nineteenth century: liberalism and individualism Their liberalism meant that they believed in the Revolution and were ready to defend its gains They stood for freedom of press, speech, assembly, and trade They resented all governmental action that would interfere with the individual's pursuit of his own good and the enjoyment of his own property They refused to become too enthusiastic over any form of government. Republic, Empire, monarchy, each in turn received their support as long as their claims to property rights, equality before the law, and personal liberty were recognized They cheered the victories of Napoleon, but when his taxes and his conscriptions reached for their pocketbooks and their sons, the bourgeoisie were glad to brand the hero-emperor a tyrant and to swear allegiance to the restored Bourbons who would recognize their rights. Their conception of society was the familiar combination of Montesquieu and Adam Smith They wished to see a government in which the balance of powers would leave each individual free to work out his own destiny, and they trusted that the strongest would find their natural places as leaders of the society. This was a comforting doctrine for men who, scorning blood and titles as a basis for social distinction, regarded wealth and the power that comes from wealth as the natural order of things.

As a class, the French bourgeoisie of 1815 were very restricted in their outlook. They did not travel nor did they read extensively They had little conception of the world beyond their own countinghouses or shop walls Their virtues were the homely virtues of middle-class respectability, and their vices were the vices bred of the love of money For both they were often satirized by the dramatists and literary men of the day, but theirs was the class destined to dominate France They, with the nobles, made up the electorate; they owned the wholesale businesses, the ships, such factories as there were, and the banks, they forced the peasants to work in their fields and the proletariat to produce their goods They set the tone for society—a tone which, after 1830, was copied by the monarch himself

THE great masses of the French people were neither nobles nor bourgeoisie. They were peasants in the country and proletarian laborers in the cities, and neither group had any voice in the councils of the nation nor any considerable stake in the civilization of the country. The Revolution, however, had been advantageous to the peasants; they, with the bourgeoisie, were its principal legatees. In the old France the peasants worked the land under many different contracts A few of them had never cast off the bonds of serfdom, a few of them had risen to the position of full proprietors. The great majority, however, had been *censiers, métayers,* tenant farmers, or merely agricultural laborers. They owed their lords a feudal due of money, kind, or labor, or they farmed the lands on shares under a contract not dissimilar to that of the sharecroppers of the cotton belt of the United States, or they rented their lands outright from the lord; or they were agricultural proletarians dependent upon a daily wage

Moreover, they were hemmed in by laws and traditions that dictated almost every move they made, from the sowing to the harvesting of their crops They paid heavy taxes to the state, and to their lord for the use of his oven, his mill, or his wine press They were forbidden to molest the game that destroyed their crops, and were forced to allow the hunting expeditions of their noble neighbors to range freely over their fields. They could be called upon for personal service on the roads, and in some cases in the lord's fields. The lot of the prerevolutionary peasant was far from enviable, even though it probably was not so sordid and miserable as the worst descriptions of peasant life under the old régime would lead us to imagine

The Revolution had done much for the peasants, but not so much as some writers would like to believe By the cancellation of all feudal dues and obligations, serfdom was abolished and the *censiers* became full proprietors In the sale of confiscated lands of the Church and the émigré nobles, the total peasant holdings were considerably increased The repeal of the game laws guaranteed the peasant against invasion of his unharvested fields by hunters The abolition of laws regulating cultivation gave the peasant control over his own crops. Other laws freed him from the obligation to use the lord's oven, mill, wine press, and so forth The crushing burden of taxation was considerably lightened, and other humiliating obligations, such as personal service on roads, were removed. The peasants, not without justice, regarded the Revolution with friendly eyes

But it was often impossible or impracticable for the peasant to take full advantage of the opportunities open to him Traditions and customs dominated the rotation of crops, the tilling of the fields, the use of the public utilities of the village The freedom that was given to the peasant did not bear its complete fruits until after the whole generation that knew the Revolution and the Empire had died. Furthermore, the work of the Revolution did not affect all classes of peasants equally To the individualists who wrote the revolutionary legislation, all feudal contracts were an anathema, but they did not recognize the fact that the lot of the tenant farmer, the sharecropper *(métayer)*, or the landless agricultural laborer was not greatly dissimilar to that of his neighbor that owed feudal obligations. It was not the actual economic predicament, but the contract, that interested the revolutionary lawgivers They held that the peasants who tilled land as tenant farmers or sharecroppers made nonfeudal contracts that were not beneath the dignity of freemen.

One other important consequence of the Revolution, as far as the peasant was concerned, was the ubiquity of mortgages on practically every peasant holding. When the confiscated lands of the Church and the émigrés were sold, bourgeois land speculators succeeded in buying up most of the estates, and then proceeded to parcel them out piecemeal to the peasants. The land-hungry country people almost to a man bought more than they could pay for, and optimistically gave a mortgage to the extent of their entire holding to indemnify the speculator. These mortgages hung like a heavy cloud over the whole countryside The interest rates were often ruinous; the peasants were usually in constant fear of losing their lands Many of the mortgages contracted before 1800 were not finally paid up until after the World War when inflation came to the rescue of the debtors.

When the Empire of Napoleon came to an end, the peasants were almost completely illiterate, and even if they could read, they were unable to obtain books or newspapers. Their intellectual life, if it could be so called, was almost entirely under the influence of the clergy, a neighboring landlord, or the government functionaries in the village Their world was bounded by their fields, and even the next village was often unknown to them Their houses were often wretched hovels shared with the beasts of the field, and completely lacking in sanitation or comfort. Their food was largely rye bread and soup, their clothing the coarsest of cloth, often made in their own home. Their labors, which were long and hard, left marks on their bodies in the form of gnarled hands and stooped shoulders that Millet and other painters of the next generation loved to record. The peasants furnished labor for the rich, taxes and soldiers for the state, and enjoyed only the barest of living for themselves But the Revolution had opened the way, which the nineteenth century was to develop, for the growth of a France dominated by small land-owning proprietors.

THE urban proletariat, although far fewer in number, were often more wretched than the peasants, and the most discouraging fact about their predicament was that the first fifty years of the nineteenth century saw their lot steadily becoming worse. Revolutionary legislation had effectively destroyed the guild regulations which had become irksome to the laborers, but the individualists who wrote the revolutionary legislation did not sympathize with the problems of the proletariat any more than had the king before them. Under the Empire the bourgeoisie riveted their ideas of social control firmly on the state through the great Napoleonic law codes It was the proletariat that fought on the barricades and, with the peasants, filled the revolutionary armies, but the Revolution was not theirs They had not the training, or the numbers, or the leaders, to mold the course of events in their favor

Revolutionary legislation forbade the workers to combine for their common advantage, on the ground that there were "no longer any interests save the particular interest of each individual and the general interest of the state." The Napoleonic codes standardized this ruling by prohibiting all unauthorized associations This applied equally to employers and employees, but it is interesting to note that the penalties imposed upon employers for combinations to reduce wages were less severe than those imposed upon employees who combined to better their salaries This fitted in neatly with the general bourgeoisie conception of liberty and equality, each individual was assured the "freedom" of contract on a basis of equality before the law. Napoleon did authorize the establishment of mutual-benefit societies among the workers, but he insisted that they must have no professional or political aims. However, in spite of all that the police could do, *compagnonnages*—loose associations dating back to the Middle Ages—did persist *sub rosa,* especially among the building workers The working classes were always suspect in the eyes of the police, some groups more than others The metal and furniture workers were considered the most docile, while the building trades and especially the printers were the most dangerous. "There are no workers," wrote an imperial *fonctionnaire,* "more insubordinate, more disposed to coalition and tumult than the printers of letters."

The lives of the proletarians were further controlled through the institution of the *livret* This was a small book necessary to every laborer; in it each of his employers testified to his satisfactory conduct. The *livret* was deposited with the employer, who kept it as long as the worker was in his service. Without it a worker could not hope to obtain a position. In any dispute between employer and employee the law recognized only the word of the former, and the employer was urged to denounce his employee to the police if there was the slightest question about his loyalty to the state or his obedience to the law. This system effectively assured the bourgeoisie that their workers would remain docile.

The urban proletariat of 1814 was not a numerous class; the great industrial concentration of the Machine Age was still in the future The class included the beggars, the hewers of wood and drawers of water, the craft workers in small shops, and the like. They worked from sunup to sundown under unsanitary and miserable conditions which gave many of them asthma, catarrh, skin diseases, lung infections, and nervous troubles. They lived in wretched quarters of the city slums under appalling conditions that defy description Like the peasants, their diet rarely knew meat, eggs, or butter, and usually consisted of black bread and cabbage soup. Their wages afforded them sustenance so near the line of starvation that a third child, if it lived, was a source of misery to its parents Also, like the peasants, they were largely illiterate or unable to secure reading matter, and it was not until the middle of the century that the journalists began to reach them with their propaganda The proletariat had little share or stake in the civilization of France; their prospect was a life of labor and want that started in childhood and ended only with death. A surprisingly large percentage of them (one out of every nine inhabitants of the city of Paris) could expect to die in the workhouse.

In 1815 the upper crust of French society, nobles and bourgeoisie, was almost completely indifferent to the lot of both the peasant and the proletarian. The socialist philosophers had not yet begun their crusade for social justice, nor had the novelists and artists yet found in the lives of the wretched suitable materials for pen and brush The mass of the people of France living in the towns and the countryside were largely excluded from the benefits of the civilization which their nation had developed, and were ignored by those who were enjoying it.

THE impact of the years of Revolution and Empire on the intellectual development of France was no less striking than it had been on other phases of French civilization The old France drew its inspirations largely from its own traditions or its humanistic education. The classics of Greece and Rome and the classics of indigenous French philosophers and men of letters formed the nucleus of the culture of the old régime. It was thoroughly French, acclimated and nourished in national traditions It is true that Montesquieu, Voltaire, and a few others among the philosophers discovered Europe, but they explained Europe to France in terms of French traditions.

The Revolution drove thousands of Frenchmen to England, Germany, Spain, Italy, Russia, and even to the Near East These involuntary travelers discovered, to their surprise, that there was a civilized world beyond French frontiers, and many of the noble nomads were able to appreciate the driving force of the world culture with which they were unwillingly confronted. After 1795 they began to trickle back into France, bringing with them the civilization of their temporary homes to enrich and fertilize the intellectual life of France. A brief roll call of the articulate visitors to foreign lands shows that de Maistre, the Duc de Richelieu, and Madame de Krudener visited Russia; Delille, Arnauld, Fontanes, Malouet, Mallet du Pan, and many others lived in England; Bonald, Constant, Portalis, Degerando, and Boufflers were among the émigrés in Germany; LaFayette, du Pont de Nemours, and Chateaubriand visited the United States. Others went to Italy, Spain, and the Near East Madame de Stael's celebrated book on Germany was one of the many discussions of the world which these émigrés offered to their fellow citizens.

The emigration, however, was only one of the contacts which Frenchmen made with the world. The armies of the Republic and the Empire did much to destroy the provincial outlook of France; they watered their horses in the Nile, the Danube, the Vistula, and even the Volga; they left the bones of Frenchmen scattered all over Europe. They brought back impressions of European civilization, as well as the art treasures of Italy, Flanders, and Germany, to the infinite gain of French culture. Furthermore, Paris under the Empire became the capital of Europe, to which the genius and the talent from the four corners of the world were inevitably attracted. The *Weltanschauung* of France probably had never been more cosmospolitan than it was in 1814 when the conquerors of Napoleon occupied Paris.

The Revolution also profoundly affected not only French but general European intellectual development The philosophers of the eighteenth century, with their naive respect for human intelligence, their boundless belief in the promise of the future, and their hatred for thoughtless tradition, with their scoffing mockery of the Church and their insistence on rational behavior, were responsible for much of the intellectual equipment of the revolutionaries. The Age of Reason seemed to be at the roots of the violence, the tumult, and the wars of the Revolution. By 1815 the Revolution meant to many only the misery of bad paper money, the horrors of the Reign of Terror, the military despotism of Napoleon, and the suffering of endless wars Many timid souls drew back aghast before the logic of rationalism, others cynically proclaimed that nothing else could be expected from men who knew no authority The human intellect, it seemed, could not be trusted. In their reaction, men fell back upon the dictates of emotion They found in the heart a suitable substitute for the mind. They asked for security rather than liberty and equality.

De Maistre and Bonald were among the first to open the attack on rationalism, but they did it with all the dialectical paraphernalia that the rationalists themselves had used. The heavy logic of their pages was almost a sufficient obstacle to prevent their message from reaching their readers. They rested their system on the propositions that "order" is the first principle of politics and that order can never be obtained without external authority. De Maistre, with incontrovertible logic, and often with brilliant wit, pushed his reader to admit that Europe could never achieve order without Christianity, and that Christianity could not function without an authoritative head, the Roman Catholic pope Bonald denied the eighteenth-century assumption that man is naturally good and that he creates his own society. With dull and ponderous argument he proved that society is the creation of God from whom all powers flow, and that God divinely constituted monarchs to rule over the social order that He created Revolution, therefore, is defiance of God's will, constitutions are a mockery of His purpose.

To these men and their disciples the Revolution meant the guillotine, profanation of churches, and strife. The cure they offered lay in spiritual and temporal authority, with divinely constituted power to use force in suppressing the brutality of man's natural impulses. As one careful and brilliant historian observes. " . . the persistence of their appeal to external authority leaves the impression that the institutions in which they placed their faith were bankrupt in everything except such authority " De Maistre did see, however, that the Revolution could not be checked until it had burned itself out He held that it, too, was God's work, to punish men for their sins, and in time it would destroy itself to return men to their natural social order.

It is obvious that these philosophers drew much of their argument from the patterns of medieval society. Their central theme, however, might well have escaped popularity if it had not been translated into intelligible language by another group of men who also went to the Middle Ages for their inspiration. The romanticists, with Chateaubriand at their head, took up the crusade to rescue France from anarchism and rationalism. The movement was already well under way in England and Germany when it was introduced into France to prepare the way for the conversion to Catholicism and monarchy. The romanticists profoundly distrusted the human intellect, but in the heart and the emotions they found truth and beauty They drank deeply of the culture of the Middle Ages, a culture scorned since the Renaissance, and urged their contemporaries to see the satisfaction, the beauty, and the security of medieval life They neglected the drab and unsavory aspects of medieval society and emphasized its pageantry and its picturesqueness.

Naturally, their medievalism, like their search for authority, led them to the Roman Catholic Church. They saw its beauty, its appeal to the human heart, rather than any theological pattern. Rivarol replied to Voltaire: "It is not a question of knowing whether religion is true or false, but whether it is necessary." Madame de Stael explained: "The work of the philosopher is to perfect administration, to encourage populations by wise political economy . . . but the dignity of the human soul means more than happiness and, above all, an increase in population, to multiply births without ennobling human destiny is to prepare a more sumptuous feast for death " Chateaubriand, after painting the beauty and security of Catholicism, declared "France, instructed by her misfortune, has finally opened her eyes; she has recognized that the Catholic religion is like an anchor which alone can quiet her restlessness "

The Catholic religion offered to these men beauty, security, and artistic inspiration They were flowing with the tide away from the hard rationalism of the eighteenth century. The movement, begun even before the Thermidor, was, by 1800, secure; in 1814 rationalism and freethinking were definitely out of style. For these men who asked for security and authority in religion it was only a short step to the embrace of the whole ideology of monarchy by divine right In a somewhat mystic way, they confused the émigrés with the heroes of Arthur's Round Table and Charlemagne's court They believed, or wished to believe, that they saw the color of the Middle Ages in the court of Louis XVIII. These early romanticists now seem to us like frightened children seeking solace on their mother's breast, but it must be remembered that they paved the way for the richly imaginative literature and art that France was to develop in the first half of the new century

If the contact with Europe and the terror of the Revolution produced a philosophy of absolutism and authority with a literature of romanticism and imagination to support it, that same contact also brought France in touch with the more forward-looking doctrines of the new century. At the turn of the century J B. Say introduced the *laissez-faire* doctrines of Adam Smith to the French and rapidly forced many of his fellow citizens to see the superiority of the reasoning of the *Wealth of Nations* over that of the French physiocratic philosophers. With Smith came the whole theory of individualistic economics, which fitted in well with the individualistic political philosophy of the Revolution The bourgeoisie discarded the economist's belief in free trade between nations, but they heartily approved of the doctrine of *laissez faire* within the state. Later in the century, Malthus, Ricardo, and Mill found France well prepared to receive their expansion of the science of classical economics.

The beginning of the new century had not been kind to many of the political doctrines of the Revolution. Napoleon had substituted glory for personal liberty, and autocracy for democracy. The restoration in 1814–1815 was made by a Europe deeply suspicious of revolutionary ideology. But France had learned much in the twenty-odd years before 1814, not the least being a general conception of popular sovereignty.

Napoleon had repeatedly recognized its validity, and the charter which Louis XVIII granted in 1814 half-heartedly admitted that the people had some right to control their own destinies The whole ideology of liberalism—equality before the law, freedom of speech, press, and association; inviolability of person and property—had been ingrained into the political outlook of millions of Frenchmen, and although, for the moment, they might admit invasion of some of these concepts, they doggedly clung to the ideals

Rationalism, too, did not completely give way before the mysticism of the romanticists and the authoritative pronouncements of the reactionary philosophers Voltaire never lost his popularity with a large section of the French people, and the "witches' dance" of the obscurantists, mystics, and romanticists tended to make him only more popular with the opponents of the Restoration. However, the men of the new century who were to build anew on the spiritual foundations of the eighteenth century had not yet taken their places on the stage of French intellectual life in 1814–1815.

CHAPTER II

THE REACTION VERSUS THE REVOLUTION

THE collapse of the Napoleonic Empire left the solution of the political problems of Europe in the hands of the allies. Czar Alexander, Metternich, and their friends could not stop when Napoleon surrendered his sword, theirs was the task of remaking the western world. Since there was no recognizable authority in France with which they could negotiate, their immediate problem was to find a French government that could sign a treaty of peace. The allies had no intention of imposing a government upon France, their only condition was that Napoleon must never again sit on the throne. There were several possible solutions in the air: the Bourbons might be restored; a regency for Napoleon's son might be created, or a new dynasty might be established. Metternich was struck by the lack of Bourbon sympathizers, and Castlereagh believed that British opinion would be hostile to a Bourbon restoration. Metternich may have favored a regency, but the other statesmen feared the influence which that would give Austria over France, since the empress was a Hapsburg. Alexander rather favored Marshal Bernadotte, who would establish a new dynasty, but Castlereagh and Metternich were hostile to the idea. Even a republic was considered, but not for long. The allies ended by temporizing and waiting for the French to express their desires, a tacit recognition of popular sovereignty.

The French were somewhat surprised at the indecision of their conquerors, but when the Parisians discovered that the Russians were not merely paying them a return visit for Napoleon's trip to Moscow, they settled down to the amusing and profitable task of selling to their invaders wine and entertainment. The average Parisian probably believed that nothing he might do could possibly affect the situation, so he, too, waited for events to shape themselves Not so the presumptive leaders of France, they were thoroughly tired of war and wanted peace, but they also wanted a government that would assure the benefits of the Revolution for France, a secure position for themselves, and, at the same time, induce the invaders to be generous in their terms A group of erstwhile trusted servants of Napoleon, headed by no less skillful a politician than Talleyrand, decided after conferring with emissaries of the Bourbon pretender, the Comte de Provence, that France could not do better than to establish a constitutional monarchy under the old royal family France had forgotten the Bourbons; children born in 1789 were already twenty-five years old, and men of forty only vaguely remembered Louis XVI. The Bourbons would surely be willing to accept the Revolutionary settlement for a chance to give up their wanderings in foreign lands.

Talleyrand undertook to sell the idea to the allies. "The Bourbons," he told Alexander, "are the best guarantees of general peace, and France desires them A regency, Bernadotte, a republic, would only yield intrigues; the Restoration alone is a principle, it is the triumph of legitimacy." This was an alluring doctrine to the men who were trying to find a principle to apply to the chaos that was Europe. Alexander hesitated; Talleyrand's fellow plotters bought an idle crowd in Paris to stir up a Bourbon demonstration. When the Russian emperor rode through the city, cries of "Vive les Bourbons!" "Vive Alexandre!" convinced the doubting czar that the principle of legitimacy was as dear to the hearts of Frenchmen as it was useful in the diplomacy of the allies The question was settled, Louis Stanislas Xavier de Bourbon, brother of the late king, was soon invited to ascend the throne of his ancestors.

The senate and legislative corps hastily declared their creator, Napoleon, and his heirs forever deposed from the throne of France, and set up a provisional régime to govern France until a regular government could be established A commission was appointed from the senate to draw up a constitution which would provide a safe and profitable place for its makers, and Louis was invited to return to his country as its legitimate, but constitutional, monarch. Alexander and the allies approved of these steps, or they never could have been effected; the autocrat of Russia even promised the constitution makers that he would defend them against the possibility of a non-constitutional king. But neither Alexander nor his allies gave France the government or the principle of the Restoration; that was the work of Talleyrand and his friends.

Louis, the pretender to the throne, was living in England more or less as the guest of the British government when he received the news of his good fortune. He was tired of his traveling, suffered from gout, and desired nothing more than a chance to return to his native land with some assurance of being able to stay. His years of exile had not corroded his good sense, and his thorough respect for the philosophers of the eighteenth century gave him some understanding of the problems which were to confront him. Charles, comte d'Artois, his brother, who did not share Louis' sound sense, preceded the new king to Paris, and assumed the title of lieutenant general of the realm, but he would take no oath to defend the senatorial constitution. When the king arrived, he, too, rejected the senate's document, but promised to grant to his people a charter that would guarantee the rights of Frenchmen. Once in Paris, he assumed a brave air and received his brother monarchs, the conquerors of Napoleon, as he believed befitted a descendant of Louis XIV. He surrounded himself with faithful nobles who had shared his exile, but he chose a ministry of men who had served the Empire, with Talleyrand in charge of foreign affairs. His first acts were to sign the peace treaty presented by the powers and to grant the Charter which had been drawn up by a commission appointed by himself.

This royal Charter was a curious combination of paradoxes, a compromise between democracy and the divine rights of kings. Its vague nature left much for usage to establish.

Earlier French constitutions had spoken of the rights of man; this document assured the rights of Frenchmen to equality before the law, to freedom of press and speech and religion, to fair trial by jury, and to undisturbed possession of property. The same Charter proclaimed Roman Catholicism the religion of the state, provided that laws should be made to correct the "abuses" of the press, and allowed for the erection of courts of extraordinary jurisdiction The Charter's preamble reasserted the divine right of kings, but tacitly it recognized the revolutionary principle of the sovereignty of the people. It established a government in which the king possessed all of the executive power, with the right to command armed forces, make treaties, and declare war, but he exercised this power through responsible ministers. The legislative power was to be divided between the king and a bicameral legislature with a house of hereditary peers and a chamber of deputies elected on a restricted suffrage. Although they had the right of petition, the chambers could not prepare a law; they could, however, accept or reject any proposal of the king. The Charter assumed a ministry, but did not state clearly whether the ministry could survive adverse legislative action The whole Napoleonic administrative and legal system was incorporated into the new régime, and the recently created imperial nobility was recognized as on a par with the nobility of the old régime.

It was obviously an imitation of the English system. To assure conservative control of the legislature, the deputies were elected by voters who were at least thirty years old and who paid 300 francs or more in direct taxation, and only men who were at least forty years old and who paid 1,000 francs or more in direct taxes could be candidates. The peers, men of the Empire as well as of the old régime, were paid a generous stipend of 30,000 francs a year, but the deputies served without salary. The impracticality of this system did not seem to daunt the men of 1814 who threw in their lot with the Restoration. France had had many constitutions in the twenty-five years that had passed since 1789, and somehow had always managed to find a government.

WITH Louis XVIII apparently seated firmly on a constitutional throne which the French people might learn to love, the allies left France for Vienna to decide the fate of the rest of Europe. Louis, however, was unaccustomed to ruling and unacquainted with the temper of the French. His court was crowded with threadbare nobles who believed that France should make good the misfortunes they had suffered in the years of her madness. These returned nobles, the former émigrés, had little political sense, but unbounded greed; like vultures they descended on the part of the confiscated lands that still remained the property of the state, and, after dividing it, began to talk about further indemnification. With an arrogant air they forced their way into the army and civil service, and demanded promotion on the basis of their services in Prussia, Austria, or Russia. Officers of Napoleon found themselves on the retired lists or even discharged; the functionaries of the Empire saw men who had not been in France for years in their offices as prefects and secretaries of state. But the boasts of these men were even more grandiose than their deeds, and to the Frenchmen who had stayed home after 1789 it appeared that the effects of the Revolution would soon be nullified. The issue soon became clearly drawn. The men who had acquired the confiscated lands were facing the erstwhile owners of their property; both groups could not be satisfied. The men with careers earned in the army and the administration under the Empire were facing the men who felt that their noble blood gave them just claims to preference in both military and civil positions; both groups could not be cared for. France began to grumble; plots—contrary to the prediction of Talleyrand—began to spring up like mushrooms.

While Talleyrand was defending the rights of small states at Vienna, and Frederick William and Alexander were planning to take Saxony and Poland, the news of this discontent in France reached Elba. Napoleon was already a little bored with his island, after he had completely reorganized the administration, there was little left for him to do The murmur of Frenchmen decided Napoleon upon a bold stroke. He would recapture France She was not hard for Napoleon to seduce; the "glories" of the Bourbons had not dulled the memories of the "Little Corporal," while the pretensions of the émigrés made him seem a great liberal With a handful of men, he landed on the southern coast of France, and, although those men who remembered his tyranny and his taxes remained cool to him, his march to Paris resembled a triumphal procession. The armies sent to capture him were transformed into loyal legions ready to follow him anywhere. There was nothing for Louis XVIII and his courtiers to do but leave France before they were put in prison

In Paris, Napoleon was received a little coldly by those men who had hoped to see France develop liberal institutions. They admitted that he had the power, but they indicated that he could never again establish the autocratic Empire Napoleon, too, realized that he could hope to retain his position only by returning to his earlier rôle of "eldest son of the Revolution"; he therefore hurriedly gathered together some of his friends and some of his critics to draw up a constitution. Constitution making in France was a familiar task, and Napoleon's Additional Articles were accepted almost unanimously by those Frenchmen who bothered to go to the polls to vote in the plebiscite The Napoleonic constitution of 1815 was obviously in competition with the Bourbon Charter; while it was a little more liberal, it provided for essentially the same things But would Europe allow Napoleon the privilege of assuring France the fruits of her Revolution?

The news of his return reached Vienna just when Talleyrand had succeeded in insinuating himself into the councils of the allies, but with the eagles again in France the powers forgot their differences. The men who had won at Leipzig were resolved never to allow Napoleon to rule again On

March 13, 1815, they declared that Napoleon's march on Paris could not be considered an act of war, it was "a crime against the social order" By leaving Elba, Napoleon had destroyed the only legal title to his existence, "he had placed himself outside of civil and social relations, and, as an enemy and disturber of the peace of the world, he had delivered himself to social reprobation." This, said Talleyrand, was not a declaration of war; it was Napoleon's death sentence The negotiations at Vienna were hurriedly concluded, for, with Napoleon in France, the leaders of Europe had other business on their hands. The partly disbanded armies were mobilized, and Europe again heard the tramp of marching feet

Napoleon, however, wished to avoid a struggle He tried to convince Europe that he intended to settle down as a peace-loving sovereign. "We do not wish to meddle with the affairs of others," he said, "but woe to those who meddle in ours." When neither pleas nor threats softened the adamant determination of the allies, he prepared for war Only his brother-in-law, the unhappy king of Naples, came to his assistance, and then too late to do anything but deprive himself of his throne. By the middle of June the imperial armies were facing the British and the Prussians in Belgium After three days of feeling around, Napoleon threw his entire force at Wellington and Bulow at Waterloo (June 18) While the battle was raging, Blucher arrived with the rest of the Prussians, and Napoleon was crushed He had ruled a Hundred Days.

Back in Paris, Napoleon abdicated in favor of his son, Napoleon II, and, when his services as "General Napoleon" were scornfully declined by the men who assumed control, he started that long journey which was to lead to a martyr-hero's death on a lonely island in the south Atlantic. Napoleon II was tacitly accepted by the Parisians, but they refused to defend themselves or him against the invaders. Carnot remarked, when asked what he thought of the possibilities of defending the city. "My opinions cannot be doubted; I voted in the Convention for the death of Louis XVI, and I have no reason to expect favors from the Bourbons, who perhaps are coming tomorrow to Paris, but as a Frenchman I believe that it would be criminal to expose this great city to the chances of a last battle and the horrors of a siege." Wellington and Blucher were masters of the situation.

AGAIN the allies were forced to consider the problem of finding a responsible government for France Castlereagh and Alexander had come to believe that the Bourbons, through their foolishness, had forfeited their claims to the throne France must have a government which could maintain itself, and there were excellent reasons for believing that the Bourbons with their unpolitically minded entourage could never be stable. Louis Philippe, duc d'Orléans, was seriously considered as a candidate for the throne. He had had sense enough not to associate himself with the émigrés, and he was believed to be a man of parts who could be trusted to use some judgment But Metternich finally decided that Louis XVIII, the *legitimate* king of France was necessary not only to the European system, but also to Austria, and one by one the other powers came to see that this was the only solution. So, while Napoleon embarked on the *Bellerophon* to go to St Helena, where he paved the way for his nephew to become emperor of the French, Louis XVIII returned to Paris, declaring that he forgave all except the "instigators of this dream" which had brought the emperor from Elba.

When the powers gathered around the table to make peace with France for a second time, they were not inclined to be as generous as they had been in 1814. France was forced to give the Saarland to Prussia, to receive an army of occupation to assure domestic peace, and to pay an indemnity for the fright which Napoleon had given Europe. This left France with the boundaries that she had had in 1789. The great powers then renewed the Quadruple Alliance as a guarantee of the peace of Europe On the morrow of the treaty, the

Holy Alliance was added to the portfolios of the European chancellors, and the League of Nations of 1815, which helped to keep peace in Europe for almost forty years, was complete.

France, however, was not to have internal peace for several months to come. The battle between the white flag with the lilies and the tricolored flag of the Revolution had to be fought out in many sections before she settled down. At Marseille the news of Waterloo was received with joy, the royalists unmercifully massacred the friends of Napoleon. In Lyon, the white flag did not appear until a month after Waterloo, but finally the royalists took a bloody revenge. Throughout the Midi—in Provence, Avignon, Languedoc, and many other places—the White Terror raged with unrelenting ferocity. The royalists found in the willingness of the French to desert the king fresh proof of their theory that the nation was honeycombed with traitors, and used every means to seek out and destroy their enemies. The government was powerless or unwilling to intervene; when General Ramel, who had not served during the Hundred Days, attempted to prevent a massacre, he shared the fate of the supposed traitors.

The unofficial terror was supplemented by governmental acts of terrorism. In two ordinances of July 24 the government revoked twenty-nine peerages and posted a list of proscribed persons. In spite of his promise to allow the chambers to designate the guilty, Louis XVIII accepted a list which his chief of police, Fouché (a regicide himself), had drawn up, and Fouché had not forgotten many of his old friends. Eighteen generals were referred to court-martial, and thirty-eight other persons of high rank were placed under surveillance. Of the fifty-six suspects only thirty-one had accepted office under Napoleon before March 23; the king had promised not to consider as treasonable acts committed after that date. Of those proscribed, several were executed, but the deaths of General Labédoyère and Marshal Ney excited the most feeling. Ney was finally condemned by the chamber of peers, his was a useless and very stupid execution which many hero-loving

Frenchmen chalked up against the Bourbons The vengeance of the returning nobles did not stop with the punishment of individuals directly connected with the return of Napoleon. They found an excellent opportunity to continue the weeding-out process in both government and society. The government functionaries were so carefully selected that only about one-twentieth of the old prefects returned to their posts A large number of the late notables, including Garat, Siéyès, Merlin, Lucien Bonaparte, and Étienne were excluded from the *Académie Française,* while Monge, Carnot, and David were driven from the *Institut.* The last-named spent the rest of his life in Belgium, but his style remained enthroned at the *École des Beaux Arts* for years to come

The permanent result of the Hundred Days and the White Terror seems to have been the chasm that they created between the two sections of the French people. The Bourbons with their white flag, their stuffy manners, and their tales of the valor of Henry of Navarre probably never could have won the affection of the nation that carried the tricolor all over Europe, but the excesses of the men who surrounded the Bourbons finally convinced a large—if in 1815 almost inarticulate—number of Frenchmen that the Bourbons must be driven from the French throne. It is interesting to note that Louis Philippe, duc d'Orléans, in 1815 almost succeeded in getting the throne which a later revolution was destined to give him, and it is equally interesting to remember that Napoleon's last constitution, his defeat at the hands of Europe, and his subsequent, romantic exile laid the foundations for the great political myth of Bonapartism which one day was to place on the throne of France another Napoleon who would say, *"L'empire, c'est la paix."*

While the White Terror and civil war were still raging in the country, the king requested the election of the chamber provided for under the Charter. The rigid electoral qualifications reduced the number of voters to about 88,000 in a population of almost 30,000,000, and thereby assured to the rich and the well born alone the blessings of representation in the councils of the nation. With the nobility and the wealthy bourgeoisie as the electorate France was guaranteed against any radicalism that did not have adequate respect for the rights of property. The franchise and the Charter, however, assured France of more popular control and a more liberal government than any other European state possessed in 1815, the chamber was elected on a broader basis than even the House of Commons in England. But the first elections, held under the emotional duress of the White Terror, did not return a chamber representative of the French electorate; the émigrés in control of the forces for coercion did not hesitate to use the power of the state for their own interests. A very reactionary chamber soon rose to plague Louis XVIII and to interfere with his program of conciliation.

IN THE France of 1815, formal political parties were unknown, but the candidates tended to group themselves into more or less well defined patterns of political thought. On the one side, the royalists—ultra-royalists they were soon to be called—wished to re-establish the old régime. On the other extreme were the independents—an assorted group with many different views—who wished to overthrow the Bourbons. In the center was the large group of moderate royalists that wished to give the constitution a chance to work The lines between these parties were not clearly defined, often the parties merged almost imperceptibly into each other because of the lack of party organization or discipline and the general vagueness of party programs. The French electoral system has never been conducive to the development of political parties in the British or American sense.

As a group the ultra-royalists were numerically weak, but they were socially prominent and intellectually awake to their desires. The party drew its chief support from the country gentry, the émigrés, and the old aristocracy living in the Faubourg St. Germain. Their political philosophy was a complete negation of all that the Revolution had stood for; their political program was aimed at a systematic destruction of the reforms of revolutionary and imperial France. They rejected the idea of popular sovereignty as contrary to their belief that God alone is the fountainhead of all power, and therefore that political society is His own creation. With this divine origin of society in mind, they reasoned that man is sacrilegious if he attempts to penetrate into the mystery of its origin or modify its development "Man can no more give a constitution to society than he can give weight to the body or extension to mass"; it is the work of God, and man cannot change it From this they reasoned that the doctrine of "equality" was unholy in the sight of God, because it was contrary to the laws of God expressed in nature, where inequalities are patent everywhere. To proclaim equality is to blaspheme the maker of the cosmos.

Society, to the political thinkers of the ultras, was based upon these inequalities between men, and it must be organized in hierarchies of social order, so that each may know his responsibilities, his rights, and his place. At the top of the social pyramid stands the king, who is God's representative on earth. Any restriction, therefore, on the power of the king is, in the nature of things, an attack on the authority of God. Below the king must stand the nobility, who in turn govern the affairs of men in the countryside. It is easy to see that these men were dipping their pens in ink that was made before the age of Voltaire, and Rousseau; their inspiration was the Middle Ages and the Counter Reformation, and their philosophy was derived from that of the sixteenth and the seventeenth centuries. It is little wonder that these men returned after the Hundred Days filled with bitterness against their fellow citizens and resolved to "wipe out the destructive philosophy that had ravaged France and that will ravage the entire world if its course is not stopped."

The political program of the ultras shows that their philosophy was not adopted without consideration of their own political ambitions They wished to return France to a state vaguely resembling the France before Richelieu, in which the king would be supreme but the government so decentralized that a landed aristocracy, preserved by primogeniture, could exert a preponderant influence in the administration In their ideal state, the Church, revitalized and wealthy, was to play a predominant rôle in maintaining social discipline. To realize their program, they hoped to set the Charter aside and make the king's will supreme, to abrogate Napoleon's concordat and his Université de France, and so give the clergy an influential rôle in the state, including surveillance over, or even a monoply of, education The nobles, who had suffered so severely from the Revolution, were to be indemnified for their lands so unjustly taken from them and for the trials that they had been forced to bear because of their loyalty to the Bourbons. From their program the ultras earned their name; they were "more royalist than the king, and more Catholic than the pope."

The ultras, although few in number, were apt in circulating their propaganda. They established a dozen or more important newspapers including *Le Drapeau Blanc, Le Journal de Paris,* and *La Gazette de France,* which vociferously proclaimed their views and threatened their enemies In addition, ultra pamphleteers and writers turned out a steady stream of pamphlets and books to back up their case. Closely allied with the ultras was the new school of literature that gained so much ground in the early nineteenth century, the romanticists They joined hands with the ultras to proclaim the errors of the Age of Reason, the beauties of the Church, and the perfection of medieval society. Led by a chief of the ultra party, the Vicomte de Chateaubriand, the romanticists tried to give the people a new appreciation of the glories of the Middle Ages with their glamorous heroes, their picturesque society, and their respect for God. By a sort of imaginative gymnastics the Bourbons became the heirs of Charlemagne and Saint Louis, and the émigré nobility became a new crop of Rolands and Olivers.

In a cloud of brilliant, if somewhat maudlin, rhetoric and poetry, the beauties of Catholicism and mysticism were used to blot out the age of rationalism, while feudalism, the anathema of the Voltairian revolutionists, was given a halo of virtue and exposed for public admiration. Before 1830 many of the romanticists were somewhat disillusioned about the connection between émigré nobles and the heroes of the Crusades, but in 1815 they entertained few such doubts

The ultras not only had their philosophers, their politicians, and their journalistic and literary propagandists, but also their secret society. During the Revolution, when free exercise of religion was forbidden, a group of devout Catholics were accustomed to meet secretly at the old seminary for foreign missionaries to fulfill their religious obligations After the concordat, in spite of Napoleon, the movement did not disband, but became the Society of the Congregation of the Virgin, which had for its objectives the revival of religious emotion, the extension of clericism in politics, and action against the Empire. In 1814, the Comte d'Artois, heir to the throne, and probably Louis XVIII himself were introduced into the Congregation as members The society itself was never large, but it exerted considerable influence through the subsidiary societies which it organized, it became a tool both of the nobility and of the Jesuits to effect their political-religious program. It organized home missionary work, great revivalist meetings, and religious processions It stirred the clergy to use the pulpit in defense of ultra principles

If the ultras wished to destroy the Charter to pave the way for a re-establishment of the old order, political, religious, and social, there was another group of the French electorate that also wished to destroy the Charter, but to give France a chance to develop more liberal institutions. This group, unorganized though it was, has been variously called independents, liberals, or the party of the tricolor. The political faith of its members was tinged by a definite hatred of the Bourbons and their reactionary followers; they could not forgive the White Terror that had followed the Hundred Days, and they saw in every act of the Bourbons and the ultras a concerted effort to destroy the fruits of their Revolution. This party was covertly antidynastic, but it was far from united on any constructive program. Some wanted the Duc d'Orléans to replace the Bourbons, others wished to re-establish the Empire on a liberal basis, and a small group wished to see France become a republic.

If the members of this faction were not united on the question of form of government, they were one in their ideas about the governing class. Few if any of them were ready to consider a democracy in which the people would rule, they could not approve any government that did not give the men of wealth and substance a preponderant position in the affairs of state. Politics, in their minds, was the proper pursuit only of the socially washed and the intellectually well groomed. Most of them had a fear of an unbridled democracy in which men of property would carry little weight. On the other hand, they could not accept the old feudal order as a satisfactory solution of the problem. Their opposition to the Bourbons was personal, and their objection to the Charter was based on the fact that it was not a sufficient guarantee of the victories that the bourgeoisie had won in the Revolution. This group was profoundly influenced by Voltaire and the Enlightenment, and held deep in their hearts a biting scorn for the returned nobility and an abiding contempt for the clergy.

It was not until 1817 that the independents arrived at any realization of unity or any position of political importance, but all through the Restoration they kept up a running fire of criticism of their enemies on the right. Their newspapers, *La Minerve, La Bibliothèque Historique,* and others, contented themselves with urging anticlerical action and liberalism as interpreted by men of substance, while their poets and cartoonists amused France with witty jibes at the men in power. After 1815 a number of secret societies, including the *Charbonnerie,* a French model of the Italian *Carbonari,* came to be associated with the chiefs of this faction, but in spite of an abortive revolt in the early twenties, the revolutionary tendencies of the independents did not bear ripe fruit until Charles X outraged Paris in July, 1830. These men were the radicals of the French electorate—as radical as landed proprietors, bankers, ex-functionaries, rich lawyers, and doctors could be expected to be

Between the independents and the ultras there was a group of men that have been called constitutional or moderate royalists This group, the most important in the chambers and the favorites of Louis XVIII, was largely made up of the more moderate and realistic elements of the old nobility, many of the men of the Empire, and a large section of the bourgeoisie They wanted to stand by the Charter and to organize around it a conservative and stable government that would provide peace and tranquillity for France. They believed that the Charter was a proper compromise between the old and the new France, and that it was their task, in the words of one of their chiefs, "to nationalize the monarchy and royalize France." Their policy was the policy of moderates; they were willing to increase the power of the clergy, but not too far, they were willing to curb the press, but not to suppress it; they wanted a government of and by the aristocracy of wealth for safe, sound, conservative principles, "to heal the wounds of the Revolution" Their newspapers, *L'Independent, Le Constitutionnel, Le Censeur, Le Courrier Français,* and others, urged France to try to resolve the old and the new into a higher unity

Closely allied to the constitutional royalists was a small but influential group of intellectuals whose dogmatism secured for them the title of "doctrinaires" These men argued that anyone who believed in legitimacy, order, and liberty would naturally rally around the Charter as the greatest safeguard against the uncertainties of both revolution and reaction. Good government, they argued, was not the product of political theory, but of a system of guarantees. In their considered judgment the Charter represented the *juste milieu* which was a perfect compromise resulting from the historical development of France whose genius was neither Jesuit nor Jacobin Royer-Collard and his fellow doctrinaires held themselves aloof from the political parties, and their long, pedantic lectures on their ideal government earned for themselves the dislike of most of their colleagues. In case of a vote, however, they could be counted upon to oppose equally the reactionary right and the revolutionary left When Charles X attempted to put aside the Charter, it was the doctrinaires that rallied a majority in the chamber to protest against the usurpations of the king

None of these groups could properly be said to represent the opinions of the great mass of the French people. But it is impossible to say what the mass of the people really thought—if they did think—about government, for they were largely inarticulate The masses of Paris seem to have had considerable sympathy for the leaders of the independent faction when they were in opposition to the clerical policy of the ultras, but whether the people approved of their constructive policy is largely unknown One thing is fairly certain, that is, that the great mass of the people in 1815 wanted peace and tranquillity, and the conservativism natural to a peasant people probably led them to approve any government that, while it did not endanger the real or supposed benefits that the Revolution had secured for them, would insure them against a recurrence of the horrors of a war

AS MIGHT have been expected, the election which was held while the White Terror was still in progress gave the ultra-royalists a powerful majority in the chamber of 1815 Liberal electors had been intimidated both by roving bands of noble-blooded thugs, and by the officials of Church and state. Only about one-half of the small electorate went to the polls When Talleyrand saw the election returns, he and his ministry resigned, hoping that the king could not get along without them Louis XVIII, a little embarrassed by the violence of the support which the majority offered him, exclaimed, *"C'est un chambre introuvable."* But Louis had not left France hurriedly in the spring of 1815 without learning something about the France he was governing; he refused to play into the hands of his ardent supporters, who soon earned the description, "more royalist than the king." For prime minister, Louis picked the Duc de Richelieu, an émigré who had lived in Russia in high favor with the Russian court. His administrative experience had been gained while he was governor of Odessa, and, although he knew little of France, he was a good choice. The rest of the cabinet were mostly men of moderate views who, like Richelieu, loyally wished to carry out the Charter. It was a ministry that represented the spirit of the king rather than that of the ultra-royalist majority in the chamber.

At first everything seemed to go well Both the peers and the deputies assured the king of their warm support and their absolute loyalty The ministry introduced a series of laws of exception which pleased the revengeful spirit of the ultra majority; a strict press law, a law for "public security," a law to re-establish courts of martial law *(cours prévôtals)* which had been discontinued in 1790, and a law of amnesty were passed in rapid succession These laws placed over a thousand prominent revolutionary or imperial figures in danger of death, prison, or exile, and provided courts that would be swift and partial in their decisions. The government could weed out its enemies and muzzle any appeal to public opinion. But the ultras were not satisfied; they wanted laws to carry out their clerical policy: abolition of divorce, ecclesiastical control of education, suppression of the Université, and a new electoral law. Richelieu's hesitancy in yielding to their demands, which he feared would endanger the monarchy, resulted in a curious struggle for power. The ultras, defenders of the doctrine of divine right, insisted that the ministry must resign because it no longer enjoyed the confidence of the majority of the elected chamber The prerogatives of the king were defended from the left of the chamber!

With the laws of exception, the White Terror broke out anew: the new courts of martial law showed their zeal in following the law of "amnesty", scores of old officers, functionaries and important figures were summarily condemned to imprisonment, exile, and even death Of the suspects who hurriedly left France to escape the rigors of the new law, one group of about four hundred migrated to Texas, while others went to Germany, England, Italy, or Belgium to find an asylum from the wrath of their enemies These measures made many Frenchmen wonder if liberty can be bought too dearly, and made them reflect on the ease with which the Revolution had upset the old order When it was understood that the ultras planned to weed the revolutionary figures from the chamber of peers, the situation grew dangerous, France's tradition for direct action was strong

The allied armies that had defeated Napoleon were still camped in France, and it was obvious to them, if not to the ultras, that too much reaction could only result in a new revolution English newspapers began to discuss the advisability of dethroning the Bourbons, who were obviously unfit to rule, and placing Louis Philippe, duc d'Orléans, on the throne. Wellington wrote to Louis XVIII as early as February, 1816, expressing the fear that he would soon find himself calling Europe to arms again unless the king of France acted vigorously in defense of the moderate French ministry against the ultra majority Nesselrode instructed the Russian ambassador to tell the king's brother, the Comte d'Artois, who was heir apparent and leader of the ultra party, that the powers were not in France "to sustain his foolishness and to hold the French throne for him to ascend with his reactionary system " Finally, the ambassadors of the great powers flatly told Louis XVIII that he could not hope to govern France with so reactionary a chamber The ultra policy was too much even for the men who had signed the Treaty of Vienna and the Holy

Alliance to make the "world safe for legitimacy" Louis was apparently not sorry for this advice, since his own convictions and inclinations were not sympathetic to the ultra party An ordinance for dissolution of the chamber was prepared secretly, and issued on the fifth of September, 1816 By this act the king turned his back on his brother Charles, and on his reactionary supporters, and looked to the electors to see if they would return men ready to support the Charter and unite royal and revolutionary France

Naturally, the ultras were furious, they upbraided Louis XVIII as a traitor to the royal cause and dubbed him "King Voltaire" The other political groups were delighted to see the king side against the reactionaries Most important of all, the upper bourgeoisie seemed satisfied, for the *rentes* went up three francs on the Bourse. In the election that followed, the ultras confidently expected to win another victory They were resolved next time to create a real royalist faction by every means of coercion available to the party in power, in the fullness of his hopes the Comte d'Artois drew up a slate of new ministers that could be depended upon to carry out the policy Richelieu hesitated to use the full weight of the administrative machine to crush the political ambitions of his late fellow exiles, but his colleague, Decazes, untroubled by scruples, denounced the ultras as black reactionaries who would drive France to civil strife if given an opportunity The elections were quiet, and because this time the liberals and moderates cast their ballots, the result was a hearty approval of the moderate constitutional royalist policies The electorate wanted the king and the Charter; they rebuked the ultras who would have destroyed the latter.

The constitutional royalists remained in power from 1816 to 1820. Richelieu kept the post of prime minister until after the foreign armies of occupation were removed from France in 1817, and then Dessoles and Decazes took over the government. The latter had become a favorite of Louis XVIII, who enjoyed the many spicy tales about his courtiers that fell into

Decazes' hands by virtue of his office as minister of the interior In the three and a half years during which the men of the constitutional party controlled France they passed a new electoral law (1817); they reorganized the finances, the army, and re-established France's position as a great power (1818); and they inaugurated a new press law (1819) Their statesmanlike policies failed in the end to achieve their goal of nationalizing the monarchy and royalizing France, largely because of forces over which they had no control They found themselves in the sorry predicament which moderates often experience: they were caught between two groups with irreconcilable interests, and their moderation was unsatisfactory to both In France, as in all Europe, men were rapidly forming two opposing factions, the reactionaries and the revolutionaries, and in neither was there sympathy for moderation. The constitutional royalists, however, enjoyed the support of the king, who saw that their policy was the best guarantee of his throne, but even the king was no match for the conflicting forces which undermined moderation There could be no real compromise between the white flag and the tricolor

The new electoral law did not alter the heavy property qualification for voters and candidates that had been imposed by the Charter, but it did abolish the indirect method of election which had so hampered the selection of liberal candidates Under this law, the qualified electors met in the chief city of the department under the presidency of a man nominated by the king They chose their representatives to the chamber directly by *scrutin de liste* This law not only gave the advantage to the town-dwelling bourgeoisie, but also removed indirect electoral colleges The ultras insisted that the new law would give France "a democratic chamber, drawn from the inferior classes"; that it would destroy the balance of political power They protested that it was based on revolutionary precedents, and that men of property would be excluded from their rightful places in the councils of the state Since the property qualifications (300 francs tax for elector,

1,000 francs tax for candidate) were unchanged, the majority in both houses disregarded these doleful predictions, and the law passed in spite of a last-minute attempt by the ultras to obtain foreign intervention

The military law that was passed in the next year was the work of Marshal Saint-Cyr, an old revolutionary soldier. It was calculated to assure to the army a full quota of recruits each year, and to regulate the advancement of officers. Conscription as such was forbidden by the Charter, so the new law avoided the use of the word, but by a quota system it guaranteed a sufficient number of "voluntary enlistments" to fill up the ranks and to supply France with an army commensurate with her proper position as a great power Seniority and service were made the basis for promotions of the officers by this law, Saint-Cyr did not overlook the interests of his old comrades in arms. This was a hard blow to the old nobility; they assumed that dominance over the army was their own prerogative, and that the upstarts who commanded the imperial armies would be placed aside. This bill, they raged, "calls to the flag the enemies of the king; it is a conspiracy against the monarchy, legitimacy, and the Charter" The law passed, but soon the nobles found ways of evading its provisions. Old army units could be disbanded and reorganized under new names with new officers appointed by the king. The men of the imperial armies could be thus retired and men with ancient names could take their places.

Richelieu in the years 1816–17 was most preoccupied with the problem of re-establishing France's position in Europe After the Second Treaty of Paris (1815) France was burdened with an army of occupation and saddled with a war indemnity. Even more embarrassing was the fact that her erstwhile enemies were closely bound together by an alliance for the purpose of keeping France from disturbing the European peace. Thus France was humiliated and ostracized by Europe. The French people grumbled about the presence of foreign armies; the French budget was strained by supporting them.

Richelieu realized that the Bourbons could not win the heart of France as long as these so-called protectors of the monarchy —they had brought Louis back to his throne in 1815—remained on French soil

Richelieu first found money to pay the war indemnity by floating a series of large loans which, to the surprise of people who doubted the financial stability of France, were enthusiastically received and even oversubscribed With money in the treasury, Richelieu reorganized the finances, and then turned to his friend, Czar Alexander, for assistance in re-establishing France's position in international affairs Alexander was sympathetic to Richelieu's requests that the armies of occupation should be withdrawn so that the Bourbons could show the world that foreign bayonets were not necessary to maintain their throne. A European congress, the first of a series of meetings of the great powers in the decade 1815–25, was called at Aix-la-Chapelle to discuss the French question. At this conference Richelieu succeeded not only in liberating French territory but also in obtaining recognition of France's equality as a great power, the Quadruple Alliance, which had been directed against France, was transformed into a Quintuple Alliance that had as its objective the maintenance of general European peace. The four powers did secretly renew their old agreement to act together to prevent France from disturbing the peace, but France had gained a voice and a vote in the concert of Europe

With his king thus accepted as an equal, Richelieu withdrew from the cabinet and turned over the affairs of government to Decazes and Dessoles to carry on the constitutional policy. After the dissolution of the chamber in 1816, the government relaxed the rigorous press policy that the ultras had supported During these first years, when France was trying to learn to govern herself by a constitution and representative institutions, political theories were more freely discussed than they had been since the stormy days of the Revolution. But the press laws were extremely harsh. To lighten the burden on the newspapers, Decazes in 1819 offered a new press law, which removed preliminary censorship By this law, the owners of newspapers had to deposit a large sum with the government, the stamp tax of five centimes, a feature of the old law, was retained, but "crimes" of the press were turned over to a trial by jury rather than by a court of correction. The deposit and the stamp tax were enough to prevent the press from becoming too democratic, for only the wealthy could print and only the wealthy could buy, but the jury trial assured the journalists that their offenses would have a sympathetic hearing The ultras naturally condemned this law as a Jacobin measure, but their resistance was powerless to prevent its passage.

AFTER France had had a few years to forget the trials of the Empire and the civil strife of 1815, moderation ceased to satisfy anyone; the men on the right and on the left came to believe that compromise was impossible and really undesirable. This situation in France was not unique; moderates all over Europe were in the same predicament In Spain, Germany, Italy, and even in England there was an increasingly large number of men who felt that the *status quo* established by a war-weary Europe after the downfall of Napoleon was intolerable, and that the salvation of Europe could be assured only by direct action—revolution. On the other hand, here was a large body of tight-lipped, determined men who demanded that the people of Europe should forget the nebulous ideas of the Revolution and return to the eternal social verities of a disciplined, regimented society. These two trends, common to Europe, were vividly reflected in French politics, and determined France's political development. The position of the moderates between the two groups of men with strong convictions became increasingly difficult.

The rising tide of radical feeling made itself evident soon after the rigors of the White Terror were over, and grew apace with the moderate liberalism of the government after 1816

New election laws gave a better opportunity for the liberals to express their views by ballot, and the relaxed press administration allowed a freer discussion of political issues The renewals to the chamber in 1817, 1818, and 1819 placed the ultra party in the position of a small minority, but their places were not always taken by men of moderate constitutional royalist views. The independents showed considerable gains. In 1816 this so-called "tricolor party" was negligible, it increased in 1818, and by 1819 it appeared that the independents might even eventually command a majority in the chamber Within this group there were men who were known to be enemies of the Bourbons, many who were suspected of being hostile to the Charter; and most of them had been prominent figures during the Revolution and the Empire With old liberals like Lafayette, wealthy bourgeoisie like Laffitte, old imperialists like General Foy, as the chiefs of the left party, the defenders of reaction were quick to recognize the threat to their hopes When the notorious Abbé Grégoire, a regicide and an avowed enemy of kings, was elected in 1820, the men around the king pretended to believe that the bloody ghost of the Revolution was making ready to stalk again.

The elections gave only an indication of the storm that was brewing in France The independent press, especially after the new press law, was outspoken in its hostility to the state of affairs It fought bitterly every suggestion for a compromise of the Revolution with the old France, and was especially caustic about the increasing influence of the clergy. Between 1818 and 1821, secret societies, some of them with legal objectives, but usually inspired with the doctrine of direct action, became increasingly numerous and ambitious. In some cases—for example, the *Charbonnerie*—they were frankly preparing for the day of reckoning with the enemies of the Revolution by laying the groundwork for an armed revolt

This growth of radical liberalism drove the defenders of the old régime back to their belief that France was inhabited largely by traitors They naturally assumed a more extreme position on the right to counterbalance the attacks of the liberals They begged Louis to give up his erroneous ways and dismiss the ministry that was unwilling to see the dangers of radicalism The clergy, which largely stood by the ultras in condemning the follies of the moderate government, fulminated against the men of the left as enemies of God and man After 1818, the reactionaries got assistance from abroad. At Aix-la-Chapelle, Alexander urged upon his colleagues the necessity for a policy of intervention to check revolutionary movements, but since there were no demonstrable revolutions at hand, his pleas fell on deaf ears After this conference, revolutionary movements seemed to spring up everywhere: students in Germany toyed uneasily with liberalism and nationalism, a reactionary agent of the czar was assassinated Metternich promptly clamped the lid down on the German revolutionaries by the Vienna and Carlsbad decrees. In Italy and Spain the stupidity of reactionary kings drove their citizens to revolt, and the leaders of Europe began to be genuinely concerned

By 1820 the growing French independent party, which seemed to result from the moderation of the constitutional ministry, came to be regarded with suspicion in Vienna, Berlin and Saint Petersburg The liberals of all Europe saw Paris as the capital of freedom, but to the rulers of Europe, Paris was the capital of world revolution The czar and Metternich began to wonder what attitude they should take if French radicalism continued to grow, while the French reactionaries appealed to them to dissuade their "King Voltaire" from following a revolutionary course It appeared as though Europe would again intervene in French internal affairs

Decazes and the cabinet became genuinely alarmed when they saw their majority dwindling before the onslaughts of the left. Decazes was too much of a conservative to think of adopting the independents' views, and although he mistrusted the political intelligence of the ultras, he felt that something must be done to keep the conservative complexion of the chamber. His proffered solution was a new electoral law that would give a double vote to the heaviest taxpayers Several of his colleagues, unwilling to follow him in this policy, resigned from the ministry, Decazes then fumbled around trying to persuade the less reactionary leaders of the ultras to join his cabinet, but he had earned the suspicion of the entire right and a compromise with him was considered dangerous. An event over which he had no control soon ended his political career.

As the European revolutionary movement of 1820 gained momentum in Italy and Spain, radicals in France became more and more uneasy. Decazes' cabinet troubles were aggravated by an act of violence that was traceable to the general revolutionary movement in Europe rather than to any act of the French government. A fanatic murdered the Duc de Berry, son of Charles and the only male Bourbon that had a chance of presenting his king with an heir to carry the family name into the next generation The assassin's hopes of ruining the Bourbons by depriving them of an heir to carry on the line were blasted when the duchess gave birth to a posthumous son of the murdered duke This act of violence, however, brought about the downfall of Decazes. By a dextrous coup, the ultras represented the unfortunate minister as the real cause of the murder. Reluctantly Louis dismissed his favorite, made him a peer of France, and again drafted Richelieu to form a ministry that would lean heavily on the right The reaction that Europe was to experience after 1820 had already begun in France

BEFORE Richelieu would accept office, he secured a promise from the Comte d'Artois that he would give the new ministry his loyal support. Even then his position was far from secure; the ministry had to depend upon the moderates and the ultras for a majority in the chamber, and the ultras were impatient to carry out a policy of repression and reaction far more drastic than Richelieu could support. Furthermore, his position was endangered because the moderate center, upon which he had hoped to count, was in the process of dissolution. The events in Europe in 1820 added to the effect of the murder of the Duc de Berry, and drove the men of the center party either to the left or to the right. In 1820, Richelieu was only the stalking horse for the men of reaction; his usefulness was limited because he would go only part way with the party of the right.

Richelieu's principal task was to undo the supposed damage done by the Decazes government. The only answer that he and his colleagues could find to their problem was repression. All over Europe the men of 1820 had a curious reaction to the events of the day: they did not question the source of political discontent, nor did they attempt to draw up legislation that might remove the hostility to the existing régimes; they saw only the symptoms and tried to remove them. Hence Richelieu devised legislation that would hold the press in line and prevent the election of men who might voice discontent in the chamber. It was an ostrichlike policy that found precedent and followers everywhere. The French chamber, in spite of the strength of the members of the opposition, was ready to follow this policy blindly. Conservatives—and the old center was a conservative faction—and reactionaries alike were appalled at the idea of a new revolution, and resolved never to compromise with it Compromise, they said, had cost Louis XVI his throne and his life; they would not repeat his mistake.

The liberal press régime of 1819 was suspended and preliminary censorship was re-established, while the regulations surrounding the establishment of newspapers were generally tightened A new public-security law was passed, aimed at secret societies as well as at individuals who might possibly become a danger to the state The new electoral law was the most effective piece of reactionary legislation; it re-established the indirect election, which gave the administration a powerful control over the choice of candidates. But, even more important, it established two different types of electoral colleges one in which all qualified electors voted, and another reserved for those electors who paid the highest taxes This gave the wealthiest citizens two votes, and assured them permanent control over the chamber.

This legislation was conceived in the dominant note of the day The revolutions and threats of revolution of 1820–21 thoroughly frightened the conservative leaders of society, and their answer to the danger was the same—suppression. The great powers gathered in the quiet little city of Troppau to discuss the question of revolution as an international problem, and the three eastern states, Russia, Prussia, and Austria, ended by assuming the congenial task of underwriting the *status quo,* if necessary by force of arms This general doctrine of the right of intervention received teeth several months later when the powers reassembled at Laibach to hear the treacherous king of Naples complain about the revolutionary excesses of his subjects and to request the loan of a European army to re-establish his rights. That summer Austrian infantry tramped in the dust of Italian roads, and order with a capital "O" returned to the peninsula. Richelieu, following the lead of England, did not lend France's support to the eastern powers at Troppau and Laibach, and thereby incurred the displeasure of French reactionaries His resignation was soon given to the king.

France under Richelieu's direction did not send troops to Italy in 1821, but French troops had an opportunity to show their efficiency in France The reaction was popular in the Faubourg Saint-Germain, on the great country estates, and in the court, but it did not strike a responsive chord in many other classes of French society. The liberals and the independents, seeing their personal liberty imperiled, their newspapers muzzled, and the ballot boxes stuffed, gritted their teeth and prepared to defend their rights as Frenchmen. That society of revolution par excellence, the Italian *Carbonari,* had been imported into and organized throughout France. Professors, students, lawyers, intellectuals, a few merchants, mechanics, disgruntled politicians, and a large number of ex-army officers were initiated into its mystic rites, and each was instructed to provide himself with a rifle and fifty rounds of ammunition. Just before the new year of 1822 began, outbreaks flared up all over France, and for a while it seemed that Lafayette might become president of a French republic. But the government was too strong, and the revolts were badly planned. A number of brave men went to the scaffold to receive their crowns as martyrs for liberty; the march of reaction could not be checked.

The suppression of the revolts, like the White Terror in 1815, only deepened the gulf between the men of the Revolution and the men of the old régime; and Richelieu's program of moderation became increasingly impossible as the two factions faced each other with hatred in their hearts. While loyal troops were suppressing the *Charbonnerie* revolts, a lonely man died on an island in the south Atlantic. He left to France, and in particular to those men who wished the fruits of the Revolution combined with order, a legacy in the form of a great myth, which was at once a comfort and a program to men sorely tried under the restraining hand of political forces that knew not French spirit. But Bonapartism was for the future, when its new prophet would appear. In 1822, the French reactionaries still had their greatest follies before them, for they were to have several years in which they could try to create a France according to their own desires.

Richelieu's suppression of the *Charbonnerie* revolts did not save him from the wrath of the ultras which his liberal foreign policy had aroused. At last he was forced to resign. When he reproached the Comte d'Artois for failing to keep his promise of support, the ultra chief and future king evasively explained that conditions had changed since the promise had been given. The changed conditions were only in the chamber. The new electoral law worked as its authors had hoped; the elections of 1821 and 1822 gave the reactionary right an increasingly large majority, and these men of the right were anxious to be rid of the moderate Richelieu and to find a minister who would do their bidding The new minister, Villèle, was not a man cut exactly to their desire, but he was more satisfactory than any of his predecessors had been Villèle was an able administrator and a first-class financier, but, although his business sense prevented him from being a perfect ultra, he was weak before the representations of the Comte d'Artois who soon became king of France, and he was willing to oblige the clerical ambitions of the Congregation He was the last man that stood with the ultras to enjoy the confidence of an elected chamber of deputies.

WHEN Villèle took office, Louis XVIII had two more years to reign, but the wise old king was losing his hold on the affairs of state He had been shaken by the unfortunate assassination of the Duc de Berry; his health was broken, and he was absorbed in a woman provided by the ultra chiefs to give him the reactionary point of view But Louis was an unrepentant moderate, and on his deathbed in 1824 he warned his brother that it was his duty to save the crown for his grandson. Louis was buried at St Denis, and then France received an exhibition not forgotten even to this day. The Comte d'Artois became Charles X with all the pomp and circumstance that had surrounded the crowning of the kings of medieval France; he went to Rheims (1825) to receive the crown from the archbishop and to be anointed with the same holy oil that had been used in the Middle Ages Obliging churchmen explained that the oil was miraculously discovered. When the ceremony was over, he methodically set himself to the task of curing some of his subjects of scrofula by the king's touch, just as Saint Louis had done before him.

Charles ruled France from 1824 to 1830, and Villèle was his prime minister during the first four years of his reign. In that time the crown accumulated enough enemies to make the Revolution of 1830 comparatively easy. Charles personally was a kindly and charming man with many admirable virtues, but political sagacity was not included in his make-up. He was an uncompromising foe of the Revolution and an ardent Catholic; it was even rumored that he had been ordained a priest. He was unable or unwilling to understand that France did not share his views; he did not appreciate the fact that the nation had a meaning apart from the king Charles, as one historian cleverly remarked, "had all the qualities required for gaily losing a battle or for gracefully ruining a dynasty, but none needed for managing a party or reconquering a country." Villèle, at his side, was too willing to oblige the royal will, and too far removed from the vital political forces of French life to communicate to his master the true state of affairs The court was frequented only by a few ancient noblemen and their wives, friends of the king's exile, who played whist and avoided any discussion of politics The real springs of France were bubbling elsewhere, in the counting houses and cafés, in the factories, in the salons of the bourgeois The court and the chamber still held the power of the state, but the only use they made of it was to destroy the Bourbon monarchy by rash and unconsidered legislation

By 1823 Richelieu's reactionary legislation assured to the ultras control of France. The press was under control, the administration had power to abrogate the rights of Frenchmen if it feared an emergency, and the chamber was rapidly losing all of its liberal color, for the new electoral law practically assured the election of reactionaries. Villèle embarked upon a policy for which the ultras had waited since 1815. The émigrés were to be indemnified for their losses during the Revolution, the churchmen were to be assured their rightful place in the state; and the power of the reactionaries was to be entrenched in France so that their authority would never be questioned again.

The first step was directed toward the preservation of the ultra majority in the chamber The Charter provided that the chamber should be renewed by one-fifth every year, so that it would always be in close contact with the prevailing political beliefs of the country When, however, the ultras commanded an absolute majority in the chamber, they could see no reason for stirring up a political debate every year, so a bill was introduced to change this system and replace it by a law that provided that the chamber should be elected every seven years. This law of the septennate was popular with the ultras, who saw in it a barrier to any encroachment upon their power, but it ruined the hopes and aspirations of the liberals, who saw themselves cut off from any opportunity of expressing their case As a matter of fact, even this law, rigorous as it was, did not save the ultras For death took its toll in the chamber, and by-elections reflected the dissatisfaction of the nation with the reactionary policy of the ultras

The indemnification of the émigrés was a policy close to the ultra hearts Those men that had suffered financially and spiritually because of their loyalty to the Bourbons and their hatred for the Revolution had long insisted that the restored Bourbons owed them a debt that could be repaid only by a complete restoration of their lost possessions Ten years after the Restoration these claims were still unsettled, because none of the statesmen was willing to endanger the crown to satisfy these demands Villèle recognized that it would be folly to attempt to upset the revolutionary land settlement, but he was a financier, and he found a way to create credits that could be used to buy off the émigrés' claims By refunding the public debt at a lower rate of interest, Villèle was able to release a considerable sum of money that could be used to pay interest on new state bonds These new bonds were given to the émigrés in payment for the damages that they had incurred during the revolutionary epoch. This clever financial juggling, which did not even require a rise in taxes, was easily pushed through the chambers which were dominated by the ultras, and in which the men who saw the interests of the old bondholders were definitely in the minority The result was that a billion francs were at the disposal of the government to satisfy the men of the old régime. The taxpayers could have no complaint at this charitable project, for not a penny more was collected from them, but the French bondholders, both in France and abroad, were considerably agitated over this audacious legislation that forced them to pay the émigrés a bounty for their treason to the Revolution. A quiver of resentment passed through the French bourgeoisie, but nothing could be done The bill earned for the ultras the cordial hatred of the bondholders, but it was popular among the men who had bought the lands during the Revolution, for the land question was now settled beyond recall

The most acrimonious debates, however, were fought over Villèle's clerical policy "This present period," said one thoughtful observer, "will be hard to explain to our descendants One talks of nothing but bishops, priests, monks, Jesuits, convents and seminaries" The ultras' clerical policy was largely responsible for the anticlericalism that was to remain a live issue in French politics for almost a hundred years The Congregation received a free hand in France during the brief administration of Villèle, and the fanaticism of its members left an indelible mark on French political life Education, naturally, was the first stronghold that the clericals stormed They insisted that the state had no right to deprive fathers of families of the privilege of educating their children as they wished. The burden of the argument was that only the Church could educate the young to be God-fearing and sturdy citizens. Villèle was willing to listen to the clericals to the extent of installing Bishop de Frayssinous as grand master of the Université de France The good bishop explained his educational ideals in the following declaration "I know that my administration ought to be paternal, but I also know that rigor is my first duty and that moderation without force is pusillanimous Those who have the misfortune to live without religion or without devotion to the reigning family ought to know that they lack the essential thing to qualify them as instructors of youth" The liberals were hunted out of the Université;

even Guizot, Cousin, and Villemain were forced to give up their professional chairs. The philosophers of the Age of Reason were forbidden authors, and the statues of Voltaire and Rousseau were removed from the Pantheon, which was made into a church. All elementary education was placed under the surveillance of the clergy, and the Jesuits opened schools unmolested by the police. The education of French youth was passing out of lay hands into the hands of the clericals.

As clericalism became more powerful in the court, the Church became bolder in expressing extreme demands The number of French bishops was greatly increased, so that they could more closely supervise French Catholicism. Christian burial was refused to people suspected of Jansenism Marriages contracted before civil authority—and during the Revolution most of them were of this character—were declared null and void, and the unfortunate couples were considered as living in the state of sin until the marriage was validated. Paupers who could not furnish proof that they were faithful to their duties as Catholics were refused state aid The drama was censored before performances were allowed. The officials of both Church and state thus joined hands in forcing people to conform to the religion of their ancestors; the ultras fancied that the events of 1815 had restored the France of 1715.

In the cities and the villages the members of the Society of Missions organized huge religious demonstrations, with impressive processions and out-of-door sermons. These traveling salesmen of religious emotion denounced liberalism as the work of the devil, and exhorted the people to remain firm behind the reactionary policy of the reigning family When the liberals scoffed at their pronouncements, the crowd was urged to destroy the enemies of God Naturally, these excesses did not weaken the anticlericalism that had been growing in France for over a hundred years New religious orders were organized on all sides, and it became legal to endow these orders if the king chose to give his consent Many Frenchmen gritted their teeth and muttered under their breath; even the pope felt that he must advise the overzealous to practice moderation.

The crowning piece of clerical legislation was the "Law of Sacrilege." Sacrilege was as rare in France as it is in other parts of the world, but it pleased the religious fanatics to pass a law through the chamber that made it a felony punishable by death to deface or molest the sacred vessels of the altar or the consecrated Host. The law was never used to execute an offender, but it was passed as a solemn declaration of faith on the part of France. The liberals scornfully pointed out that such a law had not existed since the Middle Ages and that it made human judges less clement than the Divine Judge in heaven who never failed to show mercy. The ultras gleefully explained that the new law was merely meant to send the felon before his true Judge as quickly as possible. The "Law of Sacrilege" was regarded by a large section of French opinion as definite evidence that the alliance of throne and altar was the chief obstacle to any liberal development in French political life.

By 1827 the tide began to turn. The chamber of peers first reversed in rapid succession two laws that were particularly obnoxious to the liberals. One was to re-establish primogeniture so that the great estates of the nobles could be assured of a continuous existence; another was a new and stricter press law, ironically called the "Law of Justice and Love." For their action the peers received a great ovation from the Parisian crowds. In the law courts the newspapers found protection against the rigorous administrative prosecution of "crimes of the press," when several liberal papers were dramatically acquitted in face of everything the government could do. Furthermore, the elections of 1827, in spite of the law of the double vote, returned a larger number of liberal deputies who took their places on the left, and, to add to the ministry's embarrassment, Chateaubriand, who had been treated rather shabbily by Charles X, led a group of the ultras into opposition to Villèle. The real seriousness of the situation became apparent when, at a review of the National Guard, Charles was greeted by cries of "Long live the Charter!" "Down with Villèle!" "Down with the ministry!" Charles dissolved the National Guard, but he neglected to disarm the guardsmen—an oversight that made "the Revolution of July" somewhat easier to accomplish.

Villèle's internal policy had not been everything that the ultras had wished, but it had gone far to develop their philosophy of the state. It had one rather unexpected result The party of the left, which in 1820 had been revolutionary to no small degree, was forced into the position of a constitutional party. They stood for the Charter as it had been granted by the king, and tried to prevent the radical reactionaries from undoing it In the course of the political battles Charles succeeded in foolishly placing the monarchy against the Charter, and thereby played into the hands of the enemies of his dynasty. They insisted on the Charter, and were prepared even to dethrone the king to preserve it. Finally, Charles apparently partly realized his folly, for he called a man of moderate views to form a ministry to succeed Villèle's Martignac, the new minister, was expected to return to the political system of Richelieu and save the throne, but by 1828 the center party was almost gone Men were on either the right or the left, and Martignac was not resourceful enough to create a new center.

THE French reactionaries were unwilling to see the fruits of their power confined to internal affairs alone. They were anxious to carry their doctrine of reaction beyond the frontiers, to give other peoples the benefit of their political wisdom. Richelieu's hesitancy to support the eastern powers in the prevailing doctrine of intervention brought about his downfall. Villèle was unwilling to become involved in a foreign adventure, but his colleagues forced his hand. By 1821 revolution was rampant both in Italy and Spain, and the advocates of legitimacy were urging European action to prevent the spread of radical fires to all Europe. The Austrians obtained the czar's permission to pacify Italy only after assuring Alexander that the Spanish revolution would be considered as soon as peace was restored in Naples. Metternich had no real interest in the Spanish question, but for the French ultras it seemed to provide a twofold opportunity, they could destroy a revolution and win military glory for their party and their nation After 1815 France had had little glory, and they believed that a glorious foreign war would strengthen their position in the state and endear the Bourbon monarchy to the hero-loving French Money was loaned to the befuddled king of Spain, who did not know what to make of his Cortes, and a French army of observation was sent to the Spanish frontier. Then the Spanish monarch, bribed with French gold, repeated the act of the king of Naples, and the Congress of Verona gave France a European mandate to suppress the Spanish revolution. Somehow the military promenade into Spain and the scattered engagements with Spanish guerrillas did not bring much glory to the white flag of the Bourbons It was difficult to catch the imagination of a people that remembered Napoleon

The Spanish king was replaced on his throne, and the French government presented him with a bill for services which was never to be paid, but the visions of the ultras did not subside In the Americas the Spanish colonists had taken advantage of the tumult in Europe, between the time of the First Consul and the suppression of the Spanish revolution, and had declared their independence. Greedy statesmen in Europe saw an opportunity to apply the doctrine of intervention so that it would really do some good, maybe a grateful Spain would cede some of her reconquered provinces to the friendly states that had re-established the Spanish sovereignty in the new world This idea was lurking in the minds of the statesmen at Troppau, Laibach, and Verona, and it was an important factor in the chilly attitude that the British government took to the benevolent doctrine of intervention British merchants had built up a flourishing trade with the revolted Spanish colonists, a trade which would disappear if the colonies were forced to return to their legitimate sovereign. The British foreign secretary sounded out Mr Rush, the representative of the United States at the Court of St. James, and two ex-presidents, one president, and one future president of the United States considered his proposal for Anglo-American joint action He then explained to the French ambassador that Great Britain would never allow a European army to cross the Atlantic, and France quickly said she had no intention of sending her troops to South America. Shortly after this exchange of notes, Mr Monroe sent a famous message to the Congress of the United States—a message to which the British foreign secretary had given teeth The Latin-American question, one of the two unsolved problems of the Congress of Vienna, was settled.

In the solution of the other problem which the Vienna Congress had overlooked—the Near Eastern Question—the ultras had little interest When the Greeks revolted against his majesty the sultan, the French reactionaries were inclined to follow Metternich's lead and consider them as rebels against their rightful overlord But the interest which the Russian czar and the Egyptian viceroy took in the problem of Greece forestalled any concerted attempt of the rest of Europe to ignore the question The cause of the Greek rebels, moreover, was highly popular with many classes in Europe; liberals, romanticists, and men educated in the humanistic tradition joined to deplore the brutality of Mehemet Ali, and begged their governments to save the remnants of Hellenic culture. Hard-headed conservative statesmen all over Europe wished to keep their hands off the problem, but the new czar of Russia, Nicholas I, finally decided that he must act, and his decision forced the others into line The French fleet joined with the British and the Russian to demonstrate at Navarino Bay, and ended by assisting in the destruction of the Turkish and Egyptian navy.

When Russia declared war on Turkey, French troops occupied the Morea. France was playing up to the new Russian czar, and at the same time attempting to bring glory to the ultra government.

Although the foreign ventures did somewhat distract the politicians from the burning question at home, the French people did not properly appreciate the "glories" won in foreign fields by Charles and his ministers. In 1830, just before Charles attempted the *coup d'état* that dethroned his dynasty, he tried to use North Africa as another distraction. The insolent ruler of Algeria so far forgot his manners as to strike the representative of the French king with his fan; it was just the excuse that Charles was looking for to embark on a safe campaign for French honor and glory. Algeria was duly invaded, but the control of North Africa was not to be won by the Bourbons.

THE moderate ministry that followed Villèle's was in an impossible predicament. It lacked the support of the king, and it had no party in the chamber. Martignac attempted to inaugurate a more liberal régime by relaxing the rigid ultra education policy and easing the press laws, but he succeeded only in antagonizing both the right and the left. Charles obviously did not understand what was happening. He made a tour of France, and, since he was greeted everywhere with enthusiasm, he decided that France supported his program even if the deputies and the peers repudiated it. Emboldened by this belief, he decided to form a ministry that fitted his own convictions absolutely. The Prince de Polignac, a man as reactionary as Charles himself, was called from his post as ambassador to England, and intrusted with the government of France. Polignac was especially unfitted for the post; he knew nothing about France, and he was temperamentally averse to learning about her. Even worse, from the point of view of practical politics, Polignac had visions; he claimed that the Virgin Mary showed herself to him periodically to give him advice and counsel. When the revolutionaries were victorious in every section of Paris, Polignac assured his king that the Virgin had told him that the revolt (which cost the Bourbons their throne) would amount to nothing!

When the appointment of Polignac was announced, many Frenchmen must have examined their guns and their powder The secret societies became more active, the liberals became bolder in their public discussion of the problems of the day A small group of scholars, journalists, and politicians—including that master of French revolutionary politics, Talleyrand—began to groom the Duc d'Orléans for the position of king Liberals of every complexion had to consider what might happen next They did not have long to wait, at the opening of the chamber in the spring of 1830 Charles X read a speech from the throne that showed clearly his sentiments, his ideas, and his policy Without mincing words he informed the chamber that he expected loyal Frenchmen to follow their king blindly, and darkly hinted that those who refused to do so must watch out for themselves The king tried to brand as traitors all those who did not see the world through his own reactionary glasses

This speech, coming as a culmination of almost eight years of ultra encroachment on the benefits of the Revolution, drew heavy fire from the men on the left. Two hundred and twenty-one (they came to be known as "the 221") of the 402 deputies drew up an answer to the king in which, although cautiously professing their loyalty to the king's person, they did not hesitate to point out that their rights as Frenchmen were guaranteed by the Charter. They even lectured the king on his duty to adjust his policy to accord with the wishes and the ideas of his people The address was respectful in its tone, but behind it stood the threat of direct action and the barricades if the king refused to consider the wishes of the nation This was on March 18, 1830; on March 19 the king prorogued the chamber until fall; and on May 16, 1830 the chamber was dissolved and new elections were ordered.

The electoral campaign of 1827 was repeated, but this time with even more seriousness; both sides marshaled all their available power The terrific weight of the French administrative system was at the disposal of the government; men were bribed, threatened, and coerced by prefects, mayors, and police inspectors. But the liberals could refer to the administration of Villèle and point out that beside Polignac the former was a liberal The benefits of the Revolution were at stake unless men rallied to its cause With the liberal electoral societies, the remnant of the liberal press, and traveling orators and agitators, the men of the left sounded the alarm. When the votes were counted, the liberals were found to have won a great victory. They held 274 seats while their opponents held only 143 It was Charles' move.

The king and his advisers did not seem to realize the seriousness of their position. They did not understand that France had repudiated their policy, nor did they recognize the fact that Paris was ready to resist any further encroachments on the rights of Frenchmen. The stupidity of the ultra chiefs in July, 1830, was no greater and no less than it had been during the preceding years, but in 1830 they were confronted by liberals of all shades who were profoundly convinced that neither the Bourbons nor the ultras were fit to rule France. Charles somehow believed that he could convert the French nation by a *coup d'état.* On July 25 he issued the famous ordinances that provoked a revolution. These ordinances dissolved the newly elected chamber, muzzled the press, altered the electoral law, and called for new elections on September 1. Charles apparently expected Paris to receive them quietly, for he did not even bother to inform the chief of police of his projected step, nor did he attempt to strengthen the garrison in Paris, which was considerably weakened because of the Algerian campaign "The gods make insane those whom they plan to destroy."

The ordinances were not received quietly in Paris Working men—at first the printers—who suddenly found themselves out of work, gathered to discuss the affairs of the day, and ended by pulling up the paving stones and overturning carts to make barricades. Shop and factory owners helped their employees to arm, mill owner and mill hand fought "cheek by jowl." The next day the uniform of the National Guard appeared on the streets, and while the bourgeoisie joined the workers in manning the barricades, the revolutionists took over the Hôtel de Ville as a center of operations. The rattle of musketry drifted through the windows of the Palace of Saint Cloud, but Charles X and his court continued to play whist and chess while Polignac had a vision from the Virgin assuring him of the essential safety of the situation. On the third day Paris was in the hands of the revolutionists and the streets were placarded with a poster extolling the virtues of Louis Philippe, duc d'Orléans. Thiers and his confederates were on the spot to give France her "Revolution of 1688" Before leaving for London, the old king tried to save the throne for his grandson by abdicating, but it was too late; Louis Philippe was already on his way to the Hôtel de Ville to make peace with the republicans

CHAPTER III

THE RÉGIME OF LANDLORDS AND CAPITALISTS

THOMAS MANN tells us that the July Revolution was a high point in the elder Settembrini's life. "He had gone about proclaiming to all and sundry that some day men would place those three days alongside the six days of creation and reverence them alike." In 1830 this opinion was widely shared by liberals and revolutionaries all over Europe. The "three glorious days" caught men's imagination and confounded their intellect, they appeared as the triumph of the revolutionary principles over the whole system of reaction Men, hard pressed by the restoration system in Germany, Italy, Belgium, Poland, and Spain, saw the barricades in Paris as a manifesto of liberty and equality, an inspiration for fraternity. It was not long before the liberals came to see that their idealism was misplaced; the system of divine right and ultra-royalism had been driven out, only to be replaced by a régime of landlords and capitalists with a bourgeois monarch. There was not much to choose between the two

The victory of July had come too easily. Before men had time to realize what happened, Charles X had left France in the hands of revolutionary Paris, without even waiting to see what the provinces thought about the situation. The men behind the barricades who cried "Vive la Charte!" were not prepared for so complete a victory. At the Hôtel de Ville Lafayette and his friends vaguely planned to establish a republic; the members of the chamber that had never met were talking about a provisional government; there were a few old soldiers who thought of Napoleon's son in Austria. In the confusion, Thiers and his fellow plotters found excellent ground for their Orléanist propaganda. From their historical studies, they reasoned that France needed a "Glorious Revolution" similar to England's experience in 1688; a revolution that would retain the best features of monarchial government and at the same time assure to men of wealth and breeding popular control over the state Louis Philippe, the duc d'Orléans, was their candidate for the rôle of William and Mary. They placarded Paris with posters lauding Louis Philippe, duc d'Orléans, as a prince who could be trusted to uphold the Charter, as a member of the royal family who had fought under the tricolor, as a man deeply loyal to the principles of the Revolution Before opposition could be mobilized, an Orléans monarchy was recognized as the logical solution for the crisis of the day.

The republicans at the Hôtel de Ville were skeptical at first, they were not prepared to accept another king unless there was no alternative But when Lafayette was faced with the probability that a republic would mean civil war and foreign intervention, he decided that he did not wish to assume the responsibility which would inevitably be thrust upon him. There was a touching scene; Louis Philippe informed the friend and comrade-in-arms of Washington that he, too, was a republican at heart, but that France was not prepared for a republic The general kissed the prince, and told the crowd "Here is the king we need; it is the best of republics" Several days later Louis Philippe was proclaimed king of the French and took a solemn oath to defend the Charter

The Revolution of July alarmed many of the people who helped to make it Revolution might mean the recurrence of the "terror," foreign war, and no one knew what. The prospect of a quick solution through a monarchy under a member of the house of Orléans was greeted with a sigh of relief; there would be no Constituent Assembly, no factious elections, no wrangles over constitution making The revolution had been intended to conserve the *status quo*—the Charter of 1814—not to create a new form of government. If that *status quo* could be so easily preserved, most politically minded Frenchmen were only too glad to approve the settlement.

It was the upper bourgeoisie who had made the new monarchy. They had furnished the opposition to Charles X in the last chamber of the restored monarchy They backed Royer-Collard when he formulated the response to the throne following Charles' peremptory lecture on the duties of the chamber of deputies. They had furnished their workers with propaganda and arms on the barricades, and in Thiers they had supplied the chief negotiator of the crisis These men, however, were not revolutionaries, they were bankers, property owners, industrialists, bondholders, and wealthy professional men, who stood together to defend the rights that they and their fathers had won in 1789 It was the same Voltaire-reading, property-respecting, selfish bourgeoisie that had destroyed the First Republic and undermined the Empire; in 1830 they were defending themselves against clericalism and the re-establishment of privilege based upon blood It was no accident that Royer-Collard, the doctrinaire, was their spokesman. He and his friends, Guizot, Dupin, Bertin de Vaux, and de Broglie, looked upon the Charter of 1814 as the *juste milieu* of politics, a true reproduction of the British Constitution as they understood it. Under this Charter bourgeois rights were properly respected, and the bourgeoisie were assured of their "rightful" place of leadership in society. Like Macaulay they believed that "the middle class are the natural representatives of mankind"—especially the leaders of the middle class

When Charles' reactionary religious, social, and political policies seemed about to undermine the Charter and stupidly provoked an armed rebellion in Paris, these men had no intention of allowing that revolution to go too far They were just as anxious to prevent the establishment of a democratic régime as they were to overthrow the reactionary system of the ultras. The propaganda of historians and journalists like Thiers, Mignet, and Guizot in the twenties had given a historical example of proper polity by explaining England's revolutionary history which had ended so happily with the change of dynasties in 1688. France did not need to go to Holland for a king; Louis

Philippe, trusted by the upper bourgeoisie, offered a satisfactory substitute for William of Orange While men hesitated at the Hôtel de Ville, and behind the barricades in Paris, the leaders of the upper bourgeoisie made the Orléans monarchy seem to be the only possible answer to the question of the day.

This upper bourgeoisie became the chief buttress of the throne of July. Laffitte, son of a Basque carpenter, and Casimir-Périer, son of a long line of wealthy bourgeois, were the bankers who stood closest to the throne, but the Paris Rothschilds and practically all of the French money interests added their support to the monarchy. Beside them were the entrepreneurs, industrialists, and great merchants who made up the flower of the middle class; they saw in Louis Philippe a monarch who could be trusted to allow them to expand their business and maintain their position in French society In close juxtaposition to these typical bourgeois figures were the men of the Empire who saw in Louis Philippe a king who would defend their position against the old nobility. Molé, Louis, Marshal Soult, and many others offered their swords and their administrative talents to the new monarch. The new régime was not to be the sole property of the bourgeoisie. The landlords were quick to recognize that the Orléans monarchy would afford them the same protection and influence as the bourgeois capitalists had. The July monarchy was to be a régime of capitalists and landlords banded together for mutual benefit. It is, therefore, not surprising that beside the bourgeoisie and the men of the Empire could be found the liberal nobles (or their sons) who had called for reform in the summer of 1789 The Duc de Broglie and that fox of all revolutions, Talleyrand, were typical of the men who were drawn into the orbit of the July sun Bringing up the rear guard, but extremely important in the establishment of the new monarchy, were the bourgeois professors, journalists, and lawyers; Guizot, Dupin, Cousin, and Thiers were admirable representatives of these intellectual janizaries who fought the battles of the bourgeoisie with ink and on the lecture platform. But from banker to professor, the aim was approximately the same. They wanted a conservative government that would assure the fruits of the great Revolution and the continued influence of men of wealth and talent over the government of the state

Several years later Guizot admirably summed up the principal doctrine of the men who made Louis Philippe king of the French His statement is so clear and so penetrating that it deserves direct quotation:

> Have I assigned limits to this class? Have you understood me to say where it commenced or where it ended? I have simply stated the fact that there exists in the bosom of a great country like France a class which is not tied to manual labor, which does not live from salaries, which has, in its thoughts and in its life, liberty and leisure, which is able to consecrate a considerable part of its time and its talents to public affairs, which possesses not only the fortune necessary for such a work, but also the intelligence and the independence without which that work could not be accomplished. It is the perfection of our government that political rights, limited to those who are capable to exercise them, can be extended in proportion to the extension of capacity within the nation, and such is, in our times, the admirable virtue of this government that it unceasingly encourages the extension of that capacity—so that at the same time that it sets limits to political rights by a property qualification, at that same moment it works to remove that limit by allowing men to become wealthy and to extend it and thus to raise the entire nation.

In this explanation Guizot aptly expressed the political philosophy of his friends and associates. Good government can be assured only when men of wealth and substance are in the position of power, for they alone have the intelligence, the leisure, and the foresight prerequisite to a governing class. Any distinctions not based on wealth are fallacious; according to these men wealth alone is an indication of fitness to govern. To the men who clamored for political rights, Guizot and his kind replied "enrich yourselves." This is the doctrine of the French plutocracy of landlords and capitalists, the doctrine that was enthroned in July, 1830

THE Revolution of July definitely ended the ultra and clerical program for the re-establishment of the old régime, but the creation of the Orléans monarchy opened a whole series of new questions that sooner or later would demand a solution. On the third of August, 1830, the deputies and peers met in the Palais Bourbon to discuss the Charter Conservatives like Guizot insisted that the Charter of 1814 "had been sufficient for sixteen years for the defence of the rights, interests, and liberties of the country, invoked in turn by diverse parties with diverse views, it had protected and restrained all in their turn" The people, Guizot insisted, had fought on the barricades with the war cry, "Vive la Charte!" Surely it had not lost its validity when the people were victorious To alter the Charter would be to betray the men who had manned the barricades, such was his argument. The republicans at the Hôtel de Ville demanded a revision of the Charter so that the throne would be "surrounded by republican institutions" Between these extremes stood the majority of the deputies, who wished to make slight alterations but no fundamental changes The ensuing compromise was much more satisfactory to the conservatives than to the radicals

The constitution which Louis Philippe took an oath to defend was only slightly different from the Bourbon Charter of 1814 The preamble that had militantly proclaimed the divine right of kings was suppressed, and thus the principle of popular sovereignty again was recognized. The Catholic Church lost its position as the "religion of the state," to become "the religion professed by most Frenchmen." The clause concerning liberty of the press was strengthened, and the king lost the power to make ordinances—such as those Charles made in July—for "the security of the state." There were other minor changes, but the core of the Charter, which provided for a monarchy limited by a parliament elected on a restricted suffrage—in short, the *censitaire* system—remained intact Casimir-Périer was not far wrong when he said " . many people in France imagine that there has been a revolution

No, monsieur, there has been no revolution; there has simply been a change in the person of the chief of state."

The organic laws which further developed the system of the July monarchy showed, however, that there was also a change in the men who ran the state. The titles created by Villèle were annulled, and the seats in the chamber of peers ceased, in spite of the protest of the conservatives, to be hereditary. This law effectively robbed the peers of any rôle which they might have played in French politics; since there was no limit to the number of peers, the ministry could always create enough new peers to pass its measures. Their chamber became, like the Italian senate in a later day, a distinguished body of helpless men who had no real voice in the affairs of the state. A new electoral law somewhat changed the character of the chamber of deputies. The double vote was suppressed, and the eligibility requirements for an elector were reduced from a minimum payment of 300 to 200 francs in direct taxes and from 30 to 25 years of age. In the special cases of members of the Institute or retired officers a payment of 100 francs in direct taxes was enough to qualify for the right to vote. The eligibility requirements for candidates, too, were reduced from the payment of 1,000 to 500 francs direct taxes and from 40 to 30 years of age. This law only increased the electorate to about 200,000 in a nation of 33,000,000, but, for the moment, it seemed to satisfy the demands of the people. In 1830 most Frenchmen had no great desire to vote.

Another law turned municipal administration over to the elected representatives of the wealthy bourgeoisie and country gentry. This created about "34,000 little bourgeois oligarchies" upon which the ministry could depend. Another law reorganized the National Guard. That citizen army, to which only the well-to-do could afford to belong, became one of the most characteristic institutions of the monarchy. The little bourgeois were proud of their handsome uniforms and their smart reviews, they were honored if they were elected officers in their regiment. This "grocers' janizary corps," intensely loyal to the monarchy, was always on hand to suppress disorder in the streets or workshops. It was the guard of honor to the upper bourgeoisie, and the chief prop of the July throne.

The amended Charter and the complementary organic laws assured France that she would be governed by people of substance. The new aristocracy of the nation henceforth was made up of landlords and capitalists whose breeding and income gave them the right to rule. The nobility, with the exception of the irreconcilable supporters of the Bourbons, joined hands with the merchants, bankers, and industrialists to give the nation the "benefits" of the Revolution as they understood them. But in doing this a deep chasm was driven between the rich and the poor In July, 1830, the proletariat and the bourgeoisie had fought side by side against their mutual enemy, the old privileged class. Both rich and poor cheered the Charter as a wall between themselves and clerical, feudal reaction. After July the proletariat came to realize that they had only aided the upper bourgeoisie to gain a foothold in the control of the state, and that a bourgeoisie-landlord plutocracy could be as oppressive as a clerical monarchy. The new privilege based on wealth was not so very different from the old privilege based on blood, this was especially true when "wealth and blood" joined hands to rule the state. The bourgeoisie could say, "Enrich yourselves and you, too, will have legal privileges," but it was easier to say than to do The masses were as effectively excluded from rule as they had been under the old régime

The legal justification for the July monarchy was never very clear Louis Philippe became king *of the French* rather than king *of France,* but neither he nor his supporters would recognize the theory that he owed his throne to the popular will—and justly so, for no plebiscite, no election, had ever regularized his position The Bourbons stood on their legitimacy; Napoleon, on a popular election; but the Orléans dynasty was forced to occupy the slippery legal ground between the two. The Orléans monarchy's most conservative supporters pointed to the chamber's declaration that the throne was vacant, and insisted that Louis Philippe, head of the cadet line of the old royal family, was the legitimate successor to Charles X. Many times Louis Philippe wrathfully shouted, "I am not a usurper!" but no amount of skillful sophistry could argue away the fact that Charles X had a grandson with pretensions to the legitimate throne of France. Another group of the supporters of Louis Philippe brushed aside this thesis of quasi-legitimacy, and stood manfully on the grounds of expediency. The people of Paris had appealed to the "supreme law of necessity" to defend themselves against oppression. To these men "destiny" had placed Louis Philippe on the throne. The republican thesis was avoided—for if the people can make, they can unmake, a king!

Another unsolved question was the true nature of the revolution itself The bourgeoisie who turned it to their own advantage insisted that it was merely a question of internal politics. The people fought to save their liberties from the stupidly reactionary policy of the ultras. Another group, headed by Cavaignac and including most of the republicans as well as many of the liberal bourgeoisie, maintained that the revolution was a nationalistic uprising against the whole system established in Europe in 1815 "This is not a liberal revolution," Cavaignac told Louis Philippe. "The battle in the streets was a nationalist revolution. It was the sight of the tricolor that roused the people, and it would certainly be easier to thrust Paris toward the Rhine than toward Saint Cloud." Although Louis Philippe and his friends would never admit it, Cavaignac was probably right, Paris was inflamed by the old slogan, "War against the tyrants," and that meant Metternich and the czar as well as Charles X. But this expansionist and nationalist spirit would have to find other leaders than the merchants and bankers who surrounded the July throne, before it could lead the nationalist crusade in Europe.

Louis Philippe was hardly on the throne when the republicans realized that they had not played their hand to their own advantage. The great difficulty was that republicanism was an uncertain, inchoate idea in 1830 It was based on a misunderstanding of both the First French Republic and the American republic The republicans were unorganized, almost inarticulate, and probably few in numbers. The Paris working class, which had manned the barricades and spilled its blood, was vaguely republican, and many of the sons of the men of the Convention were republican, but they did not have the strength to put through their program Some of the more moderate of their numbers made peace with the new monarchy, but many of them nursed the grievance that their revolution had been snatched from them, and next time—there would be a next time—things would be different. These men presented one of the greatest unsolved problems of 1830

At the opposite pole from the republicans were the irreconcilable supporters of the exiled Bourbons. They comprised the oldest and the proudest names of France, men who would have no compromise with the principles of the Revolution They regarded Louis Philippe as a usurper and a traitor who unlawfully prevented the youthful Henry V from occupying the throne of his ancestors Politically they were almost powerless, but socially they were very important. Their boycott of the society of the July monarchy and the men who supported it, their refusal to allow their children to marry into families that recognized the throne, must have caused Louis Philippe much personal anguish and provided foreigners with an endless source of amusement These men hated the July monarchy so bitterly that they were willing to give money to the republicans who were attacking it from the left.

While this formal opposition to the new régime was developing from the right and the left, there grew up a number of smaller groups that were later to become weighty factors in the opposition, although they were unimportant in 1830. The school of Saint-Simon was about to break up into the various brands of social radicalism which became so vociferous in the forties. Most of the men who were to become leaders of the proletariat were getting themselves ready for their rôles. In the religious camp, the liberal Catholics, inspired by Lamennais, Lacordaire, and Montalembert, were organizing their doctrines, and already they had started the program that ended by making the next revolution as friendly to the Church as the Revolution of July had been hostile to it The death of Napoleon at Saint Helena in 1821 had opened the way for another dangerous doctrine of opposition, for throughout France the myth of the glorious, liberal Empire was beginning to capture the imagination of men who had grown up under the restored Bourbons. Furthermore, Louis Napoleon, nephew of the emperor, had already launched his first claim to leadership, during a revolution in 1830 in the Papal States. Socialism, liberal Catholicism, and Bonapartism were soon to join republicanism and legitimacy in the assault on the citadel of the landlords and the capitalists. In 1830, however, Louis Philippe still had eighteen years in which to rule France as the representative of French plutocracy.

THE new king was largely unknown to France. His father, the cynical Philippe Égalité, who had sat in the Convention, who had voted for the death of Louis XVI, and who himself had died on the guillotine, left the tradition that the house of Orléans was friendly to the principles of the Revolution. Louis Philippe himself—as he never ceased to remind everyone—had fought under the tricolor in 1792, later he joined the émigrés, but he had carefully remained aloof from their plots. During the Restoration he kept away from any political connections that might commit him in one way or another. His salon at the Palais Royal was frequented by wealthy conservatives who regarded the Bourbons with suspicion, but they never succeeded in breaking through the "correct" attitude of the duke toward his cousins. As one wit put it, "Louis

Philippe had aspired to, but never conspired for, the throne" Even the final intrigue that made him king was carried on through the agency of a female member of the family. The men who presented Louis Philippe with the throne knew him to be a hardheaded, cautious fellow whose world outlook was similar to their own He was careful—ever so careful—with his money, respectable in his morals, and, though enormously wealthy, unobtrusive in his style of living. He appeared to be an ideal bourgeois king

Louis Philippe seemed to delight in the title of "Citizen King" He was proud to wear the frock coat of the bourgeoisie, to carry his green cotton umbrella, and to chat democratically with his subjects even on street corners. His elevation to the throne did not dull his business sense. Before he took the oath, he made over his entire fortune to his family, to prevent its becoming part of the crown property. As king, he undignifiedly wrangled with the chamber over the size of his civil list, and repeatedly asked for special gifts for himself and his children Many of his subjects came to think, "This king is expensive." His democracy and his financial caution pleased the bourgeoisie more than it did the old nobility or the lower classes, who expected a king to act and look the part.

Louis Philippe often did not look like a king, but he was ambitious to rule as one His theory of government would never admit that the throne was an easy chair for a figurehead During the first years of his reign his ministers were able to keep him above politics and policy, but he finally maneuvered himself into the position of a king who governs. His political ideas, however, were very elementary. The nation, to him, meant the property-owning electorate, he never asked or cared about the problems of the masses. He saw eye to eye, in most questions of high politics, with his distinguished contemporary, Metternich, and the Austrian champion of reaction came to regard the "Citizen King of the Barricades" as one of the great bulwarks of the European conservative system. His fixed idea was peace—peace at any price When men in the streets of Paris were clamoring for a reversal of 1815, Louis Philippe, over the heads of his ministers, appointed Talleyrand, the man of 1815, to the key position of ambassador to England. While the press of France issued manifestoes against the Holy Alliance and legitimacy, Louis Philippe assured the rulers of Europe that France would not attempt to alter the European system. "We must not only cherish peace," he told his subjects; "we ought also always to avoid anything that might provoke war" The "inglorious" foreign policy of this "Napoleon of peace" in time paved the way for a Napoleon who did not hesitate to mobilize the French battalions

THE great majority of the French electorate gladly accepted the Orléans monarchy as a solution for the crisis of July, but they did not agree upon the policy which the new régime should adopt Broadly speaking, the men elected to the chamber fell into two groups: the party of movement, and the party of resistance.

The party of movement was largely composed of the leftist members of the Restoration chambers. These men could hardly be called liberals, but they represented the most advanced liberalism to rally to the throne. In political philosophy they subscribed to the familiar "liberal" individualistic doctrines so prevalent in the first half of the nineteenth century: they wished to assure to the individual the fullest possible freedom from the power of the state, and at the same time to utilize the state to assist commerce, industry, and agriculture through the rendering of services that no individual could profitably undertake. They regarded with suspicion the leveling doctrines of democracy, but they professed a willingness to extend the suffrage as rapidly as the political education of the lower middle class would permit. This, they insisted, would be the logical development of the principles of the July Revolution, but it is interesting to note that the men of the left did not seriously advocate any electoral reform until they found themselves effectively excluded from power by the men of the right When they were in office, the men of the party of movement could hardly be distinguished from their more conservative colleagues, but when they were in the opposition, they stormed against the narrow suffrage, the system of corruption, and the stand-pat policy of their opponents There was one important issue between them and the party of resistance, they stood for a spirited foreign policy, which would assure for France her rightful place in international affairs In 1840 Thiers discredited the party when he led France to the brink of a dangerous foreign war, the intervention of the king saved France from a re-enactment of the tragedy of 1815, and at the same time precluded the return of the party of movement to power as long as Louis Philippe reigned in France

The party of resistance combined the men of the center, the doctrinaires, and a few of the left from the Bourbon chambers They stood firmly on the Charter, maintaining that it was the final expression of enlightened government. They saw the French limited monarchy as an excellent reproduction of the British system, which was, in their opinion, the *juste milieu* in politics. They pointed out that the Revolution of July had come "not to re-open, but to terminate the first revolution"; the people had fought on the barricades with the cry, "Vive la Charte!" The Charter, then, was the guarantee that the people demanded, and any attempt to alter the Charter was, in their opinion, a betrayal of the Revolution. They opposed political reform on the ground that the election system, with its high property qualification for political rights, was basic to good government The whole political development of Europe, they insisted, pointed to the fact that men had striven to achieve the ideal of government by men of wealth and breeding. This was the party that most nearly approximated Louis Philippe's own conception of polity, and Guizot, with his fearlessly outspoken doctrine that only the wealthy are fitted to rule, was its perfect leader.

THESE dynastic parties well satisfied the demands of the electors, but the men who had fought on the barricades, and many of the liberals, soon found that their ideals were not to be considered. The dictum, "the Orléans monarchy is the best of republics," soon sounded hollow to men who had hoped to establish free institutions in France. This left opposition was politically not very powerful, or numerically very large in the eighteen-thirties, but it was strategically situated in cities where its vociferous demands and demonstrations could create no little disturbance. The potential danger to the régime was increased by the opposition from the right, by the legitimists who wished Henry V to occupy the throne of France When their demonstrations clashed with those of the republicans, a riot almost inevitably resulted.

In addition to these political malcontents, there were several groups who opposed the new régime on intellectual, ethical, or economic grounds. The Catholics resented the anticlericalism of the July monarchy. The Saint-Simonians and other socialists, who were beginning to preach against the economic order and to demand a measure of social justice, objected to the smug assumptions of the bourgeois economists who dominated national policy. The romanticists, weaned from their earlier connection with the ultra-royalist party, resented the enthronement of stodgy bourgeois ideals. Moreover, the theretofore inarticulate proletarians, suffering from the industrialization of France, began to add their voices to the protest against the *status quo*. Fortunately for the ruling classes, the great bulk of French society—peasants and townspeople—were largely unaware of these programs of discontent. The clamor that was raised and the riots and disturbances that occurred affected only a relatively small proportion of the nation.

During the first few years of the July régime, however, these groups found ample opportunity to express their discontent. The amended Charter forbade legislation that would impose censorship on the press, with the result that the press ran wild. Violent attacks on both the government and the king were the order of the day Cruelly they caricatured Louis Philippe as "Louis le poire"—a little, corpulent man with a large pear for a head If the king could thus be mocked, it is no wonder that the ministry was covered with the most biting ridicule. But when editors were haled into court to answer for their offenses, almost invariably they were acquitted after the courtroom had been used as a sounding board for antigovernment propaganda.

With the press unbridled, it was easy to establish societies which, at bottom, were revolutionary in their aims. The secret societies that had been muzzled and dispersed under the Bourbons multiplied rapidly as the republicans came to realize that their share in the Revolution had been snatched away from them, Bonapartist committees were organized with more or less impunity, the working class in the cities was wooed by radicals of all sorts. The utopian socialists established colonies in which they taught and tried to practice the doctrines of Saint-Simon and Fourier The societies—some of them harmless and others extremely dangerous to the régime—were able to carry on their propaganda without much fear of governmental intervention, during the first months of the July monarchy. The government not only could not defend itself against them, but it could not even maintain order in the streets. The three days of revolution had given men great confidence in the efficacy of direct action; demonstrations and riots were all too common.

In the words of Casimir-Périer, France "needed to be governed"; the romance of revolution had gone too far But during the first months of the new régime France did not find a governor; the first ministry included men of all political faiths. Lafayette, the liberal republican; Guizot, the conservative doctrinaire; and Laffitte, the banker with liberal nationalist views, could never get together to formulate a decisive policy. Baron Louis and Dupont seem to have carried most of the burden of government, but there were too many conflicting political philosophies represented in the cabinet for it to direct the course of affairs. The result was that the streets attempted to rule· the people had dethroned Charles X, why should they not direct the government that followed him? The worst of the disturbances in Paris resulted from the clash of a legitimist demonstration, occasioned by a political funeral, with a republican mob, in the riot that followed, the police could not even prevent the sacking of the archbishop's palace. When the government refused to send the ministers of Charles X to the scaffold, a demonstration in the streets placed the ministry in a precarious position It was obvious to the men around Louis Philippe that the unstable political equilibrium must be ended, or the July monarchy could not maintain itself. Finally, the king called Casimir-Périer, a man of the party of resistance, to form a ministry

Périer's bourgeois supporters must have been surprised as well as pleased with the policy that he inaugurated. The prefects were instructed that henceforth the "first duty of government is, while allowing complete liberty, to re-establish order." He announced to the chamber that "peace abroad and order within" would be the keystone of his policy. In carrying out this program Périer did not hesitate to use stern measures. Republican and Bonapartist societies were driven underground by the police and the National Guard. When the silk workers at Lyon attempted to better their wretched economic position, which, in spite of the prosperity of the industry, became steadily worse year by year, the government in Paris sent troops to shoot the workers and force them into submission. Périer's system announced that the day of the barricades was over; that the July settlement was no longer open to question; and that France had found a firm hand to rule her affairs.

Périer adopted the same strict attitude toward his monarch and toward foreign powers. He forced Louis Philippe to keep his hands off policy, and to recognize—regretfully to be sure—that the king did not rule. When his proposal for general European disarmament fell on deaf ears in Austria, Prussia, and Russia, this banker-statesman increased the size of the French army in commensuration with France's position as a great power His vigorous policy in Belgium, the Papal States, and at Lisbon showed the world that a French bourgeois government could act as imperiously as any of the old monarchies Casimir-Périer was the model statesman of the upper bourgeoisie. His untimely death in the cholera plague of 1832 prevented the completion of his system, but he left a tradition, cherished by the powerful upper class in France, which later developed into the party of moral order

After the death of Périer, a coalition cabinet including Guizot, Thiers, and Molé attempted to carry on his policy, but they were unable to present the same stern front to the people, the king, and foreign countries Personal differences and the shifting political balance in the chamber made unsteady the status of the coalition. France grew restive. The attacks in the press renewed their vigor, and revolutionary societies became more audacious. In 1834 and early in 1835 there was a whole series of riots. One of them, in Paris, developed into a republican insurrection which required three days and much bloodshed to suppress The whole situation came to a head in July, 1835, when, on the anniversary of the revolution that had made Louis Philippe king, there was a desperate attempt on his life. A shudder of horror ran through the upper classes; this attempted assassination followed too closely upon the republican uprising to suit the men in power

In September, 1835, a group of laws of repression easily passed the chamber, and the government turned to a new course. Gone was the time when the press could say what it pleased, without fear of the consequences The republican and Bonapartist clubs were broken up, and their leaders found themselves in prison or exile; republican uprisings thenceforth were doomed to failure, at least until 1848. At the same time, Louis Philippe moved one step further toward the time when he could control public policy. After the passage of the laws of repression the practice of installing coalition cabinets came to an end. Guizot and Thiers faced each other on opposite sides of the chamber, and Molé showed himself to be a facile tool in the hands of his monarch. Between 1835 and 1840 cabinet instability was common, and behind it the wily, intriguing Louis Philippe paved the way for a personal government.

In 1840, a crisis in foreign policy enabled the king to stabilize his position and obtain a ministry that more nearly fitted his own ideas Thiers had forced his way into power just in time to be confronted with the Egyptian-Turkish situation. His attempted defense of Mehemet Ali led to the isolation of France in Europe, and almost precipitated a general war. Feeling was running high on both sides of the Rhine when Louis Philippe, apparently pushed by the banking interests of Paris, stepped in to prevent a catastrophe Guizot and the king saved what they could of French prestige, but the system they established practically ended the period of free parliamentary control over the government.

From 1840 to 1848 Louis Philippe, Guizot, and Duchâtel governed France as they believed the upper classes wished her to be governed In establishing their control over the chamber, they brought political corruption to a degree of perfection that probably has never been excelled. The key to their system rested in the electoral colleges which chose the deputies. Owing to the restricted suffrage, many of these colleges were very small, and with an unscrupulous politician like Duchâtel as minister of the interior with many political plums to deal out, it was very easy to corrupt a majority of the electors. What corruption failed to do could often be accomplished by dishonest electoral procedure. In addition, the ministry did not hesitate to use its power to appoint as functionaries, with fat salaries, the deputies themselves or members of their families This system assured to the ministry a majority—and that was all that it asked. Let the opposition protest as much as it wished, the government, backed by a majority that it owned lock, stock, and barrel, could refuse to change its course.

LOUIS PHILIPPE had hardly become king when his government was forced to cope with a dangerous situation in foreign affairs The sparks from the barricades in Paris scattered willy-nilly over Europe; first in Belgium, then in Germany, then in Poland and Italy, rebellions broke out and threatened to involve the continent in a general war. The Belgian revolt proved to be the most dangerous The Congress of Vienna had lumped Belgium with Holland as a bulwark against a revengeful France, but the Belgian people were not pleased with their subordinate position in the state When the barricades in Paris brought in a new king, the French-speaking Belgians decided to follow the French lead As the rebellion deepened, they attempted to bring France to their aid by calling a younger son of Louis Philippe to their throne. To Europe it appeared that 1792 would be re-enacted; that revolutionary France again would lead the crusade against oppression.

A meeting of the ambassadors of the great powers in London showed that all of the powers were ready to keep France from becoming the champion of liberty, but that only Russia was willing (and the czar was more than willing) to send troops to suppress the Belgian revolt. Czar Nicholas was ready not only to move into Belgium, but also to reduce Paris herself. The arrival of Talleyrand soothed the situation a little. He quickly renounced any unilateral action on the part of France, and urged the calling of a conference to solve the question. "A conference," he said, "is always a good way, if not to settle things, at least to draw them out"

The Polish revolt gave Czar Nicholas' troops work to do at home while the conference in London labored to end the Belgian crisis. Palmerston and Talleyrand worked together to give a European aspect to the settlement, but it was not finally concluded until after French troops crossed the Belgian frontier in the name of Europe and retired under the threat of mobilization of the Prussian army The solution was not entirely satisfactory to either the Dutch or the Belgians, but it prevented a general war, and established once and for all the impression that the July monarchy was not a menace to Europe. The ill-fated Belgian neutrality treaty finally fixed the international status of Belgium, while Leopold of Saxe-Coburg, the British candidate for the Belgian throne, and a new constitution stabilized the internal organization of the country

Louis Philippe's government did act vigorously to defend the rights of Frenchmen in Lisbon and to prevent a complete reversal of liberalism in the Papal States by Austria, but in the main the foreign policy of the July monarchy was unambitious The entente which Talleyrand established between England and France was maintained with a few exceptions throughout the régime. This English connection, because of the irrepressible nature of Lord Palmerston, was often very humiliating to the French nation. Later historians have spoken of it as an "entente, but not cordial" The understanding with England largely determined French relations with the other states. France was on good terms with Austria, whose leading statesman, Metternich, forgave Louis Philippe for his revolutionary "past" and regarded him as a conservative force in the European system France managed to keep on good terms with Russia, in spite of the clamor that the radicals raised against Russia's treatment of Poland

There was, however, one important exception in this era of peaceful relations In 1840 France almost provoked a general European war by her support of Mehemet Ali, the vigorous Turkish viceroy in Egypt. After the solution of the Greek crisis in 1829, Mehemet Ali demanded that the sultan should reimburse him for his losses at the hands of the powers. The Russians, fearful that Mehemet Ali might even supplant the sultan as ruler of the Straits, came to the assistance of the Turkish government, and in return received special privileges in the use of the Straits. England, and later Austria and Prussia, feared Russian predominance in Constantinople even more than they feared Mehemet Ali. They were anxiously waiting to join Russia as "defenders" of the sultan so that they could also enjoy privileges in the Straits. The opportunity arose in 1839 when Mehemet Ali again attempted to rebel against his overlord and despoil Turkey of Syria, Palestine, and perhaps the whole Arabic section of the Turkish Empire. England, Russia, Austria, and Prussia stood ready to defend the majesty of the sultan and acquire special rights in the use of his waters.

France, too, had been invited to join in "protecting" Turkey, but Thiers saw Mehemet Ali as a friend of France. The Egyptian army and navy had been trained by Frenchmen; Mehemet looked to France for encouragement and support. Thiers allowed France to be isolated diplomatically, and then tried to champion Mehemet Ali by a threat of war. Feeling ran high throughout Europe. In France the idea of an attack on the Rhine was popular; in Germany *Die Wacht am Rhein* was composed. Before the French battalions were put in motion, however, Louis Philippe forced Thiers to resign, and attempted to save as much of France's prestige as he could while he left Mehemet Ali to his own fate. The next year the Straits question was settled by a treaty of which France, as well as the other four great powers, was a signatory.

During the last eight years of Louis Philippe's reign, France followed the path of peace at any price, and with the bullying Palmerston in and out of the British foreign office, that often meant peace through humiliation. In the questions of Tahiti, the rights of visit and search, the Moroccan War, and the projected Spanish marriage for Louis Philippe's son, it seemed to many in France that peace could be purchased too dearly. Young men listened with admiration to the stories their fathers and grandfathers told about Napoleon and France's supremacy in Europe. The spectacle of an inglorious France offered by the government of Louis Philippe could not compete with the historical France of "the Little Corporal." French humility in international affairs inevitably played a great part in the movement that finally destroyed the régime of July

Louis Philippe attempted to distract attention from this inglorious foreign policy by the conquest of Algeria. The Algerian adventure was a heritage from Charles X. French troops, established on the coast in 1830, were confronted with the alternative of withdrawing entirely or conquering the interior Although the economists and many politicians condemned the venture as foolish, wasteful, and useless, France continued her conquest. In the Algerian chief, Abd-el-Kader, the French army found a foeman worthy of its steel, but before the Revolution of 1848 practically all Algeria was completely "peaceful." The work of colonizing and reorganizing the territory, however, was left for another generation.

THE men who came to power after 1830 did not hesitate to extend the functions of the public powers and the uses of the public treasury. They were committed to the dominant liberal individual philosophy of the day, which insisted that "the government that governs best, governs least," and that the individual must be protected against the oppressive weight of the state in his economic, social, and intellectual life; but they were willing to interpret this philosophy so that the state could perform those functions and services that would increase their prosperity and well-being, and, indeed, even curb their freedom of expression and action The construction and subsidy programs of the July monarchy greatly extended the sphere of action of the state in the economic life of the nation, while the laws of repression and factory legislation actually curbed individual freedom of action. Furthermore, in the field of primary education, the state assumed a responsibility heretofore left in private or church hands. These policies naturally were reflected in the tax schedules and in the prosperity of the public treasury.

The men who governed France under the Bourbons had uniformly shown themselves to be careful with the public credit In 1830, when the Orléans monarchy came into existence, French finances enjoyed a position of stability that must have been the envy of all Europe This favorable condition was largely due to the probity of the finance ministers who directed affairs after 1815, Baron Louis set the tradition when he refused to listen to the advice of the émigrés and assumed the responsibility for the debts of the Empire. His successors pared the expenditures of the state to a bare minimum, so that these obligations and the subsequent borrowings that were necessary to liquidate the position of France as a defeated nation could be repaid with punctuality The ease with which the Rothschilds floated the loan of 1823 was a monument to the financial responsibility of France, and in 1830 the public treasury enjoyed a prosperity that augured well for the speedy extinction of the entire public debt. This prosperity, however, had been secured by the most rigid economy, the Restoration governments resisted any and all public expenditures that were not absolutely necessary Budgets had been pared to the bone—so much that even important services to agriculture and trade were neglected

After 1830 the government was not so careful with the public pocketbook, the new rulers regarded the state in a different light, and lived in a different age These bourgeois statesmen did not consider the balanced budget as the end of good government unless that government also rendered services to agriculture and trade which no private individual could profitably supply They saw government as the fountainhead of fat building contracts, as the dispenser of profitable subsidies, and as the handmaiden of business. They also lived in an age when the danger of international conflict made it impossible to evade large expenditures for the army, the navy, and frontier fortifications, and they inherited a colonial war in Algeria in which French pride could not admit defeat Under the July monarchy France again became the country in which private budgets usually balanced, but the public budget often went into the red

The use of public money for internal improvement was one of the important works of the July monarchy In the development of transportation, the work of Louis Philippe has had far-reaching consequences on the whole economic life of the nation. Under the old régime, France had constructed an excellent system of trunk highways; Napoleon extended and improved these great military and commercial arteries during the Empire, but almost continuous use by the army left them in a wretched state in 1815 The Bourbons repaired the damage of twenty-odd years of warfare, but they were unable or unwilling to inaugurate any extensive system of expansion. It remained for the July monarchy to develop France's road system into a model for nineteenth-century Europe. There were traditionally three grades of roads in France: national, departmental, and communal; before 1830 the central government paid little attention to the second- and third-grade roads, with the result that most of them were impassable in all but the most favorable weather, and many of them were mere cowpaths that were never practicable for wheeled traffic. A law passed in 1836 created an intermediate grade of highways, between the departmental and communal, which were called "local roads of important communication." This law not only authorized their construction, but also provided regular sources of income for their extension and upkeep. Other laws extended the patronage of the government to the departmental roads, and thereby created an excellent network of all-weather highways for the French countryside. In the 1860's men looked back on the law of 1836 and the road-building work of the monarchy as the most important factor in the agricultural development of France.

Canals as well as highways received special attention from both the Bourbons and the July monarchy, but, again, it was under Louis Philippe that the greatest amount of the work was done. Nineteenth-century France inherited a highly developed system of canals from the old régime, and the France of the first half of the nineteenth century completed the network and made the canals practical for the increased traffic that had developed. Louis Philippe's government widened and deepened existing canals, linked the great river basins (Rhine-Rhone, Marne-Rhine, and Aisne-Marne), built the lateral canals that paralleled rivers where navigation was difficult, and dredged the rivers so that they could be used for heavy traffic. As a result of this work, it became possible to travel from one end of France to another by water The canals, like the highways, had an immeasurable effect on the economic life of the nation, for they provided cheap transportation for the bulky articles of commerce that theretofore could not be brought to market.

The steam-driven railroad also made its appearance in France under the July monarchy. The government, however, was at first skeptical about its practicability. In 1835, when the project to subsidize the construction of the line between St. Germain and Paris was under consideration, Thiers is credited with saying: "It is necessary to give this to Paris as a plaything, but it will never carry a passenger nor a package." In the next few years, however, the number of concessions that were demanded forced the government to consider the railroad seriously. There followed a debate in the chamber that lasted several years; every scheme proposed encountered heavy opposition. Lamartine made a brilliant and spirited plea for nationalization, but neither his oratory nor his promise that the railroad baron would introduce a new feudalism could convince the individualists that dominated the chamber. Too many men close to the government saw in the railroad a prospective business venture for themselves. Promoters and speculators were anxious for the government to grant subsidies and guarantee profits, but they did not wish to see the government in control of an enterprise that might become very profitable.

The result was that no real policy was adopted until almost ten years after the locomotive had appeared on the French countryside. The hodge-podge of concessions that were granted, however, finally made it obvious that a unified policy must be fixed upon if France were really to benefit from railroad transportation. A law in 1842 provided for a national railroad program· Paris was to be the center of a system that would radiate from the capital to the frontiers and the sea. A uniform subsidy was provided for all lines, the state agreed to provide the land and the roadbed, including tunnels and bridges; the companies were to provide the rails, ballast, station equipment, rolling stock, and working capital At first the local authorities were supposed to contribute a part of the state's share, but after 1845 the central government agreed to assume the entire burden. It was not long before the state also agreed to guarantee minimum rates of interest.

The system as adopted proved to be not very satisfactory; it was easy to find companies willing to construct certain sections of the system even without as much state aid as the law provided, but there were other sections for which it proved impossible to find a company. Furthermore, some of the companies very soon found themselves unable to meet their contracts, and the state was forced, willy-nilly, to come to their assistance By 1848 there were thirty or forty railroad companies, of various degrees of insolvency, working approximately 1,700 miles of railroad; the state itself was forced to take over and operate another 300 miles of the system. But the most unfortunate thing about the situation was that France did not, even then, have a unified and adequate railroad system. There were large sections that were still begging for construction. It was left to the Second Empire to finish the task of providing France with adequate railroad transportation.

Shipping also interested the men who governed the July monarchy. In 1840 the chamber opened a credit of twenty-eight million francs to subsidize the construction of eighteen steamships for four regular lines It was not, however, until 1847 that a company presented itself to establish regular transatlantic steamship service. The monarchy likewise subsidized the construction of electric telegraph lines, but only after the telegraph had long been in use in the United States, Belgium, England, and Germany. In 1845 the chamber provided money to construct the telegraph line between Paris and Rouen, and in the following years the system was extended to include all France.

In addition to subsidizing transportation and communication, the July monarchy embarked upon an extensive program of public building Old palaces were renovated and made into museums, many public buildings were constructed all over France, and work was begun on the building of modern Paris which Napoleon III and Baron Haussmann so ably carried on Unfortunately, in too many cases these building programs were carried out with very poor taste, and often under the cloud of impending scandal. During the entire period there were always rumors of misuses of public funds and corruption in high places, and occasionally these rumors were substantiated by public scandals that involved prominent officials and politicians.

Although many people in France recognized that the high-tariff policy established by Napoleon and continued by the Bourbons was paralyzing the economic development of the nation, the July monarchy did not appreciably alter it One deputy boldly expressed the situation during the tariff debates of 1836: "No society," he said, "can exist without an aristocracy. Do you wish to know what is the aristocracy of the July monarchy? It is the great industrialists; they are the foundation of the new dynasty. A system [lower tariffs] that would tend to alienate them appears to me to be senseless folly." The foreigners might raise retaliatory tariffs against French goods, the French consumers might have to pay high prices for necessities of life, and economic philosophers might point out the irrationality of the system that patronized inefficient industries, but the protective tariff for both agricultural and industrial products was not substantially changed It was profitable to the men who controlled the state, the capitalists and landlords who kept Louis Philippe upon his throne.

In 1836, after a parliamentary investigation, there was a slight change in the tariff schedules, but the protective system was never really endangered. All through the period the tariff question was under consideration, especially after the series of bad harvests that started in 1845 caused much discontent and distress among the lower classes, but every attempt at alteration seemed destined to fail before the powerful vested interests that profited by the *status quo*. Late in 1847, however, there was a project before the chamber that had a slight chance of success, but before it could be considered, the Revolution of February, 1848, ended the régime. As in an earlier period, the tariff policy made smuggling a regular and profitable industry that helped to create some of the staunchest defenders of the protective system.

It was the July monarchy that first recognized the duty of the state to carry through a program of primary education; Guizot's education law of 1833 proved to be one of the most important measures taken in the first half of the century "Each commune," the law stipulated, "is obliged, be it by itself or in conjunction with several communes, to provide at least one school for primary instruction; those communes whose population exceeds 6,000, and the principal cities of each department, must have a school for secondary education. Each department will be obliged to establish a normal school, be it by itself or in conjunction with several neighboring departments." The law provided that this education must be gratuitous for indigents, but all others must pay tuition; naturally, this first law did not include compulsory education for all children It also provided for the establishment of requirements for teachers, and an institution for the control of the schools. Guizot himself was willing apparently to allow the churchmen to monopolize the teaching positions, since he felt that complete harmony of Church and state was necessary for moral education, but the anticlericalism of the 1830's was too strong for any such surrender to the religious orders Accordingly, the certificate that gave the right to teach could only be acquired by passing an examination that would be set up by a governmentally appointed commission Each school was to be supervised by a local committee, on which the religious and civil authorities of the commune received prominent places The whole question of religious education was skillfully skirted by the provision that "the wishes of fathers of families will always be consulted and followed in matters of religious training"

By this law the public treasury, either local or national, was obliged to provide for the education of the young Naturally, this legislation did not bear all the fruits that Guizot may have anticipated from it; in some backward communities it was practically ignored, in others it tended to become a sort of subsidy for the children of men who could afford to pay tuition, while the children of the poor found it difficult to attend the schools But, all in all, it was farsighted legislation that started the long struggle against illiteracy in France.

While the government was willing to extend the public powers to provide services for agriculture and industry and to establish schools, it was very reluctant to interfere in the economic relations between worker and employer. The rulers of France had thoroughly absorbed the individualistic philosophy that was so beneficial to their own interests, they interpreted freedom to mean that each man be free of all restraints in his economic life, for only then could each individual seek his own best interests This meant, in so many words, that the state would keep its hands off business except to prevent combinations of individuals from destroying another individual's freedom of contract The public power, therefore, could be used to suppress a strike, for these individuals were unlawfully combining to defeat freedom of contract, but that same power could not be used to regulate working conditions, since such action would mean an invasion of individual rights As early as August 25, 1830, when the workers of Paris had not yet forgotten that they had shed their blood to make the July monarchy possible, the Parisian proletariat was told that the law and the state would never have anything to do with the relationships between worker and employer, and, furthermore, that "no demands addressed to us [the government] asking for intervention between worker and employer in questions of hours of labor or rates of wages would be received, since that would be in direct opposition to the laws guaranteeing freedom of industry" In following this policy, the police, the army, and the National Guard were used to suppress strikes and labor troubles in Lyon, Paris, and elsewhere. Several of the disturbances occasioned considerable bloodshed.

The misery created by the new industrial organization, however, finally forced even the bourgeois government in Paris to consider the question of state intervention English parliamentary inquests and the subsequent factory legislation for the British Isles gave philanthropic and socially minded people in France hopes for similar action on the part of their own state. Finally, an inquest conducted under the auspices of the Académie des Sciences Morales by Villermé created so great a sensation that the question could no longer be ignored by the chamber. A law was proposed in 1839, and finally passed in 1841, that opened the first breach in the fortress of state nonintervention. The law itself was pitifully emasculated, and almost completely ineffective as it was finally passed, but it was a recognition of the state's rights to interfere. It provided only for a limitation of the hours of labor of children; a child under eight could not be admitted into the factories, and children between eight and twelve could work only eight hours a day. Children from twelve to seventeen could work only twelve hours a day between the hours of five A. M. and nine P. M., except under unusual conditions. Children under twelve were required to go to school, or they could not be admitted into the factories Penalties for evasion of this law were provided, but no effective system for enforcement was established, so the law's beneficial effects were meager indeed.

The debates that preceded the passage of this law were very interesting. Its opponents attacked it, first of all, as a limitation of the rights of fathers of families that needed the money that young children could earn, and, secondly, as an invasion of the freedom that an industrialist must have in the conduct of his affairs. The protagonists of the law fairly shouted: "The first duty of the state is to assure itself that the children of the country grow up robust, intelligent, healthy, and moral. Industry has no right to demand that we give it discretion over childhood, the future generation." One man said that the state must tell a father who would sell his child: "This child no longer has a father, I will protect it." The law aroused great hopes among the workers and the socially minded elements of society, but it was foolish to expect a government largely dominated by the wealthy bourgeoisie to initiate a program of social reform Regulation of hours for adults—and, for that matter, the whole of the workers' program—had to wait for a government in which the voices of the poor could be heard.

The attempt to strengthen the legislation that forced each worker to carry a *livret* in which his whole past employment record could be reviewed shows well the social outlook of the upper bourgeoisie. The *livret* placed the worker absolutely at the mercy of his employer, since obtaining another position was dependent upon his present employer's giving him a clean slate in his *livret*. Many workers who, for one reason or another, were unable to get a satisfactory discharge, were forced to leave urban employment and become agricultural laborers, for in the country the *livret* was not in use. This was the only possible way for a worker to bury his past. A bill was introduced in the chamber to block this escape; friends of the bill explained that "the idea that motivated this proposed law is unfavorable to neither the employers nor the employees, but that it wished to furnish to both positive guarantees . . . the worker finds in the *livret* the story of his life, a statement of his fidelity in fulfilling his contracts, and the manufacturer finds there a sure recommendation." The protests of the workers and their sympathizers prevented the bill from coming up for a vote, but the fact that it was considered is indicative of the temper of the ruling class.

During the last years of the July monarchy the legislative machinery slowed down, and all but stopped. Soult and Guizot feared any widespread program of legislative action. In their care not to adopt any policy that might antagonize any group of their supporters, they avoided adopting any policy at all. Politics became the administration of the state in the interests of the very wealthy, and further legislation to care for the developing social, economic, and political structure of France had to wait until after Louis Philippe was driven from the throne.

CHAPTER IV

FRENCH CIVILIZATION UNDER THE CONSTITUTIONAL MONARCHIES

IN THE France of the first half of the nineteenth century there were two countries and two peoples: Paris and the provinces, the rich and the poor. The old France of the throne, the altar, and the peasantry predominated in the provinces, the new France of free thought and emerging democracy centered in the city. Paris was cosmopolitan, international, she had been a world capital under Napoleon, and she remained a world capital for literature and art Even under the Bourbons, but more especially after 1830, the liberals throughout Europe looked to Paris as the haven of liberty, the capital of liberalism; refugees from all oppressed lands found there congenial company and a measure of freedom unknown in the continental Europe of the age of Metternich Paris was not yet the comfortable, beautiful, modern metropolis with broad boulevards, great squares, and beautiful, well-stocked museums that the tourist today finds so interesting That Paris was to be built under the Second Empire. But even in 1830 she was a city well provided with gay restaurants, cafés, and places of amusement, and her high society presented a brilliant spectacle to the world.

The provinces had been less affected by the moving events of the Napoleonic era; even the great provincial cities, several of which exceeded 100,000 in population, were not in close contact with world movements. The men in the provinces rarely traveled, read only sparingly, and seldom met representatives of the outside world. It was only natural that their outlook should be restricted. Paris, too, was still both the will and the brain of France; the extreme centralization that characterized the administration of the country deprived the provincial cities of an opportunity to compete with her; the decisions that she made were still accepted in the provinces, apparently without question. The time had not yet come when provincial France forced Paris to follow her direction

In Paris and in the provinces, however, only a small part of the nation enjoyed the civilization which France was creating. The great mass of the population—peasants, workers, and petty bourgeois—remained dumb, inarticulate, excluded; their lives, their hopes, and their fears did not count in politics or in society. The Constitution excluded them from political rights; the law which guaranteed "freedom of industry" forbade them to unite for the purposes of obtaining economic rights. The difference between their yearly income and their necessary expenses was not large enough to allow them to enjoy the civilization of the land. They were the disinherited classes. Only the wealthy counted in French society. The government functioned in their interests; the lower classes labored in their workshops and on their fields so that the upper crust of society could enjoy a civilized life. For the latter, and for them alone, were the art, the music, the literature, and the science that France produced. They set the tone for society, they fixed the standards of civilization

Within this favored group of fortunate ones there were many distinctions. The legitimists, the émigré nobility, the country gentry, the Napoleonic families, and the commercial, industrial, and financial capitalists stood at the pinnacle of the social structure. Some of them were comparatively liberal, others ultraconservative, but almost without exception they stood ready to guard their position of privilege based on wealth This group might be said to include all those people whose incomes exceeded 12,000 francs a year They were usually able to own both a country villa, in which they lived during the late spring and summer, and a city house for fall and winter. Their lives were a round of parties, balls, operas, and plays Their children were educated by tutors or in expensive private schools. Their chief interests were politics, society gossip, business, and the arts. Just below them in the social scale were the middle bourgeois who enjoyed political rights, but whose incomes, probably from 6,000 to 12,000 francs annually, would not permit extensive expenditures. These people owned a city house or its equivalent, sent their children to an ecclesiastical or a state college or a convent finishing school, they talked business and politics almost exclusively. They filled the ranks of the National Guard They did not have an important part in the great social or intellectual life of France, but they knew that, if their business prospered, they could rise to the status of capitalists. These two groups, the élite of French society—probably less than a million individuals in a nation of over thirty million—were the only important people in the bourgeois civilization of the day.

Georges Weill has aptly summed up the spirit of this dominant class. He writes:

> In all these men we find common characteristics. hate of despotism, defiance against the court, pride in their aristocracy of wealth as opposed to the aristocracy of birth; aversion alike for clericalism and irreligion; love of order and regular authority, tenacity in political struggles as well as in practical life, family virtues; philanthropy toward the lower classes on condition that they remain inferior. They lacked the sentiment, the artistic sense, the poetic insight, the comprehension of democracy—all that would have been necessary to direct a people that had felt the passion for equality aroused by 1793, for glory aroused by Napoleon, for idealism aroused by the romanticists Wealth and wealth alone, solidly invested for a generation at least, gave access to this class. It remained closed to the poor, to parvenus, save for striking exceptions such as Guizot and Thiers. It remained on good terms with the middle bourgeoisie, with all those that paid taxes enough to earn the title of elector The elector there is the master of France under Louis Philippe.

And to become an elector a man had to pay 200 francs in direct taxes!

The solidity and regularity of the bourgeoisie became objects of scorn for the intellectuals who opposed the "bohemian life" of the left bank to the propriety and probity of the dominant class. The National Guard, the "proprietor," the elector, each in turn was mocked by the artists and writers of the period Sue, Gavarni, Daumier, and Monnier have immortalized the bourgeois in their satires, while Proudhon, Leroux, and others, in their political tracts, deplored their existence The privileged ones, however, never allowed the scoffers' arrows to ruffle their calm They even ignored Heine's famous remark "Never has France been so low in the eyes of a foreigner, not even in the times of du Barry and de la Pompadour. One sees now that there is something worse than the reign of mistresses; one can find more honor in the boudoir of a gallant lady than in the countinghouse of a banker." It is no wonder that they could ignore Leroux and Louis Blanc, when this biting sarcasm did not take effect

Just below the upper crust of society were the petty bourgeoisie whose yearly incomes ranged from 1,500 to 6,000 francs. Many of these men had a hard time maintaining their status above the workers, but they considered themselves as belonging to the better element of society. Unlike the upper bourgeoisie, they did not leave memoirs, nor did they create a stir in the social life. They often belonged to the National Guard, and managed their small workshops or businesses. The head of the family worked hard at his business or profession, while his wife managed her own household, often doing most of the work herself These little people were often unhappy as the result of their contacts with the wealthy in the National Guard or in business, for they had to practice the strictest economy to make both ends meet, and, thus, were unable to attain the standards of living of their wealthy neighbors The literary men of the age pilloried this class for its shortsighted, matter-of-fact, cautious outlook and its parsimony Its members were avid place hunters, sharp dealers, and schemers, but they were to become the backbone of the nation. They supported the July monarchy until February, 1848, when their defection made victorious the cause of the revolutionaries; in a later age they became the chief prop of the Republic.

BEFORE the July Revolution there had been more or less social intercourse between the very wealthy bourgeois, the old nobility, and the men of the First Empire. Napoleon had started the melting process, and the Bourbon kings attempted to continue it. Wealthy bourgeois were given patents of nobility, marriage between the old and the new families was encouraged, both the old and the new were invited to the court. It was not uncommon to find nobility and wealthy bourgeois meeting socially in the salons of the Restoration era. Under the Bourbons these salons were a characteristic institution, anyone who was anything at all had days "at home" to entertain friends and acquaintances. The salon became the clearinghouse for gossip, for political bargains, for literature and art, and even for business. It marked the re-entry of women into political life, from which they had been excluded by Napoleon. The lines in the salons were not too sharply drawn; a liberal could almost be sure of a cordial reception, even in the home of an ultra, a foreigner was welcome in all the salons, and anyone with wealth could be sure of a reception in most of them. The successful hostess prided herself on her ability to bring together diverse elements.

The July Revolution ended this easy intercourse. Partisans of the legitimate king locked their doors against men who recognized the "King of the Barricades." Sulking in their houses—in Paris they lived mostly in the *Quartier Saint Germain*—these irreconcilables revenged themselves by repeating scandalous gossip about Louis Philippe and his family and friends. "Louis the Pear," or "Louis the Apple," they called him. They refused to allow their children to marry into families that were received at court, and used every opportunity to stir up trouble for the official society. Only foreigners were welcomed into their select company.

The retreat of a large part of the old nobility left the stage free for the upper bourgeois. These prided themselves on the title "middle class"; they recognized that they were clearly the most important section of French society. Flanked by the liberal and the imperial nobility, they dominated the social life of the nation during the entire period of the July monarchy. But under the new régime there was a striking change in the functioning of social life. The salon was restricted from two sides. In the first place, politics and business came to be exclusively the work of men, carried out in the offices of deputies, lawyers, or bankers Secondly, a new institution, the club, came to compete with the salon. Men preferred to gather together in their private clubs—the Jockey Club was one of the most famous—and enjoy their cigars and drinks away from the companionship of the ladies Under the impacts of these two factors, the salon gradually changed in character Music, literature, art, and gossip became the subjects of conversation, and the custom of having musical recitals came to stifle even these topics. "The piano," said Heine, a habitué of many salons, "kills our thoughts."

With Louis Philippe as king, the court, too, underwent a profound change. Under the Bourbons, court etiquette had been stiff and formal; the palace approximated as far as possible the ways of the old régime. The new Orléans king carefully cultivated bourgeois tone; court etiquette was greatly relaxed; the king lived the life of an exemplary family man in easy familiarity with his wife and children. The royal chateau was always open to the officers of the National Guard, and court festivals were crowded with the élite of the Parisian middle class. Only on rare occasions, such as the marriage of the royal prince, was the etiquette extremely formal.

In another significant way the new régime made an important impression on the society of France. Before the July Revolution, social functions were unostentatious, and, usually, in good taste No one was ashamed to admit that he did not own a carriage or that he had to watch his expenditures carefully, but after the revolution there were a number of factors that tended to change this simplicity. The wealthy bourgeois could afford more display than, too often, their good taste knew how to curb. In a society in which wealth was the criterion for position, the tendency to display "ability to pay" will inevitably show itself. Furthermore, after 1830 France became a Mecca for wealthy foreigners, the first crop of American millionaires, fabulously rich Russian nobles, and English plutocrats These men found the life of Paris congenial, but their habits and wealth tended to debase French good taste. The tawdriness of the era infected the court itself; Louis Philippe spent large sums in rehabilitating and redecorating the palaces belonging to the state, but usually with less artistic judgment than ought to be expected from a French monarch. The society of the July monarchy bore the tone of the plutocrats who loved to splurge and to waste conspicuously, it is no wonder that the "Count of Monte Cristo" with his houses, his horses, and his unlimited credit found no difficulty in establishing himself in the good graces of the generation of Louis Philippe.

These social tendencies that were found in Paris could be discovered in the provinces—usually, however, in an exaggerated form. Even in the larger cities, the provincial salons were not so interested in politics or so up to date in literature and art, but they compensated for this by the enthusiasm with which they pursued their interests of the day; for example, in advocating the spread of vaccination, if they were liberals, or the advancement of Christianity if they were conservatives In each department there was usually an official press fed by the prefect, and an opposition press that led a precarious existence In the larger sections, especially after 1830, provincial periodicals like *La Revue du Nord* and *La Revue du Midi* began to appear in competition with the literary and philosophical journals of the capital. Here and there, in cities like Metz, Lyon, and Bordeaux, "learned societies" of one kind or another met—as in the days of the *ancien régime*—to discuss literature, science, or art. In many of the provincial universities and colleges, particularly in the north and east, the instruction was about as good as that found in the capital. These provincial societies, however, were for the wealthy alone, the poor had no influence.

The functionaries almost constituted a social caste of their own. They were the representatives of the government, and they carried out the task of administering the civil, religious, and military life of the nation These functionaries were the principal contact between Paris and the provinces, they were important personages in both the metropolis and the village. During the July monarchy, the number of civil, religious, and military officials rose to about a quarter of a million—about one adult male for every thirty in the population. They varied in importance, from the well-paid prefects, generals, bishops, and ministerial officials, to poorly paid petty judges, mayors, and other local officers. Before the Revolution, their posts were purchasable, but after 1789, and particularly after 1830, they were obtained by political "pull" Under the July monarchy the minister of the interior and the deputies were chief distributors of this patronage. Frenchmen have always been avid office seekers; one observer pointedly exclaimed, "If there were two men living in France, one would ask the other for a governmental position."

Napoleon created the prototype of the French functionary, and endowed him with an honorable position in society Under the monarchies, however, too often the hard-working, efficient imperial functionary was replaced by the ignorant, indolent types which Balzac enjoyed satirizing—men who could not find time to carry on the duties of their offices, because of their other activities or their laziness Nevertheless, a surprising number of officials survived revolutions and changes in government, particularly in the finance ministry, where there were many able civil servants who served their country well. Considering that there were no schools for the training of administrators, the level of administrative efficiency was quite high, and the functionaries often showed creditable independence For example: the Paris Court of Appeal refused to carry out the violent requests of Villèle and Polignac, in 1832 the Court of Cassation declared the state of siege in Paris to be illegal The office of prefect, under the régime of Louis Philippe, was generally regarded as a tool with which to control elections; thus, the novelists often chose this office as the butt of their satire. But the conclusion should not be drawn that the entire administrative corps was corrupt

ALTHOUGH the great mass of the people—peasants and proletarians—did not appreciably affect the course of French civilization during the first half of the nineteenth century, no discussion of French society that omitted them would be complete. During this period, many of the problems that later generations were forced to consider first made their appearance. Under Napoleon, the peasant or the worker could always find a place for himself either in the army or in a workshop producing goods to assist in the war, but after 1815 it became increasingly difficult for him to find a way of making a satisfactory living As if to make their lot worse, the gradual introduction of industrialization made the city proletarians into factory workers at the mercy of economic "laws" and crises, and at the same time it destroyed the domestic working system, thereby depriving the peasant of his home industry. Between 1815 and 1848 the law, and the ignorance of both peasant and worker, effectively prevented them from obtaining redress, it was only after 1848 that universal suffrage and the gradual extension of education placed in their hands weapons with which they could force the upper crust of society to consider their problems

The life of the urban proletariat in the old cities was extremely disagreeable, their quarters were cramped and unsanitary The worker's existence was more or less bleak, except for an occasional spree. But life in the new cities—the factory towns—was, if possible, even worse. These towns, particularly in the east and north, grew rapidly as the peasants were attracted by the prospect of better wages than agriculture could offer. Several of these towns doubled or tripled in population every ten to fifteen years. They were horrible, ugly, stinking examples of man's ability to adjust himself to miserable conditions The agricultural laborers who filled them had not counted on the ill effects of overcrowding, any more than they had considered the possibility that a business crisis would place them in the most dire need The proprietors of the land and the tenements well understood that the laborer could not pay much rent, and therefore they made no attempt to give him a decent dwelling place. The factories, like the towns, were hardly fit for human habitation. Their poor lighting and ventilation, unsanitary conditions, and dangerous machinery unprotected by guards helped to make the mortality rates inordinately high.

The urban proletarians who lived in these cities fell roughly into two groups: those that worked in the traditional shops or at traditional trades—tanners, dyers, hatters, masons, smiths, wheelwrights, plasterers, and the like—and those that were employed in the new machine-using factories, particularly in textile and metallurgic plants. It was this latter group that swelled the new cities after 1820; the former group remained more or less stationary in number, and in some cases even declined in size.

Statistics taken in the 1840's in sixty-three departments show that the factories that hired an average of ten workers employed 672,000 men, 254,000 women, and 131,000 children Women and children were especially in demand in the textile mills, since they could tend the machines about as effectively as the men, while they were paid from a third to a half as high a wage. It is difficult to ascertain any standard for the wages of the workers at that time, since the pay varied from province to province and from industry to industry It is safe to say, however, that very few heads of families received more than 600 francs a year, and that many of them received less than 300 francs a year—at a time when a petty bourgeois family with 1,500 francs could hardly afford to hire a maid.

The laborer's existence was made more precarious by the fact that his wages did not respond to a rapid rise in prices such as occurred after the bad harvests of 1845–1847, while a business crisis (and there were ten severe crises between 1815 and 1848) left him without any means of support

The workers in the traditional trades were somewhat better off than their fellows in the factories—but, even so, their lot was not exactly enviable They were forced to apprentice themselves to a master or a patron for a long period of training, before they could be admitted to regular employment. When the apprentice learned his trade, he became a journeyman, and made a tour of France. Almost everywhere he could find friends and assistance, through his connection with the secret labor organizations, the *compagnonnages*. Furthermore, the young journeyman could always hope (too often he had never more than a hope) that the time would come when he would settle down, own his own shop and be a patron, although the process of acquiring a shop became increasingly difficult as the nineteenth century went on During the July monarchy, the salaries paid to many of these traditional craftsmen increased appreciably, and a number of them were able to rise to the ranks of the petty bourgeoisie.

As a contemporary observed, one of the great difficulties involved in improving the lot of the workers was that the industrialists and shop owners "were manufacturers because they wished to become wealthy, not because they wished to be philanthropists." It is only just to say that there were exceptions; but, for the most part, the upper class did not concern itself with the condition or the problems of the poor. Nearly all economic thought emphasized the possibilities of increasing production through the machine processes, and neglected the other aspects of the economic and social problems connected with the new industrialism. But probably the most important difficulty was the fact that the dominant political theory of the day was hostile to state intervention in any form. The

English factory act of 1833 did inspire a French parliamentary investigation into the condition of children in industry This resulted ultimately in the legislation that regulated child labor in the factories, but the government was hindered in executing the law because no provisions were made for salaried inspectors The manufacturers themselves were expected to enforce the regulation! In 1847 a bill was introduced to give teeth to the child-labor regulations, but before it could be passed, the Revolution of February ended the régime There was also an attempt to reform the *conseils des prud'hommes* that judged disputes between master and worker. In these councils the employers alone had real representation. But the reform project came to nothing The establishment of savings banks for the use of the laborers was probably the most important single attempt to better their lot, but here the difficulty was that many laborers could save nothing out of their miserable salaries.

The laboring class continued to suffer severely from the revolutionary and imperial legislation that remained on the lawbooks throughout the period of the constitutional monarchies The law not only forced each worker to keep a *livret* wherein each of his employers must testify to the worker's satisfactory conduct, but also forbade all combinations or coalitions which might restrict liberty of contract or attempt to force a rise in wages. Infractions were severely punished by the courts. Strikes were regarded not only as illegal, but even as sedition against the state. The government did not hesitate to use armed force to suppress strikes, and even forced laborers to return to work. In spite of these regulations, there were numerous strikes between 1815 and 1848; several of them under the July monarchy were especially violent. The results were nearly always the same; the National Guard and the police suppressed the strike, the leaders were imprisoned, and the workers' organization was broken up Sée very aptly observes: "It is no wonder that the working class, held in check by legislation, closely watched by the administration, offered little effective resistance to the conditions imposed upon them by the masters of industry"

The workers did have several organizations through which they could express their discontent. The most effective were the *compagnonnages* of the traditional tradesmen These organizations, however, had lost much of the force that they had possessed under the old régime, and their difficulties with the law reduced their value to the worker The *compagnonnages* were secret societies of skilled laborers; they were conducted with rites and mystic symbolism believed to have originated at the time of Solomon There were several grades or ranks, each with special rites the "children of Master Jacques," the "children of Father Soubise," and the "children of Solomon", between the members of different ranks there was the greatest rivalry, which often resulted in bloody riots The *compagnons* could obtain aid in the form of food, lodging, and perhaps a job through the "father" or "mother" who kept an inn for the members They could always find companions and fellowship to tap a keg of wine, assist in a strike, or care for the sick. Most of the traditional crafts were represented in the *compagnonnages,* the building trades were especially strong, probably because of the migratory nature of the work The factory workers, however, were not members "Those groups," writes Clapham, "which were to dominate the later nineteenth century, were not even counted worth recognition . . . either because they were so few . . . or so lowly." After the Revolution of July, a group of workers attempted to establish a more democratic *compagnonnage,* the "Union of the Tour of France," in which the various mystic ranks and degrees were suppressed This organization was strong in Lyon and Toulon, but under the attacks of the government and with the changing economic structure, it failed to fulfill the hopes of its founders. The coming of the railroad dealt a body blow to the *compagnonnage;* new transportation changed the customary "Tour of France" of the journeymen, and altered the economic organization of the nation. The building trades retained the society after 1848, but it was destined to disappear.

One form of worker organization was recognized as legal—the mutual-benefit society. These societies were not supposed to have other than fraternal aims—care of the sick, burial of the dead, and the like As benefit societies, they received the patronage of the government itself under the July monarchy By 1840 there were more than 200 societies in Paris; in Lyon they counted 3,000 members, and in Roubaix, 1,500 members Theoretically, they were not organized on professional lines, the members could be drawn from all types of industry. This would prevent the mutual-benefit society from developing into a labor union Actually, however, many of these societies became training grounds for labor leaders, and veritable unions for labor interests Of course, this illegal activity was always subject to police interference.

After the July Revolution, laborers grew more and more to realize their community of interest Short-lived proletarian newspapers were founded to voice their problems, and the first of the labor leaders and proletarian philosophers made their bows in the presses of Europe. After the workers had overthrown the Bourbons, they got an exaggerated opinion of their power, but when they tried to repeat their performance against their bourgeois masters, they discovered that the National Guard would fire, and that without guns the workers could not hope to win. In Paris, Nantes, Lyon, and elsewhere, they learned between 1830 and 1839 that, unarmed, they were no match for the bourgeois National Guard, the police, and the army. It was not until much blood was shed, however, that they really believed it. Their new leaders urged them to bide their time, for theirs was the future. The time must come when their interests would be considered in French civilization.

WHILE the workers were slowly preparing themselves to take a place in the society of the future, the peasants—the other group of the disinherited ones—made no comparable progress. Their lives on the land, unstimulated by the daily hum of a bustling city, were deadened by monotonous, routine toil The peasants' sensibilities were never sharpened by contact with the bourgeoisie or struggling for an existence in the midst of their fellow men The soil, the solitude of the country and the deadening labor in the fields paralyzed susceptibilities and drowned aspirations which they might have had. Mute, ignorant, inarticulate, the peasant continued much as his father and grandfather before him; the great moving forces of the nineteenth century hardly caused him to turn in his traditional path.

Very few of the peasants could read, write, or calculate; the man who could read a notary's document would pass as a savant. But many of them had no desire to learn. "The sun," they said, "rises equally for the ignorant and the wise. . . . See that one! He can read, but he is poorer than I am" It was extremely difficult to persuade them to take advantage of Guizot's educational plan. For those who could read, there were few books. A very popular work was *L'Albert,* the peasant's encyclopedia, which supplied him with all sorts of useful information, such as cures for all illnesses, the making of beauty potions, recipes for cooking, formulas for preserving butter, and thousands of other things that the peasant might want to know. If he did not have *L'Albert,* he might have one of the almanacs that Decazes had passed out to strengthen the cause of royalism, or a book of devotions, or a book on love The houses were decorated, if they had decorations at all, with crude lithographs, and perhaps a bust of Napoleon or the Virgin, or maybe a crucifix

The peasants' heads were filled with curious lore about fairies, goblins, werewolves, and witches, but they knew practically nothing about politics Few of them had ever been beyond the village in which they were born Cooper's story of the peasant who did not know the name of the next village "because he was not from that country" probably is an excellent index of the restricted outlook of the class. The chief factor that took the peasant away from his village was military service, but only the very poorest, who could not buy exemption, went to the army. Usually, those boys that did go were agreeably surprised to find the diet and the living conditions in the army far superior to anything that they had known at home, a fact that made them willing to re-enlist after their first term of service. When they returned to the land, however, they rarely exerted any effect on the cultural level of their villages, a few years on the soil, and the soil reclaimed them. The ex-soldier was hardly to be distinguished from his fellows who had not seen "the world."

For a short time after the ultras acquired control in the early 1820's, the peasants took an interest in the politics of the chamber, for they feared that the government might upset the revolutionary land settlement and re-establish the feudal exactions. The interest, however, was short-lived—so short that a popular story of 1830 reports the following conversation between two peasants: "What is this Charter that they are talking so much about?" asked the first. "Eh, *pardi*," replied the second, "that is the wife of Louis Philippe." The politics —in fact, practically all of the ideas of the peasant—came from one or two individuals of importance in the village, the mayor or the priest, a neighboring lord, an old soldier, or the schoolteacher. The peasants liked to tell malicious yarns about their priests, and often stayed away from church, but at least once a year they were scrupulous to confess their sins, and, in case of severe illness, the priest was always called in to pave the road to the next world The mayor or the neighboring country gentleman often enjoyed a local reputation that gave him considerable prestige in the village Much of the peasant royalist sentiment arose from the fact that after 1830 many of the old nobility retired to the country, where they and their wives often played the part of ***grand seigneur*** and ***grande dame*** and benefactor to the villagers The physician who lived in the larger villages sometimes also played an important rôle, but usually the peasant was too stingy to call in a physical adviser until he had reached a stage of illness so advanced that the priest's services were every bit as good as the doctor's The veterans of the Napoleonic wars were omnipresent in the villages during the first half of the century; they told the youth about adventure and glory in foreign lands, and kept alive the name of Napoleon—the only political name that captured the peasants' imagination.

The chief interests of the peasants centered in the soil Only about one-fourth of them owned enough land to support themselves and their families, the other three-fourths earned part or all of their living on land belonging to others. It was, however, the desire of every peasant to own a "little" farm and be independent of the world; to satisfy this ambition they were willing to undertake debts which would not be paid for generations Backward agricultural methods and inherent conservatism often made their dream impossible of realization, but throughout France the increase in the petty holdings at the expense of the large and middle-sized holdings gave evidence of the tenacity and ambition of the peasants. The peasant, a creature of the soil, lived by the land and drew his strength from it, the industrialization of Europe and the rise in the demand for agricultural produce made it possible for him gradually to increase his holdings of the land that served him so well.

The romanticists, who loved the quaint and the picturesque, found in the village ample food for their imagination. The peasant had not yet become standardized in dress and custom, and each district presented its own local color Costumes, local fêtes and celebrations, and local variations in speech, made the villages the "happy hunting grounds" of people who wished to recapture the spirit of ages past. But all this colorful beauty could not hide the fact that the peasant's life was not desirable. He had only begun to learn to lighten his labor and increase his crops by newer methods of agriculture. The system had suited his grandfather; why should he change? His diet was strictly limited and woefully monotonous; his house was not good, and had to be shared with the beasts of the field. He had learned little or nothing about sanitation or control of disease, and over all hovered his dismal ignorance and stubborn conservatism that stood in the way of bettering his lot. Like the urban proletarian, he did not have much of a stake in the brilliant civilization that Heine saw in Paris.

THE economic forces that revolutionized European civilization in the nineteenth century were slower in beginning their work in France than in England, improvements in techniques and methods lagged, in spite of the combination of favorable government, comparative internal and external peace, and expanding economic horizons. Although the first stirrings of the new economy were discernible under the Bourbons, and very much in evidence after Louis Philippe became king, French society by 1850 had only begun the transformation from an agricultural to an industrial economy Population trends, however, provide sure evidence of the tendencies at work; between 1815 and 1848 the population rose from about twenty-nine to thirty-five million, and the cities absorbed the greatest part of the increase. In 1815 rural France accounted for eighty-five per cent of the nation, by 1850 the figure had dropped to less than seventy-five per cent. Paris, the metropolis, made the greatest gains; her population passed the million mark by 1850, but four other cities exceeded one hundred thousand each. The foundations for an urban industrial, social, and economic organization in which the mechanized factory would set the pace for production were well established before Louis Philippe was forced from the throne in 1848.

During the first half of the century, however, agriculture remained the backbone of French economic life. It supported about two-thirds of the population, and employed the greater part of the total wealth of the nation After the revolutionary settlement of the land question was reaffirmed, first by Baron Louis in 1815, then by Villèle at the time of the indemnification of the émigrés, and finally by the July monarchy, the danger of a re-establishment of the old régime in the countryside was no longer to be feared, and French agriculture could settle down without danger of any violent disruption of the basic framework of rural life Still very important in rural economy were the large landholdings that had played so prominent a rôle in pre-revolutionary France. Many of the old nobles had never lost their lands; others had reacquired them through purchase or as a gift of Napoleon or Louis XVIII Furthermore, in the sales of the Church and émigré properties, many of the great estates were bought outright and not subdivided. Thus, we find that large landholding was still quite common, especially in le Maine, la Vendée, l'Anjou, as well as in other sections of the country. The middle-sized estates, property of the bourgeoisie, were also very important Most of these holdings were, obviously, the direct result of the revolutionary sale of Church and émigré lands Naturally, there was also a considerable number of small property holdings which stemmed from revolutionary legislation, the sale of the public lands, and the insatiable land hunger of the peasants that often drove them to mortgage their future for an additional scrap of soil

Statistics gathered in the middle of the nineteenth century show definitely that over half of the agricultural population either owned no land or did not own enough to support their families, while a large proportion of the owners had little or no contact with the soil itself Of the 6,359,258 proprietors, over one million, the owners of the largest holdings, did not even live in the countryside, and over two million did not cultivate their own soil. Another two million cultivated their own land exclusively, but the remaining 2,200,000 properties were so small that their owners had to hire themselves out to supplement their incomes Of the 4,792,000 landless inhabitants of rural France, almost 3,700,000 were day laborers; about 700,000 were tenant farmers; 350,000 were *métayers,* and the remaining 30,000 were stewards and master valets. It is evident that, although France was a nation of peasants, she was not a nation of peasant-proprietors. The lot of the agricultural laborer who owned a scrap of land was not much better than that of the urban proletarian. There was, however, in the course of the first half of the century, a tendency, accelerated in the second half, for the small holdings to increase at the expense of the larger ones The French peasant never gave up the desire to own more land, and he purchased it a scrap at a time. One man of letters referred to this as "worm boring" which would end in destroying the only efficient agriculture in France.

The general increase in population—and above all, in urban population—had a happy effect on French agriculture, for when the peasant could find a market for the surplus produce of his lands he could afford to devote all of his time to cultivation. This was doubly fortunate, since it came at the exact moment when the domestic system (which, heretofore, had given the peasant extra employment) began to give way to the factory system of production. The peasant came to earn through his agriculture as much as or more than he had been accustomed to earn in spinning, dyeing, or weaving for the entrepreneur. Agriculture did not benefit as much as industry from inventions, chiefly because so many of the holdings were too small to make the use of improved farm machinery profitable, but the farmer did reap excellent profits from the new road, canal, and railroad construction, particularly after 1836. Some of the simpler new methods of farming—better seeds, better stock, and new crops—contributed to raising the level of agricultural production.

The medieval practice of allowing a large part of the soil to remain fallow every year was disappearing before newer theories of crop rotation, and, at the same time, lands that had formerly been uncultivated were gradually brought under the plow. This greatly extended the total yearly arable acreage of the country, and introduced new crops, particularly fodder; this, in turn, allowed for an increase in the number of animals and a decrease in the area formerly utilized for pasture that could be released for formal agriculture. The most reliable statistics indicate that between 1815 and 1850 the total amount of plowed land increased from twenty-three to twenty-six million hectares. This increase was due in part to utilization of former pastures, and in part to the use of heretofore uncultivated lands

Cereals remained the principal crop, employing over half of the arable fields; during the thirty-odd years of the monarchies, although the total area planted with grain increased only fifteen per cent, the harvest grew over fifty per cent This followed as a consequence of better agricultural methods and the use of better seeds. Nevertheless, a good crop produced hardly more than France needed for herself, a poor harvest, as the situation in 1846 illustrated, decidedly affected the price of the grain. As it is today, the production of wine was then an important agricultural industry Up to about 1835 there was a slight increase in the total wine acreage, but after that date it remained comparatively stationary. Yet, between 1805 and 1850 the yield from the vineyards almost doubled. The cultivation of the sugar beet, started under Napoleon, declined in the years immediately following 1815, but after 1837 it became very profitable, thanks to the tariff The processing plants ceased to be small local units; sugar manufacture was placed on a factory basis Production, however, was limited to the north of France, where the culture was combined with that of cereals

The livestock industry, too, made considerable progress, both in the number and the quality of the animals. The total number of sheep—animals well suited to the backward system of agriculture—increased from twenty-seven million in 1815 to thirty-two million in 1850, more important was the fact that the animals of 1815 were poor both in size and in the texture of their wool, while those of 1850 were excellent specimens, resulting from a cross between earlier natives with, first, the Spanish merinos, to produce wool, and second, with the English sheep, to produce more meat. Cattle also improved in number and quality, the best estimates for 1815 and 1850 indicate that the number increased from seven to eleven millions, and the average weight from less than three hundred to more than three hundred and fifty kilograms apiece. Since the bread-and-potato diet of most of the peasants was rarely varied with the meat that they produced, this increase was obviously due to the demands of the meat-eating urban population.

THE industrial development of Europe in the first half of the nineteenth century was largely dependent upon the combination of steam power, cheap iron, and the use of machinery, which made large-scale factory production feasible and profitable. Although the economic structure under the Restoration gave very little evidence of this new system, the beginnings of the machine age became discernible after 1815. In 1817 a steam engine, established in a spinning factory at Rouen, was a great novelty; before 1830 there were about fifteen hundred steam engines, of low horsepower, in France. French industry, however, even by 1830 lagged pitifully behind England's; in the British Isles, while Napoleon was governing France, the use of steam and machinery had been generalized and expanded to such a degree that English industry was able to maintain a position of world primacy throughout the entire century. It was only after 1830 that French industry made great strides; the use of the steam engine became so general by 1855 that a thoughtful observer could report: "The steam engine has won an important place in the public's attention in the last twenty to twenty-five years . . we can say of it that we are moved by steam."

The English assisted in the introduction of new industrial techniques into France, at least sixteen hundred skilled laborers and factory managers migrated from England to France before 1830, and many more went in the period after the July Revolution. These men acted as instructors for the French, and, in the formative years, were the backbone of the factory system on French soil Not only British technical men, but also British capital, found it profitable to go to France Several of the most important textile and metallurgical establishments were owned and directed by Englishmen, in the first half of the century it was not necessary for them to go to Africa, Asia, or the Americas to find a lucrative field for exploitation

It was the textile industry that felt the first impulse of the new machinery and methods, particularly in the production of cotton textiles, which had the dual advantages of a cheap supply of raw materials (the cotton gin had been invented in 1793), and a freedom from the traditional production systems that hampered the wool, linen, and silk industries. Between 1812 and 1847, French raw-cotton imports jumped from ten to fifty-five million kilograms a year; mechanical spinning increased the fineness of the thread from No. 80 to No. 300, while the amount of thread produced per worker increased from two to fourteen kilos per day. Naturally, the price dropped considerably By 1848, French cotton production, especially in Alsace, was a well-established machine industry with over thirty thousand factories The whole process—spinning, weaving, bleaching, and printing—was carried on through a machine technique. The woolen industry, too, made great strides; in 1812, France used sixteen and a half million kilograms of wool; in 1850, eighty-nine million. The factory system accounted for much of the increase, although in 1850 there was still a large amount of wool produced in the cottages by hand. The new machinery, however, made it inevitable that the entire woolen industry would eventually become a factory industry. Linen was the slowest of the textiles to develop a factory-production technique; traditions were strong, and the machinery developed was imperfect; only about one-fifth of the total was produced in the factories. After 1835, the silk industry made important progress Machinery to handle the raw silk, developed in England and Germany, made an extension of factory technique profitable, and by the middle of the century the silk industry had become very significant in French economic life

French metallurgical industry, too, made some progress under the July monarchy New techniques and machines were imported from England and Germany, and the foundations for a modern iron industry were well established. The French iron industry, however, had not reached a very high level by the end of the July monarchy; most of the iron was still smelted by charcoal rather than by coke, and the small producer was still firmly entrenched. French iron was not so cheap as the German or so good as the British; without the tariff, the industry would have had either to reorganize itself completely or to go out of business.

There was hardly an industry that was not somewhat touched by the new mechanical methods of production, but in France the changes came slowly For example, machine production of paper was definitely established as early as 1827, but thirty years later a considerable amount of French paper was still made by the old methods. The steam printing press, first used by the London *Times* in 1814, was introduced into France in 1824, but it was not until 1844 that it was used to print books Frenchmen invented machines or processes that often were not used in France until after they had long been successful in England or Germany.

A glance at the size of the industrial plants illustrates conclusively the fact that the French had not accepted the full implications of the division of labor. In the Paris of the 1840's only seven thousand workshops employed ten or more laborers, while thirty-two thousand were one- or two-man establishments. It was only in the textile factories and a few iron works that large-scale division of labor was really accomplished. But even in the textile industry, the plants were often quite small, while the iron industry as a whole was conducted much as it had been in the eighteenth century, with many small charcoal-using forges producing the bulk of the iron. The rationalized large-scale industrial establishment was decidedly an exception to the rule.

The domestic system of production, however, was definitely on the decline. Although in some of the new industries—for example, in ready-made shoes—the "factory" was only one step in a system that resembled the cottage domestic production much more than it did the factory system, the day when a peasant could supplement his income by spinning, dyeing, weaving, or some such work for an entrepreneur was rapidly waning. France stood between the new and the old, but the new system had taken roots that precluded a return to the ways of the eighteenth century.

One factor that slowed the development of large-scale industry in France was her comparative poverty in coal Between 1815 and 1850, the yearly production of coal increased from 880,000 tons to 4,500,000 tons, but the consumption increased from 1,412,000 tons to 7,250,000 during the same period. This meant that France was forced to import English, Belgian, and German coal every year to supply her needs, and, naturally, the price of coal was always comparatively high. Another factor that worked to resist economic revolution was the tariff policy of the monarchies. Napoleon's continental blockade continued to be the center of French tariff thinking long after the Empire was overthrown. The tariff created a hothouse condition in French industry; sheltered behind the absolute protection of high tariff walls, the inefficient small industrial units continued to be profitable to their operators. The French producer did not have to meet the open competition of British, Belgian, or Rhineland factories that would have ruined him unless he completely reorganized his system, and he was too conservative to make unnecessary, sweeping adjustments in his traditional methods of production French conservatism, French tariff policy, and a lack of certain basic raw materials probably were the most important factors that retarded the development of French economic society.

THE commerce of France was largely confined within the boundaries of the country; her total foreign trade for 1830 did not amount to more than $7.50 per person. The chief commodities for export were wines and liquors, silk, china, glass, and leather goods, while coal, raw cotton, sugar, and ironwares were the most important items of import. The few colonies left to France after 1815 were treated as adjuncts whose existence had no meaning apart from their connection with France Fish and furs came from the islands in the Gulf of St. Lawrence; sugar and tropical products from the Caribbean islands The Indian towns supplied products of the East, and the Senegal provided an African trading post. But the overseas commerce, with either colonies or foreign nations, was not of great importance to the average Frenchman; France was still working under the mercantilist doctrines of foreign trade. The unwillingness of the government to make commercial treaties that would conventionalize rights of entry is indicative of the persistence of the mercantilist leanings of French lawgivers.

Internal commerce was already rather highly developed by the first half of the nineteenth century. The needs of Paris and the other large cities involved a complicated system of supply. Grain, wine, and brandy merchants, wholesale dealers in cloth, leather, and iron products, were common in all the important sections of the country. France's distribution system had reached the point where the fair was no longer of prime importance. Regular establishments with fixed domiciles cared for the wholesale and retail business in the cities, but in some districts the roving peddler with a pack filled with varied treasures still supplied the needs of the peasant. Retail trade, however, was primarily the business of little people with humble, specialized establishments and limited ambitions; by the middle of the century the small shopkeepers made up a regular social class whose voice was soon to be heard in the councils of state In many trades—for example, in the clothing industry—the shopkeeper and the craftsman were often the same person, the industrial organization did not include middlemen.

To facilitate the commerce of the nation, the Bank of France, established by Napoleon, acted as a clearinghouse for credits The bank was at once semiofficial and popular, it acted as the friend of every small trader, by discounting paper of even petty proportions, and it assisted in the control of the treasury of the nation During an age when the commercial check was unknown and the coins were usually heavy silver or gold, the bank held the right of unlimited issue of paper currency, and thus largely controlled the credit of the nation. After 1817, several provincial banks were established in competition with the Bank of France, but they were to be short-lived, the crisis of 1848 gave the central bank an opportunity to deal with its competitors and to re-establish its monopoly The commercial policy of the bank was conservative and sound; its sane control over French business through note issues is reflected in the statement that there was but a gradual increase in the notes in circulation: 172,000,000 francs in 1820, 239,000,000 in 1830, 251,000,000 in 1840, and, including the provincial banks which were soon to become branch banks, 378,000,000 in 1847 The bank in 1848 had a share capital of 92,250,000 francs, and, except for a few months after the Revolution of February, there was never a question of its ability to meet its obligations. It was always in a position to lend to municipalities, to departments, and to the central government, and, although the captains of industry complained that the bank would hardly loan a franc even to a growing industry, its rôle in French economic and even political life was of great importance to the nation. Clapham writes that in 1848 the Bank of France completed "a half century of sound, successful management and steady expansion, in a political atmosphere which had often been far from healthy."

During the first half of the nineteenth century the French did not play the rôle of international leaders in finance which characterized them in the latter half of the century. On the contrary, France was a borrowing country, England, Holland, and Belgium poured capital into France in the form of loans to the French government and investments in French enterprise. The Rothschilds, the Barings, the Hopes, and other international bankers floated French loans, since strictly French houses were usually not strong enough to provide the necessary money French savings during this period were, as a rule, reinvested in either land or private commercial or industrial enterprises. Although the law provided for the establishment of limited-liability joint-stock companies, comparatively few were founded. During the eighteenth century the French had learned to fear trusting their money to anything but land, a strongbox, or a business that they could control themselves There were, to be sure, a few true joint-stock companies founded to carry on banking, or public utilities like gas works, railroads, or waterworks, but most of the investments ran true to earlier forms. During the reign of Louis Philippe, many corporations were formed in which stock was issued, but, although the shares were transferable and even sold on the Bourse, these companies (*sociétés en commandité sur actions*) were really merely sleeping partnerships During this same period, a number of swindles resulting from unsound or even dishonest promotion made the French even more cautious of the enterprises to which they intrusted their money. It was not until after Napoleon III ruled in Paris that France became an almost inexhaustible source of capital for both industrial and governmental enterprise

THESE social and economic patterns of French society were vigorously attacked, either entirely or in part, by philosophers and publicists of all shades of opinion. The principles of liberty, equality, and fraternity that the eighteenth century had developed, and the facts of the new economy that the steam engine, the machine, and the technique of mass production were producing, provided ample inspiration for reformers who wished to alter the emerging bourgeois system Their volleys of criticism, however, rarely penetrated the chamber or the house of peers, and seldom made an impression on the council of ministers; they had no meaning to the kings who occupied the throne, and no significance to the preponderant part of the electorate. Smugly, the official society accepted the *status quo* as final, and ignored the rebukes as well as the suggestions of the dissenters.

Not all of the condemnation came from men tinged with social radicalism The principle of liberty was open to diverse interpretations, it could be used by those who saw in liberty the absence of state restraint and interference with the individual, as well as by men who envisaged liberty as inadequate without state intervention to protect the underprivileged. The facts of the new economic society, too, could be regarded as natural phenomena that were subject to discoverable laws, or as social forces that man might direct and control for the creation of a better society. The philosophers, who saw absolute individual liberty as the remedy by which all ills of society could be cured, and regarded the economic life of mankind as a phenomenon regulated by natural laws, attempted to solve the problems of the age very differently from the thinkers who demanded state guarantees for the liberty of the poor, and regarded the evolution of society as subject to the will of man.

Under the Restoration, when the political argument between the new and the old régime occupied the center of the stage, the French counterparts of the English classical economists were the most important weavers of social and economic theory. J. B. Say introduced Adam Smith to France, and he and his disciples tried to convince their fellow countrymen that liberty—absolute liberty for industry and commerce—provided the only tenable basis for economic polity. In their eyes, the economic life of the nation was subject to discoverable natural laws, which, like the laws of science, were beyond the control of man Since these laws were inherent in the functioning of economic society, they argued, any attempt on the part of government to interfere with their course would result only in disaster. Accordingly, they advised absolute freedom of action for each individual. This would permit competition to operate for the benefit of society as a whole. No one could gather too much profit, each man would be prodded to exercise his ingenuity in affairs, and all would eventually benefit through lower prices and greater production. The economists did not halt their doctrine of freedom at the frontiers of the state; free trade between nations would, they insisted, allow each state to produce those commodities for which it was well suited, and allow all states to reap the benefits of trade. War, tariffs, and bounties must disappear from economic policy, and then man could develop a truly intelligent economic society.

In their thinking, the state was a necessary evil essential to public security, but potentially dangerous to economic life. The activities of the state must be strictly limited to little more than the duties of the policeman; it must keep order, provide public works, and prevent organized groups from tampering with free competition and individual economic liberty. Thus, the economists disapproved of any state interference between employer and employee, except to prevent either of them from unlawfully combining to destroy liberty of contract. Wages, hours, and conditions of labor were not subjects for statutory law, since they were regulated by economic laws. The economists strongly attacked the French tariff policy as an unwise interference with the natural course of trade. The leaders of French society were quick to appropriate for their own that part of the economist's doctrine that best suited their interests, but they adamantly refused to listen to any ideas, such as the tariff doctrine, that did not seem to correspond with their own special needs

The system of the economists was a classic structure of sure proportion, its exact syllogisms, its facile explanation of all events, and its alluring promise of ever-increasing production and consumption made many converts Some of the writers tried to soften the harshness of their prescription for the poor, by attempting to teach the capitalistic aristocracy that it had social obligations toward the lower classes, others felt that any aid that might be given to the proletariat would, in the long run, make their lot more miserable, since it would only invite an increase in births and thereby increase the numbers in competition for the available jobs For example, M Duchâtel wrote concerning the institutions for care of foundlings: "It is an encouragement to vice and improvidence, an invitation to parents to free themselves from their sacred duty to care for their children, they [the institutions] are the cause of the evil that they pretend to alleviate" As a matter of fact, the foundling children were cared for so well that less than ten per cent of them lived to be eight years old—but that was not the point; the strict economist saw any such institution as an invitation to increased births, and thus a stimulus to greater misery for the poor. On the other hand, men like Benjamin Delessert, de Gérando, and others worked to give to the poor the benefits of medical attention, an opportunity to save their money, and even to obtain a rudimentary education Had the bourgeoisie understood and followed the suggestions of de Gérando's *De l'Esprit d'Association* and *Traité de la Bienfaisance Publique,* "they would," writes Weill, "have prolonged their power and justified the theories of the economists"

As the industrial system developed, and the sufferings that it brought in its wake became more widely known, a reaction against the philosophy that preached freedom but justified wage slavery was inevitable One of the first attacks came from Sismondi, an erstwhile disciple of Adam Smith His *Nouveaux Principes d'Économie Politique* (1817) presented a glaring picture of the abuses of industrialism After presenting the much-admired British industrial organization as a system for creating a nation of paupers, Sismondi demanded government intervention to save the lower classes from slavery worse than that practiced in the plantation economies His protests were almost immediately seconded by the prefect Villeneuve-Bargemont, who wrote on the misery of the proletariat at Lille, and Dr Fodere, mayor of Strasbourg, who discussed the actual problems in Alsace. Several liberals, including Voyer d'Argenson and Beauséjour, took up the cry in the chamber of deputies, but no proposed solution ever had a chance against the complacency of the bourgeoisie. The idea that men ought to seek "social justice" and divide the "fruits of nature," as well as the assertion in the chamber that "in France there are more men that have no bread than there are men that have too much wheat," only irritated the ruling class. "Social justice" had no place in the thinking of even those men who spoke the loudest against the political injustice of the reactionary ultras

While the economists and these first critics of the French system were basking in the full light of publicity for their ideas, another small group of almost unknown men were tending uncertainly toward the doctrines of socialism. Saint-Simon, Fourier, and the English reformer, Robert Owen, the fathers of the new doctrine, gave the generation of the first half of the century a new approach to the problems that industrialism had posited for society The socialist ideas—altered, expanded, vivified, and put into fighting form by subsequent proletarian philosophers—have proved to be one of the most significant forces in French society. During their own lifetimes, Saint-Simon and Fourier did not attract wide attention; their disciples and imitators, however, were destined to force the complacent bourgeoisie to give some attention to their protests.

Fourier's doctrines, developed in obscurity, were aimed at giving society a new pattern for organization that would provide social justice and introduce harmony into man's life The creation of free associations in colonies or *phalanges* was the central point of his proposal, these colonies—co-operative islands in a bad capitalist world—were each to be more or less economically independent, and the individuals who comprised the colony were to be allowed the greatest freedom in their choice of occupation It was an idealistic type of communism, probably doomed to failure from the very beginning The few *phalanges* that were established on the Fourier model did not work out according to the master's plans.

Saint-Simon was never able to distill his ideas into a complete system; his disciples were responsible for Saint-Simonianism! According to his views, society was divided into three groups of producers: industrialists, philosophers, and artists. These groups must unite their efforts in a new form of government, to secure the amelioration of the lot of the poor through a more equitable distribution of the goods of the world. After Saint-Simon's death, his disciples attempted to erect his doctrines into a socialist religion, with dogmas, rites, and a sort of priesthood However, their extravagant program for supplanting the entire existing social organization with this new cult does not alter the facts that the Saint-Simonians probably had a better grasp of the economic situation than any other group in the early years of the July régime, and that the literature which they published in *Le Globe* and elsewhere was both stimulating and substantial. Their insistence that the moving-dynamic forces of world development pointed to association as the keystone for the new society, and that human exploitations must be a concern of the state, since the family no longer could meet the problem, showed an understanding of the forces at work utterly lacking in the councils that surrounded the July throne.

The July Revolution was hardly over when the Saint-Simonian cult was broken up, but the idealism of Saint-Simon did not disappear Auguste Comte branched out to develop his doctrine of Positivism; Pierre Leroux founded *La Revue Encyclopédique,* edited a new encyclopedia, and finally ended by becoming a prophet of a new religious-social doctrine that men mistakenly labeled socialism Other Saint-Simonians went into business, and became wealthy capitalists; some reappeared after 1850 as advisers to Louis Napoleon. Moreover, the movement had attracted enough attention to act as instructor to the younger group of reformers who were to appear on the French scene after 1840. After the time of the Saint-Simonians, the day when a socialistic, proletarian philosophy would make a bid for power in France could not be long postponed; this emotional, half mystic, self-appointed advocate for the poor and the downtrodden broke ground that could be sowed with the seeds of the doctrines of Blanc and Proudhon, Marx and Engels, and Jaurès and Sorel.

Many names, famous for the day, are included among the reformers who mounted the tribune after 1840. Paul Louis insists that no other period in French history is so rich in social theory and social criticism as the eight years preceding the February Revolution. Leroux and Lamennais appealed to religion; Blanc and Cabet to socialism and communism; Proudhon to a modified anarchism. They found allies in the republican camp, in men who felt that political freedom would solve the social and economic problems. Lamennais, who started in political life as an advocate of reform in the Church, turned to social problems after the pope in 1832 condemned his religious movement. He did not work out a system, but his battle cry was for war on the oppressors of the poor; war without violence, perhaps, but with every weapon of propaganda and politics, to give the children of God their just dues. The society which Leroux hoped to create would provide each with his needs and require from each his best labor. He believed in the perfectibility of man and human institutions; he held out to his readers the prospect of a heaven on earth, while his philosophy, which rejuvenated the doctrine of transmigration of souls, assured everyone of his eventual enjoyment of a future terrestrial paradise. By 1848 his system was complete, but it was too learned and abstract for the proletariat, and too mystic and disorganized for the intellectuals Leroux's greatest service probably came from the bitter attacks which he made on the plutocracy of the day

Louis Blanc, who had a larger following than any other radical of the 1840's, contented himself with a less ambitious program; he urged the reorganization of society so that the state would assume the rôle of guarantor for each individual's economic security Every man, according to Blanc, has "the right to work" and to earn a livelihood To assure this right, the state should maintain "social workshops," establish a system of social insurance to care for the sick, the aged, and the unemployed, and, in general, act as the father and guardian of the people. Blanc's faith in the state and his practical suggestions received a rather shabby trial in 1848—a fact that showed his successors that his system required more "iron and blood" than the idealist socialist was willing to employ in making his program. Cabet, another socialist, envisaged a communistic paradise in which money was no longer used, no one bought or sold commodities, and a generous, all-powerful state cared for the needs and regulated the labor of the individual. Cabet's ideal was popular with the proletariat, but it was so far removed from practicality that in 1848 there was no hope for its receiving a trial.

Probably the keenest mind that attacked the problems of social justice in the 1840's was Proudhon's. He rejected both socialism and communism and did not create a "system," but he was a relentless critic and a deep thinker. He struck at the very root of bourgeois society with his brutal statement, "Property is theft" Many of his disciples never got further in his pages, for his syllogisms and his logic are closely knit and difficult to follow, but for those who could understand his analyses, his books became a mine of ammunition for the struggle of the proletariat. Practically all later proletarian writers, including Marx himself, are deeply in debt to Proudhon for his critical analyses of the problems and evils of industrial society

These prophets of social justice found allies among the republicans, who were hoping to establish a more equitable political system for France. Ledru-Rollin, Pagès, Lamartine, and others, were not ready to go the whole way on the road of social radicalism, their program merely envisaged a political democracy, but they were not slow to recognize that they and the socialists were assulting the same citadel of power in the 1840's However, when the monarchy with its restricted suffrage was out of the way, it did not take the republicans long to see that political and economic democracy are not exactly the same thing

The radicals failed to make a dent in the serenity of the established ruling caste until after 1848 The red flag on the streets of Paris and the vociferous demands of a wild mob were necessary to impress upon the aristocracy of wealth the fact that their class really was in danger. In their search for a justification and a slogan to oppose the cries for social justice, they hit upon the ideal of "moral order." This became the watchword of the next generation of the upper bourgeoisie.

THE July Revolution was directed as much against the French Catholic Church as against the Bourbon government itself. The crowds that fought on the barricades saw in the alliance between throne and altar, and in the clerical program of the Jesuits and the ultras, one of the principal threats against their liberty So anticlerical was the sentiment that Louis Philippe, in spite of his own preferences, hesitated to go openly to church during the first half of his reign In 1831, after a legitimist demonstration that ended in a riot, the crowds invaded and sacked the archbishop's palace without the interference of the government and the National Guard. The crucifix disappeared from the court of assize; traditional religious processions were forbidden; and the ministry forced the Church to give to the regicide constitutional bishop, Grégoire, a funeral appropriate to his rank in the clergy. In the early days of the July monarchy the Church, at a low ebb of popularity, lost most of the ground that it had won under the Bourbons.

This popular and official disfavor resulted from the clerical policy of the ultra-royalists, which forced France to associate the Church with repression and reaction The Restoration's first act had been to do all that it could to root out radical and liberal members from high places in the clergy, and to establish in their stead men of noble blood and conservative tendencies. This had been followed by a rapid extension of the power and influence of the Church in every phase of French society Through the surrender of the Université de France, education had been turned over to the clergy, a whole series of laws and ordinances like the "Law of Sacrilege" had strengthened the Church's hold. The Congregation exploited the home missionary field by sending purveyors of emotional religion throughout the country, while the establishment of new orders of monks and nuns, with the re-establishment of the Jesuits, gave the Church a legion of able defenders to strengthen its position and prestige The fact that the clergy closely associated itself with the ultras brought the wrath of the liberals upon the Church, and in 1830 the accumulated record of ecclesiastical pro-Bourbon actions made the Church an object of severe attack.

However, even under the Bourbon government there were tendencies at work within the Church that were aimed at a divorce between the throne and the altar, and a reconciliation between the Church and liberty. A small group of ardent Catholic reformers, who hoped to free the Church from the association with the reactionaries, attacked the problem at its very foundation—the close connection between the Church and the state By opposing ultramontanism to Gallicanism they hoped to wean the Church from its close reliance on the powers that controlled the state, and to give it a broader base by appealing to the religious sentiment of the entire nation. The Gallican element in the clergy, which undoubtedly was the stronger, had worked hand in glove with Charles X and the ultras They saw the French Church as an institution with interests *vis-à-vis* to the pope. There was, however, a minority committed to ultramontanism that wished to recognize, unreservedly, the power of the pope over the entire Church without state interference In 1817 a young Breton priest, Lamennais, opened the new attack against the prevailing Gallicanism of the day; by 1830 he had developed a doctrine about the place of the Church in French society Like Saint-Simon and Jouffroy, his contemporaries, Lamennais appealed to the younger generation to attack the *status quo* as "one of the most prodigious follies that the human mind could conceive." He pointed out that the continued association of the Church with the reactionary state could only result in disaster for the former. Submission to the state—that is, Gallicanism—amounted, according to him, to submitting the Church to slavery; Lamennais wished the Church to give up the "crumbs from the table of the state" that made the Church an institution for state repression, to recognize the pope as the universal spiritual monarch, and to depend upon the people for support. After July, 1830, Lamennais and his friends founded *L'Avenir,* an ultramontane paper, in which they expounded their doctrine. Liberty became their watchword for the Church; they insisted that the Catholics ought, as citizens, to demand liberty of press, education, association, and conscience. The truths of the Church would then win out, and the Church itself would become a modern, independent institution.

The doctrines of *L'Avenir* created a great storm. Naturally, the conservative, pro-Bourbon clergymen who sat in the bishops' chairs condemned them as a heresy aimed at separation of Church and state. Finally, Lamennais decided to carry his case to Rome. Gregory XVI probably would have preferred to stay out of this fight of the French clergy, but

Lamennais made necessary a decision on his part; *Mirari Vos,* his encyclical letter, was unfavorable to the new idea. Lamennais retired to the country, and wrote *Les Paroles d'un Croyant* (1834) in which he pointed out that in the inevitable choice between a conservative, royalist Church and democracy, his choice was democracy. The book was placed on the *Index* by the pope, and Lamennais left the Church.

His departure temporarily left the Church in the hands of the Gallicans, but before long his followers devised a dialectic that allowed them to re-enter the field. The condemnation of liberal ideas that was involved in *Mirari Vos* could be treated, they said, as relative rather than absolute. There could be no reason, they argued, for Catholicism not to prosper under the July monarchy, or even under a republic, as well as it did under the defunct legitimist régime. After all, France was Catholic, and there was no reason why it could not be liberal as well. The views of the liberal Catholic party, advocated in press, parliament, and in many pulpits, helped considerably in the defeat that Voltairian anticlericalism came to suffer before the middle of the century, and, at the same time, paved the way for a revolution friendly to the Church in 1848.

It was not liberalism, however, that played the decisive rôle in the rehabilitation of the Church. As we have seen, the bourgeoisie that took over power in 1830 soon found that the liberalism they had talked of then was a conservative doctrine. On the left of the victorious bourgeoisie stood the republicans and socialists, whose political and economic doctrines sounded like dangerous heresy to the dominant class. The Church might teach people how to bear privation and suffering in this world, so that they could enjoy the next, but if the Church failed to do this, men like Pierre Leroux might convince the masses that heaven was to be attained on this earth through radical political action. This thought drove many a wealthy man to reconsider his attitude toward the institution that baptized and married his children, and that might silence the complaints of his workers To this very practical reason a deep philosophical basis was added After 1830, Cousin became the most popular teacher of philosophy; his eclecticism came to replace Condillac's sensualism, which had so contributed to irreligion Cousin's doctrines contained a vague spiritualism that led to many conversions among his readers. Less serious, but equally powerful, was the fact that irreligion went out of style after the revolutionary bourgeoisie and liberals had made themselves masters of the government Talleyrand, who had held aloof as long as the Church was the handmaiden of the ultras, gave them a *bon mot* "There is nothing less aristocratic," he said, "than irreligion." Before he died, his reconciliation with the Church was so complete that his former episcopal office was recognized. Thus, many factors converged to bring the bourgeoisie back to the Church

The latter itself was not slow to take advantage of the new situation. From the pulpit in Nôtre Dame, Lacordaire told his bourgeois congregation: "Property is one of the fundamental bases of society, not only because it assists the conservation and distribution of life, but also because it is the guardian of the liberty and the dignity of man. Harmony has been established between the rich and the poor of a kind that the ceaseless toil of society results in a voluntary, just, charitable division of the goods of this earth." The poor were poor because they chose to be improvident; the rich, who were careful of their substance, rightly acquired superfluous wealth, and they could, therefore, afford to be charitable. This was a comforting doctrine to hear from the pulpit, a doctrine that would not alienate the wealthy The establishment of the Society of Saint Vincent de Paul, of the order of the Little Sisters of the Poor, and of other such charitable organizations, provided the bourgeoisie with convenient means for distributing their charity, and appealed to the social idealism of their youth Popular teachers like Buchez and Ozanam—the latter one of the greatest Catholic intellectuals of the century—won the young men for the Church, and since the daughters of the wealthy were almost always entrusted to the convent for their education, the Church appealed not only to the elders, but also laid a firm foundation for its future by winning the flower of the bourgeois youth. By 1837 Saint-Marc Girardin could say in the chamber of deputies: "Gentlemen, whether you wish it or not, in the past six years religion has taken an ascendancy that we could not have predicted."

In winning the wealthy back to the fold, the Church lost its hold on the poor; the legal country—that is, the electors—returned to their religious duties, but the disinherited classes tended to fall away. One priest insisted that only fifteen per cent of the Parisian proletariat were believers. Proudhon wrote in 1844 that among the workers of Lyon many families had broken all contact with the Church; they were not even baptized, married, or buried by the priest. In many sections of the countryside, too, the peasants broke with their traditional religious customs. One observer remarked that not more than a dozen individuals attended mass in the villages. A priest, in 1839, complained: "Impiety has left the great to descend to the people. It has abandoned the cities to invade the villages." Lacordaire found among the peasants "an almost total absence of faith, an infinitely small number of communions and confessions, and an immense scorn for the priest." It would almost seem that the disinherited ones felt that the Church was always a friend of those in power (first the ultra reactionaries, and then the July monarchy's plutocrats), but never a friend of the poor and the oppressed.

The Church leaders, however, were not so worried by the falling off of the masses, since they could see their conquests among the bourgeoisie. But that was not enough. The new leaders wanted political power as well as spiritual influence, and under Montalembert they finally succeeded in forming a political party. This was most embarrassing to the ministers of Louis Philippe; after the labor disturbances in the early years of the new régime the government had welcomed the return of influence to the Church. Molé had quietly allowed the Jesuits to return, and Guizot had continued to favor the Church as the "greatest school of respect that had appeared on earth." When a Catholic party appeared on the political scene, the government remained neutral, for it was not ministerial policy that Montalembert attacked, but rather the Université with its monopoly on higher education. First of all, the Catholic party proclaimed its liberalism, and then demanded that liberty should be extended to education. The men in the Université were astonished by an attack in the name of liberalism from a Church party. Their leaders defended themselves by asking what sort of liberalism could be expected from the Jesuits. The conflict finally entered the chamber, and by 1848 it became one of the many factors that destroyed the July monarchy.

By that year the Church enjoyed a position in French society that its most sanguine supporters could not have foreseen in 1830. It had finally achieved a break with the reactionary policy of the old régime, and had established itself in the confidence of the wealthy bourgeoisie It championed a type of liberalism that fitted well with the prevailing political philosophy, and it had carefully kept its skirts clear from radical economic doctrines that might cost it the support of men of property. The new pope, Pius IX, was still regarded as a liberal who would reconcile the doctrines of Roman Catholicism with the new bourgeois civilization of Europe.

THE first half of the nineteenth century witnessed the flowering of romanticism in letters, in music, and in the fine arts; it has, however, been impossible to relate the movement to the political, social, and economic forces in French society—except in a very general way. It would be fantastic to say that the romantic movement of 1830 had much connection with the reactionary party that provoked the July Revolution, even though it is true that Chateaubriand led the romanticists into the ultra camp in 1815; and, although the movement reached its full development under the July monarchy, it would be equally absurd to contend that romanticism was inspired by the stuffy bourgeois ideals that dominated French society after 1830 Romanticism was a European movement, it was well under way in Germany and England before the French made their significant contributions. As a general European movement, it was probably more closely related to the *Zeitgeist* of post-revolutionary Europe than to the vicissitudes of political and social forces in any particular geographical area.

The movement was a revolt against the literary and artistic canons of the seventeenth- and eighteenth-century classicism. As such, it took vigorous root in French intellectual soil, because it provided the generation that came of age in the 1820's with an escape from a situation that to many seemed intolerable The general disillusionment after 1814 deprived youth of any satisfaction that it might have had in the dream-cities of the eighteenth-century philosophers, the excesses of the Revolution had frightened men out of faith in rationalism; the vast horizons that war and administration had provided for the generation of Napoleon were closed, and the restrictions of Restoration Europe prevented the youth from using their imagination in politics. There was left only business or, as Artz says, "the road to Xanadu." The romanticists turned in upon themselves to be free of the restraints of their age; they created in their minds "an east, impossibly oriental . . . forests, impossibly primeval, and periods, impossibly medieval. The romanticists were straining to escape into a dream-world to muffle the ache of the actual"

In creating a world more nearly to their liking they ran amuck in the china shop of classicism. They refused to limit their vocabulary to the purified French that the grammarians of the seventeenth and eighteenth centuries had created; they ignored the logical, concise rules by which classicism dictated style and subject matter, they scorned the classicist demand that the world must be described in generalities devoid of emotional content. The revolutionary leaders had overthrown the old régime and had proclaimed the rights of man, the individual; the romanticists were overthrowing the classic style and proclaiming the right of individualistic expression. In the eighteenth century the ego, and the hopes and fears of man's soul, had not been considered suitable or dignified subjects for artistic expression. These nineteenth-century literary revolutionaries to whom the individual was the supreme reality reveled in recounting man's joys and sorrows, his trials and privations, his fear of death, his awe in the presence of the eternal and the supernatural. Where the eighteenth century spoke of the sickness of the age, the romanticists spoke of the suffering of the human heart. If the sad, disillusioned figures—the Renés and the Manfreds—that suffer in their pages are an index of the feelings of the romanticists, they were unhappy beyond all comparison.

The men of the new style refused to view nature through the eyes of long-dead Latin poets, and insisted on the validity of their own emotional reactions. With Goethe, they professed a scorn for human reason, which "man has used to make himself more animal than the beasts," but they placed great confidence in the truth of the human heart and emotions. In their battle against the rationalism and the sensationalism of the *Philosophes,* they created a religious spiritualism, a mystic surrender to the eternal truths and the emotional satisfactions inherent in religious worship. It was not necessarily an acceptance of the dogmas of the Church, but a glorification of the religious experience which the Church ritual and services provided for the human heart. Towering cathedrals, stained glass, the scent of incense, the richness of organ music and of chants—these were the values that were set in opposition to the rationalism of the freethinking philosophers.

In their fight against classicism the romanticists rightly turned to the Middle Ages for support. They ransacked preclassical literature to find justification for their own literary heresy. Dante, Shakespeare, and the Provençal lyricists became their allies in the literary free-for-all that raged in the daily and periodical press, in the theater and the bookstall, and in the art gallery The men of the first half of the nineteenth century welcomed this fierce battle in the arts as a pleasant diversion They were forbidden to discuss politics freely; they had lost interest in the old-fashioned religious debate The arts gave them a respite from ennui. By 1830, the romanticists had almost conquered the field. For better or for worse, the classicists were forced to give ground and allow the "wild men" of the fine arts to prepare the way for the artistic development of the modern world.

The romanticists drew their inspirations from nature, from the distant in time and space, and from the picturesque; they reveled in solitude, in their own suffering and world-weariness. They painted and described a world of gallant men, beautiful women, and harrowing experiences. They created new literary vehicles, new color and tone combinations, to express the outpourings of their ideas. They gave France the lyric poetry that earlier literary movements had neglected; they created a new drama to enrich the French stage; they introduced a vital, colorful note into both painting and music. Much of the literary work of these men is vague, hazy, carelessly done, and inferior, but their leaders, Chateaubriand, Lamartine, Victor Hugo, de Musset, Gautier, and others, have left an indelible mark on French literature The school maintained its hold on French letters until 1848, but even by 1840 a new note was sounded when Balzac and the men who were to develop realism in literature began to appear on the French scene.

In painting and music as well as in literature the romanticists made significant contributions. They found a stiff and formal art devoid of emotion; romanticism enriched both the pallet of the artist and the subject matter of his canvases. In their presentation of picturesque cathedrals, intimate nature scenes, and stirring historical incidents, the romanticists experimented with color and style to give greater life and meaning to their art Delacroix, the greatest master of the romantic school, produced paintings full of an emotional fire that had not been seen in painting since Rubens What Delacroix did for French painting, Berlioz did for French music. Parisian musical taste was somewhat debased, and French music in general did not show the vitality that characterized the German, but Berlioz was a composer of the highest originality, and in the development of the modern orchestra he stands second only to Wagner In both painting and music, emotional feeling and new color or tone combinations assisted in creating a new synthesis of beauty.

There were, however, gaps in the French romantic movement; neither sculpture nor architecture found a romantic interpreter The classical ideals of the Empire continued to dominate these two fields, with deadening effect. In the field of interior decoration, an attempt to revive the Gothic style often resulted in a facile and vapid eclecticism Literature, music, and painting were suitable media for romantic expression, and in those fields the romanticists won great triumphs.

PHILOSOPHY in France, unlike the lofty idealistic systems developed in Germany, was never able to transcend the political problems of the day. The Restoration lived either by the theocrats, Bonald and de Maistre, or by the sensationalist disciples of Condillac. The first group solved all problems by giving credit to God and the pope; the other by quoting the eighteenth century. De Maistre's defense of the "rights of God" against the rights of man interested the young generation no more than did Laromiguière's eighteenth-century ideologues Both systems were intellectually bankrupt Between them there grew up the philosophy of eclecticism which Victor Cousin and Royer-Collard succeeded in establishing at the Sorbonne. The German philosophers, Hegel and Schelling, as well as Plato and Aristotle, were introduced into France and accommodated to French taste This provided a spiritualism which did not go as far as theocracy, but definitely evaded the traps of eighteenth-century rationalism. As the July monarchy was the happy medium for politics, the eclectic philosophy provided the happy medium for thought. It was a philosophy not too deep for either the romanticists or the bourgeoisie, and it soon became almost the official thought of the July monarchy

Eclecticism's contributions were not particularly significant, but, while it reigned at the Sorbonne, a great though neglected French philosopher began to establish his system. August Comte, a spiritual heir of French eighteenth-century thought, dropped the armchair philosophy of that century, and developed Positivism He sternly refused to consider the absolute, the first cause, and contented himself with a purely scientific study of secondary causation Science, he insisted, must be applied to all phenomena; and his research did much to create a science of society His doctrine of positive proof was one of the significant contributions of his generation It was not until after 1848 that Comte attempted to found a religion of humanity, with bizarre and complicated rites; his first work was that of a scientist rather than that of a prophet

In the France of that period the taste for rationalization of the present had a more profound effect on the writing of history than did the teachings of von Ranke and the men of the critical German historical school. The generation which came of age in the 1820's was largely ignorant of the history and traditions of their nation; they were not even clear about the Revolution which was the predominant influence on their lives However, having lived through such cataclysmic changes, their interest in history was unbounded, and between 1820 and 1848 a whole galaxy of historians appeared on the French scene to explain French traditions In Michelet, French history found its romanticist; in Guizot, its philosopher Between these two stood the journalists, Thiers and Mignet; the radical, Louis Blanc, and the democrat, Lamartine. Guizot interpreted the history of his nation—of all Europe, for that matter—as a process preparing for the advent of the bourgeoisie to power. He helped to decorate the mental furniture of his generation with the comforting bourgeois doctrine that the middle class is the very backbone of society. Michelet asked every actor in French history what he had done for France, and the poor wretch stood or fell, in Michelet's pages, by the measure in which he had contributed to the glory of his country The journalists and the radicals were primarily interested in the great Revolution, and each of them found that the "facts" of history could be fitted into patterns that supported his political beliefs. None of these historians in the first half of the century had the critical judgment or the training that was developing in the German historical seminar, but their enthusiasm and their literary brilliance earned for them a place in the thinking of their contemporaries; their histories, if not scientifically accurate, were, at least, extremely readable.

Philosophy, history, and literature encouraged the foundation of a number of reviews, some of which enjoyed a fame only in their own time, while others have come down to us in the twentieth century. *La Revue des Deux Mondes* from its very beginning in 1831 was assured of success, its dignity and simplicity, as well as its variety, appealed to the intelligent bourgeoisie In time it absorbed its principal rival, *La Revue de Paris,* to become the most important periodical of its day. *La Revue Encyclopédique,* also founded in the 1830's, attempted to carry on the traditions of the great encyclopedists in the new spirit of the nineteenth century. Its editors gave to the journal a lofty, progressive, democratic tone, but their social and economic radicalism prevented the review from attaining great popularity with the conservative bourgeoisie. *La Revue Britannique* gave to French readers translations of the English periodicals that dealt especially with political and economic subjects. There were also a number of provincial reviews, such as *La Revue du Nord* and *La Revue du Midi,* and several ill-fated proletarian journals that could not hope to find economic support Under the July monarchy the daily press, too, showed considerable vitality The first exuberant crop of political newspapers withered under the restrictions of the laws of 1835, but all through the period the number of substantial newspapers with a regular public continued to grow Under the constitutional monarchy the taste for reading daily and periodical journals became fully established.

In spite of the exhaustion that followed the Revolution and the imperial wars, the generation that followed Napoleon made substantial contributions to the civilization of Europe It is true that French philosophers and historians were probably less important than their contemporaries beyond the Rhine, and that, with the exception of the work of Berlioz, French music could not compare with that of Italy or Germany, but in other fields of human activity French genius was the equal of any in Europe French romantic men of letters and painters broke ground for the whole subsequent literary and artistic development of the century, and themselves left canvases and literature unexcelled by those of any of their foreign contemporaries French scientists and political thinkers were well in the forefront of their times For a society that had its intellectual, emotional, and physical resources so lavishly squandered by a war lord, the French made an astonishing recovery in the years following 1815

CHAPTER V

THE END OF THE CONSTITUTIONAL MONARCHY

BETWEEN 1840 and 1848 the July monarchy presented a brave front to the world. There was practically no disorder in the streets, no desperate attempt to overthrow the régime by force; the conservative government, which appeared to enjoy the confidence of the nation, gave ample evidence of great stability, and the throne, buttressed by the upper ranks of society, had every indication of permanence. This was in contrast to the first ten years of the régime, when the police, the army, and the National Guard were often called upon to defend the settlement of the July Revolution against its real or supposed enemies. In that earlier period, workers in Paris, Lyon, and elsewhere, despairing in their miserable conditions and unable to see hopes for the future, rose up against both their employers and the state itself (1831–1835). Republican secret societies like the "Seasons" had made desperate if futile efforts to revise the decision that Lafayette took in 1830. The legitimists made at least one daring attempt to re-establish the Bourbon monarchy when a princess of the blood appeared on French soil to claim the crown for Henry V (1832). The fact that the good lady gave birth, while she was in prison, to a child of doubtful fatherhood, placed her cause in a ludicrous light After the death of Napoleon's son in Austria, Louis Napoleon, the nephew of the great emperor, assumed the rôle of pretender, and twice tried to rouse the army and the nation for an imperial restoration. The first attempt in Strasbourg (1836) was laughed off as the act of a rash boy, but the second invasion (1840) earned for Prince Louis a prison sentence. As long as the army, the National Guard, and the police could be relied upon, the stability of the régime was really not in danger; but these republican, royalist, and Bonapartist adventures managed to keep the country in a state of expectancy during the first decade in which Louis Philippe sat on the throne

These first ten years were also characterized by ministerial instability; the chamber presented the nation with one governmental crisis after another. Often the problems that brought about ministerial changes were less the result of conflicting political credos than of conflicting personalities, but to the outside world it appeared that the French cabinet utterly lacked permanence Louis Philippe utilized the conflicts between the political leaders to work himself into a position of real power in the state In the early days of the régime, the ministers had forced him to take a distinctly subordinate place in the formation of policy, but Louis Philippe would never admit that the throne was an armchair in which the king reigned while his cabinet ruled the country. Gradually he insinuated himself into a position of power, which the crisis in foreign affairs of 1840 consolidated It was the king's intervention that saved France from almost certain disaster when Thiers defied Europe in the Egyptian crisis, the timid bourgeois, who formed the electorate, were very grateful. The ministry that ruled France from 1840 to 1848 was the king's ministry, and, without shame, defended the king's right to assist in the formation of public policy. In one way or another, however, the electorate was persuaded to give that ministry its support during the remaining years of the régime, so Louis Philippe could always insist that he ruled France according to the Constitution.

The king and the ministry had no active policy. As rulers of France during the last eight years of the monarchy, they resembled nothing so much as an extinct volcano. Soult, who headed the ministry, and Guizot, who directed it, saw the maintenance of the *status quo* as the final word in political expediency The men who first achieved power in 1830 had already rounded out the revolutionary program of July as they understood it, the system was complete, and nothing was left to be done but to administer it. When they were attacked from the right or the left, they replied with bland assurance that the "system of July" was the perfect political instrument, the best safeguard for the development of the material and moral progress of the state. "All the policies," said Guizot, "promise you progress, but the conservative policy alone will give it to you, since it alone can succeed in giving you order and peace."

The tragedy, as far as France was concerned, rested in the fact that Guizot's cynical disregard of the protests from the majority of his opponents in the chamber was founded on a deep reality. The greater part of the opposition had no more constructive policy than the government They, too, were politically bankrupt Thiers and his friends regarded the settlement of the July Revolution as the happy solution for France's political problem, and their real complaint was that Guizot, rather than they, held the reins of power. They assailed the government for its corruption, its inglorious foreign policy, and royal meddling in the affairs of state, but they did not show any real understanding of the social and economic forces which were gradually outmoding the whole political system of the monarchy. Tocqueville aptly summed up the situation with the sardonic remark: "I have spent ten years of my life in the company of great spirits who constantly worked themselves up without producing heat, and who employed all their perspicacity to discover great issues without ever finding them." The men who made Louis Philippe king—whether they sat in the government or on the opposition benches—had already created their ideal political system, after 1840, public policy disintegrated into the task of administering the closed corporation that men called the state

The ministry maintained a majority, but had Thiers or even Barrot, who sat on the other side of the chamber, enjoyed the favor of the king, it is highly probable that he also could have persuaded a majority in the chamber to vote with him. The key to the majority was political corruption and inertia

A large number of the deputies would have voted for any government that did not attempt to alter the *status quo* of the Charter, another section was made up of men indebted to the ministry for political plums; and the remaining group was composed of those that feared an adventurous foreign policy. Through corruption, the government could discipline its majority and make "converts." Guizot and Duchâtel brought political corruption in France to an all-time high Doubtful deputies or members of their families received lucrative positions in the civil service. In many cases the votes of a majority of the electorate in small districts could be purchased outright for ministerial candidates; government contracts and subsidies were never wasted on men who could not help the ministry to retain power. There was always a faint rumor of financial scandal, which amused rather than shocked the leaders of French society. The courage of the beneficiaries of this system was manifest when a law that proposed to forbid a deputy from accepting another government position was voted down by 198 ballots, of which 130 were cast by functionaries Naturally, the politicians who were not in with the "feeders at the public bin" complained of corruption, but the electorate in 1842 and again in 1847 overruled these complaints, to return a comfortable majority for the conservative ministry

The electors approved the conservative government largely because they feared an adventurous policy. During the first ten years of the July régime, the men who made the Revolution of 1830 actively worked to build up a political system; legislation affecting roads, railroads, canals, schools, banks, child labor in factories, and many other things was written in the statute books After 1841, with the exception of the railway bill of 1842, which had long been under discussion, there was not a single important piece of legislation passed by the chamber. It was not that there were not things to be done—the tariffs, the questions of abolition of slavery, reorganization of the public debt, postal reforms, and other matters of public policy were prominent in the debates of the period—but, in each case, vested interests of a group of electors gave the government an excuse for neglecting definite action The government feared to alienate the plantation owners in the question of slavery, the manufacturers in the tariff question, the National Guardsmen in the case of a reorganization of the public debt. The deputy was not wrong who said in 1847: "What have we done in the past seven years? Nothing! Nothing! Nothing!"

But this pleased many of the electors, for they feared that any widespread embarkation on a policy of reforms must ultimately result in political changes that would deprive them of their monopoly of the government. The political reforms that were demanded took two aspects: on the one hand, an extension of the suffrage to allow anyone who paid 100 francs direct taxes the right to vote; and, on the other, a series of prohibitions that would exclude from the chamber all persons who held another position of any kind from the government. There were radicals who talked about universal manhood suffrage, but even the men who proposed to admit the 100-franc taxpayers to the electorate were considered dangerous, for they would add another 200,000 names to the electoral rolls, and the balance of political power would undoubtedly slip from the upper to the middle bourgeoisie. Thus, the men who wished to keep a firm hold upon the state found it easy to justify the "system" that kept a ministry satisfying to themselves in office. Guizot sternly refused to consider the reforms; to the men who wanted to vote, his only advice was "enrich yourselves" so that you will have the right to vote. The electors went to the polls, and solemnly approved this policy of absolute resistance

The ease with which the government met political crises between 1840 and 1848 strengthened the conservatives' opinion that this system of resistance was politically impregnable. Once, however, it appeared that the whole foundation of the monarchy was in question. In 1842 a carriage accident resulted in the death of the Duc d'Orléans, the king's eldest son.

The duke had been very popular with the people, and his supposed liberalism had been the hope of the men who wished to alter the political *status quo*. The duke's son, a mere child, was now the successor to the throne, and France faced the prospect of a regency as soon as Louis Philippe should die For a moment, the question of the monarchy raised by the Revolution of 1830 seemed about to be opened; the chamber was in a position to dictate the personnel of the regency, or accept the recommendation of the king. The regency law, which passed over the liberal wife of the dead Duc d'Orléans in favor of a conservative son of Louis Philippe, was dictated by the king and passed by the chamber, 310 to 94. The men veering toward a republic saw that legal France had no doubts about the stability of the Orléans monarchy.

GUIZOT'S foreign policy in the 1840's gave rise to a series of minor crises in the chamber, each of which was successfully circumvented The foreign policy of the Orléans monarchy was a matter of dispute from the very inception of the régime The Revolution of July had been a nationalist as well as a political revolt, men on the barricades in 1830 felt that they were fighting as much against the Treaty of Vienna and Metternich's Europe as against Charles X and his reactionary policies However, the compromise that put Louis Philippe on the throne ignored the nationalistic program, so that the political aspirations of the bourgeoisie could be attained without the danger of foreign intervention Louis Philippe was the guarantee to Europe that France would not seek to alter the Vienna settlement. He recognized that his rôle was cut out for him, he posed before his countrymen as the "Napoleon of peace," and he quietly told his fellow monarchs that France could be depended upon to resist any disturbance in the international *status quo*

The cornerstone of Guizot's foreign policy rested on an understanding with England. Shortly after the Egyptian crisis,

Palmerston, who was regarded as the chief conspirator in the isolation of France, was forced out of the British foreign office, and Aberdeen, his successor, seemed to be a man who would understand and appreciate France's needs. But the presence of Aberdeen or Palmerston in Downing Street did not alter the fact that the so-called English *entente* meant that France must play second fiddle to England in the concert of Europe. To make matters worse, the period after 1840 was filled with friction between French and English interests both in Europe and abroad. The British were committed to a suppression of the slave trade; with their navy patrolling the African coast, it was inevitable that France and England should have harsh words over the question of visit and search. In the Mediterranean region, French and English interests conflicted in Greece and in Morocco. The British and French ambassadors at Athens usually found themselves supporting opposite sides in Greek politics, and the British did not hesitate to use their navy to enforce their will The exigencies of France's colonial war in Algeria led to a conflict with the sultan of Morocco; the brusque intervention of the British foreign office humiliated and annoyed the French government. In Tahiti, the conflict between Catholic and Protestant missionaries led to intervention by a French battleship and the arrest of Pritchard, an Anglican missionary. When the French cabinet was forced by the British to pay an indemnity, the French nation was highly indignant After 1846, Palmerston returned to Downing Street in time to make the question of the Spanish marriages an important and almost belligerent issue between the two countries In spite of the exchange of visits of the royal families, the *entente* between France and England—as French historians have pointed out—was not an *entente cordiale.*

These pinpricks forced Guizot away from the English connection into a closer understanding with Metternich. In doing this, he placed France again in the position that she had occupied under Charles X, a force for preserving the conservative *status quo* of Europe In the Sonderbund affair in Switzerland, and the questions of liberalism in the Italian peninsula, France became a defender of the Vienna system. "You and I," Guizot wrote to Metternich ". . . struggle to preserve and heal modern society from the evils of anarchy We are able, without special and apparent conventions, to understand each other and to assist each other; there are not two policies of order and conservatism." Guizot and Metternich agreed in the question of the radical Swiss cantons, on the projected Prussian constitution, and both made representations to Pius IX when he seemed to carry the Catholic Church into the camp of the liberals The brusque invasion of the "rights" of the Holy Father by Austria in 1847, which for the moment allied Mazzini, Charles Albert of Piedmont, and Pius IX, found France supporting Metternich while Palmerston and the *London Times* offered lofty and friendly advice to the Italians

Guizot had carried the French government far from the sympathies of the French people The Metternich system meant the humiliation that France had experienced ever since 1815. The hopes and aspirations of the Italians were re-echoed in liberal and nationalistic circles of France The government that so far forgot French traditions could not hope for popular support. The essential difficulty for Guizot's policy rested in the fact that he and the king were resolved upon peace at any price. This led them, first, to accept humiliation at the hands of the English, and, secondly, to align France with the forces of reaction in central Europe Such a policy could not endear them to men who were reading the history of the great Revolution and the Empire, nor would it satisfy Frenchmen who wished to feel proud of their position in world affairs While Guizot managed to find a majority of peace-loving business men, country gentry, and paid government officials to support this foreign policy in the chamber, he succeeded in alienating the rest of the people of France that had any interest in politics.

Louis Philippe attempted to gratify the patriotic ambitions of his people, through his conquest of Algeria. One of the last acts of Charles X had been to dispatch a military expedition to north Africa The July monarchy expanded this punitive measure into a bid for empire on the southern coast of the Mediterranean Sea A whole new crop of military heroes was created in the course of the adventurous wars with the Mohammedan tribesmen, but the nation seems not to have been particularly impressed by the glory reflected upon the French flag. One writer, after explaining that the modern age was witnessing the decline of the Latin race at the expense of the German and Slavic races, wrote: ". . . I see Russia march to the conquest of the Bosporus, England to the conquest of high Asia; France, through Algeria, to the conquest of the desert. . ."

Thus, in foreign policy as well as internal affairs, Louis Philippe's government failed to attract the support of a large section of the French people. The maintenance of the *status quo* had virtues that were recognized only by a comparatively small section of the nation, and even if that small group did elect the deputies to the chamber, the general discontent with government policy created a situation that was dangerous to the stability of the régime "France is bored," one politician exclaimed. But it was more than just ennui; France was actively discontented with the do-nothing, pusillanimous methods of her governors. It is now obvious not only that a majority of the politically minded individuals in France did not approve of the policy of resistance, but also that these people were not included in that select company that elected the deputies The mass of the people who received little or no benefits from the rule of the conservatives were unable to make their opinions articulate in the councils of state, and there was nothing to be done about it until a breach could be made in the walls that surrounded the electoral laws of France.

THE opposition to Guizot's system found various means of expression After 1840, and particularly after 1845, a coalition of the left and the left center, the old party of movement, carried forward a legal, dynastic opposition In the streets, the secret societies, and through the press, another group of men—social and political radicals—were teaching a theory of opposition that at bottom was illegal and antidynastic. From the pulpits, and through the Catholic party, a third group taught doctrines for which, apparently, they were willing to fight, even if this course might place them in opposition to the king and the Charter These doctrines ranged from a mild program of social reform to plans for a complete overhauling of the social and political institutions of the state. The reformers included wild-eyed proletarian radicals, thoughtful students and philosophers, men of letters, and conservative bourgeois politicians In one way or another the régime had succeeded in alienating the sympathy of most of the intelligence of France; conservatives and radicals were driven to join hands against it.

The dynastic opposition in the chamber came from the old party of movement, of which Odilon Barrot and Thiers, chiefs of the left and the left center, were leaders well endowed with inspiring oratory and skill in parliamentary tactics Their opposition, however, was not based on any deeply rooted issues between themselves and the government majority, they objected to Guizot's methods more than to his political philosophy. They were ardent nationalists, and advocates of a spirited, independent French foreign policy; Guizot's lack of backbone toward England and his subservience to Austria appeared to them as a betrayal of the national pride. They insisted that a limited constitutional monarchy could not function properly unless the king kept himself above party politics, and this belief was greatly strengthened by Louis Philippe's obvious preference for Guizot and the party of resistance. Accordingly, they raged against the king's interference in the free play of parliamentary practice and the ministry's habit of allowing the king to participate in the direction of policy In and out of the chamber this dynastic opposition talked knowingly about their "policy," but they never gave any clear indication that they had a policy—or, for that matter, an understanding of the needs of their country. When they found it impossible to break Guizot's majority, they became advocates of reform—a reform that would alter slightly the complexion of the chamber so that they, rather than Guizot and Soult, could govern France.

Here and there in the chamber there were bright spirits who grasped the fact that the politics of the day were extremely unrealistic Lamartine and de Tocqueville, for example, reached the conclusion that state polity which considers only the interests of the upper classes fails to meet the needs of the new civilization. Lamartine started his public life as a romantic poet and an ultra-royalist. After 1830 his thinking veered sharply to the left, and by 1848 he had attained the position of a prophet of democracy The presentation of his "social convictions," as well as his warnings against the evils of plutocracy, failed to make an impression in the chamber, but they did give Lamartine an importance in the eyes of Paris that commanded authority in February, 1848 De Tocqueville returned to France from a study of the emerging Jacksonian democracy in the United States, to tell his fellow citizens of a great "discovery." Democracy, he said, must be the next stage in the evolution of western civilization; through democracy it would be not only possible but inevitable for Europe to realize the revolutionary ideal of equality De Tocqueville refused to ally himself with the left in the chamber, since in his opinion its members were illiberal, self-seeking, and hostile to the rights of the individual. The prophets of democracy found a few kindred spirits in the chamber, but their influence on the councils of the state was imperceptible.

The greater part of the radical party was outside of the chamber—indeed, often outside of the limits of the law itself. The September laws of 1836 made it illegal to question the régime; this did not end the questioning, but it did make the republicans, socialists, and Bonapartists change their labels They called themselves democrats or radicals. The thing that they had in common was a concentrated dislike for Louis Philippe, the conservative ministry, and the high property requirement for suffrage; they were antidynastic, antirégime, and anti-Guizot Beyond that their cohesive interests were few. The republicans saw salvation in universal suffrage and republican institutions. The Bonapartists (there were very few of them) hoped for a Napoleonic restoration based on popular will The socialists regarded political reform as only a means to a far-reaching social and economic reorganization of society As long as they were in opposition, they could work harmoniously together and even ally themselves with the left in the chamber, but once they were victorious the inherent differences in their political aims became strikingly evident.

In *Le National,* the ablest and most important radical newspaper, the republicans found an effective mouthpiece, but they were unable to create an organization The deaths of the elder Garnier–Pagès (1841) and the elder Cavaignac (1845) and the defection or retirement of several other chiefs had a discouraging effect on their spirits The remaining leaders, Godfroy Cavaignac, Pagès, Argo, and others, vacillated between hopes for a social revolution and the belief that they could achieve their aims through suffrage reform within the framework of the Orléans monarchy The more radical of the republicans combined with the socialists in organizing another newspaper, *La Réforme,* it was founded as a joint-stock company with 200,000 shares costing five francs each This gave the little people an opportunity to own their own organ of discontent. Pierre Leroux, Louis Blanc, Godfroy Cavaignac, Étienne Argo, and other chiefs of the radical parties were among the first subscribers, and Ledru-Rollin, a brilliant young radical lawyer who won great fame among the leftist parties, became its first editor. *La Réforme* pilloried the property-owning bourgeois conservatives, and clamored for political and social reorganization

These antidynastic radicals could not hope to make a dent on the chamber; their sole strength lay in the cities, and even there they could not command an organized following. Their press and their pamphlets made a few converts among the petty bourgeoisie and the proletariat; occasionally they had an opportunity for a demonstration provided by a political funeral or by a lawsuit following the arrest of the editors of their newspaper, but it must have been evident that they were weak in numbers and practically powerless in politics The plight of the real social radicals, the socialists, was even worse than that of the republicans. The people whom they wished to help could not read their books, let alone understand them, and the majority of the bourgeoisie would have nothing of their dogmas. The only hope that remained for the radical parties rested in the realities of the national life. French society was marching inexorably in their direction

Far to the other pole in political philosophy, a small group of men espoused a lost cause, legitimism. They had their newspapers, *La Quotidienne* and *La Gazette de France*, which kept up a running stream of criticism of the régime. *La Gazette* and several of the legitimist orators joined hands with the radicals to demand universal suffrage, a tactic that would most embarrass the government, but dissension within the party made their programs more noisy that effective. Berryer, one of their leaders, sorrowfully told Lamartine: "If there is any chance [of a legitimist restoration], it is not within the sight of man; it is on an unknown horizon" In the 1840's there was little reason to hope that the grandson of Charles X would ever occupy the throne of his ancestors.

The Catholic party stood somewhere between the groups that wished to drive Louis Philippe from the throne and the reformers that wished merely to oust Guizot. This party was mildly hostile to the July monarchy because of the anticlericalism inherent in the Revolution of 1830, but its chiefs were willing to work with any government that would comply with its demands. The core of the Catholic party was formed around the ultramontane followers of Lamennais. That religious reformer had left the Church, but his disciples remained within the fold to salvage what they could of liberal Catholicism. They argued that the Church must be able to function under a bourgeois monarchy or even a republic, and that it probably could hope for better treatment under such a régime than it would receive under a legitimist monarchy that used the Church as a political tool The Church, they reasoned, must demand basic liberties, and as long as those liberties are recognized, the Church can have no objection to any government. After 1840 the party received support from most of the French bishops in a campaign for liberty of instruction—in other words, a campaign to break the power of the Université and place education under the control of the Church. The Catholic leaders included laymen like Montalembert and clerics like Lacordaire, each in his own way a brilliant and influential orator Considering the great strides that the Church had made in the reconversion of the bourgeoisie, and that the Catholic party, clothed with the mantle of liberalism, was allied with the parties of opposition, the movement presented a grave danger to the government of Louis Philippe. It was the work and propaganda of this Catholic party that was largely responsible for making the Revolution of 1848 almost as proclerical as the Revolution of 1830 had been anticlerical. The Catholics had earned for themselves a place in the councils of the revolutionaries.

THE programs of discontent were founded on very real social and political problems that the king, the government, and a majority of the electors found it best to ignore. Apparently, the ruling class completely failed to understand that the moving forces of nineteenth-century civilization inevitably were creating new social and economic patterns that required government attention. The radicals could demand political reform and relief for the poor, but the rulers of France smugly assumed that their régime would be secure as long as the wealthy and the wellborn were satisfied. In doing this, they overlooked the fact that a successful revolution would be possible as soon as a large section of the population of the great cities was alienated from the government. The industrial society that France was developing worked great hardships on two numerically important urban groups—the proletariat and the petty bourgeoisie. The new economic order threatened the very life of the one and the independence of the other. But the government refused to consider their plight, and thereby drove them into an alliance against the entrenched privilege of the upper class.

The wretched predicament of the proletariat, discussed earlier, presented a social problem that became more serious every year. The industrialization that filled the coffers of the wealthy weighed heavily upon the poor. In 1840, out of every 10,000 young men called to the army from industrial departments, 9,000 were rejected as physically unfit for military service, out of every 10,000 called from agricultural departments, 4,000 were sent home. A forty per cent disability should have indicated a serious situation, but even a ninety per cent disability failed to stir the state into action. The proletariat were living under impossible conditions—long hours of labor at starvation wages, poor and insufficient food, unsanitary and badly cramped living quarters, working conditions dangerous to life and limb. The class was definitely outside the pale of French civilization. Their lives illustrated with horrible accuracy the working of the Malthusian principles.

The governing classes, pointing to the doctrines of individualism and classical economics, denied that they had any responsibility for the problem. They assured the proletariat that the Charter guaranteed liberty, equality, and fraternity, and explained that the privilege of voting was within the reach of every man. To be sure, there were no legal barriers to prevent the worker from becoming an elector, but the economic hurdle was nearly insurmountable. Talk about bettering his economic position was sheer claptrap, for even the children of the workers had practically no way of rising above the precarious economic condition of their fathers The ruling classes were begging the question Articulate radicals, who insisted that it was the place of government to do something in behalf of the poor, and the workers, living together in cities and heirs of a tradition for direct action, made this verbiage about liberty and equality dangerous to the régime. The day when government must intervene in the solution of the social problem could not be postponed indefinitely

The economic crisis that appeared in 1845 made more vigorous the demands for some relief for the proletariat. A series of bad harvests forced up the price of food; in 1845 wheat sold for 19.75 francs a hectoliter; in 1846 for 24.05 francs; in 1847 for 29 francs. Potatoes and other cereals followed the same price trend It was only the importation of Russian wheat that saved France from the worst horrors of a famine. Wage levels not only did not follow the ascending price of bread, but actually declined The harvest failure was common to all western Europe—in Ireland it brought on the horrible potato famine—and very early it caused a sharp reduction in the demand for manufactured commodities An industrial crisis followed The factories closed their doors or worked only part time. The whole economic structure of France went out of order. Even there the causes for misery did not cease, for the introduction of the railroad worked havoc with the traditional transportation system. The teamsters, porters, and the like found themselves without employment, and drifted into the cities to swell the crowds competing for a chance to work. Unemployment and high food costs caused terrible suffering among the poor The harvests of 1847 were normal, but the hungry years could not be ended until the industrial cycle had worked its way out of the depression. By that time Louis Philippe was no longer king of the French

The plight of the landless peasantry was often just as wretched as that of the urban workers, and the bad harvest meant hunger and death for them as well as for the proletariat, but the peasants were scattered all over France, and their ignorance added to their geographical distribution to make collective action impossible. The city workers were concentrated, often horribly so They could discuss their problems with each other, and listen to an occasional agitator's analysis of the situation Some of them had learned to read, and they were gaining a little experience, in mutual-aid and secret societies, toward the day when collective action would be possible In the industrial cities, and particularly in Paris and Lyon, communistic secret societies, like the Cabetists and the Dabouvistes, began to take hold among the workers. Naturally, the movement was feeble at first, but by 1848 it had reached extensive proportions. The city slums were an excellent incubation grounds for radical doctrines The worker came to believe that "the exploitation of men by men" was an evil that he could remedy, and when the opportunity presented itself in 1848, the workers manned the barricades to force the upper classes to recognize that they, too, were men.

While the workers faced slavery, starvation, or worse during the 1840's, the petty bourgeoisie and the small master craftsmen also discovered that their position was becoming increasingly precarious. The machine and the new business technique created a competition that they were often poorly equipped to meet; their little workshops and specialized shops were no match for the steam-powered economic institutions of the new society They held on, but often it meant that their standard of living was forced down, and their outlook was darkened. To make matters worse, they were obliged to shoulder the greater share of the rising costs of government, but bearing this growing tax burden did not entitle them to political rights The increased revenues came from indirect taxation; only direct tax payments made a man an elector. In 1835 the state required 1,047 million francs, in 1840, 1,363 million francs, and in 1845, 1,629 million francs. The governing classes did not hesitate to spend money if they could see an advantage to themselves The increasing costs, however, were not met by direct taxation; indirect taxes were easier to collect, and they had a broader base The upper bourgeoisie knew how to shift the burden from themselves to the people below In 1835 direct taxation accounted for 270 million francs of the state's income, and in 1845, 291 million, but indirect taxation in the same period rose from 560 to over 800 million francs a year The little people absorbed the increase, and it is small wonder that they were anxious to make their voices heard in the councils of the nation.

These little people—shopkeepers, clerks, master craftsmen, and the like—were hard hit by the depression and the high costs of foodstuffs that followed 1845. They felt the pinch, and found means for expressing their discontent. They, too, lived in the cities, and had their secret societies. They, too, read the literature of the philosophers of discontent. The books advocating communism and socialism did not find much response, but the propaganda of the republicans in *Le National* and *La Réforme* made many conversions. This petty bourgeoisie—later to be the chief prop of the Republic—got its first effective indoctrination in republicanism during the hungry forties. The defection of these little people from their loyalty to the régime was to have far-reaching consequences. They filled the ranks of the National Guard, the monarchy depended upon its "grocer-janizaries" to defend it in the street The more wealthy members of the Guard came to advocate Thiers' and Barrot's reform measures, while many of the rank and file, petty bourgeoisie, became actively infected with republicanism.

The socio-economic problems of the proletariat and the petty bourgeoisie did not start the Revolution of 1848 Human beings will submit to an unbelievably heavy burden before they will revolt of their own accord They murmur, complain, and feel sorry for themselves, but it is an open question whether socio-economic conditions are sufficient in themselves to stir up enough men in a society for a successful revolution. Human misery, however, creates a social powder keg that, when a problem or a provocative incident applies the torch, is capable of blowing a political and even a social régime to bits. The spark that inflames the social problem is often in itself quite harmless, in another situation it would die out without any great disturbance. This seems to have been the case in France after 1845 The political opposition, which was primarily directed by men almost as conservative as the government itself, inflamed a social situation that proved dangerous enough to destroy the whole settlement of the July Revolution.

IN THE spring of 1847, French taste for history was gratified by the appearance of three new books. Lamartine's *L'Histoire des Girondins,* and the first volumes of Louis Blanc's and Michelet's histories of the Revolution. They created a sensation Apparently, Frenchmen found something in the history of their fathers' time that was lacking in the stuffy political life of their own. The story of the Revolutionary age opened vistas of important movements and events, stirring pictures of heroic deeds, and visions of great men; and it recalled both the grandeur and the misery of democratic and revolutionary idealism It invited comparisons between the hopes of the revolutionaries and the situation of their own day. In their own way, these histories were foundation stones for the revolt against the conservatives who ruled France. The opposition in the chamber loudly proclaimed that they were men of the Revolution, while their opponents were denounced as men of the reaction. The mere fact that the whole performance was given by two groups of middle-class politicians calling each other names did not interfere with the romantic associations that Frenchmen came to attach to the conflict

The program of the opposition was mild enough, so that no

one should have become confused about its real importance They had two proposals the first, to enlarge the suffrage; the second, to reform the system of corruption The reformers proposed to admit to the electoral rolls men who paid a direct tax of 100 francs, as well as doctors, lawyers, notaries, professors, and other individuals whose position in the community warranted electoral responsibility In case any arrondissement failed to have at least 400 electors, that number would be made up by including as electors the highest taxpayers of the community. This measure would enfranchise about 200,000 new electors, and increase the size of the chamber by 79 seats The other bill was devised to check the policy of corruption, by limiting rigidly the positions in the civil service which a deputy could hold In this way, the worst abuses of Guizot's system could be controlled.

These are hardly the measures of revolutionaries—indeed, they have a chimerical air even as a reform program They would not basically alter the complexion or the outlook of the chamber, and they would certainly not assure a better hearing for the fundamental social problems facing the nation At best, the balance of political power would slip into the hands of the middle bourgeoisie. The reform would have replaced Guizot with men who saw eye to eye with Guizot on most of the fundamental problems of French government Naturally, the program had the full support of the opposition in the chamber, but it was doomed to failure from the very beginning. The ministry could point to the recent elections, and cynically insist that "if the country wanted reform, it would be easy to see its desires" Obviously, the country was not interested, for Guizot's majority had been strengthened by the elections. When the reformers pictured the ministry's methods of electing deputies by corruption as an attack on representative government, Guizot coldly informed them that the very essence of representative government was the submission to the will of the majority "Have a majority," he remarked, "then you can pass the reforms that you wish"

The king backed up his ministers, for their policy of resistance to change was his policy. When Guizot entertained doubts about the wisdom of his attitude, the king explained to him "I am absolutely resolved not to leave the constitutional régime . . you have a majority . if the constitutional régime should wish me to dismiss you [that is, if Guizot should lose his majority] I will do my duty, but I will not make the sacrifice in advance for ideas which I do not approve." When the demands for reform became louder and more persistent, and members of his own household began to push for a change, the old king only became more stubborn. "There will be no reform," he insisted, "I do not want it. If the chamber of deputies should vote for it, I have the peers to reject it, and even if the peers should adopt it, my veto is there."

It was useless to look to the king or the government for reform; whenever a vote was called, the conservative majority wheeled into action to defeat the measure Was the nation equally cynical about the question? The English reformers of the same period had roused public opinion against a conservative chamber by great mass meetings and monster petitions; the French reformers asked themselves if similar tactics might not shake the calm of an obstinate French cabinet. In May of 1847 a plan was suggested A great reform banquet would be held for the champions of the opposition in the chamber. This would provide a satisfactory sounding-board for their program, and at the same time give ample evidence of the strength of the reform party The press gave the banquet much publicity, and the deputies invited all their friends. Any liberal elector or politician willing to pay ten francs for a meal could attend; this price insured the reformers against the attendance of the proletariat. On the ninth of July, 1847, about twelve hundred well-to-do, politically minded Frenchmen ate an excellent dinner at the Château Rouge while an orchestra played the *Marseillaise* and other revolutionary airs. The orators who followed the last course filled the room with well-turned denunciations of the cabinet and corruption; they compared the régime of the day with that of the last days of the Restoration in 1830, Guizot and the king playing the unenviable rôles of Polignac and Charles X. They earnestly advocated political reform as the cure-all for the evils of France. In spite of their ringing phrases, the most revolutionary thing about the whole affair was the music played by the orchestra. The mere fact that the diners did not drink to the health of Louis Philippe did not indicate any serious intention of dethroning him.

Several days later, at Mâcon, a banquet was given in honor of Lamartine, the author of *L'Histoire des Girondins.* The poet-historian set the tone of the gathering by announcing that "France has known a revolution of liberty and a counter-revolution of glory," and that the day would come when she would know a "revolution of scorn" After this dinner, the habit of political banquets spread like wildfire. The idea appealed to middle-class Frenchmen, for to advocate reform after a good dinner was a pleasurable experience During the fall and winter of 1847, some 17,000 well-dressed men sat down to seventy banquet tables to eat good food, drink excellent wine, and listen to enthusiastic orators The provincial politicians, grateful for an opportunity to display their forensic talents, pushed the program in the provinces with all their might. The rosy glow that surrounded the presence of good food and drink made their oratory more vigorous and spectacular.

At first the antidynastic leaders refused to associate themselves with the banquet campaign; men like Louis Blanc considered "the political revolution as merely a means; the social revolution was the goal" Finally, however, they too joined the movement, and an occasional republican or even a well-dressed socialist appeared at the speaker's table. The usual toasts were "to the national sovereignty," "to the institutions of July," and so forth, but these newcomers often added toasts "to the Convention" or "to the rights of man and of the citizen." On several occasions, two banquets had to be held in the same city when the antidynastic leaders refused to drink "to the health of the king," but they were uniformly peaceful gatherings that ended with everyone feeling that he had done his duty for state and fatherland.

The entire campaign had a fantastic air of unreality. The word "reform," so widely and loosely used, was never exactly defined, though it meant to a majority of the diners merely a slight reform in the franchise; it had much deeper connotations for many of them, and men on the street came to attach real, revolutionary implications to the whole movement The men who paid for the banquets were, for the most part, substantial bourgeois citizens who had no intention of exposing their society to the dangers of real civil strife But the loose talk of revolution that was bantered about under the influence of good food and drink gave the whole movement a radical tinge. These men, however, were—after all was said and done—the principal beneficiaries of the July Revolution; they merely wished to make a slight alteration in their political machine rather than any sweeping change in the régime. However, they were playing with fire, for, as one French historian writes, "They worked with unpitying ardor to destroy the régime that they greatly feared to see disappear."

The king and the cabinet were as unimpressed by the banquet campaign as they had been by the opposition speeches in the chamber. On the twenty-eighth of December, 1847, Louis Philippe, in a speech from the throne, referred to the movement as "an agitation fomented by hostile or blind passions" The king informed the chamber that he was convinced that a strict adherence to the Charter would "satisfy all the moral and spiritual needs of our dear fatherland" Guizot, more explicit than the king, assured the chamber that his ministry, which operated within the framework of the Charter, "would not preside over the disorganization of the conservative party and the ruin of its policy." Although the government's majority dropped to thirty-three, it was obvious that there would be no reform. When the king of the Belgians heard about the situation in France, he wrote to the Duke of Saxe-Coburg. "My father-in-law will be chased out as Charles X was"

The reformers were about ready to concede that all the food and wine had been consumed to no avail, Guizot's position, apparently, was still impregnable. They were resolved to carry through their movement by legal means, but a way to triumph had not yet shown itself Just when they were groping about for new tactics, an incident developed that carried the whole question into the streets of Paris and forced a revolutionary solution. A clique of obscure adherents of the reform program proposed to give a banquet to a group of radical officers of the National Guard The twelfth arrondissement, in which the banquet was to be held, was hardly a fashionable section of the city, and it was very likely that the demonstration would attract a rowdy crowd. The reformers were embarrassed; they did not wish to become associated with any riots that might ruin their case with the electors, by linking reform with real revolution The timid deputies were searching for an excuse, when Guizot came to their rescue by forbidding the banquet This act of the government relieved them of their embarrassment, but at the same time forced them to protest the invasion of the rights of Frenchmen Odilon Barrot dramatically accused Guizot of denying a right which even Polignac had recognized.

After some discussion, the reformers decided that the banquet must be held but that it would not be a regular banquet The "guests" would hold a parade, march to the banquet room, drink a toast to reform, and allow the leaders to be arrested. This would make a test case for the courts, to decide between the government and the rights of citizens. The parade caught the imagination of the press; it was to be organized with each group in an appointed place—the National Guard, the students, the deputies, and others When plans were well under way, the prefect of the police announced that both banquet and parade were illegal, and must not take place The Municipal

Guard received rations and ammunition, as a measure of police preparedness The reformers hesitated, and finally surrendered ignominiously by calling the whole thing off

It is easier to start a demonstration than it is to stop it. The press had played up the parade, a number of well-defined groups had made extensive preparations to participate, and the whole population of Paris knew about the plan. On the twenty-second of February, the scheduled day, a large crowd gathered on the Place de la Madeleine and the Place de la Concorde, in spite of a rainstorm, the police order, and the action of the reform chiefs There were a few cries, *"Vive la réforme!" "À bas Guizot!" "À bas le ministère!"* but by and large it was a good-natured assembly However, when the troops arrived, to disperse the crowd, its temper changed for the worse. There was a scuffle, stones were thrown, a barricade appeared on the corner of the Place de la Concorde, and a Parisian riot was soon under way. Demonstrations against both the government and the troops broke out in several sections of the city, but by midnight the streets were cleared What the next day would bring no one knew, but the government decided to prepare for the worst.

No French government could be without plans to suppress a riot in the capital. Experience had shown that Parisian temper was notoriously short, and a riot might easily prove fatal to the régime. The Monarchy of July depended upon the Municipal Guard, a section of the regular army, and the National Guard, to supplement the regular police authorities. The National Guard was, in the last analysis, the chief prop of the government in case of a crisis. Louis Philippe felt secure in his belief that the bourgeoisie would fight his battles in the street. Unfortunately for the régime, it was not in close contact with the feelings of the citizen army, the National Guard. The ranks were filled with little people of the petty bourgeoisie, who had been estranged by the policy of the conservatives, and almost the entire corps in Paris had been actively sympathetic with the reform program. Certain arrondissements were more radical than others, the first, second, third, sixth, and ninth, for example, were ardently opposed to the ministry, but only the tenth, from the Faubourg Saint Germain, could really be considered proministerial. A statement by Montalivet, an officer in the cavalry regiment—which, naturally, included only very wealthy, proroyalist members—is indicative of the temper of Louis Philippe's janizaries: "The cavalry of the National Guard," said Montalivet, "has not indicated loyalty to the ministry; it has come to maintain order and the institutions of July." On the twenty-third of February the drums of the National Guard summoned this citizen army to form its ranks, but the guardsmen who met at their appointed posts were not ready to play the rôle assigned to them.

The riots of the preceding day had aroused tempers and stirred up resentment in several sections of Paris; this fact, combined with a vague taste for excitement and the thrill of disorder, brought a crowd on the streets during the morning of the twenty-third. Here and there an overturned cart, the paving stones, and miscellaneous débris, were utilized to make a barricade. A few of the crowd brought muskets; a few more provided themselves with arms by looting the gunshops. The army was busy tearing down street fortifications and breaking up crowds when the National Guard appeared on the streets, presumably to take up positions and maintain order. But before leaving their assembly posts, nearly every regiment of the National Guard had talked over the task of the day, and had decided to act as guardians of the crowds against the wrath of the troops, as well as guardians of the monarchy against the attack of the crowds This decision, apparently spontaneous with each regiment, cost Louis Philippe his throne Once in the streets, the Guards stood between the troops and the rioters, while their cheers for reform showed that they belonged behind the barricades. "When the harassed military moved against the insurrection," writes Guedalla, "they found that the auxiliary force had interposed itself in the attitude (if with somewhat less than the grace) of the Sabine women; and the National Guard, which should have been the last police force of the monarchy, melted into a vaguely cheering mass of middle-class politicians" Now the revolution was armed.

The king was shocked to learn of the defection of this trusted bourgeois body, there seemed to be nothing to do but separate himself from Guizot. At two-thirty on the afternoon of the twenty-third the ministry resigned, and Molé was summoned to form a new cabinet. Guizot's friends were worried, but the crowds in the street received the news with acclaim. The bourgeois National Guard went home, assured that its job had been well done; the king, to be sure, had not mentioned reform, but Molé's appointment seemed to indicate the end of the system of resistance. In the poorer sections of Paris and in the student quarter, however, there were men who could not distinguish between the conservativism of Molé and Guizot. They stopped fighting, but they did not give up. A crowd broke into the armory in the Latin Quarter and distributed weapons to the people The radical newspaper, *La Réforme,* demanded that the entire population of Paris be armed and enrolled in the National Guard, and that the Municipal Guard be dissolved.

During the evening a great mob assembled in the Faubourg Saint Antoine, and, with banners and torches, but without precise plans or leaders, began a victory parade through the city. They turned into the Boulevard des Capucines, and came to the foreign office, where Guizot made his home. Derisive shouts and stones thrown at the windows indicated their contempt for the fallen minister The government had stationed troops around the building to protect it from the mob, and as the demonstration grew more bitter, these guards became more and more nervous Finally, the colonel became involved with the crowd, a shot was fired, then a volley. When the smoke had cleared away, fifty-odd persons were found killed or wounded; the "massacre" of the Boulevard des Capucines was already a *fait accompli* This occurred about nine-thirty in the evening By midnight, all Paris had the news An angry mob paraded the bodies through the streets, to show what the government had done, Molé resigned his post, barricades were thrown up all over town, and the king asked Thiers and Barrot to form a ministry and save his throne

The July monarchy probably could have saved itself The insurrection was only in Paris, and even there it was neither well armed nor well organized There is a strong presumption that the regular army and the provinces would have backed the government if it had put the capital in a state of siege and crushed the rebellion by force of arms. Paris was not France, as later rebellions were to prove. But Louis Philippe was old, he had lost his nerve, and he hated the idea of real civil war When his National Guard shouted for reform and even joined the men behind the barricades, he decided against an appeal to the country and abdicated his throne. The fighting was furious, and ominously near the royal palace itself; the loyal troops could not break the rebel lines, and were themselves forced to retire. The republican and socialist leaders took over the Hôtel de Ville and directed operations as best they could, while they made hurried plans to establish a new régime

The last act of the constitutional monarchy was played in the chamber on the twenty-fourth of February Louis Philippe had left for England, and the chamber was aimlessly discussing the revolt, when the Duchess of Orléans appeared in the room with her son and begged for the establishment of a regency. While the chivalrous deputies were considering her petition, a mob invaded the chamber and demanded its adhesion to the provisional government. Lamartine made a speech, and the claims of the Count of Paris were passed over The politicians went to the Hôtel de Ville to open a new chapter in French history

CHAPTER VI

THE REPUBLIC OF THE REVOLUTIONARIES

FEW men were prepared for the collapse of the July monarchy, but the events of February left no time for expressions of surprise. Men in the chamber of deputies, on the barricades, and in the offices of the reform newspapers immediately began to discuss the problem of finding a government to assume control. The editors of *Le National* and a few bourgeois republican politicians drew up a list of names to be offered as a provisional government; when the list was read to a wild crowd on the street, several changes were proposed, and adopted on the spot. Then the editors, the crowd, and the politicians straightway went to the chamber of deputies, where a bill was being discussed to establish a regency. The session was rudely interrupted; the list of the proposed provisional government was read, a vote of questionable legality was taken, and the new régime was acclaimed But *Le National's* list was not the only one to be drawn up. In the offices of *La Réforme,* the more radical journal, another list was made which contained most of the names that had been adopted in the chamber, but, in addition, several socialist republicans who were far from welcome to the bourgeoisie A riotous crowd on the barricades duly "elected" *La Réforme's* list, and proceeded to the Hôtel de Ville to install them in office The other men had gotten there first, and had already assumed the reins of power. A compromise gave the nominees of both lists a place in the governing council that would direct the affairs of France until a more regularly elected body could be assembled.

Clothed in the mantle of authority provided by popular acclaim, this provisional government assumed the responsibility for restoring order and ruling France. The cabinet posts were distributed among the nominees of *Le National,* the four social radicals, among whom were Louis Blanc, socialist philosopher-historian, and Albert, unknown, half-literate worker, were made "secretaries," with the right to deliberate in the councils of the government. Lamartine, whose European literary reputation was calculated to inspire international confidence in the revolution, became minister for foreign affairs, and during the first trying weeks of the régime his oratory and his personality saved the government from several severe crises. Ledru-Rollin, a Jacobin republican, became minister of the interior, and the aged Dupont de l'Eure, a representative of the first revolutionary age, was president. The new government included all shades of republican opinion, from the social radicalism of Louis Blanc to the conservative bourgeois republicanism of Marie, who became minister of public works. This compromise was necessary if the government were to retain the confidence of both the mildly reform-minded bourgeoisie and the radical crowds that had manned the barricades, but in making the compromise the provisional government opened all manner of difficulties for itself and for France.

The first decisions had to be made before Paris had settled down to an orderly life. The revolution was over, but the excitement of street warfare, the thrill of victory, and a vague fear that the spoils of revolution might be snatched away made it practically impossible to restore sufficient order in the streets to permit a calm consideration of the problems of government. The Hôtel de Ville was literally deluged with petitions, with delegations demanding that the government act on every conceivable matter—aid for Poland or Ireland, suppression of slavery or vivisection, enactment of social legislation, and so forth. From morning until night the government was forced to review a parade of demands that apparently called for immediate action. Naturally, all of them could not be granted, but the petitioners had to be assured that their requests would receive careful and considerate attention. On several occasions, when mobs filled the square below the Hôtel de Ville, the government, with no force other than its moral authority, was faced with the possibility of another revolution. In these trying days the ubiquitous Lamartine proved to be the masterful orator who could satisfy most of the petitioners with promises or convince them orally that their requests were impossible.

In the first week of its existence, the provisional government turned out a surprising amount of work. After much soul searching about its right to commit the nation, it issued a declaration to the effect that henceforth France would be a republic But when a mob demonstration before the Hôtel de Ville attempted to force the adoption of the red flag of social revolution as the national emblem, the government balked. Lamartine harangued the crowd. "The red flag," he shouted, "has been carried only around the Champ de Mars . . . the tricolor has been carried around the world with the name, the glory, and the liberty of the fatherland." Most of the crowd was satisfied, and the government announced that the tricolor, with the inscription "République Française," would be the official flag of France. The government also hastened to assure France that the proclamation of this republic would not bring in its train the horrors of the "terror" associated with the First Republic On the twenty-fifth of February it announced that "in its opinion the death penalty for political offenses [was] abolished," and that this *wish* would be presented for the definite ratification of the national assembly

In the sphere of economic affairs the government adopted policies that were soon to cause grief. On the twenty-fifth of February, a young worker, armed with a rifle, and bearing a petition, made his way through the crowds in the Hôtel de Ville. His pale face, blue eyes, and haggard look made the romantically inclined see in him the incarnation of the spirit of the victorious people. As a matter of fact, he represented a small obscure group of disciples of Fourier, and his petition was unknown to the mass of the Parisian workers. He demanded that the government should recognize the right of each man to work, and that it should organize labor to assure a "minimum for the worker and his family" There was an impressive scene, that ended in the issuing of the fateful decree whereby government "engaged itself to guarantee the existence of the workers by labor" On the following day, another decree created the national workshops to provide the unemployed with an opportunity to earn their living These national workshops, created as a necessity, appeared symbolic of the victory of the revolution. On the twenty-eighth of February, after refusing to create a ministry of progress or of labor for Louis Blanc, the government replied to a workers' demonstration by establishing a commission in the Luxembourg Palace to investigate conditions of labor and to make recommendations for labor legislation. To the bourgeois republicans this commission appeared a convenient way of sidetracking the socialists and at the same time of avoiding further commitments to radical Paris.

In its attempt to organize public peace, the provisional government was forced to recruit its own army. A radical republican, Caussidière, had already occupied the prefecture of police, armed his followers, and refused to take orders from the mayor of Paris, his policemen could be depended upon to act only against a counter-revolution. The government decided to create twenty-four battalions of the National Mobile Guards, an organization modeled on the "Volunteers of the Charter of 1830." The recruits, enlisted from the crowds under arms on the barricades, received one franc fifty centimes a day to become the defenders of order. At the same time, the question of democratizing the National Guard received considerable attention. The "property requirements," [1] which kept the proletariat out of the ranks, were considered incompatible with the new philosophy that proclaimed that the only

---

[1] The fact that the Guardsmen had to furnish their own uniforms, rifles, and other accouterment prevented the poor from joining the National Guard

free citizenry is an armed citizenry On the eighth of March the government undertook to equip the National Guard with arms and uniforms, and enrolled the entire population in its ranks

Thus, in the first week the new government prepared the way for the eventual destruction of the Republic. The recognition of its responsibility to provide every man with an opportunity to earn a living, and the creation of the national workshops without adequate study of the problem, committed the state to a program which, in 1848, was unrealizable. At the same time, the laborers received a way to voice their demands through the commission in the Luxembourg Palace, and to enforce their wishes with the arms that were freely placed in their hands The road to June, 1848, was already opened.

THE provisional government had hardly assumed control in the Hôtel de Ville, when France began to recognize its right to displace the Orléans monarchy *Le Moniteur* printed daily lists of high officers of the army and navy who offered their swords to the new régime; even the forces in Algeria, under two popular princes of the house of Orléans, recognized the revolution, and the princes, refusing to question the will of France, went into voluntary exile The Church, too, rallied to the revolution As early as the twenty-fourth of February the archbishop of Paris ordered the priests in his archdiocese to celebrate mass for the victory of the insurrection, and in a pastoral letter, on the third of March, approved the change in government The provincial bishops quickly followed the archbishop's example; the revolution appeared to be well disposed toward the Church, and the clergy readily appreciated that religion might prosper better under a friendly Republic than under an anticlerical monarchy. The liberty trees, planted throughout the country to celebrate the victory of the barricades, invariably enjoyed the blessings of the clergy, and the revolutionaries burned the house of M. de Rothschild rather than that of the bishop. When the civil service and officialdom followed the example of the armed forces and the Church in recognizing the authority of the usurpers, the government at the Hôtel de Ville rested easy in the thought that the great centers of potential resistance to their authority had willingly disarmed themselves and had joined the movement started on the barricades.

For the most part, the provinces received the news of the revolution quietly. The banquet campaign had taught the bourgeoisie that Louis Philippe's government was corrupt, and the workers, from experience, had learned that they could expect nothing from the monarchy. There was some disorder, but no attempt to reverse the decision of Paris. The outbreaks that did occur are illustrative of the stage of development that the French industrial revolution had reached. They were mostly antimachine riots or raids on the state forests. In Lyon they assumed large proportions, when the workers burned buildings and smashed machinery; in Alsace the rioters directed their attacks against textile factories, in the vague belief that thereby they could rid themselves of the new productive system In other sections of the country, the enemy was the railroad, somehow, the locomotive and the iron tracks were associated with the misery of the poor Often it was only after the arrival of a commissioner from Paris, who brought assurances of a new order, that the passions of the underprivileged were quieted The organization of the new régime occasioned considerable confusion in the provinces In several cases, two or more agents, with conflicting instructions, were sent to the same locality; in other instances, the authority of the revolutionary commissioners was disputed by local officials. By and large, however, France accepted the revolution in Paris without question One provincial wrote· "People here say that if Louis Philippe has been sent away it is a good thing, and that he deserved it" No one seriously challenged the right of the capital to give leadership to the nation.

IN 1848, revolutions all over Europe started with an appearance of success that seemed to the optimists to open bright vistas of development, but a closer investigation of the factors and the forces involved furnishes ample evidence that the hopes were built upon sand. The revolutionaries in France had a common enemy, but no common goal Together they had fought against the entrenched interests of the party of resistance, but when they had to construct a new governmental edifice they consulted divergent architectural authorities. In France the ideas of social radicalism, Jacobin democracy, and liberal republicanism, under the banner of "liberty, equality, and fraternity," had stood shoulder to shoulder against standpat conservativism Only when they triumphed did their strong ideological differences become apparent The problem was further complicated because the border lines between the three ideas were vague and indistinct, and because in the camp of the liberals there was a curious mixture of republicanism and monarchism While the several political philosophies struggled for supremacy at the ballot boxes, in the press, on the streets, and on the barricades, the Napoleonic ideal of democratic order and discipline, propounded by a political adventurer, found an opportunity to build a structure based upon force.

Of all the groups, the social radicals were numerically the weakest, and, probably, the most confused ideologically. There was no Lenin in the France of 1848 to direct the revolutionary program, and the *Communist Manifesto,* published in 1848, had not yet become the scriptural text for proletarian thought. In place of a unified command and a fixed dogma, there was a whole galaxy of rival, petty, proletarian leaders, each with his own little theory for solving the social question. They were generally agreed that "the exploitation of man by man" must come to an end, but their plans for the reorganization of society ran the whole gamut of political theory, from a religious anarchism to pure communism Each leader had his own followers, his own catechism, and usually an intense dislike for his rivals During the first few months of the revolution the radicals played a rôle entirely out of proportion to their real strength. The freedom of press and assembly which the February Revolution brought in its train provided a magnificent spawning bed for new doctrines Every available wall space was plastered with notices, proclamations, and manifestoes, dozens of newspapers appeared on the streets for a few issues, to disappear when financial embarrassment proved too great a handicap. Books, pamphlets, and brochures, dealing with every conceivable subject of political and social reorganization, were hopefully offered for sale. Each of the high priests of the radical party saw to it that all of his works were made available to the public.

It was in the "club," however, that the prophets of social reform made their greatest impression. By March, all Paris was honeycombed with clubs modeled on the traditions of the great Revolution; every available building, theater, and amusement hall became a session room for one club or another. There were clubs for every profession, for every province, for every political faction It was, however, the radical club, grouped about this or that proletarian leader, that was the most conspicuous. In an effort to make their work more effective, superclubs appeared which were composed of delegates from the cell clubs, but confusion of thought and division of command precluded any really united effort. There were two union clubs that bid for leadership The one, "Club of the Revolution" or "Club of Barbès," opened for business with the proclamation " . . As yet we have only the name of the republic, we must make the fact. Political reform is only the instrument of social reform The republic must satisfy the workers and the proletariat." The other union club, organized by Blanqui—the "Club of Clubs"—adopted "the Declaration of Rights of Robespierre," a catalogue in which there was a sharp distinction between republicanism that respected the rights of property, and republicanism that respected the rights of man The intense, personal rivalry between Barbès and Blanqui extended the rivalry between the two clubs, and effectively split the efforts of the social radicals.

Even if they had been unified in thought and action, the radicals of 1848 were fighting for a lost cause, because France was wholly unprepared to accept their doctrines. Their strength was confined to the cities, and even there they could count only on a minority. French society had developed a strong bourgeois class before it created a class-conscious proletariat The leaders of the social radicals realized this fact only too well. They sent delegations into the provinces to enlist as much support as possible for their cause, they joined the Jacobin democrats in an attempt to hold up the elections to the constitutional assembly until after France had had an opportunity to be educated for social democracy; they even offered suggestions that sounded very much like "dictatorship of the proletariat." After the elections had decided definitely and finally against them, the social radicals attempted to carry out their program by force The first trial led to a noisy demonstration and an uproar in the assembly; the second to the barricades and several days of terrible fighting. After these June Days, social radicalism was driven underground for twenty-odd years

Whereas the social radicals saw the revolution as a departure along the road of social reorganization—even a step in advance of the Convention and the First Republic—the liberal republicans wished only to consolidate the revolution as a victory against the standpat conservative system that the July monarchy had developed. The liberal ranks were filled with republicans who had rallied to the monarchy in 1830, and monarchists who rallied to the Republic in 1848. Their solution for the problem of government was a parliamentary régime that would guarantee the rights of man and his possession of property against the overwhelming power of the state, and at the same time would offer an opportunity for government to adjust its functions to fit the most pressing needs of society

Since the monarchy had failed to achieve this program, the liberals were willing to try a republic, but neither the Republic nor the monarchy could claim their unswerving allegiance. Although universal manhood suffrage was soon to give this group an overwhelming majority in the constitutional assembly, the liberals were not altogether converted to the principles of democracy The counting of noses, which was the practical way of discovering the general will, might not necessarily yield the desired results To guard against any revolutionary equalitarian democracy, these men wished to establish guarantees of person and property, which the state must respect.

In the first months of the provisional government, the liberal republican philosophy attracted practically the entire bourgeois class and most of the peasantry The violence of the radicals gave them ample opportunity to propagandize the nation France was literally flooded with newspapers and brochures, ridiculing, mocking, and condemning the programs of the so-called communists. The liberals appeared in the revolutionary chaos as a pillar of strength that would support the parliamentary tradition, and at the same time block any violent attacks on the sacred institutions of family, property, and individual liberty Their "reasonableness" and lack of political experience eventually proved to be a basic weakness, but in the spring of 1848 the majority of Frenchmen looked to the liberals for leadership

The bridge between the liberal republicans and the social radicals was formed by the Jacobin republicans; in the test of strength of June, 1848, however, it became apparent that the Jacobins would stand against the so-called communists even if they could not completely agree with the liberals. The Jacobin republicans leaned heavily on the traditions of the Convention and the First Republic To assure the success of their program, they were willing to create republican institutions by force, if it should prove necessary. Ledru-Rollin, the most popular leader of this group, ably explained its beliefs and aims, in his instructions to the commissioners in the provinces

"As apostles of the revolution," he wrote, "we will defend it by our deeds, words, and teachings"; the "dogma of liberty, equality, fraternity" must be translated into action by "abolition of all privileges, imposition of taxes according to the size of fortunes, progressive inheritance taxes, freely elected officials, trial by jury, equal military service for all, free and equal education . . . a democratic reconstruction of industry and credit, and voluntary association instead of egoistical compulsions." Here we see in formation the ideology of the petty bourgeois republican. It was Ledru-Rollin's election instructions, however, that revealed his uncompromising republicanism. He asked the commissioners to see to it that true and tested republicans, the "republicans of yesterday," should be placed in the positions of influence for the coming elections, for "they hold in their hands the destinies of France. They should give us an assembly capable of understanding and achieving the work of the people." Furthermore, he insisted that only "old republicans," as against opportunist converts to republicanism, should be considered as candidates for the coming assembly. In another circular, he wrote to his agents: "What are your powers? They are unlimited . . . the victory of the people imposes upon you the mandate to consolidate its work." The great mass of the French could not make a clear distinction between this individualistic equalitarianism, which would not hesitate to use dictatorial methods, and the social doctrines of the "communists." The rabid republicanism of the neo-Jacobins made few converts, in spite of Ledru-Rollin's position as minister of the interior in the provisional government, but the suggestion to insure republicanism by influencing the elections brought a cry from the conservatives in the name of liberty, and rallied the bourgeoisie and the peasants to the cause of liberalism against Ledru-Rollin as well as against Louis Blanc, Blanqui, and Barbès.

To the right of these three republican philosophies there slowly emerged a doctrine destined to dominate the Second Republic—the doctrine of moral order. It was a political panacea of the wealthy and the wellborn, that found ample support after the republicans failed to reach a plausible compromise between social radicalism and liberal republicanism On the morrow of the February Revolution the erstwhile electors found their political structure swept away; the king was gone; the chamber, elected on a restricted suffrage, was broken up; and rampant republican democracy seemed to be enthroned. But even these obstinate political facts had not robbed the electors of their wealth, their social prestige, and many of their vested interests. They still owned the land, the workshops, the factories, the banks, and the great commercial establishments. They still could assume their rôle as leaders in society. When the radicals clamored for communism, and high taxes on the great fortunes, these men naturally were drawn closer and closer together. In the crisis that they faced, it was only natural that they should fall back upon the formula that Casimir-Périer had used against the rioters and equalitarian revolutionaries in 1831. "Moral order" was a convenient rally cry for all those who wished to conserve property and position. It was not until after June, 1848, that the party began to grow, but, even in March, the seeds of moral order were well planted.

But moral order, like social radicalism, offered a program open to various interpretations. In general, its proponents fell into four main categories: conservatives, who were anxious to try out the Republic if it could be controlled by "sound men"; Orléanists, like Thiers, who wished to re-establish the parliamentary Orléans monarchy; legitimists and Catholics, who would restore the Bourbons with certain guarantees of basic liberties; and a small, vociferous group of imperialists who cried *"Vive Napoléon!"* and hoped to place Louis Napoleon on the throne. As long, however, as these groups had a common enemy in the traditional republican camps, they all found it more or less expedient to work together. It was only when they got control that their basic conflicts came to light.

The great differences in world and political outlook that

animated the leaders of France boded ill for the fate of the Republic proclaimed in February, 1848 The little group of men trying to guide the destinies of their nation from the Hôtel de Ville realized only vaguely the explosive nature of the political air of their time; optimistically they inaugurated policies, and issued proclamations that sharpened the basic conflicts between the leaders and the interests of their country, without, apparently, understanding that they were digging a trench in which to bury their hopes and aspirations. The governments that followed them continued to struggle with the problems posited by the revolution, and one by one the political philosophies and the parties that espoused them were destroyed, or forced underground, until Napoleonic imperialism captured the field. Such was to be the end of the idealism of 1848.

FROM the outset, the provisional government was forced to grapple with problems of state as thorny as the political debate that the revolution evoked. While the distressing state of the public treasury was only one of many conditions that threatened to undo the Republic, it was probably the most important, since it involved the economic stability of France. By 1848, the public debt had reached an all-time high. Unlike the Bourbon régime, the July monarchy had never shown itself to be oversolicitous about a balanced budget, and the years 1840–1848 had witnessed progressive demands on the public funds that could not be met from ordinary taxation. The pacification of Algeria, and the tremendous expenditure on the army, the navy, and the frontier fortifications following the war scare of 1840, had allowed the military departments to dip deep into the national pocketbook; subsidies for railroads, and the construction of canals and highways made further inroads on the public revenues; and, lastly, the inevitable graft and corruption, all too common under the July régime, completed the exhaustion of the treasury. Several large bond issues totaling over 800,000,000 francs had proved insufficient to repair the damage, and when the revolutionary government assumed control, it found the coffers empty

The first minister of finance, Goudchaux, was a practical banker, but he resigned quickly rather than face the impossible situation. His successor, Garnier-Pagès, with less knowledge of finance than optimism, struggled manfully with the problem of pulling the Republic out of the red His task was made more difficult by the general panic that followed the revolution. Both public and private credit had been inflated before 1848, on the unwarranted assumption that France was destined to a long future of internal and international peace. The revolution rudely shattered this dream, and the subsequent scramble for solvency produced a severe crisis. When the Bourse opened on March 7, the five per cent government bonds, which had sold at 116, dropped to 89; the next day they fell to 75, and subsequently even sold under 70. Stocks and bonds of all kinds followed the same trend, as banks attempted to liquidate their holdings, and discount rates on commercial paper rose out of all proportion Money tightened, and values, especially of luxuries, dropped. A fancy carriage valued at 5,000 francs in 1847 brought only 150 francs; horses valued at 2,000 francs dropped to 60 francs; even real-estate values fell almost as sharply. Industrialists, caught in the panic, closed their factories; merchants, bankers, and traders faced bankruptcy. The optimistic assurances of the provisional government failed to inspire any confidence in the future, espepecially since the government withheld information about its own solvency.

In an effort to force the government to come to their assistance, a crowd of bourgeois bankers, traders, and business men literally stormed the Hôtel de Ville with a petition urging the government to suspend all payments for three months. To Garnier-Pagès this looked like a recognition of universal bankruptcy, which he could not admit; he announced that the government would honestly and courageously face the problem of re-establishing public credit and confidence, even if such action should entail the selling of the crown jewels, the king's silverware, and the public forests. None of these sales was made The state's first move was a raid on the savings banks, by declaring that deposits over 100 francs were unredeemable in currency. State bonds and treasury notes were given to the depositors, in lieu of hard cash. Since this paper was worth from twenty-five to forty per cent less than par, the decision was almost tantamount to partial confiscation. The government offered bonds (five per cent) for sale at par, and urged patriotic citizens to buy them, and, if possible, to make outright donations to the state. Many citizens, particularly among the proletariat, naively brought a part of their savings or their jewels as gifts to the state, but the great mass of the bourgeoisie calmly refused to let their patriotism become an expensive virtue that would force them to pay 100 francs for a five per cent bond, when five per cent bonds were selling for 70 to 75 francs on the Bourse.

During the first few weeks of the new régime, the Bank of France continued its services, but finally the crisis affected even that pillar of financial strength A sudden suspicion that the bank could not meet its obligations led to a run, and on the fifteenth of March the bank closed its doors The government, however, unable to leave so potentially valuable an ally in the lurch, authorized the bank to issue 350 million francs in banknotes, which were declared to be legal tender. This prompt action saved the bank and gave it a new prestige in the French financial world. At the same time, the government authorized the creation of a discounting agency, *Comptoir National d'Escompte,* to give assistance to business men. These discounting agencies were founded in the principal commercial cities, and financed by the state, the municipality, and a group of private business men. They helped to loosen credits and thaw out frozen paper; in 1848 they did a business of 243 million francs.

Even though the economic crisis continued, and the government's own need for revenue was hardly satisfied by these measures, they did tend to relieve the worst of the panic The conservative, property-respecting bourgeois republicans in the provisional government refused to consider inflation or the confiscation of the estates of the Orléans family Since it proved impossible to raise money by a bond issue or a sale of short-term treasury notes, there remained only the expedient of an increase in the taxes, to place the treasury in a sound condition After much discussion, it was decided to impose an additional forty-five centimes on every franc of direct taxes. This gave the provisional government some of the money that it needed to carry on its functions, but, at the same time, it provided the enemies of the Republic with effective political ammunition, in a country in which direct taxes were so greatly disliked.

ANOTHER question which apparently contained as much dynamite as the economic crisis was the problem of the elections Universal manhood suffrage had been proclaimed, in a naive belief that this instrument would assure democratic control, but the leaders of the leftist parties soon came to realize that universal suffrage would in no way assure the kind of democratic control that they had envisaged unless the nation of peasants, workers, and petty bourgeoisie could be educated in their philosophy. This fact led Ledru-Rollin to use his office as minister of the interior much as his Orléanist predecessors had done—namely, as a convenient tool for influencing elections. At the same time, the socialists came to believe that their only hope for electoral success rested in delaying the elections for the assembly until after they had educated France. In the acrimonious debate that developed, the conservatives attacked Ledru-Rollin, the radicals threatened another revolution, and all factions vigorously bombarded the country with political literature. Lamartine might say, "if France chooses badly, so much the worse for her," but most of the politicians were convinced that France should conform to their own pattern of action.

Closely associated with the problem of electing a constituent assembly was that of choosing officers for the National Guard. After the revolution, the state undertook to equip the rank and file of the Guard with both rifle and uniform. This removed the obstacle that had prevented the proletariat from joining the citizen army, and broke the bourgeois monopoly of its ranks. But if the officers were to be elected before the recruits had a chance to organize and know one another, the probabilities were that the old bourgeois officers would continue in control Naturally, the proletarian leaders wished their people to secure a share in the command, and, quite as naturally, the bourgeoisie wished to retain their posts of honor. Moreover, many members of certain élite corps, which heretofore had been composed of only the very wealthy who could afford the special uniforms, were resentful that the illiterate and the socially unwashed were attempting to elbow their way into these regiments. The democratic arrangement, they thought, would spoil the *esprit de corps* as well as the smartness of the organization. Thus, the reorganization of the National Guard provided a thorny problem for the men in the Hôtel de Ville.

These questions were not to be settled in the calm deliberation of the council chamber. The Revolution of February and the demonstrations that followed had inspired great faith in direct action and mass pressure. On the sixteenth of March, the bourgeois National Guardsmen, in full uniform, staged a demonstration for the benefit of the provisional government. The next day, the clubs and the proletarians staged a counter-demonstration which, in point of numbers, greatly overshadowed the one of the day before. In each case, the mob before the Hôtel de Ville finally allowed itself to be broken up, after a number of fine speeches from the members of the government. But tempers were wearing thin, for the election was in the offing, and the government was suspected of double-dealing. A month later, the radical leaders, convinced that they could not win in the elections, decided upon a bold stroke to force postponement. They organized a monster parade for the sixteenth of April, to show their real strength. At first, it looked as if the government must fall; but before the demonstration reached the Hôtel de Ville, the bourgeois National Guard arrived to defend the government against the workers. By merest chance, General Changarnier also appeared, to consult Lamartine about foreign policy. He immediately took over the task of placing the troops so that they could effectively hold the demonstrators under control. When the crowd reached the square, it was obvious that they were checkmated by the armed Guardsmen, who cried, "Down with the communists!" "Long live the provisional government!" Lamartine called it "a victory without combat," when the crowds broke up after a few empty speeches from the government.

Whether the bourgeois National Guardsmen saved the government from real enemies on the sixteenth of April may be open to question, but the results of that act seem clear today. The failure of the demonstration to postpone the elections—or, indeed, to do anything—spelled the defeat of the program of radicalism. At the same time, the fact that the bourgeois National Guard had "saved" the government placed that government under greater obligations to the wealthy in Paris The elections, which were soon to follow, clearly demonstrated that France, too, was still under the influence of the upper bourgeoisie

THE elections for the constituent assembly were held on the twenty-third of April. The novelties of universal manhood suffrage and candidates without property qualifications produced a campaign such as had never been seen under the constitutional monarchies. Demonstrations, placards, pamphlets, and speeches were aimed at attracting the votes of the masses. The wild talk and tumultuous demonstrations of the radicals in Paris had made uneasy the people in the provinces, but the news that the mobs in the great cities were armed by the government filled the peasant proprietors and the bourgeoisie of all ranks with real terror. Many saw either civil war or submission to the demands of the "communists." When the bourgeois National Guard broke up the demonstration of April the sixteenth with a show of force and the cry, "Down with the communists!" these people took heart, and prepared to send "sound" men to the national assembly. The socialist and Jacobin radicals appeared to menace home, family, and property; and since they failed to utilize the one line of attack that might have attracted the peasants to them—that is, cancellation of mortgages and debts—these men of the left could not expect much support outside of the great cities. Their case was further damaged by Ledru-Rollin, when he attempted to create "official candidates" from the "republicans of yesterday." In the provinces the so-called "republicans of yesterday"—that is, pre-February republicans—very often were ill-balanced individuals, black sheep in their own families, whom the majority of their neighbors regarded as addlepates.

In spite of this suspicion of the radicals, nowhere was the Republic itself distrusted. It was accepted not only as an accomplished fact, but also as the solution of the government problem that practically everybody claimed to support. The dethroned kings—if they were mentioned at all—were classed with the Merovingians or other historical characters No one dared to suggest a restoration. With very few striking exceptions, the men who had been prominent in the politics of the July monarchy rallied to the new régime, and assured their prospective electors of their undying affection for the Republic and the principle of universal suffrage. The majority of the candidates for the new assembly, however, were new men in politics—doctors, notaries, lawyers, business men, and landowners who theretofore had avoided public life The tumult of the revolution, the threats of the radicals, and the demands of their friends and neighbors brought them out of obscurity to make them representative of the sovereign people of France.

The polling of the votes went quietly enough; it was Easter, and in many districts the whole male population went to church, and then, in strict alphabetical order, formed a procession and marched to the polling place to cast their ballots. The first disturbance came after the election, when, in Limoges and particularly in Rouen, the workers took to the barricades to reverse the decision of the ballot box. Some blood was shed, the hatred between bourgeoisie and proletariat was deepened, and a milestone on the road to the June Days was erected, but the disciplined companies of the bourgeois National Guard defended the decision of the polls.

TO MANY observers, the results of the election were nothing short of remarkable. They had expected universal manhood suffrage to produce a new kind of representative who should typify the democracy of France. It did produce a new type of representative, but not such as they had expected Very few men were elected who could not have met the property qualifications for a deputy under the old monarchy; indeed, a large number of the men who sat in the chambers of Louis Philippe's government were returned to the republican assembly The novelty of the new candidates arose from their political naivety. They were painfully sincere in their desire to do their duty by their constituents, they were eager to create a political system that would give stability to their country, but they were ignorant of the mechanics of parliamentary politics. They had no well-grounded political philosophy, nor did they understand the traditions of their own country. Well-meaning but politically untutored, this assembly was the delight of the orator who found that his words carried weight in the decision of the hour.

When the politically wise counted noses in the new assembly, they found that the vast majority represented the vaguely liberal, bourgeois republican tradition. They were men who read *Le National* or its equivalent, and wished to create a régime that would assure progressive political reform, but at the same time guarantee property rights, the home, and the Church.

Out of the nine hundred deputies, about seven hundred fitted into this category They were business and professional men who had recently rallied to the Republic as the most satisfactory solution for the problem of government. The right and the left had each about a hundred deputies The men of the left, recalling the traditions of the First Republic, called themselves the Mountain They were, however, not entirely in agreement among themselves The Jacobin republicans were almost conservatives beside their colleagues, the social radicals or "communists." On the right were the remnants of the monarchist parties which hardly dared to fly their own flag. In their ranks were Bourbon legitimists, Orléanists, an occasional imperialist, and the most ardent of the Catholics. But neither the right nor the left had any real power in the assembly that was to dictate the constitution for France in 1848.

The assembly first met on May fourth in the Palais Bourbon; there was an impressive scene when the provisional government accounted to the duly elected representatives of the French nation. Lamartine rose to great heights of eloquence in his idealistic account of the work of the government that had emerged from the Revolution of February He glossed over the conflicts which existed within its ranks, and failed to warn the nation against the possible unfortunate results of the fiscal and social policies that the government had adopted. The assembly was allowed to believe that there would be clear sailing ahead for the Republic because of the wisdom of the men who had seized power in February. In its innocence of what was in store for it, the assembly voted that the provisional government merited well of the country. Lamartine was at the height of his popularity, men were already asking for his favor, in anticipation of the day when he would become president of the Republic.

The first act of the assembly was to organize the executive power. After much discussion, the assembly decided to elect a commission of five to govern until the constitution could be written and put into effect. Arago, Garnier-Pagès, Marie,

Lamartine, and Ledru-Rollin were finally elected to the commission. The inclusion of Ledru-Rollin was demanded by Lamartine, in the hope of splitting the Mountain party in two, but his insistence on associating the Jacobin republicans with the government cost him much of the popularity that he had enjoyed when the session opened. Since the executive commission was made up of the most important members of the provisional government, and had called most of the rest into the ministry, the assembly started on its course with the same helmsmen that had been guiding the affairs of France since February. They continued to rule until June

ALTHOUGH the assembly suited the taste of the provinces and the bourgeoisie in the cities, the clubs and the proletariat could find little satisfaction in it. Obviously, again the men of wealth and substance would dictate the constitution of France, and even if this assembly was apparently more liberal than previous ones had been, there could be no doubt that it would be solicitous for the desires of men of property The bloody outcome of the uprisings in Limoges and Rouen left no question in the minds of the radical leaders about the ultimate end of their hopes. They realized that they must either control or destroy the assembly, if the social revolution were to be saved. In the Polish insurrection and the thorny question of the organization of labor they found an excuse to demonstrate their potential power, and, they hoped, to cow the assembly into submission. The proposed demonstration was announced and organized with full publicity, and although it should have been patent to everyone that a riot might well result, the executive commission did not take extensive precautions to prevent trouble

On May fifteenth, an immense crowd of workers, loafers, and agitators, with more than a vague taste for disorder, started from the Place de la Bastille to cross Paris toward the Palais Bourbon, where the assembly was in session. The demonstrators were unarmed, but their latent hostility to the assembly should have been a warning of coming danger. When the crowds reached the Palais Bourbon, the show apparently was over, for it was neither well organized nor effectively led. The armed guards of the palace appeared sufficient to protect the assembly against the unarmed crowd. Then, through ignorance, stupidity, or cowardice, de Courtais, who commanded the guards, ordered their withdrawal, and the mob invaded the assembly hall itself There was considerable disorder The deputies refused to move or speak until their chamber was cleared, but several of the club leaders spoke, and the clamor became general. Finally, one of the invaders announced that the assembly was dissolved, and invited the mob to go to the Hôtel de Ville to form a provisional government. The Revolution of February was to be re-enacted.

It was May fifteenth, however, rather than February twenty-fourth. This assembly had been elected by the whole nation, not by just a small group of electors. The mob and the radical leaders did not realize this distinction, nor did they reflect that the temper of the Parisian bourgeoisie had changed since Louis Philippe had been driven from the throne. At the very moment when the mob was shouting in the assembly chamber, the drums of the National Guard were beating in all sections of the city, and before any provisional government could be installed in the Hôtel de Ville, troops were on the street to break up the demonstration and restore order. Since the proletariat had neglected to bring arms, their coup was suppressed without bloodshed, and the leaders were clapped into prison. May fifteenth, however, was merely the rehearsal; the next time that the workers went into the streets to enforce their will, they brought their guns and powder.

When the assembly met that evening to continue the work that had been interrupted, it was a more serious group of men. The temper of the mob indicated that all was not well, and that another clash must be expected soon. Louis Blanc, who had had nothing to do with the demonstration, was severely criticized because he had been forced to talk to the invaders

The executive commission, whose prestige was considerably diminished, agreed to act with great energy to prevent a recurrence of the events of the day. May fifteenth deprived the radicals of their natural leaders, and at the same time it showed up the weakness of the executive authority of the national assembly.

No longer was there any doubt that the assembly had become estranged from the Parisian proletariat; and the public was beginning to become aware of an estrangement between the assembly and the executive commission The more conservative members of the assembly, thanks to their experience in the parliaments of the July monarchy, gradually assumed a rôle out of proportion to their numbers. They resented the presence of Ledru-Rollin, and even of Lamartine, in the executive commission, and began to undermine the government's authority by bringing up all possible objections to its policy. At the same time, the by-elections of June fifth and sixth produced alarming evidence of a change in the temper of France. The new deputies were men of either the right or the left—men like Thiers and Molé, who had little sympathy for any republic, or men like Leroux and Proudhon, who had no sympathy for a bourgeois republic And, among the others, Louis Napoleon Bonaparte, nephew of the emperor and pretender to his throne, was elected in Paris and in three other departments. A radical, revolutionary, social republic; a monarchical restoration, or a Napoleonic empire stared France full in the face.

The election of Louis Napoleon caused the most confusion. His past record included two desperate, if badly planned, attempts at *coups d'état,* a daring defense in court, a romantic escape from his prison at Ham, and a series of books and pamphlets on military, scientific, and social questions The assembly considered him a dangerous man, and feared his potential popularity with the people. Prince Louis had great faith in his destiny, and played his hand with great care. He had made an appearance in Paris shortly after the Revolution of February, only to leave again at the request of the provisional government. While the prince lived quietly in London, his henchmen, particularly the faithful Persigny, directed Bonapartist agitation in France. They painted him as all things to all men—to the bourgeoisie his name represented order and discipline, to the army and the nationalists it meant glory; and to the proletariat his pamphlet on the extinction of poverty made him almost a socialist. Behind it all stood the tradition of Bonapartism and the thwarted liberal Empire, which the exile and last writings of the great Napoleon had willed to his family. By the middle of the century, the legend of Bonapartism had developed a powerful appeal, and it was not long before *"'Poléon, 'Poléon—nous l'aurons,"* and even *"Vive l'Empire!"* could occasionally be heard in the streets of Paris. Earnest talk about "the Little Corporal" again was rampant in the villages. With some justification, the politicians in Paris were anxious to prevent the popularity of Louis Napoleon from spreading.

The assembly took a circumspect attitude toward Louis Napoleon's election to its benches, when it became known that a regiment of the regular army had replied *"Vive l'Empire!"* to the cry *"Vive la République!"* of a regiment of the National Guards. If the army was captivated by the name of its most famous leader, the régime might easily be in grave danger. Louis Napoleon intervened before the assembly decided to reaffirm the banishment of his house from French soil, by discreetly resigning his seat, but not before he had a chance to tell France that "if the people impose duties upon me, I shall fulfill them." The first Napoleonic crisis was past, but the name of Louis Napoleon was not to be forgotten.

NONE of the problems that confronted the national assembly loomed larger than that created by the national workshops. They had been established at the demand of the Parisian mob shortly after the provisional government assumed control in February, but neither a consistent plan nor a well-considered philosophy was evolved to direct this revolutionary institution Presumably it was the brain child of Louis Blanc, but neither he nor any of the socialists had anything to do with its organization Marie, minister of the interior, and Thomas, a young engineer who was made director, were responsible for planning the whole undertaking. Marie was hostile to the idea, and wanted nothing more than to demonstrate its impracticability, Thomas saw the problem almost entirely as a question of organization. The result was that a mammoth, complicated machine was erected to administer the workshops, but little or no effort was expended to secure effective plans, useful projects, or even proper tools The armies enrolled in this revolutionary organization planted trees, fixed roads, dug ditches, filled up the ditches, and loafed Very little was accomplished that had any great value to French society

The ranks filled rapidly. The revolution accentuated the economic crisis, and many laborers, especially those employed in the luxury trades, were added to the already large unemployed population of Paris. As the news of the workshops spread abroad, unemployed from all France and even from foreign lands streamed into the capital to fill the ranks. The exact figures are uncertain; by the fifteenth of March, there were about 6,100 enrolled, by the first of April, about 23,000, by the fifteenth of April, about 36,000; by the twenty-sixth of May, about 87,000; and in June, over 100,000 In March, the bourgeoisie regarded it as a socialist dream, but by June it had become a horrible proletarian nightmare The cost was tremendous. It soon proved impossible to give every man work for every day, and a system was evolved whereby the enrollees received part pay for no work, and full pay only a few days a week. This led to abuses; even a few petty bourgeois wine sellers and small shopkeepers managed to enroll for pay without work, while many cases of falsified identity revealed the fact that some individuals were receiving two or more salaries The cost rose to the point where the government had to find 170,000 francs a day to support the workshops. Obviously, this could not go on.

Before the elections, the government had used the workshops to split the proletarian movement. Then men were organized in the *Club central des ateliers nationaux,* and in the elections they voted for the bourgeois lists rather than those of the socialists. After the election, however, it became increasingly evident that the workshops were developing their own philosophy of social revolution, a philosophy that even Thomas apparently began to share. The events of May fifteenth, when a large number of the men from the workshops participated in the demonstration and the violation of the assembly, decided the government that the workshops must be closed. The government abruptly dismissed Thomas, sent him to the provinces under semiarrest, and began to take counsel on the most effective means for closing the Pandora box that caused so much fear.

It was easier to talk about abandonment than to accomplish it. The workers had also been enrolled in the National Guard, and armed from the state arsenals. The men in the workshops could count on the sympathy and support of the entire proletarian population of Paris, for the people were becoming more and more fearful for their promised social revolution Alexis de Tocqueville, himself a deputy in the assembly, described the situation as follows: "I found in the capital a hundred thousand armed working men formed into regiments, dying with hunger, but their minds crammed with vain theories and visionary hopes I saw society cut in two—those who possessed nothing, united in greed; those who possessed something, united in common terror. There were no bonds of sympathy between these two great sections; everywhere the idea of an inevitable and immediate struggle seemed to be at hand." His conclusion that "a great battle fought in the streets of Paris" alone could end the crisis may have been hindsight, but it was none the less true.

The showdown came on June twenty-first when the government announced that the workshops were to be closed. To soften the hardship that this order would bring, the government invited all men of military age to join the army, and told the others that employment on roads in the provinces would be available to them. To the Parisian, the army meant death in Algeria at the hands of the Mohammedans, and work in the provinces meant exile. It would be impossible to get 100,000 men with their families to leave the city. On the twenty-second of June, a crowd, crying *"On ne partira pas!"* appeared in the streets, and marched to petition for the rescinding of the order. When Marie refused, the delegation left him with the threat that arms would decide the issue. The Revolution of February was still fresh in the people's minds, and the proletariat, better armed and organized than they had been in February, felt sure of success. They did not realize that the bourgeoisie and the provinces, which either actively assisted or remained indifferent in February when Louis Philippe was driven out, would now take up arms against them. It was one thing to overthrow the power of Louis Philippe and the party of resistance, but quite another to attack the assembly which had been elected by universal suffrage.

"Revolutions," writes de la Gorce, "all follow the same course—they start with promises, and the crowd applauds: then, as none of the promises are realized, the applause changes to murmurs; the murmurs grow to the measure that the deceptions multiply; finally, at the hour when the last illusion vanishes, the revolt begins—the revolt, which, if victorious, leads to anarchy, and vanquished, compromises liberty for a long time to come. Thus broke out the insurrection of June." This June Insurrection is one of the grimmest events in French history; civil war is always bitter, but when the issue is drawn on a class line, it is, if possible, even more terrible. On the morning of the twenty-third of June, the workers, bearing arms, appeared on the streets, and quickly established their control over a large area, in the center of Paris, and extending from the Pantheon to the Porte Saint Denis The paving stone and débris again assumed the dreadful rôle of stuff for barricades, and a large section of the city became a fortified camp. Several attempts to halt the revolt by peaceful negotiation failed, and by noon blood began to flow again in the streets.

The tragic aspect of the battle was that the workers had only despair on their side; the battle must be fought, but there was no chance for them to win anything but death Their presumptive leaders had been imprisoned after the affair of May fifteenth; in spite of their apparent strength and early victories, they were disorganized and poorly armed, and they were fighting against overwhelming odds. As the battle progressed, there were but few of the cheers that usually accompanied French street fighting. This was a grim fight to death, in which the worker saw his choice narrowed to a rifle bullet or slow starvation. Men, women, and children manned the barricades to meet the onslaught of the combined forces that the government could muster against them, but after four days of terrible fighting they were forced to give up.

At first, many of the members of the chamber and the government itself feared that the loyalty of the troops and the Garde Mobile could not be trusted. In the elections, the rank and file of the army had voted for the radical candidates, and the Garde Mobile came largely from the lower classes of the city. But discipline counted, and both the army and the Garde Mobile remained true. In addition, the government could depend upon the Parisian and provincial companies of the National Guard Before the fighting was over, the railroad transported thousands of provincials to Paris to help to subdue the insurrection. "These men," writes de Tocqueville, "belonged indiscriminately to every class of society; among them there were many peasants, many shopkeepers, many landlords and nobles—all mingled together in the same ranks" The old nobility, he said, turned out to a man, "from the petty squire squatting in his den in the country to the useless, elegant sons of the great houses—all had remembered that they had once formed a part of a warlike and governing class ." Provincial peasant or noble, Parisian and provincial bourgeois—all had an intense fear and hatred of the radical proletariat, and, once joined in deadly conflict with them, would show no mercy. Up to the last, it was the rule to give no quarter to anyone taken in arms or suspected of having had a part in the conflict. The ruling class hoped once and for all to dispel the wild dreams of social equalitarianism.

The struggle necessitated a reorganization of control on the side of the assembly. The executive commission proved incapable of directing the conflict, and, as often in times of stress, authority gravitated into hands most capable of exercising it. General Godfroy Cavaignac, son of a constitutional, brother of a republican leader, and himself a hero of the Algerian wars, assumed command in the moment of stress, and efficiently directed the operations. Politicians such as Thiers wanted to evacuate Paris, and return with the entire regular army to take it by siege. Cavaignac threatened to shoot Thiers, called up all the troops he could find, and finally emerged victorious. He deserved well of the bourgeoisie; but since he did not aspire to play the rôle of a Napoleon, he was thanked within a very few months by an overwhelming defeat in the presidential election.

The struggle gave rise to great heroism and great tragedy. When the battle was at its height, Monsignor Affre, the archbishop of Paris, who had welcomed the establishment of the Republic, offered himself as mediator between the contending parties. He was killed by a stray shot, before his errand of mercy could be accomplished Several generals, who had made names for themselves in Africa, met their deaths in the streets of Paris; and thousands of homes, both bourgeois and proletarian, lost fathers, brothers, or sons in this battle that neither accomplished a social revolution nor saved the bourgeois Republic. This was the greatest tragedy of all: the June Days drove deeper the chasm between the workers and the bourgeoisie, without guaranteeing victory to either. Its real outcome was to pave the way for the Second Empire, and, like the White Terror of 1815–16, to leave a legacy of class hatred that would flare up again in 1871.

CHAPTER VII

THE REPUBLIC WITHOUT REPUBLICANS

THE June Days opened a new chapter in the revolution; General Cavaignac emerged as chief of the executive power, and Paris, in a state of siege, was occupied by the army, the National Guard, and the Garde Mobile The inevitable reaction followed The press was again curbed, the clubs were placed under supervision, the "faithless" companies of the National Guard were disarmed and disbanded, and "sound" men were established in the places of power. The workshops were dissolved, but the workers were partly assured that they would be able to buy bread, by the inauguration of public works, the promise of limited tax exemption for private construction, and provision for a dole. An attempt at reforming the public taxing system in the interest of the bourgeoisie failed, but, in spite of resistance, the tax of the forty-five additional centimes, which the provisional government had levied, was collected, so that the state could carry out its functions. The government also took measures to bring some relief to both the holders of public *rentes* and the men whose saving accounts had been raided by the provisional government. These were social, military, political, and financial measures that pointed toward the government of moral order and the Empire.

The assembly proceeded immediately to the task for which it had been elected, the writing of a constitution. There were, however, few men in the assembly who had pondered deeply on the problems of framing a republican régime; even the ardent republicans themselves were most superficial in their thinking. These men had infinite faith in Montesquieu's checks and balances, and little knowledge of the actual workings of a government De Tocqueville, himself a member of the committee that prepared the first draft of the constitution, wrote that the assembly "bore little resemblance to the men, so certain of their objects and so well acquainted with the measures necessary to attain them, who, sixty years before, under Washington's presidency, so successfully drew up the American Constitution." The committee began its labors in May, and, in spite of the turmoil of June, prepared the constitution for presentation to the assembly by July. The haste of the founding fathers of the Second French Republic was obvious; their constitution was a hodgepodge of confused political theory borrowed from previous constitutions and from conflicting political theorists—a state paper literally loaded with idealistic hopes and impractical regulations, that was foredoomed to failure.

It opened with an elaborate, inflated declaration of the rights and duties of Frenchmen, in which good advice and bold assertions intermingled to confuse the reader. In organizing the government, this constitution rigidly separated powers, and provided for a complicated system of checks and balances to maintain that separation A single legislative assembly of 750 members, elected by universal manhood suffrage for a three-year term of office, controlled the legislative function. A president, also elected by universal manhood suffrage, but for a four-year term, controlled the executive branch. The president appointed ministers responsible to himself, but no way was open to him whereby to dissolve a recalcitrant legislative chamber that might refuse to approve his measures. The legislators, moreover, enjoyed parliamentary inviolability, while the president could be impeached, and even tried for any misdemeanor in office. To sum up their work, the framers made it practically impossible to change one phrase of the Constitution legally; they wished France to enjoy forevermore the fruits of their wisdom.

The British ambassador wrote in his journal, on the day on which the Constitution was adopted: "I think any impartial examination must lead to the conclusion that it is the very worst that ever reached that finishing stage of manufacture. With no original idea, it is so confused in its expressions and contradictory in its provisions as to be unintelligible to many of its authors, and undoubtedly impracticable in execution" It required less than three years to prove the essential wisdom of this observation The assembly did not ask for a popular ratification of its work, before trying this ridiculous document on the French people. On the contrary, by sternly voting down that suggestion by a great majority, the assembly tried to force France to accept this practically unrevisable constitution. It was, in the opinion of many of the framers, the only way of keeping France republican. The reaction in the country after the June Days ran strongly against the republican ideal; and the supporters of monarchy grew daily in stature and in strength, while the republicans continued to lose prestige The men of the assembly put their faith in the rigid mold that they had made, for they feared that the republic would soon be governed without the republicans

ONCE the Constitution was out of the way, France settled down to the problem of selecting a president for her new republic It was not long before the obvious possibilities were narrowed down to General Cavaignac, the victor of the June Days, and Louis Napoleon Bonaparte, nephew of the late emperor. There were other candidates proposed, and others ran for office, but they were either men who had been connected with the discredited provisional government, or radicals who did not stand a chance for success. Cavaignac was the choice of the assembly, for he had saved it when the Parisian proletariat took to the barricades His austere republicanism, which had severely repressed any suggestion of a military dictatorship, appealed to the middle-class idealism of the liberal republicans, and his background of bourgeois respectability, as well as his republican traditions, made him a perfect representative of the men who wished to establish a liberal bourgeois republic. But it was Cavaignac who had suppressed the June revolt, and governed France in the months that followed. No one forgot that his victory was a victory over Frenchmen. His stern impartiality in meting out both favors and punishments, while he was chief executive of France, earned him many enemies Men of more subtle intelligence despised his gaunt appearance and his almost inarticulate speech, while the opportunist politicians ridiculed his strict insistence on his republican ideals. Cavaignac was a candidate for the presidency, but his defeat was inevitable He could count on the support of only the liberal bourgeoisie that hoped to create a republic.

Louis Napoleon Bonaparte, on the other hand, had the advantage of being personally unknown and politically unconnected with either the February Revolution or the June revolt, and he had a name known to every Frenchman Undaunted by the assembly's first refusal to admit him to its benches, the prince had his name presented in the by-elections, and, to the surprise of many, he was elected in Paris and four other districts. Since the assembly could hardly refuse him a seat after this show of popularity, Louis Napoleon Bonaparte returned to France to assume office. His maiden speech went badly; his second, hardly better; for unless Louis Napoleon was careful he always spoke French with a German accent, and his stage presence was awkward and ineffective. The assembly mistakenly assumed a lack of ability, and discounted him as an unimportant political figure, but the prince, with immeasurable faith in his star and his destiny, presented himself as a candidate for the presidency of the republic.

His suite in the Hôtel du Rhin became a mecca for old soldiers who wished a glimpse of the nephew of their leader, for an idle crowd that came to cheer or ridicule this "false" Napoleon, and finally, for the politicians who, ear to the ground, slowly discovered that France would probably elect Louis Napoleon to be her president In the thirty-three years since the exile of the emperor, France had forgotten the misery and remembered the glory of the Empire. She had forgotten the horrors of foreign wars, and remembered the order, the discipline, and the conquests for which the eagles had stood. The inglorious years that had followed, when a moth-eaten émigré nobility and a money-grabbing plutocracy had ruled on the Seine, had dimmed neither the glamour nor the brilliance of the name Napoleon.

Louis Napoleon appropriated the legend that the emperor had left, and made it his own. In his own right, he had added, for the romantically inclined of his age, his participation in the revolution at Rome in 1830, his daring, if somewhat impractical, attempts at the overthrow of Louis Philippe; and his colorful escape from the prison at Ham. Furthermore, Louis Napoleon's life had not been spent in vain pursuit of pleasure; he had educated himself, and cultivated his prose style so that the bold manifestoes that all France could read carried more weight than the halting sentences that he pronounced from the tribune in the assembly. In pamphlet and brochure he had expounded the doctrine of Bonapartism, and even ventured into the more difficult disciplines of both social and natural sciences by a study of beet sugar and an essay on the extinction of poverty. If the politicians in Paris were slow to see that Louis Napoleon was an excellent presidential possibility, France was quicker to grasp the idea, and it was France —that is, the nation of peasants, bourgeoisie, and proletarians— that would elect the president of the republic.

The leaders of the conservative party in the assembly, the party that came to be known as "moral order," finally came to see an advantage in the candidacy of Louis Napoleon. After the June Days, the bourgeoisie slowly withdrew their allegiance to the Republic, and the more liberal leaders of the last days of the July monarchy—Barrot, Thiers, Molé and their friends—began to regain the prestige that they lost after February. These men accepted the Republic only as a stopgap; they really preferred a monarchy, and they looked forward to an early restoration. General Cavaignac's austere republicanism disqualified him for the rôle of a General Monck, but in Louis Napoleon they believed they saw a man who could easily be led to turn over the power to a legitimate monarch. Since no one of their own number stood a ghost of a chance for election, these men decided to support Louis Napoleon, in the belief that he could be used for their purposes. Never were politicians more deceived in their judgments, but on this ground the conservatives decided to support Louis Napoleon at the polls. He responded graciously to their approaches, and met their plans with an enigmatical, half-dreamy smile that convinced them of his political stupidity.

With his name, his record, his promises to all men, and his conservative mentors to plan his campaign, Louis Napoleon won an easy victory at the polls His name alone gave him the support of almost the entire peasantry. Of the seven million votes cast, he received five and a half millions. "Stupid provincials," writes Guedalla, "felt vaguely that they had elected an emperor, but in Paris, where they knew everything, he was only a president"

On December twentieth, the prince took the oath to defend the Constitution and remain faithful to the democratic republic; when he had finished his oath, he added: "I will see the enemies of the fatherland in all those that try to change by illegal methods that which France has established" This was December, 1848; in December, 1851, came the *coup d'état,* and in December, 1852, the proclamation of the Second Empire.

THE new president took up his residence in the Élysée, and soon established a household that was too military to suit the elder statesmen who had sponsored his candidacy after they were assured that he would be elected. In choosing his cabinet, he first approached Lamartine, who refused, and then appointed Odilon Barrot prime minister. The cabinet contained only one republican, and he resigned very shortly. From the point of view of the Orléans monarchy, it was a liberal government. Indeed, practically the entire cabinet was made up of members of the old party of progress; but, in the light of the months that had followed February, it was extremely conservative. From the beginning, this ministry found itself in conflict with the assembly, which decided to prolong its life so that it could enlarge on the basic laws of the republic. But this assembly no longer represented France, the election of Louis Napoleon rather than of Cavaignac indicated that the people wanted a conservative government.

During the first few months of his office, Louis Napoleon established precedents which were greatly to enhance his power. The first was in a conflict with his ministers Out of a natural curiosity to see his own record, he called for the files relating to his ill-fated attempt at a *coup d'état* in 1840, and at the same time demanded that the ministers submit to him the telegrams dealing with the affairs of state There was an indignant refusal, a threat of resignation, and finally an apology from the president; but, although he did not get his own case record, more of the telegrams were henceforth sent for his examination. Several weeks later, the cabinet came to blows with the assembly. Should they resign? The president calmly announced that the ministry enjoyed his confidence, and there would be no need for their resignation. This definitely placed the cabinet under his wing, if he could retain it, he could also dismiss it without consulting the assembly. The third incident arose out of a mistaken idea on the part of certain members of the Garde Mobile and a threat of rebellion from the Jacobin republicans. It appeared for a moment that the disorder which had been so common the spring before would again trouble Paris, but on the morning of January twenty-seventh the capital awakened, not to an attempted rebellion, but to find herself strongly invested with troops Criticism has been made of the overwhelming show of force, but it is made on the assumption that the government ought to give every rebellion a sporting chance. Louis Napoleon calmly announced that the romance of street fighting was over; order must prevail

The president became personally very popular. In the uniform of a general he reviewed troops, who did not refrain from the cry, *"Vive Napoléon!"* and even *"Vive l'empereur!"*

In a frock coat he visited charitable institutions, inspected hospitals, and filled the ceremonial rôle of his office. He was cautious in every move, in spite of the suggestion that his hour had come, he carefully avoided the opportunity for a *coup d'état* that the situation of January twenty-seventh afforded. After all, he had waited many years, why not wait until success would be without question? He became the despair of ministers by his insistence on a general amnesty for the rebels of June, by his vague suggestions for social and economic reform, and by his occasional, alarming show of independence, but largely they believed that he was a man who could be led, a man who would suit their plans for an eventual restoration In his early days in the Élysée, the prince-president did nothing that would alter this impression He had reached the presidency from almost complete obscurity, and he believed, almost fatalistically, that his star would lead him to greater triumphs.

THE Revolution of February loosened the tension all over Europe. Hardly had the news of the victory over Louis Philippe crossed the frontier, when the Metternich system in central Europe crumbled to the earth. First in the smaller states, but finally even in Berlin and Vienna, the principles of liberty, equality, and fraternity were proclaimed with cheers and promises of new constitutions. Czar Nicholas of Russia alone was able to sit serenely on his autocratic throne; the others were overwhelmed by the enthusiasm of the revolution. There was a nice distinction, however, between the revolution in Paris and the revolutions elsewhere The Revolution of February was a social and political movement; the issues of the other revolutions were confused by association with the doctrine of nationalism. This complicated the French revolution, since representatives of every nationality of Europe, from Irish to Bohemian, prepared petitions begging for the assistance of the revolutionary French government; in some cases, such as that of the Poles, the petitioners were vociferously supported by the mobs on the streets But the provisional government, and later the assembly, carefully eschewed the suggestion of intervention. Lamartine was dilatory and evasive; later foreign secretaries were blunt in their refusal to allow France the doubtful honor of heading a European nationalist crusade.

After the June Days, Bastide, foreign minister, wrote to an ambassador: "We will not engage in any war in which all Europe would be against us, and in which we would have no assistance. I say no assistance, for the German democrats at Frankfort, whose first act was to make an emperor, would primarily see in the war only an occasion to found and consolidate a united Germany. . ." Nothing could be more explicit; revolutionary France was and would remain neutral; her leaders were not inspired with any crusading zeal for European liberty This policy probably worked to isolate France, but at least it saved her from the disaster that war might well have brought. In November, 1848, however, revolution reached Rome, and French policy had to be reconsidered. His Holiness, Pius IX, at that time still regarded as the first great liberal to occupy the chair of Saint Peter, was hunted out of Rome after he had attempted to give the Romans a liberal régime Cavaignac offered aid and sage advice, for French prestige was at stake. The pope replied evasively, and took refuge in the kingdom of Naples; his advisers preferred to be rescued by Austria or Spain rather than by republican France. It was a question that had to be considered when the new president took office in December Catholic France owed assistance to the pope; republican France sympathized with the Roman republicans, neither Catholic nor republican France wished to see Austria restore the pope But the reaction was already under way in Italy and throughout the Hapsburg lands, and Austria might soon be in a position to suppress the Roman republic

Louis Napoleon, himself an old Carbonarist and a participant in the Roman revolution of 1830, found choice very difficult. There were three possible policies. to do nothing, and leave to Austria the restoration of order in Rome, just as she was restoring order in the Quadrilateral; to go to the aid of the Roman republic, in which case he would bring not only all Europe but also most of France down on his head—a policy which his ministers would never support; and, lastly, to go to the aid of the pope and try to effect a liberal restoration If successful, this last policy would enhance his own prestige, and, successful or not, it would be popular in France, for France was rapidly becoming less republican, and even some republicans were friendly to the liberal pope, since Pius IX had not yet appeared as the author of the denunciation of progress. The cabinet finally decided to follow the third policy, and Louis Napoleon, as much out of hatred for Austria as love of the pope, gave his consent.

After Austria's striking victory over the north Italians there was little time to lose, for Austria would gladly send her troops on to Rome to restore Austrian order in the peninsula. An expedition of 7,000 men under General Oudinot sailed from Marseille on the twenty-first of April, on the twenty-ninth it was bivouacked within a few miles of Rome. Somehow, the French believed that the Romans would welcome the French army as a deliverer from the power of Austria; they believed that the Romans would realize the futility of their republic and welcome the French "restorers of order" with open arms. The Romans, however, had other ideas, and, to Oudinot's surprise, he was quickly repulsed when he moved on to Rome itself.

The immediate demand for reinforcements put both Napoleon and the assembly in an awkward position; only the cabinet was prepared for this outcome The assembly, which no longer represented the opinion of France and which soon was to be completely discredited at the polls, was largely republican. The thought of suppressing a sister republic caused many frantic gestures in the chamber and was summed up in an ambiguous resolution. Napoleon had consented to the expedition in the belief that it was just what the Romans wanted and needed. Now that the military honor of France was involved he had to continue, but he was resolved to do what he could to save Rome from complete reaction. The ministers, who had foreseen that the expedition might result in war on the Roman Republic, offered to resign; as in January, the resignations were not accepted

At the same time that reinforcements were dispatched to Oudinot's army, Napoleon sent de Lesseps, with vague orders, on a mission to convince the Roman republicans that a French restoration was not only their sole hope, but also a far more satisfactory solution than the Austrian army would offer them Some writers regard this mission as an attempt to play for time until the French army could be re-enforced. This view is not in accordance with the facts, although it was the ultimate result of de Lesseps' blunderings. There were confused negotiations in which de Lesseps exceeded his authority, and the Romans built up dream castles The elections in France for the new legislative assembly on May thirteenth returned a majority for the party of "moral order," men who advocated forceful intervention The republicans, defeated at the polls, again tried bullets. Louis Napoleon crushed the incipient rebellion before it really started. With "moral order" in the saddle in France, the hopes of the Romans vanished Oudinot's army received orders to advance, on July third, after almost a month's siege, the French armies entered Rome.

The restoration of the pope was the prelude to the Second Empire. Napoleon, more or less unwillingly, had crushed a phase of Italian unification, and made himself acceptable to the French Catholics. By the same action his régime was identified with the authoritative reaction that spread over Europe in 1849 "Moral order" was to be the introduction to the Second Empire.

THE June Days split French society wide apart. On the one side they created the party of "moral order," which hesitantly supported Prince Louis Napoleon for the presidency, and on the other side it developed the party of republican solidarity, a coalition of the social and Jacobin republicans. The men who stood between these two extremes, the men of the liberal republic, were soon to find their position untenable. After the election of Louis Napoleon, the assembly, which had made the constitution, was loath to end its own life. The majority of that assembly was made up of liberal republicans, who viewed with alarm the spectacle of Louis Napoleon, a Bonapartist pretender, and his monarchist advisers, composing the executive branch of the state. On the other hand, the assembly could not fail to see that the socialist dreams were crushed but not extinguished by the June Days, and that the Jacobin republicans were slowly driven to make common cause with the remnants of the extreme radical party. The assembly alone contained a majority of liberal republicans. It no longer represented France, but it could not conceive of a republican France after it gave up control It was not until the spring of 1849 that the constituent assembly was finally persuaded to disband and allow the nation to elect the legislative assembly for which the Constitution provided.

In the election of May, 1849, the men loosely grouped in the party of "moral order" won a striking victory. This party had been more or less directed by the so-called committee of the Rue de Poitièrs; it had collected about 400,000 francs to placard the nation with antiradical and proconservative propaganda, and, although the committee did not pick the candidates for the provinces, it acted as a co-ordinating agency. Bourbon legitimists, Orléanists, Catholics, Bonapartists, and undecided conservatives of all kinds made up the allies in the ranks of "moral order" The erstwhile opposition to Louis Philippe and Guizot provided the bulk of the leadership, and Louis Napoleon's government gave as much assistance as it decently could under the republican system. While the party acquired about 450 of the 750 seats, the party of republican solidarity obtained about 180 This surprising strength of the radicals was the result of eight to ten months of strenuous campaigning in the country and the city by the advocates of the social republic. They dropped their theories of socialism and republicanism, and, as did their opponents, appealed to the basic interests of their prospective supporters. The sober bourgeoisie told of the need for order, discipline, and the protection of property, home, and Church, the radicals talked of redistributing the land, abolishing debts, shortening working hours, and raising salaries. The result was that the party of the left—the Mountain—appeared in the legislative assembly with a strong minority. Many of the chiefs of the liberal republicans failed even of election to the new assembly; Lamartine, Marie, and Garnier-Pagès discovered that the country could do without their services. The men of 1848 went down between the reaction to the right and to the left; there was no room for the middle.

The reappearance of the left, in spite of the June Days, gave the men of property a scare, and gave the radicals a feeling of importance out of proportion to their real strength. Ledru-Rollin, on whom the leadership of the party of republican solidarity devolved, came to believe that the left would soon dominate the nation. The French troops in Rome gave him an excuse to test his strength. Early in June, the radicals published a proclamation intimating that the war against a sister republic was unconstitutional, and, if necessary, that the Constitution must be put in force by resistance in the streets of Paris. On the eleventh of June, Ledru-Rollin challenged the minister of foreign affairs; he declared, a little hysterically: "The constitution has been violated; we will defend it by all means possible, even by force of arms." On the next day proclamations and defiances followed a call for a demonstration. The scenes of the revolution from February to June, 1848, seemed about to be re-enacted, but this time Louis Napoleon, not a provisional government or an executive committee, held the reins of executive power.

At eleven o'clock on June thirteenth, a great demonstration started at the Château d'Eau to carry a protest to the legislative assembly. Uniformed National Guardsmen from the poorer districts, members of republican societies, and proletarians marched toward the assembly hall, with Ledru-Rollin and his friends at the head of the parade. At the Rue de la Paix, a column of regular cavalry cut the demonstration in two, and quickly cleared the streets. Ledru-Rollin and a small group hastened to the Conservatoire des Arts et Métiers, and started to direct a rebellion against the government. Loyal troops quickly arrived, broke up the meeting, and arrested some of the conspirators Ledru-Rollin and a few of the others escaped to exile in England, but their hopes of a revolt were definitely ended. That evening Louis Napoleon and a group of generals and staff officers made an inspection tour of Paris. As they rode by, there were cries, *"Vive la république!" "Vive Napoléon!"* and even *"Vive l'empereur!"* France had found its strong man who would govern.

The news of the abortive revolt ended the hopes of the Roman republicans, but the capture of Rome by the French army several weeks later did not end the Roman question in French politics. Louis Napoleon had agreed to the suppression of the Roman republic, but he was not prepared to accept the reaction that occurred in Rome when the pope and his court returned. As a youth, Prince Louis had participated in a Roman revolution; as a man, he hated to be the instrument of repression. Furthermore, the pope had pointedly failed to single out France when he thanked the "Catholic powers" for his restoration. When it became obvious that Pope Pius IX was an ex-liberal, and that only the blackest reaction could be expected from Rome, Louis Napoleon, without consulting his ministers, sent a strongly worded letter to His Holiness. "The French Republic," he wrote, "has sent an army to Rome not to stifle Italian liberty, but to regulate it by preserving it against its own excesses." In a spirit of bravado, he added: "When our armies made the tour of Europe, they left everywhere, as the token of their passage, the destruction of feudal abuses and the germs of liberty; it shall not be said that in 1849 a French army could act otherwise or leave other results."

These were brave words, that startled men in France no less than in Rome. The elder statesmen who had been managing the prince's affairs were shocked to hear their "young man" express himself so independently. The Catholic majority in the legislative assembly, which had regarded Louis as a puppet and the republic as a transition to a monarchy, did not like to see the president step out alone, especially in the name of liberty. They deeply resented the rebuke that he had given the pope in the name of Catholic France. There was a serious debate in the chamber, in which Barrot lamely defended the chief of state, and contrived to avoid reading Louis Napoleon's letter in his own defense By assuming a half-apologetic tone for the president, the cabinet won a vote of confidence in the chamber, but it was a victory for the cabinet at the president's expense. On the last day of October, 1849, Colonel Edgar Nye carried to Barrot a letter in which Louis Napoleon peremptorily demanded the resignation of the cabinet. Twice had Louis Napoleon sustained this cabinet when the assembly voted "no confidence"; the cabinet now had the confidence of the chamber but not of the president, and their resignations were in order. In the new cabinet that President Napoleon appointed, he became his own prime minister, and thus freed himself from the tutelage of the "elder statesmen"

WHEN Louis Napoleon returned to France in 1848, he had not a single friend prominent in French political life, and very few who were known in either the social or the business world. It was his name, and the tradition for which it stood, that gave him the election to the presidency. After he assumed office, he found himself surrounded by chiefs of the party of "moral order," elder statesmen who saw him as a stalking-horse for the re-establishment of the monarchy. In the elections of 1849, when it was necessary for one candidate to drop out of the race in this district or that to assure the victory of a conservative, it was almost inevitably a Bonapartist that had to step aside. To the despair of his real friends, Prince Louis fondly believed that he did not need a political party, even that a party might be a hindrance to him After his experience with the Barrot cabinet, Louis Napoleon slowly began to change his mind, and the party of the Élysée, or the president's party, began to grow in the chamber. There were a few obvious Bonapartist chiefs. Napoleon's half-brother, de Morny, experienced in business and society, shrewd in political sense, and inflexible in will, soon became a leader in the president's circle Persigny, the companion of his exile and the comrade of his earlier plots, was one of his closest advisers Rouher, an "ex-official candidate" of M. Guizot, and Baroche, a business man who saw in Napoleonic discipline the safety of the bourgeoisie, added stability and financial prestige to the president's plans. There were others, who, by reason of their debts, their convictions, or their ambitions, were willing to join the president's party so that they might share in his prosperity in case he achieved the throne of emperor.

The new ministry, however, was not largely drawn from this embryonic party of the Élysée. The prince-president took two steps forward and one step backward. The new cabinet represented minor chiefs of the men of "moral order" whose names would not outshine his own, and who, for one reason or another, were willing to replace Barrot's "elder statesmen." Louis Napoleon had no intention of locking horns with the legislative assembly just yet; indeed, during the first half of 1850 he made himself most agreeable to the majority group in general and to the Catholics in particular. The Falloux laws on education and the electoral laws of the thirty-first of May were peace offerings that he presented to the men of the right after the dismissal of his first cabinet.

The Falloux laws were the fruit of a decade or more of Catholic agitation The Catholics had resented the monopoly of the Université ever since 1815; during the reign of Louis Philippe they had found it possible to attack that monopoly in the name of liberty of instruction. It was not until 1850, however, that political alignments made it possible for them to do anything effective M Falloux, Louis Napoleon's minister of education, was a monarchist, but first of all he was a Catholic. There is good reason to believe that he was willing to give up his legitimist aspirations in return for relief for his Catholic friends. The laws that he proposed did not suppress the Université, but they considerably weakened its power. In the first place, the prefects were made responsible for the school teachers in their departments (January, 1850) and, secondly, to the religious orders was granted liberty of instruction in the primary and secondary state schools (March, 1850) The first law greatly increased the president's powers, the second entrenched the Catholics in the educational system of France. The question of education was settled for a generation, and Louis Napoleon, by allowing the Catholics to have their way, earned for himself the support of the Church. He had given to the churchmen relief that even the monarchy had been unwilling to grant

The first months of 1850 also saw the co-operation of the president and the chamber in antirepublican measures. It was forbidden to celebrate the anniversary of the February Revolution as a fête day, and the "trees of liberty," which had been planted so optimistically in 1848, were systematically cut down as "traffic hazards." These acts were typical of the trivial, tactless measures that clearly illustrated that the republic was anything but republican. Even the liberal republicans began to "see red"; those short-lived "trees of liberty" became symbols of the unhappy fate of liberty in the French nation. In March, 1850, there were by-elections in thirty constituencies, the lines were clearly drawn between the "reds" and the "whites," and, to the horror of the conservative majority in the chamber, two-thirds of the districts went "red." In April there was a by-election in Paris and Eugène Sue, a wealthy novelist who had been converted to socialism, was returned to the chamber. There was a flurry on the exchange, *rentes* fell, foreigners left Paris, and everyone assumed that June, 1850, would bring another uprising; June was the month of revolution and rebellion.

The party of "moral order" took counsel If Frenchmen insisted on voting "red," there was only one thing to do: the electoral law must be changed so that to the people who would vote "red" could be denied the right of suffrage. At first glance, there appeared to be nothing that could be done; a change in the Constitution would be legally impossible until 1851, and even then it would be practically impossible. The authors of that iron document, however, had been as careless in their phrasing as they had been in their thinking. Plainly, they intended to grant universal manhood suffrage, but while the Constitution forbade any residence qualification for deputies, it neglected to make that provision in the case of electors. It had been, clearly, the intention of the framers to dispense with all qualifications, but since that intention had not been expressly stated, the legislative assembly did not hesitate to impose a residence qualification. The law of May thirty-first required each voter to prove three years' residence before he could vote, and it accepted as proof the evidence of the tax collector. It was practically impossible for a nontaxpayer to establish the right to vote. This law automatically disenfranchised at least three of the ten million voters. Louis Napoleon himself, as a wag pointed out, could not have met the electoral requirement. When the men of the "moral order" rejoiced over the ingenuity of this law, which disenfranchised the "vile rabble," they could not foresee that it might be turned against them.

The Falloux laws and the electoral law of May thirty-first marked the last co-operation between the president and the assembly. During the next year, the conflict that had been latent in the Bonapartist inclusion in the party of "moral order" broke out with vigor, and ran its course to the *coup d'état* of December second, 1851.

IT WAS during the parliamentary vacations of 1850 that the political imbroglio inherent in the situation of "the republic without republicans" came to a head. Louis Napoleon's term of office was half over, and all shades of political opinion looked anxiously to 1852, when a new president could be expected. Political interest in the year 1852 was heightened by the fact that the legislative assembly would also be re-elected that year. It became common for men to speculate about the "crisis of 1852" Would France emerge as a social republic, a monarchy, or an empire? Few believed that the *status quo* could possibly be maintained

After the abortive revolts of January and June, 1849, republicans of all shades again could be found working together, but by 1850 their predicament was sorry indeed There had been talk of a rebellion in June, 1850, it did not occur, for the very obvious reason that Louis Napoleon would have crushed it without hesitation In 1849 he had shown a distinct unwillingness to give revolt a sporting chance The republicans in 1850 found their societies spied upon, their newspapers harried by the police and taxed out of existence, and their leaders in exile or prison. In 1850 their power was neutralized—but in 1852 Louis Napoleon would be out of the Élysée, and there surely would be confusion and disorder The republicans muttered ominously about their part in the coming crisis. But by pointing to the day when Louis Napoleon would become a private citizen as the day of social revolution, they made the prince-president appear as the very pillar of society, order, and good government.

The monarchists were hardly less helpful to the reputation of the president The old ministers of the July monarchy openly visited Louis Philippe in England, and on his death, General Changarnier had a regal requiem mass celebrated in his honor at the Tuileries Louis Philippe's unpopularity in France, however, did not end with his death, and even if his ministers still loved the old gentleman, many Frenchmen felt that he had got his just dues in 1848 The supporters of the Bourbons were even less discreet A delegation of them visited the grandson of Charles X—they called him Henry V—and invited him to reascend the throne of his ancestors. Henry V, with typical Bourbon stupidity, issued a circular dated August thirtieth, 1850, in which he instructed his followers to be sure that his return to France would in no way entail a recognition of popular sovereignty He would not compromise his "divine right" by an appeal to the will of the people. This document, indiscreetly published, severely discredited the legitimist cause Both Bourbon and Orléanist sympathizers further placed themselves in a bad light by hinting at the possibility of a monarchical *coup d'état.* Louis Napoleon, it seemed, was the defender of the poor against the monarchy, and the protector of the bourgeoisie against a social revolution.

But talk of revolution and *coups d'état* accustomed men's minds to the idea that the Republic was only a stage of transition, and the prince-president did not hesitate to use this notion to aid his cause. His ambition was not limited to a four-year term as president, he believed firmly that it was his destiny to re-establish the Empire. He utilized every possible occasion to show himself to the French people and to the army. During the cholera epidemic, when other men fled from the dread infection, he tirelessly visited hospitals; the opening of a new stretch of railroad or the laying of a cornerstone invariably saw the president in attendance. He reviewed troops, and rode through the streets of Paris, without undue precaution to safeguard his person; here was a man that was "not afraid to show himself." Indeed, that was just what Louis Napoleon wanted. For years France had not been able to see the nephew of Napoleon; now she must have an opportunity.

In the late summer and fall of 1850, the president planned a series of tours of France, to advertise himself and test his popularity. It was a hazardous thing to do, for if he were not well received, his prestige and his cause would suffer. The first tour was to be through "enemy country": Burgundy, Franche-Comté, and Alsace, where the republicans and socialists had many supporters. The trip was carefully planned. Officials were urged to encourage a welcome reception, friends went ahead to smooth the way, and every detail was worked out in advance. But it is nonsense to say that the people who welcomed the president were driven to do so by official pressure, for France was not yet under the control of an imperial dictatorship. Journalists went with the president to record his successes and his failures. Although even his friends would not assert that he was everywhere received cordially, both his friends and his foes were surprised at the enthusiasm that his presence provoked. The reporter for *The Times* of London wrote from Metz: "I have observed nearly the same thing here as in the other towns . where it was believed that an unfriendly population existed . . . he has been received coldly or hostilely for the first few hours or the first day, and afterwards with very kindly feeling." At Lyon, where disaster was predicted, the president "happened" to arrive on the Feast of the Assumption, which, by chance, was also the birthday of Napoleon I. The peasants had gathered in the cathedral city, about a thousand veterans of the Napoleonic wars were mustered in review, and the timid bourgeois hailed the prince as the preserver of order. If the republicans were hostile, their expressions were drowned out by the raucous battle cry of the old veterans: *"Vive Napoléon! Vive l'empereur!"* At Strasbourg, too, Louis was well received, contrary to the predictions of both his friends and enemies; while the trip from Alsace to Paris, in spite of torrential rains, afforded a continuous demonstration of his personal popularity. The peasants, and the inhabitants of the small towns, literally loaded him down with flowers and praise.

The trip through Normandy on his second tour was a joy to his friends. No socialist artisans or factory workers marred the blessings and approval that clergy, bourgeoisie, and peasants showered upon his head. The permanent committee of the legislative assembly and his foes in Paris read the newspapers with dismay. There was nothing unconstitutional about the trip, and the prince-president could not be blamed if the populace hailed him with *"Vive Napoléon! Vive l'empereur!"*

but it was distinctly unsatisfactory to Louis Napoleon's enemies. When the troops on review took up the same cry, the men who wished to restore the monarchy or to retain the Republic began to consider their future actions with greater care.

In his speeches, Napoleon was careful to pose as the champion of a stable society. "What the people acclaim in me," he said, "is the representative of order and a better future." The threats of a republican rebellion and a monarchist *coup d'état* made this man of order seem even more necessary. Gradually, a movement got under way to give him another four-year term. It was the clause in the Constitution forbidding the re-election of the president that made 1852 appear as the year of crisis. By allowing Louis Napoleon to run again, they could avoid the crisis. Before the assembly met in the fall, fifty-two of the eighty-five departmental councils had petitioned for a revision of the Constitution. When Napoleon hinted in a speech that he would not avoid responsibilities that France might impose upon him, the legislative assembly should have considered these petitions with greater care.

After the vacations, Louis Napoleon greeted the legislative assembly with the information that he would preserve order by use of the regular army if it should prove necessary, and he hinted that his orders would be obeyed as much because of his name as because of his office He then called the attention of the assembly to the problem of revising the Constitution so that he might serve a second term

The fat was in the fire. The Constitution allowed a minority to block any revision, and it was highly improbable that a sufficient majority could be mustered to alter the document. By 1850 the assembly was divided into three parties. The party of "moral order" was split wide open by the question of restoration; the out-and-out monarchists could hardly wait for the return of a king, and the Bonapartist party of the Élysée began to show a definite unwillingness to remain under the tutelage of the monarchists Since the republicans still retained their position on the left of the assembly, it was impossible for any one group to obtain a majority. In the discussion that followed the proposal for revising the Constitution, it soon became obvious that not only would the proposal be defeated, but also that a deadlock between the president and the legislative assembly would be inevitable.

In such circumstances, the control of the army became of vital importance. By virtue of his position, Louis Napoleon had command of the army, but the military official who held the rank of commander-in-chief was General Changarnier. Like most of the French generals, he had made a reputation in Africa and had returned to Paris to play politics. At first, Changarnier felt that Louis Napoleon was a fool for not making a *coup d'état* in January, 1849, but after the monarchists again became powerful in the chamber, he placed his hopes on a restoration. Changarnier apparently played with the idea of becoming a French General Monck when the hour of decision should come. The English General Monck played much the same rôle in the French monarchist thinking of 1848–51 that William and Mary and the "Glorious Revolution" had had in the thinking of 1830. A clash broke out, however, before the hour for the general's appearance as a General Monck arrived. At a review of the troops the infantry remained absolutely silent when it passed by the stand, but the cavalry broke out with cries, *"Vive Napoléon! Vive l'empereur!"* Louis Napoleon discovered that a subordinate general had ordered the infantry to remain quiet, and had the unfortunate man sent to the provinces. Changarnier attempted to save his subordinate, and on January third, 1851, spoke quite hostilely of the president before the legislative assembly. On January fifth, Louis Napoleon removed Changarnier from his post.

Fortunately for the president, Changarnier had not been very discreet. He had often spoken openly about the prince in a very disparaging tone, and in December, before a large gathering, he had discussed ways and means of imprisoning Louis Napoleon in Vincennes. When the "elder statesmen" fluttered to the Élysée to protest against the loss of their general, Louis asked Thiers: "Do you request me to retain as my commander-in-chief the man who boasted that he would drag me to Vincennes?" That practically ended the question. The legislative assembly could not even pass a vote censuring the president, because the republicans hated Changarnier as much as they hated Louis Napoleon.

Louis Napoleon installed in command of the Paris army divisions a man whom he could trust, and then turned to the problem of finding a satisfactory minister of war to manage his military plans. For some time before Changarnier's dismissal, Napoleon's friends had been grooming General Saint-Arnaud for the position He was younger than the political generals, and had an abiding contempt for assemblies as well as a deep distrust of the crowd He was known to be absolutely unscrupulous, deeply in debt, and something of a showman The only drawback was that he was unknown, and, unless something happened, would probably remain in Algeria as an obscure division commander. A military reputation, however, is often only a matter of a little printer's ink. A campaign against the natives was organized, and the Parisian press breathlessly followed the brilliant career of a new hero. By the time he was needed, General Saint-Arnaud, the sunburned darling of Paris, was ready to take his post as director of Louis Napoleon's army. After de Maupas was installed in the position of prefect of police, the stage was entirely set for the *coup d'état*.

The president, however, hesitated to push his advantage. During the spring and summer of 1851 he sought to prolong his power by legal means. But the legislative assembly was not able to pass an amendment to the Constitution, for the men in 1848 had done their work so well that revision was practically impossible. Along with the deadlock over the revision, other questions irritated the relations between the president and the assembly, and loose talk about a *coup d'état* became more and more common. It was hard to tell whether a coup by the monarchists in the assembly or by the president was more expected, but when several promised crises failed to materialize, the people grew skeptical of all stories.

THE president played his hand well. When it became obvious that the Constitution would not be revised, he made a bid for the support of the men who feared disorder as well as of those who saw the monarchy as an instrument of repression To the one he promised, "France will not perish in my hands", to the others he said that he could always be sure of the support of the assembly for repression, but whenever he "tried to do good, to ameliorate the condition of my people," then the assembly showed only "inertia and apathy" "If France recognizes that no one has the right to dispose of her future without her consent," shouted Napoleon, "France has only to say so; my energy and courage will not fail her." Although a minority in the assembly had blocked revision of the Constitution, seventy-nine out of eighty-five of the departmental councils voted a petition for revision. Was France asking the president to cut the knot?

Instead of repeating his tour of France, the president retired to the palace at St. Cloud for the parliamentary vacations in 1851. With a few of his intimate advisers he planned his campaign for the next few months. Some thought that he should launch the *coup d'état* at once; others that it must be postponed until the legislative assembly returned to Paris. The major bit of strategy decided upon was the proposal to repeal the May law regulating suffrage. When this measure was passed, it appeared to be a political blunder on the part of the president His strength obviously came from universal suffrage, and this law disenfranchised about three million voters. It had been aimed at the radical proletariat, but it equally affected the landless peasant population By espousing its removal from the statute books, Louis Napoleon could pose as a defender of the spirit of the Constitution and a champion of French democracy

The proposal met with strong opposition in the assembly. The men elected to defend the people's rights were playing into the hands of the prospective dictator. By opposing the removal of the May electoral law, the legislative assembly appeared to be conspiring to defeat the Constitution, and when the proposal was voted down by a majority of six votes, the assembly lost heavily in the sympathies of the people. It was so nicely calculated a method of earning disrepute that some historians have ventured to attribute to Louis Napoleon the chief rôle in obtaining the defeat of the measure. Such a thesis, however attractive, is not tenable; but there is no doubt that the assembly's refusal to reconsider the electoral law greatly aided the prince-president's cause.

During the fall of 1851, rumors of *coups d'état,* rebellions, and counterrebellions ran rampant in Paris and in the provinces. Although Louis Napoleon tried to calm the fears and repudiate the tales, the last act of the republic was about to be played. Between 1850 and 1851 the party of the Élysée had made many converts; the bourgeoisie, which had rallied to the party of "moral order" after June, 1848, did not find it hard to move into the camp of the imperialists Throughout France there were men who gladly lined up with the prince when it appeared that he had a good chance to establish the Empire. Lawyers, hard put to keep out of debt; business men, menaced by socialist or republican agitation; clergymen, who saw the president as the protector of the Holy Father and the patron of Catholic education; soldiers, whose expenditures outran their income and who hated the conservative, bourgeois foreign policy; a motley crew of adventurers, who sought place and preference—these were the men who, for one reason or another, were willing to support the most amazing political adventurer of his age. There was a "red scare," especially prepared to convince the doubters that society ought to be saved, and the president and his friends made their final plans

The orders that ended the Republic of 1848 were issued late in the evening of December first, 1851. Nothing unusual could be detected The president's Monday evening reception was in progress and well attended; de Morny had been conspicuously present at the Opéra Comique; and Paris was quiet and unsuspecting. At about eleven o'clock, de Maupas, Saint-Arnaud, de Morny, and Persigny joined Louis Napoleon in the president's study, money and orders were passed out, and within a few hours the *coup d'état* was a *fait accompli.* Proclamations were printed in the dead of night behind locked and guarded doors, the police arrested politicians who might have organized resistance before they had time for breakfast, Paris was systematically plastered with manifestoes, and troops of the regular army took up strategic positions in the city. The French capital awoke on the second of December to find that the long advertised *coup d'état* had taken place, and de Morny, newly installed in the ministry of interior, informed the provinces of the joy of Paris over the news.

The proclamations from the prince's own pen were masterfully written There was a decree dissolving the "reactionary" assembly which had "conspired to violate the spirit of the Constitution and blocked the fulfillment of the desires of France." The May laws were repealed, and, it seemed, the Republic was saved from a monarchical plot Within two weeks, the people would be given the right to approve or disapprove, in an open election, the president's action. This decree was followed by proclamation to the army and to the people of France. The prince associated the army with the glory of the name Napoleon, and reminded it of the duty to preserve order and peace. To the people, he denounced the intriguing assembly, which only wished to establish a monarchy, and asked France to judge between himself and the politicians who had deprived the nation of its rights The manifesto ended by proposing a new constitution, closely modeled upon the Consulate, which France could accept or reject in the elections which were to take place

The plans were so well laid that resistance was difficult, for this was no half-organized affair like the ordinances of

July, 1830 The workers, who were the first to read the proclamations, received the news without fully realizing its import. Their first response was, "Now we can vote again," or "Bravo, he fooled the assembly" The proletariat had little love for the delegates who received twenty-five francs a day for their work for the state, and who had deprived them of their right to vote. Furthermore, the monarchical tinge of the majority had aroused their suspicions and fears. The petty bourgeoisie, who were the next to awake to read the news, saw beneath the verbiage the iron hand of the dictator, but they were ready to be consoled by the thought that a dictatorship might aid business. It was the wealthy, the last to get out of bed, who gritted their teeth, but they had no intention of fighting the regular army, and since the drums of the National Guard had been thoughtfully broken in, they could not summon the citizen army to fight their battles. When the prince, in a general's uniform, rode through the city on the morning of the coup, it appeared that Paris was ready to accept his action.

There was a little opposition The delegates to the legislative assembly who had not been honored by an early morning arrest painfully tried to legislate the *coup d'état* out of existence, but the bayonets of the army were unmoved by their oratory After their arrest, when a number of the delegates refused to allow themselves to be set at liberty, they were loaded into vans, under pretext that they were to be moved to Vincennes, taken out into the country, and forced to walk home—an action that wounded dignity more than person. In the working-class district a few deputies tried to organize a rebellion Although the workers were apparently not interested, one of the deputies, Baudin, succeeded in getting himself killed under circumstances that were to make him a hero fifteen years later. It was not until late in the week that any real opposition developed. On Thursday, to save the troops from fatigue, they were recalled into the barracks, and the streets were left unguarded. The republicans believed the vague rumors that the provinces were in revolt and the *coup d'état* about to be repulsed. They therefore organized barricades and prepared to resist. The massacre that followed was as much the result of nervousness in the ranks of the army as of opposition from behind the barricades, but it served the purpose of warning the bourgeoisie against the "reds," and of converting many of the doubters in the party of "moral order" to the belief that Napoleon's solution for the problem of government was the correct one. The bloodshed, however, stained Napoleon's record, and earned for him the hatred of a section of the proletariat in Paris.

After ending the political existence of the Second French Republic, Louis Napoleon stood convicted of breaking his oath as president, of trampling on the aspirations of republican and monarchist politicians, and of staining the streets of Paris with blood Nevertheless, France, by and large, accepted him as her leader. There was some scattered opposition in the provinces, but a whiff of gun-smoke from the regular troops quickly restored calm The *coup d'état* was probably a political necessity, and the efficiency with which it was executed seemed to justify Napoleon's boast that he was the man "to end the era of revolutions"

CHAPTER VIII

THE EMPIRE, AN AUTHORITATIVE RÉGIME

THE revolutions of 1848 were apparently predestined to failure. They started with great promises and high hopes, but they were directed by men who proved themselves quite unable to cope with the political forces of the age. The result was reaction. Louis Napoleon's *coup d'état* in France was in complete harmony with the general trend in Europe; the aspirations of German, Hungarian, and Italian revolutionaries had already been trampled under by military or police régimes when the French army broke up the assembly in Paris. The great difficulty in France had been that the victors of February had only one thing in common—their hostility to Guizot's government After Louis Philippe was gone, the victors did not know how to compromise their programs, and when the radicals asserted that "property is theft" and that "the state owes every man a living," the bourgeoisie and the peasants saw that the revolution could go too far. The party of "moral order," and, finally, the Empire, resulted inevitably from the concatenation of circumstances that produced the June Days, the Constitution of 1848, and Louis Napoleon Bonaparte

The prince-president posed as the savior of society. His position was greatly strengthened by the uprisings that occurred in Paris and in the provinces on the morrow of the *coup d'état* If the "reds" were willing to fight against the odds that were offered to them in December, 1851, there could be no doubt that the president had protected France from the horrors of civil strife that would have undoubtedly followed the threatened "crisis of 1852." Some of the socialist and republican uprisings undoubtedly were *bona fide* attempts to prevent the establishment of the Napoleonic dictatorship, but others were the creation of the army and the imperially minded functionaries who wished to convince France that "society" was really in danger. Émile Zola's brutal line, "My father saved the town, have you seen the corpses?" is a classic The corpses were there, but Zola's reader knows that they were the bodies of duped workers ruthlessly murdered to convince the wealthy that prompt action had saved life and property. Real or trumped-up, the uprisings served their grim purpose; society was duly "saved," and the dictatorship assured.

Louis Napoleon pretended, however, that no definite steps would be taken until the nation had had an opportunity to ratify his action by a plebiscite; on the morning of the coup he had promised to allow France to judge between himself and the assembly When the plebiscite was held, the people were asked to vote "yes" or "no" to the proposition· "The French people wish to maintain the authority of Louis Napoleon Bonaparte, and delegate to him the necessary powers to make a constitution along the lines proposed by his proclamation of December second." Over seven million votes were cast for the proposition, and only six hundred and forty thousand against it. Doubting politicians "saw the light," and joined the imperial cause. There is good reason to believe that a majority of the people really wished to see an affirmative vote in the plebiscite. It is true that the press was rigidly under control, and that the socialists and republicans were subjected to the closest police surveillance, but the best observers are probably correct in pointing out that the mass of the peasantry and the bourgeoisie were ready to accept the dictatorship of Louis Napoleon as a shield against radical political action. Furthermore, as the proposition was stated, the electors were given the choice between the known of the prince's dictatorship, and the unknown of possible political anarchy; it is hard to vote for a leap in the dark. Louis Napoleon saw, in the overwhelming approval of his dictatorship, popular absolution for his broken oath to defend the Republic

Buttressed with this tremendous popular support, Louis Napoleon assigned the problem of making a constitution to a handful of his legal-minded friends, and turned himself to the task of governing France. In rapid succession, he struck down the chief centers of resistance to his dictatorship; since he was saving society from the "reds," the republicans and socialists suffered most from his repression, but other potential enemies of his régime were not overlooked. In dealing with the "radicals," all moderation was put aside, and the whole machinery of the state was mobilized to crush "revolutionary activity." By decree the prince-president delegated to himself the right to exile anyone who belonged to secret societies or engaged in subversive activity. To insure prompt action, he created new courts, the so-called "mixed tribunals," to purge the land of its enemies. A lawyer, a general, and a prefect sat in each department to administer the law; their sessions were secret, and their decisions were beyond appeal. Over twenty-six thousand persons were arrested; more than fifteen thousand of them were exiled to foreign lands, or to Algeria, or even to French Guiana; more than five thousand were placed under police surveillance; and only about six thousand were fully acquitted. The fact that the Second Republic had been as ruthless after the June Days, and that the Third Republic was to be even more brutal after the Commune of 1871, can hardly be presented as justification for the unnecessary severity of these measures. In justice to Louis Napoleon, it should be added that, probably remembering his own days of prison and exile, he showed great clemency after 1852, and in 1859 granted an unconditional plenary amnesty to all political offenders.

The severity of the "mixed tribunals" was only one measure of repression. A whole series of decrees closely regulated the rights of press and assembly, even to the point of licensing cafés and wineshops that might become centers for political discussion. The press law was similar to the more repressive measures taken by previous régimes, except that it contained a unique feature whereby a newspaper was permitted two offenses before the government would suppress it. This practice of allowing two "bites" introduced a note of humor that lightened an otherwise serious situation. Most of the press was silenced, but several clever editors throve on the system The journalist had to learn to write so that his real opinions appeared between the lines, or with such fine irony and subtlety that the onus of discovering malice in his sentences must fall upon the government Some of the papers played a jolly game with the censor, after one "notice" they would behave for a while, so that the "bite" would be excused. They would apologize profusely for "mistakes," and print news in juxtaposition so that only the blind could fail to see the inference After 1859, it was not uncommon for liberal editors to discuss liberty in Italy or the United States of America in such a way that no one would miss their opinion about French internal affairs. But the censorship effectively ended anything closely resembling a political debate; it was just a game to see how big a "bite" the journalist could take before his knuckles were rapped.

While the republicans and socialists were suffering under the lash of the president, the house of Orléans received a blow from the same whip. In 1830, Louis Philippe had evaded the rule that his property should fall to the crown when he became king, by giving it over to his son Louis Napoleon denounced this arrangement, and confiscated the lands and the property which, he declared, rightly belonged to the state. This confiscation, too, was a measure of dubious legality which was severely criticized by the friends of the late monarch. But Louis Napoleon, with unnecessary brutality, insisted that the Orléans family could live very comfortably on the hundred million francs which still remained in its possession. This "first flight of the eagle" caused a little flurry among the advisers of the prince: several of them resigned, others looked thoughtfully down their noses at the precedent which had been established. But neither doubts nor resignations could make Louis Napoleon reconsider his action.

With the loot which this punitive expedition against the house of Orléans supplied him, the president hoped to make many converts to his cause. The money was used to endow workingmen's mutual-benefit societies, burial associations, orphanages, and asylums. Part of it went toward the improvement of slum areas, part to establish the Crédit Foncier land-bank societies to provide money for peasant and bourgeois properties, and part to provide public baths, to reorganize pawnshops, and to establish a primitive sort of employment bureau. By making a large number of people his accomplices in the raid on Louis Philippe's fortune, the president hoped to create vested interests that would not welcome a return of the Orléans kings to the French throne. At the same time he was able to urge the workers to believe that Bonapartism would give them what the socialists had only promised.

Louis Napoleon promised France that his *coup d'état* would end the era of revolution. While he crushed the republicans and socialists, he reformed the National Guard out of existence. That bourgeois army was the only organization that possessed the arms necessary to equip a revolt, and the prince-president did not make the mistake that Charles X had lived to regret in 1830. The National Guard, he insisted, was incompatible with the principle of equality, since it allowed one section of the population to organize an army to which the rest of the people could not afford to belong. The Guard, Louis Napoleon assured France, had served its purpose in the past, but under the new régime it was unnecessary. It was disbanded and disarmed. France was assured that the regular army was adequate to defend her interests and to keep order in the country. This measure was in accord with other decrees that banned revolutionary songs and slogans, which might arouse passions and lead to unfortunate conflicts in the streets. The pattern of dictatorship does not vary much, whatever the time or the society.

The unlimited power that he had seized gave the prince-president an opportunity to carry out many programs that his late ministers had passed over as impossible Impossible they may have been with a wrangling assembly to consider them, but now the president could accomplish with a stroke of the pen what weeks of debates had failed to do. During the winter of 1851–1852, Frenchmen must have read their newspapers much as Americans did during the early months of the administration of Franklin D Roosevelt, every day brought a new proposal or a new decree. Louis Napoleon's imagination embraced the entire matrix of French society By decree, the railroad network, which fifteen years of debate had failed to complete, was regulated Canals, tramways, telegraph lines, roads, and harbors were poured from the dictator's lap to the gaze of an astonished France Pure-food laws, regulation of Sunday labor, and slum sanitation followed in rapid succession. The national debt was converted from 5 to 4½ per cent, and very few took advantage of the proffered option of redemption at par, since the prince was careful to delay his reform until there had been a general rise of values on the Bourse. Frenchmen must have rubbed their heads in wonder; here was a man who was doing things.

Professor Simpson insists that the president took "a childish delight" in playing "the rôle of Aladdin," and that "he could not resist a temporary excursion to the part of Robin Hood" Both rôles made his orthodox bourgeois advisers uneasy Had society been saved from socialism by a mad socialist? Advisers remonstrated, friends urged caution, and his enemies shook their heads. "The president," wrote one man, "has the perverse ingenuity of a madman and the self-confidence of a fatalist. He says he wants eighty millions to fill up the deficit, and that the richer classes are alone to pay them. He speaks about income taxes, progressive taxation . . ." The president's entourage tried to convince him of the "wicked folly" of his ways, and some of his friends temporarily left the Élysée. But Louis Napoleon had faith in his star, which had led him from obscurity to the pinnacle of power Why should he doubt its guidance once he had achieved his ambition?

On January fourteenth, 1852, Rouher and his co-workers finished their labors of constitution making The new document was a thing of beauty in the simplicity of its organization The president, elected for a ten-year term, was, in effect, all-powerful; the whole machine of government revolved around his office The ministers were responsible to him; the senators were appointed by him; the members of the legislative body swore fealty to him The senate held its sessions in secret, and its function was limited to interpreting the Constitution. The legislative body could reject any measure, but it could not ask questions, nor, for all practical purposes, amend legislation The fact that the president and the legislative body were both elected by universal manhood suffrage gave the Constitution an air of democracy more apparent than real. Louis Napoleon aptly remarked. "Indeed, I wish to be baptized with the water of universal suffrage, but I do not intend to live with my feet in the water."

The Constitution, however, had possibilities of developing a democratic government. Unlike the monarchical charters, this constitution began as an authoritarian system and finally produced a liberal régime. Louis Napoleon was not altogether hypocritical when he exclaimed, at the first joint meeting of the senate and the legislative body: "What do I see before me? Two chambers, one elected under the most liberal electoral law in the world, and the other—appointed by me, it is true—but independent because its members are irremovable." It is true that the senators could be independent; the president could neither swamp their chamber with new appointments, nor could he remove the men whom he had clothed with the toga. But the president did regulate their salaries; and in 1851 the senators were provided with a handsome income that few men would care to endanger. The legislative body, it is true, was elected on the broadest suffrage known to mid-century Europe, but through a system of official candidates and a censored press, the president could and did assure himself that its members would be loyal and docile followers Before the last act of the Empire was played, the democracy inherent in the Constitution had been allowed to replace the dictatorship, but in 1852 the liberal parliamentary Empire was still seventeen years away.

By the Constitution of 1852 France remained a Republic, but it acquired no particularly alert intelligence to guess that the Empire was not far away. The remaining liberty trees of 1848 were hurriedly dug up, the inscriptions, *"Liberté, Egalité, Fraternité,"* were removed from public buildings, and it became a crime to celebrate the anniversaries of the February Revolution. In the cathedral of Nôtre Dame the prayer was no longer for the president of the Republic, but *Domine salvum fac Ludovicum Napoleonem;* in the Théâtre Français, the cipher "R. F." on the state box gave way to the monogram "L. N" The civil code again became the Code Napoléon, the imperial eagles again were mounted on the military standards, and the inscription, *"République Française,"* disappeared from the tricolor Although Louis Napoleon announced to the chambers that he would "preserve the Republic" against violence, observers noted the significant fact that the portraits of the late emperor were being labeled Napoleon I. The Republic remained in name, but the Empire was already clamoring to be proclaimed.

Louis Napoleon hesitated to take the step, several auspicious occasions were passed up without any change in his title. In September, he made another tour of France, this time the way was smoothed out by loyal prefects and a disciplined populace. Everywhere the president was greeted with acclaim. It was at the end of his tour, in Bordeaux, that the prince made up his mind, and in his speech undertook to allay the fears that troubled many of the upper bourgeoisie "There are some," he said, "who say, 'The Empire, that means war', but I tell you, 'The Empire, that means peace.'" *"L'Empire, c'est la paix"*—those were brave and probably sincere words in the fall of 1852, but they sound hollow in the light of the events that were to come. The prince continued. "We have immense waste territories to cultivate, roads to open, harbors to deepen, canals to complete, rivers to render navigable, railroads to link into one. Facing France over against Marseille we have a vast dominion to assimilate to France . . . Everywhere we have ruins to raise again, false gods to trample under foot, truths to make triumphant. That is how I interpret the Empire, if indeed the Empire is to be restored. Such are the conqu[illegible] contemplate."

A week later the senate hurriedly took counsel and offered *a senatus consultum* for the ratification of the people of France. The plebiscite that followed gave seven million eight hundred thousand votes for the Empire and only a quarter of a million against it; it was a more striking victory than the plebiscite that followed the *coup d'état*. On the second of December, 1852, the anniversary of the coup, the battle of Austerlitz, and the coronation of Napoleon I, Louis Napoleon was proclaimed emperor of the French. He assumed the title Napoleon III, but assured France and the world that he recognized the governments that had followed the brief reign of Napoleon II. A third dynasty now occupied the throne that Czar Alexander and Metternich had found so vacant in 1814.

The proclamation of the Empire did not involve any considerable changes in the Constitution of 1852; it had been framed with the Empire in mind. There were, however, important changes in Louis Napoleon's mode of living. As president his income had been insufficient to care for his expenses, as emperor he commanded a civil list that was worthy of his position. The Tuileries again saw the regal splendor that only a military household could flaunt before the world—gold braid, bizarre uniforms, liveried pages and flunkies, recalled the days of the great Napoleon. After the *coup d'état* the president had punished his enemies; after the restoration of the Empire the emperor rewarded his friends. Saint-Arnaud became a marshal with 300,000 francs in yearly income; the others who had aided in the *coup d'état* were richly rewarded, each according to his service and his abilities, so that none should have reason to regret past actions. As his fortunes rose, Louis Napoleon's relatives, most of whom had been of no assistance to him in his struggle for power, swarmed into Paris to claim the bounty due to the family of Bonaparte Although the will of Napoleon I had excluded them all, except the old King of Westphalia and his son, Prince Jerome Napoleon, the new emperor was generous in his grants to these less enterprising relatives. In those first days, the court needed all the prestige that it could muster, for Europe regarded the new Empire as distinctly *parvenu*.

Louis Napoleon's most urgent need was for a wife who could provide him with an heir. For a moment he had toyed with the idea of adopting the grandson of Charles X; but since such a procedure was absolutely impossible, Prince Jerome Napoleon was recognized as the successor to the throne. That young man, the only Bonaparte who looked like the late emperor, was an outspoken republican, but he never allowed his convictions to interfere with his expectations At best this recognition was only a stopgap measure. If Louis Napoleon's Empire were to have any semblance of permanence, he must marry and have a son In the years of his exile, the prince had cannily refrained from any legal alliances that might jeopardize his destiny; the English woman, Miss Howard, whose presence in the Élysée had caused some gossip, retired to the imperial peerage, and Louis Napoleon began his search for an empress.

It proved more difficult to find a suitable wife than it had been to clear out the recalcitrant assembly Strong-arm methods might win Paris, but the hand of a royal princess required other tactics. The snobbish society of the reigning families was reluctant to give one of its daughters to a Napoleonic usurper, his throne was still shiny and unscratched, and its newness did not argue permanence. The polite inquiries that the emperor's representatives made in London and in the Germanies were coldly rebuffed This was hard on French pride, and difficult for the embarrassed suitor. A little patience probably would have yielded the desired results. After all, the vacant throne for a princess was in Paris, and even if it was new, it was better than most of the tawdry chairs in central Europe. But Louis Napoleon was forty-five years old, and he felt that he could not wait until the crowned heads decided that he was worthy of a royal princess He needed an heir, and the heir ought to make his début as soon as possible.

During the fall of 1852, he began to pay marked attention to a young Spanish noblewoman who had frequented his presidential court. Gossips had it that Mlle. Eugénie de Montijo would soon take the place of Miss Howard Events proved otherwise, for Eugénie became the empress of the French, not the emperor's mistress Few of his advisers approved the emperor's decision, but Louis Napoleon never asked for their counsel. To his ministers and to the people he announced that his marriage was a love match which must bring happiness both to himself and the nation. Mlle Eugénie de Montijo had beauty and charm—virtues scarce enough among royalty—but her pedigree did not bring prestige to the French throne. Ingenious genealogical researchers discovered an illustrious family tree, but skeptics knew that commoners had contributed to the empress's inheritance. Louis Napoleon forced his fellow sovereigns to accept her as an equal, and she provided the Empire with a male heir. But France never learned to love her, in spite of her beauty and charm

By the spring of 1853, the actors of the Empire had taken their places. The men of the *coup d'état*—Morny, Saint-Arnaud, Persigny, Magnan, and others—were firmly ensconced in positions of power, and the show of the Empire was ready to begin. France looked expectantly to her new rulers; the bourgeoisie and peasants hoped for peace and prosperity, the laborers for relief from the economic crisis, and churchmen for favors for their church. It was ominous that the rulers were, almost to a man, "new men," but there were many who hoped that the "new men" would lead the country out of its troubles.

THE rulers of Europe received the news of the *coup d'état* of 1851 with mixed feelings; it was a relief to know that the reaction had finally and definitely reached Paris, but it was annoying to see the nephew of Napoleon I in control of the government of France The king of Sardinia, who was looking for an ally against Austria, alone showed any cordiality in his recognition of the *fait accompli,* the other crowned heads of Europe would have preferred to see a more legitimate sovereign on the throne in Paris. When it became obvious that the Empire probably would be re-established, the four powers that had defeated and exiled Napoleon I hurriedly took counsel. Since none of them felt that it would be practicable to intervene, they contented themselves with giving Prince Louis Napoleon advice against aspiring to higher honors than those of dictator-president Louis Napoleon, ignoring this sage advice, hastened to assure Europe in his speech at Bordeaux, *"L'Empire, c'est la paix,"* and began his inquiries about a bride who might present France with an heir.

After the Empire was re-established by a plebiscite, the states of Europe were asked to accord their recognition The title Napoleon III caused the powers some embarrassment, but, in the end, all Europe, with the exception of Russia, regularly recognized Napoleon III as emperor of the French. Czar Nicholas' reactions were interesting. He had approved the military *coup d'état* as a proper measure in the general European reaction, but he could not approve the open recognition, in the plebiscites, of the democratic principle of popular sovereignty. He ended by swallowing everything but the title "My Good Brother" which was usual in letters between sovereigns; in his letter of recognition he referred to Louis Napoleon as "My Good Friend" Several of Napoleon's ministers wished to refuse to accept this slight, but Louis Napoleon averted a crisis, and pretended to thank Nicholas. He is reported to have said, "One endures one's brothers, and one chooses one's friends" The studied insult, however, rankled, and in time the emperor of the French repaid it with stronger measures than mere words

This conflict with Russia over recognition was much deeper than it appeared on the surface. Louis Napoleon, the nephew of the man whom the powers had exiled to Saint Helena, represented the exact antithesis of Czar Nicholas, the defender of the *status quo.* Czar Nicholas was the only ruler on the continent whose position had not been altered by the revolutions of 1848, he was the uncompromising foe of all the "isms" that stood for revolution and change, and his armies were the chief prop of the territorial settlement that had been created in 1815. It was the Russia of Czar Nicholas that had ruthlessly crushed the aspirations of Hungarian nationalism, and squelched the king of Prussia's attempt to unify north Germany. In 1851, Russia was the undisputed policeman of central Europe, and her czar was the very embodiment of the reaction. His position was such that when one spoke of "the emperor" it always referred to the czar of all the Russias, and only conservatives used his name without bitterness in their voices.

Louis Napoleon, on the other hand, was an enemy of the Treaty of Vienna, an exponent of popular sovereignty, and a friend of the doctrine of nationalism. The treaties of 1815 had banned his family forever from the throne of France, and had drawn the boundaries of Europe quite differently from those in the maps made by Napoleon I. As a result of these treaties, France, isolated and suspected, had been forced to eat humble pie in European affairs for over three decades. Furthermore, the new emperor of the French was an avowed advocate of the doctrine of nationalism and national self-determination; this doctrine, opposed to that of legitimacy, was a convenient weapon against the Treaty of Vienna, and at the same time appealed to his mystic philosophy His career, both before and after December second, 1852, gives him a secure place, along with Fichte, Mazzini, Bismarck, Wilson, and Hitler in the calendar of the saints of nationalism. Although liberty was a *rara avis* both in Paris and in St. Petersburg, the men who proscribed liberty from their realms stood for diametrically opposing forces in European high politics

It was probably no accident that Louis Napoleon's France and Czar Nicholas' Russia ran afoul of each other, and it was probably even less of an accident that the Near East should have become the theater of their conflict At first glance, the difficulty in the Near East seems to have arisen from a squabble between the Greek Orthodox and the Roman Catholic clergy over the use of the Holy Places in Jerusalem, but a closer examination shows that the whole problem of the Ottoman Empire, a problem that the Congress of Vienna had been unable to attack, was involved in the question that provided Europe with its first real war after 1815 Ever since Francis I had made an alliance with the Turks in 1536, and especially after the grand capitulations of 1740, France had played the rôle of protector of the Christians in the Ottoman Empire. In the latter half of the eighteenth century and the beginning of the nineteenth, Russia began to insist upon her prerogative as protector of the Greek Orthodox Christians, and, while France was engaged in the Napoleonic wars and weakened in the post-Vienna world, the Russians had obtained favors for their protégés at the expense of the Latin Church. As president, Louis Napoleon tried to win a little favor with the Catholics by reasserting France's position as guardian of the Roman Church's rights in the Holy Lands. The sultan agreed with the French remonstrances, and the Latin monks received a firman that extended their privileges at the expense of the Greeks.

At this juncture, Russia intervened to demand "justice" for the Greek monks. The unfortunate sultan found himself once more in the center of a European conflict. Firman followed firman; neither side was satisfied. Then the czar decided that the time was ripe to open the broader questions that existed between his government and Turkey, to further Russia's avowed aim in the Near East—the eventual control of Constantinople and the Straits On March first, 1853, Prince Menchikoff, an admiral and the aide-de-camp of the czar, appeared in Constantinople, bearing demands and threats The vague text of the document that he asked the sultan to sign would have given Russia the right to intervene in Turkish affairs at almost any time that she might wish to do so Menchikoff's mission pushed the question of the Holy Places into the background, and brought both England and Austria into the discussion. The powers were hardly disposed to sit back and allow Russia the privilege of settling the Near Eastern question by herself.

The British ambassador at Constantinople, Stratford de Redcliffe, a remarkable man, whom the czar had rejected as British ambassador to St. Petersburg as *persona non grata,* skillfully maneuvered the situation to a point where Menchikoff found every avenue to success blocked. In high dudgeon, the Russian mission returned home, and on May thirty-first, 1853, the czar dispatched an ultimatum to Turkey, with the threat of occupying the Danubian principalities. During these events, the French government had stepped aside to allow the English to defend the sultan. Napoleon's ministers advised against any measure that might endanger the peace, but he decided to send the French navy to the Near East, with instructions to second the British. When the Turks did not give a satisfactory answer to his ultimatum, the czar ordered his troops to occupy the provinces of Moldavia and Wallachia. The fat was in the fire, and none of the statesmen of the day wished to be burned in the act of pulling it out. Czar Nicholas did not want a war, but he could not back down, because his prestige was involved. Prince Albert well expressed the British dilemma: "We cannot remain spectators," he said; "we cannot see Turkey destroyed, but, if we give Turkey aid, it means European war." The emperor of the French knew that a war would mean that his army would have to do most of the fighting, this would be unfortunate, but the Roman Catholics felt that war would be less of an evil than Russian and Greek Orthodox control of the Holy Lands Austria's dilemma was even more serious, she owed Russia a debt of gratitude for Czar Nicholas' assistance in the Hungarian revolution, but Russia was potentially Austria's most dangerous enemy, especially in the Near East

The powers temporized In Vienna, the ambassadors frantically sought a compromise that would resolve Russian and Turkish interests to the satisfaction of Europe, but Stratford de Redcliffe managed to advise the sultan so that the compromise was unacceptable to Russia Six months went by, and Russia found herself maneuvered into an isolated position Finally, the sultan demanded that the czar's army evacuate the Danube area, and, when Russia refused, Turkey declared war. Again England and France sought to temporize, but they were almost committed to the defense of Turkey In November, the Russian Black Sea fleet destroyed a Turkish transport squadron; martial spirit ran high in England and France, and willy-nilly they drifted toward a war. In February, the czar refused to take notice of an Anglo-French ultimatum; and in March, England and France declared war on Russia. Napoleon III announced to his subjects that this was a war of defense, but it is significant that he had already started to dream about a new map of Europe

The war itself was a stupid affair; it even proved difficult to find a place to hold it Almost pure chance determined that the Crimea should be the goal of the Anglo-French expedition. The editors of *The Times* of London discovered that there was a town named Sebastopol in the Crimea, and assumed that it must be an important Russian harbor. *The Times'* pontifical announcement that the capture of Sebastopol "is an essential condition to permanent peace" decided the site for the war, and by the time the Anglo-French expedition got around to storming Sebastopol, the Russians had fortified it so that a 350-day siege was necessary to capture the city. The military problems in the Crimea were interesting to the authentic as well as the armchair strategists of the day, but there was an air of unreality about the whole campaign. The Crimea was far from any vital area of any of the powers; had the czar allowed the allies to take it without a struggle, it would hardly have crippled the Russian Empire. It almost seems as if the belligerents deliberately chose this out-of-the-way place for fighting their little war so that no real interests would be molested. Indeed, there was no good place for fighting as long as the Germanies refused to allow their country to reassume its traditional rôle as the battlefield of Europe

The stupidity of the war was further illustrated by the fact that typhus fever, cholera, and other epidemic diseases proved far more destructive of human life than the powder and lead that the contenders so laboriously transported to the Crimean peninsula. Individuals showed great bravery under fire, the French Catholic nuns and Florence Nightingale and her sisters earned for themselves a well-deserved niche in the hall of fame, but the whole affair offered very little "glory" to the flags of the contenders. The heroism of the soldiers and nurses was overshadowed by the inefficient and blundering conduct of the war For almost two years, men faced each other in the Crimea before it was possible to write a treaty of peace.

No sooner was war declared than the belligerents began to urge neutrals to join them to save civilization and take care of any interests that might be about. Russia's potential allies in the Balkans feared to move because of the presence of the Anglo-French navy; Sweden excused herself from an adventure in the north that probably would not greatly benefit her own interests The sentiment in the Germanies was mixed The Austrians were anxious to humiliate Russia and play an important rôle in the Near East, as well as to secure the friendship of France and England in case the Italian question should boil over again. Prussia, on the other hand, coolly pointed out that while the Near Eastern question held little or no interest for the German Confederation, Russia's friendship was very important to the safety of North Germany. The result was a declaration of neutrality All Austria could do was to obtain the evacuation of the Danube by Russia, and to assure the English and French of her sympathy for their cause Austria's position was difficult, her statesmen feared Russia's influence in the Balkans, and hated Russia for the assistance that they had been forced to beg in 1849 In the summer of 1855, when Piedmont-Sardinia joined the western powers with the obvious intention of securing their friendship against the day when the Italian question would come up again, Austria's predicament became sorry indeed Finally, the Austrians threatened to intervene in the war unless Russia would be willing to go to a peace conference. This diplomatic intervention, plus the fall of Sebastopol and the death of Czar Nicholas I, decided the issue. Russia sued for peace.

The Crimean War cost France heavily. Her soldiers bore the brunt of the fighting, and her treasury paid a large share of the bill The only significant gain to France was a tremendous rise in the prestige of her armies and her emperor In 1852, Louis Napoleon had been considered a *parvenu,* an adventurer who had elbowed his way to the French throne; his request for a bride had been rebuffed, and his court had been boycotted by the ruling families of Europe The Crimean War made him the ally of England, Austria, and Sardinia; members of the proud and ancient families of Hanover, Saxe-Coburg-Gotha, Savoy, and Hapsburg visited his capital, and accepted him and his *parvenue* empress as equals. Victoria and Albert became intimate in his household, and even visited the tomb of his uncle in the Invalides The haughty Romanov czar, who had refused him the title of brother, had been humbled by his arms, and Russia was forced to send a representative to Paris to negotiate a treaty that would become the new law for Europe. France paid in blood and in gold; Napoleon obtained prestige and recognition. In 1856, when one spoke of "the emperor," he meant the emperor of the French

The Congress of Paris of 1856 was a great personal triumph for Napoleon It was the most important European meeting since the Congress of Vienna, which had banned the Bonapartes from Europe, and it was held in the capital of the nephew of Napoleon I. Furthermore, it coincided with the first Parisian exposition and the birth of Napoleon's son and heir. The gold braid of the diplomats lent color and prestige to the court of the new emperor of the French, and France, holding the undisputed hegemony of the continent, basked in the glamour of the occasion. But the Treaty of Paris seems meager indeed when one considers the sacrifices which had been necessary to bring Russia to terms. The Black Sea was neutralized, the Danubian principalities were moved another step toward their eventual consolidation into the kingdom of Rumania, and the Danube was placed under an international commission. The powers guaranteed the integrity of the Ottoman Empire, and accepted the sultan's decree guaranteeing to the Christians equality with his non-Christian subjects The congress also laid down a series of international laws regulating maritime warfare

The treaty did not satisfy the Italian or Polish ambitions which Louis Napoleon had considered near to his heart; nor did it make any formal alterations in the Treaty of Vienna. The British insisted that the clause in the Vienna treaty that forbade a member of the family of Napoleon to occupy the throne of France was a dead letter, and that any attempt to alter the document of 1815 would be decidedly unwise. The canny French bourgeoisie that read this treaty could hardly have escaped the opinion that their money and their sons had been squandered to bring prestige to their emperor, but this first flight of the eagle came when opposition to the régime would have been impossible. France cheered her soldiers, and grumbled about the costs.

THE first years (1852–60) of Louis Napoleon's régime have been, conveniently, called those of the authoritarian Empire. It was during this period that the emperor governed France with all the power of a dictator. Political debate, discussion of public questions—indeed, any manifestation of critical public opinion—was strictly forbidden. Louis Napoleon assumed that France wished to be cured of the instability that had been so general in public life after 1848. His anodyne for the pathological condition of French society was a strict prescription of order, discipline, and silence He alone assumed the responsibility for administering the cure The constitution that he gave to the nation, and the administrative machine that he inherited from his uncle, gave to the new Caesar ample political power to carry out his program. After the raucous debate that had followed the Revolution of February, the calm of the Empire gave to French politics an illusion of peace and quiet that was gratifying to all conservative-minded Frenchmen Underneath the political calm might rage storms of hate and criticism, but the dictator-emperor, armed with overwhelming power, imposed silence and order on French society.

The man who came to direct the French state was one of the most enigmatical characters of French history—a dreamy-eyed adventurer who had a fatalistic belief in his star "I believe," he wrote to a friend, "that from time to time men are created whom I will call providential, in whose hands the destinies of their country are placed. I believe that I am one of those men. . " Throughout his early life—in face of ridicule, humiliation, exile, and imprisonment—Louis Napoleon never lost sight of his "destiny." In 1856, with the birth of an heir, a victorious war, and international prestige to bolster this belief, the prince-president-emperor must have marveled at the course of events that so well justified his faith Napoleon III knew well how to be charming; he inspired confidence and even love in the hearts of those who worked with him, but he never made close friends An emperor must live a life apart His political beliefs were a curious mixture of conflicting currents of his age He had no faith in parliamentarianism, but he professed an admiration for the British system of government He avowed his faith in the judgment of the people, but he carefully controlled and limited the people's freedom of choice He was a man of 1848 in that, unlike most rulers of the day, he had sympathies for the lot of the poor and believed that something could be done for them, but he was also a man of 1850, in that, like the rulers of his day, he was fearful of movements or ideas which originated in the underprivileged classes He was a nationalist, and a friend of struggling nationalisms all over the continent, both by conviction and knowledge that the doctrine of nationalism must undo the Treaty of Vienna, but, as a ruler of France, he had many misgivings over the fulfilment of a doctrine that would create a powerful Germany and an Italy on France's eastern frontiers His own religious beliefs were probably very unorthodox, but the clergy and the Church were powerful allies in the task of organizing a disciplined society, allies whose assistance Louis Napoleon valued highly in the first years of his rule. Napoleon III worked hard at the job of emperor, but his indecisiveness, his humanitarianism, and his mysticism prevented him from filling the rôle as efficiently as his uncle before him had done

The men around the emperor formed a curious combination of adventurers, careerists, and "respectable" bourgeois politicians. Many of them, associates in the *coup d'état,* had staked their lives and their reputations on his success. Others were ambitious and conscientious men who rallied to the Empire, with its doctrine of order and authority, because in it they saw the promise of a society in which political disturbances would not upset their normal course of life. Many were caught by the glamour of the name "Napoleon" and the promise of a career in the imperial service which might compare favorably with the careers earned under another emperor. No small number of the "imperialists" were men who first made their political débuts under Guizot The Empire was to be, in many ways, a continuation of Guizot's system; parliaments were not to alter the course of ministerial policy, and prosperity, induced by public works, was to be offered to the nation in lieu of lost liberties The military entourage of the emperor which provided the gold braid of the Empire was crowded with men who began their careers under the monarchy, accepted promotion and honors from the Empire, and ended by presenting their swords to the monarchists who were to make possible the third French republic.

The internationalism that had been so apparent in the court of the first emperor was also in evidence in the court of the nephew Walewski, the son of a Polish lady and Napoleon I, became foreign minister Napoleon's half-brother, Morny, brought a Russian wife into the circle Persigny kept the English orientation well to the fore; the empress, a Spaniard, introduced Spanish influences into the court; and Italians and Germans, friends of the emperor's youth and exile, completed the cosmopolitan picture. It is small wonder that the Second Empire again turned French attention to the whole continent of Europe.

Furthermore, the principal currents of French politics were well represented in the imperial entourage. The empress made a fetish of the cult of Marie Antoinette; she surrounded herself with relics of that unfortunate queen, and attempted to identify herself with her A handful of tame royalists attended her court, and gave the impression that the empress, if she thought of politics at all, was a legitimist Prince Jerome Napoleon was an outspoken republican, and made a point of acting as protector of the least revolutionary branch of the left opposition, but he could be depended upon not to allow his opinions to stand in the way of his own interests. The emperor chose as economic advisers a group of the disciples of the late utopian socialist Saint-Simon, whose wealth had drawn any revolutionary teeth which their chief's doctrine may have had. Louis Napoleon himself—jokingly, to be sure—often remarked that he was an Orléanist, the empress a legitimist, and Jerome a republican. Only Persigny, he said, was truly an imperialist

With this motley and varicolored crew, the ship of the Empire left port to take French society to the promised land. The direction of the state very largely revolved around the person of the emperor; he met his ministers in council once or twice a week, but their deliberations in no way resembled a parliamentary cabinet meeting. All problems were discussed and settled by Napoleon III and the official immediately concerned. The ministers and officials, however, played a considerable rôle in the affairs of state. Louis Napoleon had great respect for the opinion of an "expert," and usually the bureaucrats could find an "expert" to recommend the minister's point of view. Inertia, too, provided a means for controlling the emperor, when his orders failed to coincide with the ideas of the bureaucracy, inaction often nullified the imperial command. It was common knowledge that although Louis Napoleon directed the Empire, he did not dominate it as his uncle had before him The personnel of the régime changed very slowly; because of indulgence, laziness, or dread of new faces, Louis Napoleon hesitated to remove an appointee. The names that made the *coup d'état*—Persigny, Rouher, de Morny, Saint-Arnaud, Magnan, Espinasse, and others—remained the names of the Empire There were occasional shifts in office, but the personnel remained surprisingly stable. This situation slowed up the normal rise of young men in politics, and the ambitious were almost inevitably driven to seek satisfaction in business or in covert opposition to the régime.

The Constitution assigned only a very limited rôle for the deliberative chambers, and, for the most part, the senate and the legislative body were willing to play the part given to them. Sometimes, however, the senate became restless in its dignified, but more or less helpless, position. It was filled with men accustomed to directing affairs—high church dignitaries, generals and admirals, top-rank state officials, ex-ministers and ambassadors, and industrial, financial, and commercial capitalists. They were appointed for life and their number was fixed by law, but the Constitution limited their part to an obscure rôle in the state affairs that men of action, used to command, often found irksome On a number of occasions, this senate attempted to expand its field of activity to gain some control over the policy of the administration, and once the emperor felt it necessary publicly to remind the senate that it was not, and should not consider itself to be, a house of peers.

The predicament of the legislative body was equally sorrowful for men who wished to take an active part in the direction of the state The great majority of its members, however, were mere "stooges" for the imperial government. By the system of "official candidature," much more rigorously applied than it had been under the monarchies, the emperor's government assured itself of a docile chamber Even with this precaution there were a number of incipient revolts On several occasions, Montelambert, who had rallied to Napoleon III after the *coup d'état,* poured out his wrath at the gag rule that the Constitution imposed upon the chamber. The chamber resented a budget which could not be discussed and passed by sections, and the imperial practice of waiting until the very end of the session to present "must" legislation was gall and wormwood to the more enterprising members of the legislative body. After de Morny was named president of the chamber in 1854, the delegates became more reconciled to their predicament. De Morny, a suave man of the world and affairs, championed the rights of the legislative body as far as the Constitution would allow, and he became a personal friend of each deputy, a friend who could be counted upon for reliable favors. He relaxed the discipline in the debates enough to accommodate the natural desires of men for self-expression, and at the same time deftly directed the chamber along the road of the Empire. At the end of the first term of office *Le Moniteur* congratulated the legislative body for its efficiency; in five years it had passed nine hundred and seventy-nine laws.

The administrative system of the First Empire, with slight changes, was intact when the Second Empire made its début. Under pretext of decentralizing this complex system, Napoleon III greatly extended the powers of the departmental prefects, to allow them the right to make decisions that heretofore had been reserved for the central authority. This measure did not allow for more local self-government, it created a "little emperor" at the head of each department Along with the extension of the prefects' power came an extension of the rôle of the *procureurs généraux* who bore approximately the same relation to the minister of justice that the prefect bore to the minister of the interior. They were the public prosecutors-in-chief, with general supervision over the *procureurs impériaux* (district attorneys), but they also supplied the government with carefully prepared digests of public opinion to assist in the formation of policy. At the top of the machine, Napoleon III organized the council of state, a familiar institution in French administration This body of high officials prepared laws and decrees, ironed out problems of administration, and acted as the high administrative court. The machinery of state functioned smoothly and efficiently under the dictatorship. France was used to a government by functionaries, and for the first few years of the Empire, she willingly accepted the favors of Napoleon in lieu of her own liberty.

The legislation of those years affected every walk of French life. In the civil service and the army, retirement and pensions were regulated to attract to the professions a better type of individual and to allow young men a more important place in the government's service A new military recruiting law did away with the evils attendant on the law of 1818, which had encouraged brokerage offices, the "merchants of men," where the rich could buy exemption from which the state reaped no advantage. The harshness of the military code, especially in times of peace, was greatly reduced, and the army was reorganized and refurnished to match the dignity of a Napoleon.

The emperor will always be remembered as a builder. Railroads, canals, roads, harbors, and telegraph lines were only more conspicuous fruits of Napoleon's administration. Cities, especially Paris, were rebuilt and beautified. Public buildings like the Halles Centrales, the new Louvre, and hundreds of others rose to adorn the cities. Public parks and new boulevards brought light, air, and greenery into the heart of Paris, and at the same time ended the "age of street fighting." As a builder and a patron of building, the emperor tried desperately to justify his dictatorial régime as well as its intolerance of older political forms.

Napoleon also was interested in the problems of the proletariat. Had he not written a pamphlet on the extinction of poverty? In spite of the discouragement of his bourgeois advisers, he pushed through some reforms aimed at the socialist utopian dream of his pretender days. His slum clearance and his honest attempt to improve workingmen's dwellings did not solve the problem of French slum areas, but did better the lot of a few workers. The mutual-benefit societies sponsored by the Empire, and later the embryo trade unions that Napoleon III encouraged, gave the proletariat valuable experience in concerted action. Finally, the sanitation reforms, and the first attempts to regulate adulteration of food and drink, gave impetus to the movement for government regulation over the conditions of life. The Empire was never quite able to endear itself to the proletariat, but it did more for them than any preceding government had been willing to do. Thiers' attitude toward the "vile multitude" had little place in Napoleon's more humanitarian thinking

The finances of the Empire were somewhat unorthodox for their time. Louis Napoleon surrounded himself with economists who urged expansion. The disciples of Saint-Simon, who in 1830 were considered to be addlepated idealists, came into their own after 1850 Michel Chevalier, apostle of free trade; the Pereire brothers, founders of the Crédit Mobilier;

Guéroult, a journalist friend of Prince Jerome, and others of the school of Saint-Simon became intimates in the councils of the Empire. Credit and trade were the keystones of their doctrine. Credit would allow expansion in trade and create new wealth, credit, they believed, would overcome all problems. In the Crédit Mobilier, a bank for business enterprises, and the Crédit Foncier, a landbank for the bourgeois and the peasants, the Empire found institutions that greatly expanded the economic horizons of France, and in no small way contributed to the rapid development of French economic interests.

The tremendous expenditures of the Empire on war, public works, and social welfare greatly exceeded the outlays of previous régimes The Empire in its early years, unlike former régimes, did not have to depend upon the deliberations and consent of the elected representatives of the nation for its right to spend the nation's money. In 1852, the senate presented Napoleon with the right to open extraordinary credits, above and beyond the budget allotments, at any time that it seemed necessary. This right proved indispensable in financing the increased costs of government activity. The enormous expenditure, however, did not impair the public credit The government dropped the older methods of floating bonds through a small circle of powerful bankers, and opened its books to the entire nation The results exceeded all expectations Small investors all over France welcomed a chance to purchase "baby bonds." The treasury had no trouble in replenishing its coffers, and the market price of French bonds remained firm City, departmental, and national indebtedness rose rapidly, but so did the wealth of the nation. In spite of the older "orthodox" financiers' predictions of bankruptcy, financial disaster did not overtake the régime.

THE Empire drew its principal support from the prosperous bourgeoisie, the Church, and the peasantry. It was the party of "moral order" without the conspicuous leaders of that party who had been outmaneuvered in 1851. The men who most willingly rallied to the dictatorship were those that had been most frightened by the tumult of 1848. In their eyes, the Empire stood in the path of red Jacobinism, communism, and anarchy to protect Christian, capitalistic society from the horrors of class war They saw the Empire as the support of home, Church, and established order; it assured them social stability, discipline, and an opportunity to carry on their business unmolested

The great mass of the wealthy bourgeoisie would have supported any government of the right; many of them may have regretted their loss of liberty under a dictatorship, but they could console themselves with the thought that strong evils require strong medicine. When the Empire showed itself ready and willing to pour wealth into their laps, the bourgeoisie, apparently, gave up their recent associations with semi-liberal parliamentarianism. The wild boom of stock and real-estate speculation that followed in the wake of the imperial policy opened vistas of prosperity that allowed greed to still many half-expressed longings for liberty. Fortunes were to be made under the Empire, and their makers were willing to support Caesar as long as Caesar provided such bounties. Fear of leftist political action, and ambitions to reap great wealth made the bourgeoisie into imperialists. But the Empire also brought war, and with war came higher taxes and conscription The bourgeoisie did not relish this side of their "safe" government. After 1860, their grumbling and dissatisfaction were factors partly responsible for changes made in the Constitution. Baron de Rothschild well expressed their point of view when he said, *"L'Empire, c'est la paix; mais pas de paix, pas d'Empire!"*

Closely associated with the support of the bourgeoisie was the support of the Church. Ever since the 1830's the bourgeoisie had been returning to the Church, and the Church had been catering to the bourgeoisie. The threats of the "reds" brought these naturally conservative forces into alliance. But the clergy had other reasons for rallying to Louis Napoleon.

The Empire was able, and apparently willing, to make concessions to the Church beyond even the generosity of the Bourbon monarchs. Louis Napoleon well realized that the clergy would be valuable allies; even as president, he had shown himself pliable in the question of education. He had, in part, carried out the "Catholic policy" when the pope was restored to his "rights" after 1849. He had reaffirmed, through the Crimean War, France's intention and ability to defend the privileges of the Church in the Levant. As emperor, he went further in his honeymoon with the clergy, he and his ministers were punctilious in according every courtesy to the clergymen. The state smiled upon new congregations, allowed the establishment of Catholic secondary schools, extended and aided organizations like the Little Sisters of the Poor and the Society of Saint Vincent de Paul. It also increased the salary of the bishops, and created, out of money taken from the house of Orléans, a fund for retiring aged priests. When the clergy saw wineshops closed on Sunday during church hours, and discovered that the state would forbid the sale of certain antireligious literature, it did not require any great effort to make them into supporters of the Empire.

In the entourage and the ideals of the Empire, however, there was a latent anticlericalism that eventually caused a break in the alliance between Church and state. Before the pope got around to crowning Louis Napoleon, the foreign policy of the Empire put the French emperor out of the good graces of the Church, and the ceremony never took place. Prince Jerome, all through the period, remained as determinedly anticlerical as the empress was proclerical; he and his friends saw to it that the civil marriage retained its dominant position and that the organic articles, which had been attached to the concordat, were not repealed. Although the Church did acquire an important position in education, it was not allowed to supplant the Université. In the end, Napoleon's foreign policy, which loosened the flood of Italian nationalism, brought the intimate relationship between Church and state to an end.

It was the vote of the peasantry that had swelled Louis Napoleon's majority in his election to the presidency and in the plebiscites The old soldiers in the villages had made the name "Napoleon" into a grand symbol for the country-folk. The peasants, either led by their priests and mayors or captivated by the ideal of the Empire, continued to support the régime, but, ironically enough, they derived few immediate benefits from the dictatorship. Only the most progressive of them took advantage of the Crédit Foncier to improve their lands. The improvements in transportation which were later to bring great benefits were neutralized by the disasters that struck their vines, their potatoes, their silk, and their wheat. The wars in the Crimea, in Italy, and overseas meant higher taxes and a continual drain of young men for the army. The peasants, however, supported the Empire with their votes, their taxes, and their sons, as long as Napoleon III sat securely in the Tuileries. Their inherent conservatism and their political ignorance made them ready to accept the *status quo* with all its disadvantages rather than to risk an adventure in reform, the outcome of which could not be foreseen In the later years of the Empire, when the cities consistently returned "unofficial" candidates to the legislative body, the government could maintain its majorities by the solid block of "official" candidates elected from the countryside.

The plight of the old political parties was pitiful indeed Their newspapers were either silenced entirely or placed under a surveillance which precluded any real opposition to the régime. A great difficulty that the editors encountered came from the fact that the newspaper business had become very profitable The extension of literacy brought new subscribers, and the discovery of advertising brought a golden stream of wealth to the publisher. Few editors were willing to risk the loss of income through indiscreet publications The censor's job was made easy merely because he existed; the threat of suppression was usually enough to hold the press in line. There were, however, a half dozen or so of papers that might be termed opposition journals; the republican *Siècle* was even protected by Prince Jerome himself Occasionally, the censor's "warning" was necessary to impose a proper respect for the *status quo.* Silence on political questions was not limited to the newspapers; the clubs and the cafés were strictly forbidden to allow political discussions of any kind. With such an atmosphere, it is no wonder that Cousin wrote: "All resistance is dead No one dares to speak in the provinces or to write in Paris." When the present writer was in Germany in the summer of 1937, an intelligent German told him: "When I read the newspaper, I believe the death notices and the date—they are probably correct." Almost the same remark was made during the Empire by a French economist who complained: "No one speaks to us except the government, and we do not believe what it tells us." The France of the middle nineteenth century could not turn on the radio to listen to a Swiss, Dutch, or English news broadcast. Political debate practically died out from lack of fuel.

A closer observation, however, will reveal traces of the old political parties. The legitimists, in their salons in Paris or on their estates in the provinces, did not give up their loyalty to Henry V. They boycotted the society of the Empire, and tried to raise their own prestige by acts of charity and kindness to the peasants in the villages neighboring their châteaux. During the Crimean War, several of them came out openly to champion the czar as the defender of authority. But legitimism meant little in the political affairs of the state. The Orléanist chiefs saw most of the bourgeoisie rally to the Empire, but they knew that the conservative upper middle class would rally to any government that came to power. They contented themselves with writing sarcastic attacks on the government and its supporters in foreign journals, and with repeating malicious stories and epigrams in their salons. It was during this period that Thiers wrote his *History of the Empire,* de Tocqueville his *The Old Régime and the Revolution,* Guizot his history of *The English Revolution,* and his *Memoirs.* In their historical studies, these men found solace for their impotence in political life. It was not until after 1860 that the old Orléanist party made any headway in the political scene

The one citadel of conservative royalist power that the Empire could not storm was the Institute. In the august ranks of the Academy could be found uncompromising enemies of the régime. For a while, Louis Napoleon considered the founding of a rival institute, this idea was dropped, however, in favor of creating a new section, the Academy for Moral Science (administration, politics, and finance) to which he nominated the ten members. The little warfare between the Academy and the régime, however, was not dangerous to the Empire. The emperor was willing to joke about it himself; when he met de Broglie, who had written kindly of the eighteenth of Brumaire, Louis Napoleon remarked: "I hope, Monsieur le duc, that your grandson speaks of the second of December as you have spoken of the eighteenth of Brumaire " Napoleon's dictatorship was not of the modern, totalitarian, streamlined variety; he did not attempt to "liquidate" all his enemies nor to "co-ordinate" all French institutions.

The republican opposition to the authoritative régime was more dangerous and more persistent than that of the royalist politicians. On the morrow of the *coup d'état,* Louis Napoleon was particularly severe with the men of the left. This severity made his government, in all its manifestations, anathema to radicals of all kinds. From exile, Victor Hugo, Edgar Quinet, Louis Blanc, and dozens of others poured out their wrath and hatred in books, brochures, and newspaper articles that were smuggled into France. *L'Histoire d'une Crime, Napoleon le Petit,* and other works of Hugo, provided inspiration for hundreds of young men who found the Empire system intolerable. In France, the republican ideal was kept alive by students who scorned their professors for selling out to the Empire, by workers and petty bourgeois who refused to be bribed by promises of prosperity, and by intellectuals who clung to the dreams of a liberal or even a social republic. The funerals of republican leaders filled the churches with men spoiling for a demonstration or a riot, and the police found it next to impossible to uncover the secret societies that sprang up in all the industrial cities. Most disturbing was the recurrence, at regular intervals, of plots to kill the emperor. On several occasions, chance or bad marksmanship alone foiled attempts on Louis Napoleon's life.

In 1857, the election of a new legislative body gave the enemies of the Empire their first opportunity to express their hostility. The government announced that it "considered it just and good policy to present for re-election all the members of the legislative body," and the whole machinery of the administration was brought into action to assure a favorable vote. Unofficial candidates were not allowed to publish professions of faith; all political discussion in any way hostile to the government's candidates was rigidly suppressed. After some hesitation, the older parties decided to present a list in opposition to the official candidates. Louis Blanc advised the candidates to resign as soon as they were elected, rather than take the oath of allegiance to the emperor; this would turn the election into a mere demonstration of anti-imperial opinion. The elections gave 5,471,000 votes for the official candidates and 665,000 votes for all the others; five deputies of the opposition took seats in the legislative body. This vote was a show of strength for the government, but Louis Napoleon could hardly draw too much satisfaction from it. The six hundred and sixty-five thousand voters who had repudiated his candidates were the city people who were politically conscious; the five and a half million were peasants and bourgeois who, indifferent to politics, would support any government in power. Louis Napoleon could not escape from the realization that a large minority of the people interested in politics objected to his rule.

This uncomfortable situation became ominous to the government on January fourteenth, 1858, when there was a desperate attempt to murder the emperor as his carriage arrived at the opera. The bombs killed eight and wounded a hundred and fifty more, but the emperor and empress escaped unscathed. The would-be assassin was an Italian named Orsini, who had prepared his bombs in England with the assistance of several of his compatriots. His avowed aim was to kill the emperor because of Napoleon's failure to do anything for Italy. The affair had important repercussions on both the internal and the foreign policy of France For a time feeling ran high because the British authorities had failed to nip the plot in the bud, but the most important, immediate result was a return to the program of repression of 1852. In an address to the legislative body, Louis Napoleon broadly implicated in the plot the men who had voted against his régime, and added: "You will aid me to discover means to reduce to silence the extreme and factious opposition."

The first measures were aimed at consolidating the military power so that it could most easily be used in case of a Parisian revolt. At the same time, Louis Napoleon provided that, in case of his death, the empress would become regent, and he created a private council which would become the council of the regency to assist Eugénie to govern until the prince imperial should reach maturity. These measures were followed by the passing of a law of general safety—or, as it was called, "law of suspects"—which re-established all the rigors of the tribunals of 1852. By this law the minister of the interior received the power to imprison, exile, deport, or place under surveillance, practically any citizen who fell under the suspicion or displeasure of the government. There was some debate about the measure, but it passed with an overwhelming majority.

Billault, the minister of the interior who had failed to prevent the Orsini attempt, handed in his resignation, and Louis Napoleon intrusted his post, with the greatly enhanced powers that the new law had conferred, to General Espinasse. The general was one of the men of the second of December; his theory of government was the simple, direct conception of a ruthless soldier Force was almost an end in itself. Quoting Louis Napoleon's declaration of 1849, when he suppressed the abortive June revolt, Espinasse fairly shouted· "It is time for the good people to be reassured and for the wicked to tremble." His appointment was enough to strike terror into the hearts of hundreds of Frenchmen, a feeling that his actions amply justified The régime of deportation and drumhead trials that had been used in 1852 was repeated all over again. When Espinasse had done his job well, Louis Napoleon removed him; but in his place he put Delangle, the president of the court that had tried Orsini

At the end of six years of absolute rule, Louis Napoleon had consolidated his power over the country. He had given to France material blessings in the form of railroads, telegraph lines, steamships, broad boulevards, and public buildings. He had opened credits to the business and the landed interests of the nation, and had started France on the road to new prosperity. He had won fame for French arms, prestige for the French government, and "glory" for the French flag. But he had not mollified the opposition that his dictatorship had aroused, and at the end of six years he was forced to return to the policy of repression and laws of exception that had been necessary when he usurped authority. The next twelve years were to see a gradual modification of the autocratic régime, but Louis Napoleon's enemies never forgave him the repressions of 1852 and 1858 and the dictatorial methods with which he controlled the state.

CHAPTER IX

FRENCH CIVILIZATION UNDER THE EMPIRE

UNDER the Second Empire, France regained the hegemony of Europe, and Paris again became a world capital The radiance of the imperial court, the prestige of "the emperor," and the magnificent new buildings and boulevards, gave the old city a glamour unknown to the Restoration and July régime. After the Treaty of Paris (1856), a continual parade of kings, princes, statesmen, and distinguished visitors came to pay their respects at the Tuileries and to give color to the French capital. It was an age when expanding economic developments gave great wealth to the business and landed classes of the western world, and Paris inevitably became the mecca that provided a fashionable background for ostentatious display of the clothes, the carriages, and the jewels of the cosmopolitan society of aristocrats and plutocrats On the new boulevards of the French capital the élite of the entire occidental world found amusement and brilliant company, and in turn they gave Paris a splendor unequaled by any other city in Europe.

At the Tuileries, Louis Napoleon and his beautiful empress maintained a court of great elegance. The etiquette was more formal than it had been under the July régime, and the military flavor was more pronounced than it had been since the time of the great Napoleon. It was a court sufficiently glittering and colorful, with bizarre uniforms, lovely women, and distinguished foreigners, to give a proper setting for the imperial dignity of a Bonaparte Anti-imperialistic historians and publicists have roundly condemned its extravagant, lavish parties and displays; there is much material, from which to write a scathing story of the "saturnalia of the Empire," in the elaborate balls, exotic festivals, and expensive parties of the first ten years of the régime. Louis Napoleon was very much in love with his empress in the first years of their marriage, and the gay rounds of pleasure and excitement provided for her amusement were often in striking contrast to the misery that the economic depression of 1855–58 and the horror that the war in the Crimea inflicted on millions of the lower classes.

During the first two years after the *coup d'état* the Tuileries was conspicuously avoided by the established society; the courts of Europe were cool to the *parvenu,* and the nobility of France boycotted the usurper. But after the Crimean War, and especially after the Austro-Sardinian War, it was impossible to ignore the man whose armies had humbled the czar of Russia and the emperor of Austria The vacancies occasioned by the boycott of the legitimist nobility and the friends of Louis Philippe were filled by the members of the imperial peerage, the élite of the bourgeoisie, and distinguished foreigners. Although the empress may have regretted the absence of French blue bloods, it cost the court but little in prestige.

In the second period of the Empire, and particularly after 1860, the imperial court retained its brilliance, but lost much of its gaiety. The disasters that followed the emperor's foreign policy, especially in Mexico and central Europe, had a sobering effect on all French society. Louis Napoleon's chronic illness made him less genial, and his progressive dissatisfaction with the empress's charms cast a pall over the Tuileries. Eugénie became serene, and interested herself in her son's education and career; she saw in his coming régime the consolations which that of her husband could not offer. Louis sought satisfaction in his mistresses and in his study of the life of Caesar He embarked upon this historical labor out of personal interest, and a desire to justify his own career by historical analogy. In the 1860's the parties and balls of the court continued, but the fun was gone; a mask of merriment covered the fact that the social functions of the court had become hard work.

The upper circles of French society well reflected the splendor of the imperial court The lavish construction program of the government, and the enormous expansion of credit nicely coincided with the expanding economic opportunities to give to the wealthy such funds as even the plutocrats of the July régime had not enjoyed. This new wealth was manifest in the great mansions that appeared along the new boulevard of Paris, in country villas, in sumptuous personal accouterments. The conspicuous waste of the great and the near-great gave the French capital a tone and a brilliance which won a world-wide reputation.

The class structure, however, did not greatly change The France of the Empire saw a general rise in the standards of living. This, after 1860, affected practically every social class, but in 1870, aside from the increase in wealth, there was no great change in the social orders that had existed in 1850 The Empire did not herald an era of social revolution; like the régimes that had gone before, it was the property of men of wealth and substance, and although Louis Napoleon harbored and encouraged semisocialistic measures for the benefit of the poor, the Empire reaffirmed the control of the upper bourgeoisie over French society.

The progress of urbanization, however, gives indication of the social changes that were in store for the France of the twentieth century. In 1851, 74.4 per cent of the population lived in rural France; by 1870 the figure had dropped to 68.9 per cent. The attraction of the metropolitan centers was great; Paris almost doubled in population in the twenty-year period, and Lyon, Marseille, Bordeaux, Lille, and other large cities followed the same trend

This movement to the cities considerably increased the number of little people—petty bourgeoisie and proletariat—in French urban society; the movement was to accelerate greatly after 1870. It was not, however, until the very last years of the Empire—and really not until after 1880—that these little folk were able to play any considerable rôle in the making of

France. The bloody June Days and the stern discipline of the *coup d'état* decapitated the proletarian movement by removing its leaders, and the petty bourgeois did not come to realize their strength or their interests until the irreconcilable radical republican party showed them a way to power. During the Empire, both of these social groups in the French cities were being prepared for the part that they came to play under the republic

Louis Napoleon, himself a man of "'48" with hazy ideas about the social problem, did much to prepare these people for their rôle He patronized savings banks and mutual-benefit societies, and allowed the repeal of laws that prevented labor associations and strikes Prince Jerome Napoleon even attempted to create an imperialist workingman's movement that would make the proletariat into allies of the Empire. The emperor sent French laborers to London to the international congress where they heard Marx and Mazzini, and saw the superior working conditions of their English brothers; and the imperial government, in connection with the world exposition of 1867, patronized a congress of workingmen in Paris. Thus, although the Empire was stern and strict, it assisted the workers to equip themselves for their future rôle in history

The peasants, under the Empire, reached an upward turn in the road about 1860. In 1852, Delisle wrote an account of French life in the country to prove how little it had changed since the thirteenth century, only eight years later, when de Lavergne published his study of rural economy, it became obvious that the locomotive was in the act of changing rural life. The growing markets made possible specialized agriculture, and an increased money income gave the peasant a measure of security by allowing him either to acquire more land or to bury gold coins against a rainy day The more enterprising landowners were benefited by the emperor's Crédit Foncier, but most of them, although they were the backbone of the

Empire, received little directly from imperial bounty. The peasants learned to limit their families so that their lands would not be divided by inheritance, they gradually improved their agricultural techniques, and they slowly rounded out their scattered holdings. But the process was slow; French rural economy lagged painfully behind the economies of the advanced countries of the world.

VISITORS to the Paris world fair in 1855, and especially to that held in 1867, had ample objective evidence of the forces that were altering European life. The steam engine, the machine, applied science, and the products of the new industrial factory provided the *leit motif* for the exhibitions, and the intelligent visitor could hardly have failed to realize that a new world was about to open before him. France was slower than England in adopting the new economy as her own, but after 1850 she was irrevocably committed to face the adjustment that the machine imposed upon Europe. The sleepy calm of the countryside was now broken by the rumble and the whistle of the locomotive; in industrial areas, steam engines belched out clouds of ugly, black smoke; the Bourse became more active; and the easygoing commercial and social habits of the older régime began to give way before the brusker, more businesslike manners of the age to come. The middle ages were rapidly dropping out of sight, as the nation moved on in the direction of the industrial society of the future.

Louis Napoleon's "star" had led him to the French throne at a fortunate time; by the middle of the nineteenth century France was almost ready to take full advantage of the so-called industrial revolution, which had already altered the face of English life, and which was destined to remake the society of the entire world. In 1820, France had only sixty-five steam engines of low horsepower; by 1830 she had six hundred with about ten thousand horsepower; by 1850 she had over five thousand with about sixty-six thousand horsepower.

In view of this growth, it is not surprising to find almost fifteen thousand steam engines, with nearly two hundred thousand horsepower, in the France of 1860. These iron slaves were to set the tempo of the new economic life, and the emperor arrived on the scene just at the time when steam power began to make a deep impression on French society

A necessary concomitant of the generalizing of steam power was the development of machinery of all kinds. By 1850, the textile industry was almost entirely given over to machine production, and many other industries were rapidly following the same path. Furthermore, it was at about the middle of the century that English methods of making iron and steel came to be widely used in France. The coke process was destined to free the forge from the forest, and allow the creation of a large-scale metallurgical industry Science, long the tool of those who sought after the riddle of the universe, had finally been adopted as a child of the factory, and the new applied science very soon began to inject fresh blood into the economic structure. Lastly, the new business forms, which facilitated co-operative action in the raising of funds for new enterprises—and, at the same time, were mature enough to organize and manage large-scale industrial and commercial ventures—reached a stage of development, at about the middle of the century, that tempted the French entrepreneurs to embark upon new and more extensive programs. Thus steam power, machines, new metallurgical techniques, and new business forms paved the way, after 1850, for a great increase in the productivity and the capital wealth of France.

By ignoring these fundamental forces, which were at work long before the *coup d'état* of 1851, historians and publicists friendly to Louis Napoleon have been able to credit his régime with the building of industrial France. This view is too generous to the rule of the dictator. While it is undoubtedly true that Louis Napoleon did co-operate fully with the forces which were to accelerate French life, it is too much to attribute that development entirely to his régime. "Napoleon III," writes an eminent French historian who recognizes the emperor's policy for what it was, "desired to use his power to increase the material prosperity of France, and ameliorate the lot of the manual laborers He counted upon economic activity to distract the French from politics Industrial and financial enterprises and great public works were provided to enrich the bourgeoisie and employ the workers, and finally to attach them to the Empire by giving them wealth to compensate for loss of liberty."

With ever-mounting government subsidies, credit, and construction, the Empire "primed the pump" of French economy. The cornucopia of the emperor poured forth railroads, steamships, telegraph lines, public buildings, and new streets and roads. Easy credit, under government auspices, for all types of enterprise, tempted private individuals to increased activity. Such a policy inevitably joined hands with the basic forces latent in French economic society to produce a burst of economic expansion, and eventually to raise the standards of living throughout the entire nation. Thus the Empire re-enforced, rather than created, the trend that was to introduce the new economy in France. The emperor's power to exert influence upon the economic development of the nation was practically unlimited In December, 1852, the senate awarded to him the right to authorize any work of public utility or enterprise of general interest, without consulting the elected representatives of the people He had the authority to grant concessions, and to authorize the creation of joint-stock companies, by mere administrative action. These powers, broadly interpreted, gave him enormous influences over the emerging industrial society. Armed with this power, Louis Napoleon chose as his advisers a number of the surviving disciples of Saint-Simon who, although they now occupied important positions in French society, held true to many of the ideals of their master. Saint-Simon and his disciples had hailed the machine age as the new era in which men could be free. They had seen amelioration of the lot of the poor, and great social and moral progress, in the expanding horizons opened by the machine and steam power. They conceived it to be the duty of government to open credits for industry, commerce, and agriculture, and to stimulate economic life through vast public works projects that would increase the wealth and the potential earning power of the nation

One of the first things to receive imperial attention was transportation facilities. Louis Napoleon found France with some three thousand kilometers of railroad in 1850; when the last act of the Empire was being played in the war with Prussia, France could boast of over seventeen thousand kilometers of usable railroads. The emperor and his advisers saw the railroad as most important in the development of economic life. Their faith was not misplaced; the railroad soon became the fundamental factor that linked French economy into a single unit The following table will show the remarkable increase in the use of railroad transportation under the Empire:

	1850	*1869*
kils of railroad	3,000	17,500
passengers	4,271,000	44,000,000
kilometric tons of freight	314	6,270

Though a great expansion would undoubtedly have occurred no matter what government ruled in Paris, that does not alter the fact that the Empire did adopt a farseeing railroad policy that did much to accelerate the speed of railroad expansion.

French ocean transportation, too, received important assistance from the Empire. In 1857, the government subsidized three steamship navigation companies to establish regular contacts with North, Central, and South America The Empire saw a significant increase in the French merchant marine, but the time was still distant when steam would replace the sail as the important motive power for French ships.

With Saint-Simon's disciples as the imperial advisers, it is not surprising to find that the Empire made easy credit available for both industry and agriculture. This credit expansion was facilitated by the discovery of large gold deposits, in California and Australia, that greatly increased the world supply of the yellow metal that stood behind paper credit After 1850, France enjoyed a "favorable balance" of trade; gold flowed into her vaults at a great rate as the gold-exporting countries availed themselves of French commodities. The discount rate in Paris dropped to three per cent, and the entrepreneurs were encouraged to plan new enterprises The imperial government's contribution to easier credit took the shape of a land bank, the Crédit Foncier, and a commercial and industrial bank, the Crédit Mobilier. The latter was largely under the influence of Jewish *haute finance,* and soon spread its activities even beyond the frontiers of the nation, it helped to build the French, the Spanish, and the American railroads, to extend harbors, to construct gasworks, to build the famous Rue de Rivoli, to finance transatlantic shipping, and dozens of other such enterprises. In the end the Crédit Mobilier got in beyond its depth, and, when the Bank of France refused to come to its aid, ignominiously collapsed

The Crédit Foncier was more conservatively directed, and was destined to a more stable, if less spectacular, development than its contemporary. It was modeled on the land banks that Frederick the Great had created in Prussia; the bank's primary purpose was to give aid to the conservative landholding bourgeoisie and peasantry whose support was necessary to the régime. The initial government subsidy of ten million francs, given to the bank to assure a reasonable interest rate on loans, was largely raised by the confiscation of the Orléans property, so that the beneficiaries of the bank would find their best interests opposed to an Orléanist restoration. During the entire period of the Empire, the Crédit Foncier enjoyed a practical monopoly of all mortgage business—except, of course, person-to-person loans. It was allowed to receive deposits, in addition to transacting its regular business of loans on real estate, and its efficient and businesslike direction gave the bank great stability and usefulness. It was never necessary for the imperial government to increase its first subsidy.

In addition to its extension of transportation and credit facilities, the Empire became famous for its public works program. There were several motives behind the great building activity of Louis Napoleon's government His Saint-Simonian advisers saw that public building would give employment to the poor and contracts to the bourgeoisie, and, at the same time, would greatly increase the total wealth of the nation. The emperor, like the dictators who preceded and who would follow him, was ambitious to leave his mark on the country in the form of stone and mortar And, finally, public works, which infuse new blood into the economic life of a state, are the usual expedient of governments that try to bring the state out of an economic depression. The public works program might well be regarded as Napoleon's PWA, a weapon forged to combat the depression which began in 1845.

The building program of Napoleon III is everywhere visible even in the France of today Paris especially benefited from the refurbishing which the Empire undertook to carry out. Colossal sums of money were made available to clear out rookeries in all sections of the city; great, broad boulevards which opened the city to "light, air and infantry" were cut through the crooked, rambling, narrow labyrinths of the streets of medieval Paris Order replaced disorder; easily accessible streets replaced the old battlegrounds of French democracy, the narrow lanes made famous by the barricades. Along these new boulevards the bourgeoisie speculators, enriched by government purchases, fat contracts, and the expanding economic system, built beautiful new homes and business houses that changed the face of the city. At the same time the government was building the new Louvre and Tuileries, the Halles Centrales, and dozens of other public buildings by which Napoleon III truly earned the title, "the builder of modern Paris." It is true that some of the contemporary landmarks of that great city date from the post-imperial era, but, even so, many of them—the Opéra, for example—merely followed in the wake of the Empire.

THESE public works, subsidies, and new credits, coming as they did simultaneously with an era that saw war in the Crimea, in Italy, in China, and in Mexico, constituted a severe strain on the public pocketbook The flippant remark, "Our children and grandchildren can easily pay the bill," which Zola brutally put into the mouth of an imperial favorite, gives an instructive clue to the financial measures that supported this expenditure At no time could regular taxation cover the expenditure of war and public construction, but the dictator did not have to wrangle with the representatives of the nation in his search for credit. Louis Napoleon gave himself the right to raise extraordinary credit whenever it appeared necessary, a practice which was not checked until the last years of his reign Under the old monarchies it had been customary to float new government loans through the agency of the great private banks with international connections, the Empire departed from this procedure by opening its books to public subscription all over the nation, and, to the surprise of the orthodox financiers, the new issues were usually oversubscribed. It was obvious that, despite the expenditure, the nation's credit was in excellent condition—a fact that made an energetic administrator like Baron Haussmann impatient to finish his labors in rebuilding Paris.

Timid souls protested at the ever-mounting national, departmental, and communal debts, bankruptcy and ruin, they insisted, would be the only outcome of such reckless finance. The friends of the emperor blandly replied to these dour predictions that the government was creating national wealth, and, when that wealth was created, the debts could easily be paid. The Empire, it should be noted, did not march into bankruptcy; indeed, when Bismarck exacted indemnity for the war of 1870, France after 1871 gave astonishing proof that she had waxed rich under Napoleon III.

In spite of this public display of opulence, France was not free from financial difficulties, especially during the first ten years of the Empire. In 1855–56, central and western Europe again faced famine, when the crops failed. Acute suffering in both town and countryside visited the little people, as the price of living mounted beyond their financial ability to pay To make matters worse, a panic gripped Europe in 1857 The bad harvests had coincided with the Crimean War, which prevented wheat importations from Russia. Europe turned to the grain fields of the United States to feed herself. But peace came in 1856, and in 1857 exceptionally abundant harvests in Russia forced the price of grain down from 30 to 24 francs a hectoliter. The American speculators who had amassed large stocks of grain to sell in Europe were ruined. Their bankruptcy helped to unbalance an unstable credit situation; a bank in Cincinnati closed its doors, and within a few months the panic had spread to New York and Europe, bringing insolvency and distress in its train. England, the Germanies, and the Scandinavian countries were harder hit than was France. But even in France the prompt action of the government merely alleviated the crisis.

This year of 1855–56 was the last time in modern history that Frenchmen faced the grisly specter of famine. The crisis showed the absolute necessity of cheap railroad and ocean traffic, and after 1860 these two means of transportation assured Frenchmen that grain—from the ends of the earth, if necessary—could be supplied to keep them from starvation It was not, however, the last time that a financial panic would destroy speculators, wipe out savings and credits, and create unemployment and misery. The crisis of 1857, indeed, was only a mild introduction into the possibilities of disaster that the new economic structure could produce. However, only for a moment it crippled the railroad and building expansion; by 1859, the boom was again under way, when the benevolent government found new sources of credit and opened new contracts. In a later age, the French were to learn that, in tying themselves into the new machine and finance economy, they exposed themselves dangerously to all the vicissitudes of the world economic system.

THE most famous, and in some ways the most far-reaching, economic measure of the Second Empire was the adoption of tariff reform. The question had been in the air for three decades; the Germans with their Zollverein, the British, and even the people of the United States had adopted sweeping customs revisions before 1860, and there had been considerable discussion in France in the 1840's about the advisability of a more moderate tariff policy. The monarchy, however, had feared to take the step; it remained for Napoleon III to undo his uncle's prohibitive tariff system. As prince-pretender, Louis Napoleon had supported the high-tariff policy, but when he became emperor he gave ear to the counsels of the liberal school of economists, who convinced him that the custom laws obstructed French industrial development by allowing outmoded manufacturing and commercial methods to continue. This, they argued, unnecessarily oppressed peasant and worker by maintaining an artificially high cost of living. It appealed to the emperor to picture himself as the modernizer of industry and the friend of the poor, and, at the same time, he believed that he could see important political advantages in an expansion of trade.

Even before the famous treaty with England, Louis Napoleon had taken advantage of the articles in the tariff laws of 1814 and 1836 to reduce the duties on foodstuffs and raw materials necessary to industry. The crop failures had justified his first measures, but the emperor had wider plans in view. On the eve of the world's fair in 1856, his government announced that it intended to make sweeping reductions in the tariff schedules When vested interests raised a loud clamor, *Le Moniteur* promised that there would be no change in the existing laws until 1861. "French industry," it went on to say, "warned of the intention of the government, will have plenty of time to prepare for a new commercial régime."

In 1859, the emperor requested an investigation of the tariff on grain, and, in no time, real opposition to any change was mobilized. There were good harvests in 1858 and 1859, which depressed prices considerably. The landlords had suffered from scarcity in the years before; now they suffered from abundance They insisted, of course, that the tariff reductions of 1855–1856 were responsible for their plight, and turned to the manufacturers to find allies against any further inroads on their beloved tariff schedules Napoleon, anxious to be off to the Italian war, capitulated to this agricultural-industrial coalition, just as the July monarchy had done before him. Any legislative tariff reform seemed quite out of the question; even the tame deputies in the legislative body would oppose it. There was, however, a way to enact tariff reform without consulting the legislative body. The senate, in 1852, gave to all treaties the force of law, even though they might be contrary to existing domestic legislation. A treaty of commerce, then, could make a breach in the Chinese wall that defended the antiquated industrial structure of France.

The way was opened by Michel Chevalier, one of the Saint-Simonian advisers of the emperor. Chevalier was in London in 1859, acting as presiding officer for an international congress on weights and measures; before he returned to France he discussed with his friends in England the whole question of a tariff treaty, and obtained the consent of Gladstone to open negotiations. On his return to France, Chevalier persuaded Rouher and Louis Napoleon that a treaty with England that would replace the prohibitive customs duties with moderate protective schedules would not only benefit French economy, but also strengthen the bonds between England and France. In view of the problems that the Italian war was creating, this idea appealed strongly to the emperor, and in a few weeks Chevalier was back in England, to discuss details of the proposed treaty.

The negotiations between Chevalier and Cobden, the leading English exponent of free trade, were kept a deep secret, so that hostile pressure should be unable to influence the progress of the treaty. It was not until January fifteenth, 1860, that a letter signed by Louis Napoleon and published in *Le*

Moniteur Universel exposed the intention of the government to inaugurate sweeping reforms in the tariff system A careful reading of Louis Napoleon's communication leaves little doubt that Chevalier's hand guided the pen. "For a long time," he wrote, "one has affirmed as truth that it is necessary to increase the means of exchange to make commerce flourish, that without competition, industry stagnates and maintains high prices that slow up consumption, that without a prosperous industry which creates capital, agriculture itself remains in its infancy." He went on to say that tariff reductions would accomplish the desired aims, and bear excellent fruit for every class of society. Eight days later, the treaty with England was signed, and shortly later, published in *Le Moniteur*.

This treaty proved to be the wedge that cracked the whole system of prohibitive duties; within the next seven years, the French government signed similar treaties with Belgium (1861), the German Zollverein (1862), Italy (1863), Switzerland (1864), Norway, Sweden, the Hansa cities, Spain, and the Netherlands (1865), Austria (1866), and Portugal and the Papal States (1867) Since each of these treaties embodied the principle of "the most favored nation," they had an important effect on the whole European tariff structure by introducing moderate schedules, and ending, for the moment at least, the tariff wars which so disturbed European economy. The emperor and Chevalier have often not received their full credit for this policy, it has been customary to ascribe the primary rôle to Cobden, the English free-trade enthusiast. Dunham, however, after an extensive study of the evidence, writes as follows: "The international trade of Europe owes much to Napoleon III, who announced the new commercial policy . . .; it owes much also to Richard Cobden, the champion of free trade and principal negotiator of the Anglo-French treaty . . .; but it owes still more to the man who conceived the idea and began the negotiations of the treaty of 1860, Michel Chevalier."

The troubles of the emperor were not ended with the signature of the treaty It was soon evident that French manufacturers not only disapproved, but actually were ready to fight the change The government tried to placate them by imposing the maximum tariffs allowed under the treaty (25 per cent to 35 per cent ad valorem) and by opening an imperial loan to manufacturers. The loan was intended to provide easy money for the modernizing of French industrial establishments which British competition, in spite of the moderately protective schedules, would necessitate. Many of the manufacturers did not need or did not wish to take advantage of Napoleon's offer, but in several cases the loans rendered striking services to industry.

To ascribe the great increase in French and world international trade, that followed on the heels of the new tariff policy, entirely to the treaties of commerce would place too much emphasis on one factor in the economic development of modern Europe. Although, undoubtedly, the liberal tariff schedules had far-reaching effects on French commerce, it is also true that they coincided with the intense economic activity that followed the introduction of steam power, cheap iron, and machinery. Furthermore, the new policy was adopted just when the gold fields of California, Australia, and Colorado began to pour streams of the yellow metal into world commerce to expand credit and to oil the wheels of trade. Lastly, the policy came into effect when war in America, central Europe, and Asia distorted the normal processes of trade, to accommodate the needs of the armies. These factors, as well as the tariff treaties, must be considered in any discussion of the victories of the new industrial economy.

THE acceleration of industrial tempo in France became especially apparent after 1860, when the railroad network was approximately completed, but even then it did not show the vigor that British industrial development had already experienced and which the Germans and Americans (United

States) were to experience in the next decades Some critics ascribe this inferiority to French inability to organize, others to French artistic individualism which refused to allow factory discipline to regiment its expression. Proof of either of these contentions is still to be produced, but it is possible to explain other forces that have contributed to the relative backwardness of French industry in comparison with that of England, the United States, and Germany. Coal—or, rather the lack of large quantities of good coal—has stood in the way of French expansion. Until the railroads were complete, lack of fuel was often an absolute barrier to expansion, and even after 1860 lack of good, cheap fuel was a decided handicap. Much of the coal found in France does not make good coke, and most of the coal is scattered widely, is of mediocre heat value, and is often expensive to mine. Since French coal output was never able to supply the local market, tariffs and freight charges have maintained a price in France well above the prices in neighboring countries.

This lack of coal helped to keep the French iron industry dependent upon wood. It was not until the second decade of the Empire that the transition from charcoal to coke was definitely established in the metal industry, and only then did the French metallurgical plants, in spite of their handicaps, begin to approach the efficiency of their English rivals. By 1869, France, using the Bessemer converter and the Siemens furnace, managed to turn out a million tons of iron and steel which was more than the product of any of the other states, including the German Zollverein, in continental Europe, and second only to England's. This iron and steel, converted into cutlery in Auvergne, boilers at Saint Denis and Belleville, guns and rails at Le Creusot, and surgical instruments and machines in Paris—to mention only a few of the centers of the industry—came to play an important rôle in the economic life of the Empire

The expansion in the textile industries, particularly cotton, rivaled that in metals, for prominence under the Empire. By

1870, the textile mills in Alsace competed with those of Lancashire in the world markets; the thread was finely spun, and the dyeing and printing were artistic and of first-class quality. The hand loom was almost extinct. France, as a whole, however, had made no such progress as Alsace, but the cotton-textile industry was well established. When the American Civil War finally dried up the principal source of raw cotton, suffering in the textile districts of France was every bit as acute as it was in England. During the Empire, the woolen industry became more and more dependent on imported raw materials. In 1850, the French clip supplied three-fourths of French needs, by 1870, about four-fifths of the wool had to be imported from abroad. This was partly due to the introduction of British machinery especially fitted to handle the short Australian wools, and partly because French merino had lost its quality As in former times and even today, the French woolen industry best produced light fabrics suitable for women's apparel—export novelties, artistic productions suited to the hand loom which persisted in France long after it had disappeared in England.

The most famous French textile industry, that of silk, received a severe blow in the 1850's. A disease struck the silkworms, and the production of raw silk dropped from about twenty-five million kilograms yearly, in 1840, to a mere seven million in the decade of 1856–1866. There was some improvement before the end of the Empire, but the disaster nearly ruined the silk industry by opening the field to oriental competition, which persisted after the local situation in and around Lyon was eased. The linen industry, too, faced a crisis under the Empire, but, unlike silk, which recovered after 1870, linen was doomed to slow strangulation. Linen production was a cottage industry until about 1860, but even when it turned to power and machinery it was unable to compete on equal terms with the lusty cotton factories. The latter half of the nineteenth century was to see an absolute decline in the production of linen cloth.

At the exposition of 1867 it was evident that many other industries had turned to machinery. "It is one of the predominant characteristics of modern industry," wrote the reporter of the jury of the exposition, ". . . that the machine has penetrated all its parts. In all branches of industry, going through one after another, is this invasion which is for the general good." The manufacture of paper, agricultural machinery, beet sugar, and clothing with machine techniques gave indications of the future that the machine held open to industry. But the process of acclimating the machine to French soil was slow, and slower still was the development of large-scale industrial establishments In 1852, some 6,500 "factories" were using power-driven machinery totaling only 76,000 horsepower, an average of 11.7 for each establishment. Twenty years later, there were 23,500 "factories," with 338,000 horsepower, an average of 14 4 for each. The true meaning of these figures becomes apparent only when it is remembered that these statistics include only those for the really great metallurgical and textile plants; the average "factory" probably used a small steam engine generating only four to eight horsepower. Obviously, although the machine and the steam engine were changing French industry, they were slow in doing so, and their effect was not as revolutionary as it was in England, or, later, in Germany.

It was also under the Empire that France developed a new retail system. The traditional outlet for goods was the small, specialized shop, which often combined the functions of merchant and craftsman; every French city was literally honeycombed with small shops that could enjoy only a very limited business. The merchandising methods were those of the bazaar; there were no fixed prices, no advertising, no displays. The price of any commodity was a personal matter between the merchant and his customer. In 1852, the Bon Marché was opened in Paris; three years later, the Louvre; in 1865, the Printemps; and, in 1869, the Samaritaine These new establishments were department stores, destined in the twentieth century to enjoy a world-wide reputation. They bought merchandise of every conceivable sort in large quantities, and at prices that the little merchants could not hope to find; they sold at a fixed price, low enough to insure rapid turnover, since their profits depended upon volume of sales. Although the department stores of the Empire were not the colorful, palatial marts of trade that they are today, it did not take them long to establish themselves in the Parisian—and later, in the provincial—economic life.

The small shop, however, was not to disappear. It was only after 1870 that the little people began to feel the keen competition of the large merchants, and not until 1900 did they see their very existence threatened by the newer economic forms. The French clung doggedly to the small individualistic retail outlet, just as they did to the small industrial establishment; even to this day, the visitor to many French towns is forced to wonder whether the system does not amount to "taking in each other's washing."

IT WAS in industry, transportation, and commerce that the most striking changes came to French economy, but agriculture continued to play a predominant rôle in the French economic system A large proportion of the wealth of the nation, and forty-nine per cent of its active population, found employment on the land.* Furthermore, in spite of the disasters and crop failures of the middle 1850's, agriculture prospered under the Empire According to a fairly reliable estimate, the gross value of farm produce in 1850 was about five milliard francs. The same authority estimates that land values, on an average, increased from 1,850 francs per hectare in 1862 to over 2,000 francs per hectare in 1870. There was a sizable increase in the total number of hectares under culti-

* According to the census of 1862, agriculture employed forty-nine per cent, industry, manufacturing, mining, construction, and transportation, thirty-one per cent, commerce, seven per cent, the liberal professions, state and public service, thirteen per cent

vation, and, more important, a significant increase in the yield per hectare, in most products The peasants of 1870 had not yet achieved the comparative comfort that the future had in store for some of them, but they were leaving the hungry years of the eighteenth century well behind.

Many factors were responsible for this development. Cheap transportation and expanding markets undoubtedly had a primary influence. The growing cities needed meat, grain, cheese, fruit, eggs, vegetables, and wine, and foreigners were able to take a larger amount of French wine, fruit, and luxury vegetables. Up to 1860, the amelioration of conditions in the country was largely due to the increased total acreage put under cultivation through drainage projects, breaking new land, and reducing the amount of land left fallow After 1860, it was due to better methods of cultivation and the use of machinery. In the 1840's a German chemist proved that manure was not sufficient to restore the minerals necessary for efficient agriculture. By 1860, the science of agricultural chemistry began to affect the yield of many French farms; a new industry, the making of artificial fertilizer, was firmly established in France, and the imports of guano and nitrates became regular items of French international trade.

In comparison with their more advanced neighbors, however, the French farmers were backward both in the use of fertilizers and machinery. The French system of tenant and *métayage* farming, and the comparatively small individual holdings so characteristic of the French countryside, were not conducive to a widespread introduction of mechanized agriculture. The number of metal plows increased considerably, but most of the grain was still sown, harvested, and threshed by methods that were rapidly becoming obsolete in Belgium, England, and America. The French farmers were too conservative and too untutored to adopt more modern methods. Nevertheless, there was a striking difference between the rural France that returning émigrés had seen in 1814 and that through which the Germans passed in 1871. New crops, better culture, and better breeds of animals had combined with an enlarged market to give to the French peasant a more hopeful economic future.

WHILE new methods in industry, agriculture, and commerce were changing the physical environment of France, new crosscurrents in the philosophical, moral, and literary climate of Europe went far to alter the intellectual environment as well. It is impossible to note all the intellectual tendencies of an era like that of the Empire and condense them into a simple generalization; the new forms were usually the expansion of forces latent in the previous generation, or of ideas developed by foreigners and adopted in France to suit the Gallic traditions. To say that philosophy gave way before science, that realism supplanted romanticism, that materialism and positivism usurped the place of sentiment and idealism, is in part true, but the statement is too clear-cut to be entirely true. The various "isms" are difficult to label, and often, precisely when it seems that the older form is dead, it will be found blooming luxuriantly in another corner of the field. The march of intellectual understanding, however, did move apace with the development of industry and society, and to observe some of the important variations that it introduced into the French scene is instructive to an understanding of the age of the Second Empire.

In the fields of philosophy, science, and historical criticism, the scholars of the Empire entered upon new roads that were to lead to undermining many of the traditional conceptions of the world. As early as 1855, Abbé Gratry, in his two-volume *Logique,* expressed his fears that the new pantheistic and atheistic systems of thought were corrupting the fundamental values to which Frenchmen should cling. Eight years later, Renan published his *Life of Jesus,* a convincing bit of evidence that even the deity of Christ was no longer accepted by many French intellectuals The publication of Renan's masterpiece coincided with a rising tide of philosophic and scientific speculation that, basically, was deeply antireligious. It is indeed, not surprising that the pope at Rome deemed it necessary to condemn modernism, in most of its manifestations, by the *Syllabus of Errors*. Nor is it surprising to find that the papal condemnation was heartily approved by the churchmen in France who saw their traditional beliefs continuously under fire.

The philosophy of Hegel had an important impact on French thinking; behind Hegel, the idealist, it was easy to find Hegel, the unrepentant rationalist, whose ideas could easily be acclimated to the soil plowed by the French philosophers of the eighteenth century. His doctrine of the identity of opposites which placed good and evil within the same frame, and his conception of the absolute relativity of truth, fascinated men who were tiring of the eclecticism of Cousin. The idea of the "becoming," with the inevitable, dynamic interaction of thesis, antithesis, and synthesis, could not fail to impress a century that could witness the forward movement of society in spite of the efforts of conservatives. The Hegelian system gave Frenchmen a new approach to the age-old problems that have troubled man since he began to explain himself, but the Hegelian explanations were highly unsatisfactory to the conservatives in French society, who saw in them the contradiction of all fundamental values. The good Abbé Gratry condemned Hegel and his French disciples as enemies to religion, family, and morality.

Alongside this German importation, there was an indigenous French philosophy, equally dangerous to the old traditions, which gained wide acceptance among French intellectuals; this was the doctrine of positivism. Auguste Comte and his disciples refused to accept anything as real which could not be scientifically demonstrated. This thinly veiled materialism fitted well into the thinking of a generation that had seen the rise and fall of romanticism in literature and politics, and which was on the point of hailing the sciences, with their mathematical laws and precision instruments, as the hope of mankind

Indeed, it was from the scientists that the new intellectual impetus flowed the strongest. The scientific discoveries of the preceding two hundred years fell into place in the third quarter of the nineteenth century when the atomic table, the laws of thermodynamics, the new conception of electricity, the germ theory of disease, and the concept of biological evolution (as expounded in 1859 in Darwin's *Origin of Species*), introduced new confidence into the writings of the materialists who were to make the modern world These men *knew* that their science opened new paths, heretofore unexplored, to the understanding of the universe, and any visitor to the world's fair of 1867 could hardly escape the conclusion that their efforts might well go far to remake the physical environment of man. By science, a new terrestrial paradise, even more magnificent than that dreamed of by the eighteenth century, might well be contemplated for the human race. This was salvation, but hardly the celestial salvation of the men of the Church.

In other fields, too, the new quest for learning by men armed with sharper tools than their forefathers possessed, invaded and upset the strongholds of conservative thinking. Historians, archeologists, and etymologists began to unlock the doors of the past by rigorously applying scientific methods to the problems of history and civilization; Babylon, Egypt, and Syria were rifled for their secrets; the same rigorous textual criticism applied to new documents unearthed by excavators was also used to analyze the Bible itself. The churchmen were horrified, the conservatives shocked, but the students pressed on eagerly to unfold as much of the truth as was possible. Naturally, many conclusions were hastily drawn; many, however, were backed by incontrovertible evidence that forced men to alter their concepts of man and his historical evolution on this earth.

The literary life of France of the third quarter of the century was deeply tinged with the reaction that set in all over Europe after 1848. Romanticism, after winning for the creative artist his freedom from rules and forms, collapsed in the general disillusionment following the failure of the revolutions. In France, the new form of realism was tinged with positivism and pessimism, as men like Flaubert and Saint-Beuve took the center of the stage. The lives, hopes, fears, and failures of men and women who were real rather than romantic pictures of the distant in time and space, became the subjects for literary treatment. In the theaters, too, men like Dumas and Augier rejected the historical themes for scenes from contemporary life, and did not hesitate to write in the coarse, often vulgar, language of everyday use. It was a movement from the same intellectual soil that produced Renan and the scientists that insisted upon a positivist solution of their problems.

In the fine arts, the men with the brush followed the men with the pen away from romanticism The romantic painters had broken the rules of the classicists, and now, in their turn, the realistic painters replaced the romanticists' style and subject matter with new modes of expression. The art galleries of the world are well stocked with the works of the artists who insisted on painting, realistically, the stooped shoulders and gnarled hands of their fellow men. Courbet, a leader of the school, shocked his conservative contemporaries as much with his canvases as Renan or Darwin had with their books He was called a socialist, an insulter of religion, and a profligate. His realistic presentation of the female nude, *Les Baigneuses* (1853), aroused great indignation and was excluded from the exhibition. No matter—realism was to have its day in art, and before the Empire collapsed it was recognized as a form acceptable and valid.

To music, the French of the Second Empire made no spectacular contributions. While great musical operatic history was being made by Wagner in Germany and Verdi in Italy, the French could boast only of the Italian Rossini, the German Meyerbeer, of Gounod, Thomas, and a few others. Their contributions, particularly to the Opéra Comique, are still valued, but hardly place them among the great immortals One French writer explains that it was a period when French musical training did not prepare the people to understand the new musical forms, and the bourgeoisie would neither pay nor work for this *art d'agrément.*

Many French republican historians, particularly of the prewar era, regard the Empire as merely an unfortunate interlude between the second and the third republics, and Louis Napoleon is, in their pages, the bogeyman who checked the natural growth of French society. Such a view cannot be adopted today by even the most ardent supporter of France's liberal democratic régime. The Empire did stay the process of political education, but it also prepared France both economically and culturally for the development of those free institutions which she enjoys today. By greatly expanding the economic basis of French life and by opening new horizons to the French mind, the men of the third quarter of the nineteenth century made a significant contribution to the society and the government of their children.

CHAPTER X

THE LAST ACT OF THE EMPIRE

IN SPITE of his avowed renunciation of foreign conquests before he assumed the purple, Louis Napoleon's Empire, like that of his uncle, was destined to end with a disastrous adventure in foreign affairs. In 1852, he explained that his victories were to be won on the terrain of domestic affairs. There were highways, railroads, and canals to be built, harbors to be dredged, waste lands to be reclaimed—a program of peace, which, in his opinion, would satisfy the lust for glory of the new Empire. When adversity dogged his foreign policy, in the second decade of his reign, and France failed to see that his adventures were related to her vital interests, the emperor must ruefully have remembered his brave words, *"L'Empire, c'est la paix."* Many of his subjects shrugged their shoulders to inquire what it all meant, and far too many of them, for the safety of the Empire, wished to repeat the clever remark of a famous French banker: *"Pas de paix, pas d'Empire!"*

Was it Caesarism, Bonapartism, or mere mischance, that led Louis Napoleon into the mirage of foreign glories? The answer to this question, if it could be given, would be instructive to a new generation plagued with dictatorship; unfortunately, we can hardly provide the irrefutable answer that so direct a question must call for. In any case, we know that the imperial régime involved France in three major wars and a whole series of minor adventures in foreign fields, each of which cost heavily in both blood and gold. The promise of peace given in 1852 sounded hollow in 1870, when the imperial army met the Prussians at Sedan The Empire brought "conquests" in the domestic field, but it also brought adventure and ruin in the field of world affairs.

None of these adventures in foreign affairs was universally popular in France. The Crimean War was accepted more or less calmly, but, even so, there was considerable grumbling after the war entered its second year. The Italian war was even less popular, the cost of the war and the dangers to which it exposed France, as well as the discomfort that the Holy Father experienced, made thousands of Frenchmen actively opposed to the venture. The Syrian, Chinese—and, particularly, the Mexican—adventures aroused deep distrust in all sections of French opinion, while the disquieting rush of events in central Europe, for which the emperor was unjustly blamed, made many Frenchmen wonder what could be the matter with the foreign office on the Seine. Finally, the Franco-Prussian War—for which, at first, there seemed to be a little real enthusiasm—brought the Empire to the shambles, and opened the way for the Republic.

A major difficulty in imperial foreign policy developed from Louis Napoleon's confusion of his personal inclinations with the interests of France. He was a man of 1848, a nationalist, and a believer in the self-determination of peoples. He found it difficult to oppose even the unification of Germany, which any politician could have seen was contrary to French interests, because at heart he believed that the German people had a right to create a German state. He supported the national aspirations of Italians, Poles, and Rumanians, on the same grounds. This doctrine of nationalism allowed him to justify revision of the treaties of 1815 which were made against his family. Those treaties were a continual reminder of the failure and defeat of the First Empire, and he considered it his mission to undo them. Furthermore, Louis Napoleon was the first French ruler since 1815 who saw French policy in terms of world affairs. He was interested in developing French influence in Asia, the Americas, and Africa, at a time when Frenchmen did not understand the possibilities of modern imperialism and had no sympathy with colonialism in any form. The confusion that resulted from the emperor's point of view was heightened because many of his own advisers could not agree with his programs, and so Louis Napoleon felt obliged to maintain a shadow diplomatic service of his own, separate from the official service of the Empire. This often led to curious misunderstandings and, for France, unpleasant surprises, when the emperor's inclinations and the national interests of France, as they were interpreted by the diplomatic corps, dictated opposite courses of action.

By 1860, the opposition to the imperial foreign policy was reflected in the internal affairs of France. In an attempt to regain support that he had lost, Louis Napoleon began a progressive relaxation of the authoritative régime, and this ended, in 1869, in the creation of the parliamentary Empire, just before the régime went down before the guns of Prussia at Sedan. It is a strange story, the emperor discovered after 1860 that the sworn enemies of the Empire came nearer to approving his foreign policy than did the men who were the chief props of his régime. Napoleon chose to attempt placating the enemies of his internal policy rather than abandoning his aim to alter the map of Europe; in the attempt he completely reversed the political philosophy of the *coup d'état* of December, 1851. Unfortunately for him, his concessions did not endear him to his enemies, and he never regained his friends.

AFTER the war in the Crimea, Louis Napoleon enjoyed a prestige in Europe unequaled by any other French ruler since his uncle. His armies were recognized to be the best in the world, and his court was the most brilliant in Europe. The extensive program of public works planned and under way seemed to give assurance that he intended to carry out his promise, *"L'Empire, c'est la paix,"* in spite of the fact that he had been "forced" to fight Russia in the opening years of his reign. There were, of course, economic depressions, and everyone was not completely satisfied with the imperial program, but, with the Catholics, the bourgeoisie, and the peasants behind the régime, the future looked bright for the development of the imperial system. This promise of peace and prosperity, however, was rudely shattered, when, on New Year's Day, 1859, Louis Napoleon publicly addressed the Austrian ambassador with the fateful words, "I regret that our relations with your government are not so good as in the past, but I beg you to tell the emperor that my personal feelings toward him have not changed." It was "a bolt from the blue sky," and Europe nervously watched the preparations for war

Behind this menacing speech of the emperor there was a snarl of intrigue and conspiracy that can be traced to days before Louis Napoleon, pretender to the throne of France and a member of the Carbonari, took part in a Roman revolt in the early 1830's. Italian patriots and friends of Italy had worked, prayed, fought, and died for Italian unity. It was Austria, the pope, and the Italian princelings that stood in the way of their dreams, and the friends of Italy for over a generation had schemed to push these obstacles aside. As president of the French Republic, Napoleon's power to assist the revolutionary forces in the peninsula was limited. But as Napoleon III, emperor of the French and arbiter of Europe, he could give more concrete form to the schemes for Italian unity. The Crimean War, into which Cavour led the armies of Sardinia, opened a way for a grateful France to assist the Italians, and the attempt of Orsini on the life of the emperor vividly recalled the fact that Napoleon was neglecting Italy. In 1858 readers of *Le Moniteur* might have guessed, from the prominence given to Italian affairs in the official journal of the Empire, that Napoleon was planning "to do something for Italy."

Indeed, that is what he planned to do. During the spring and summer of 1858, Louis Napoleon's personal physician made a number of mysterious trips to Turin, where he closeted himself with Cavour, the artful prime minister of Piedmont-Sardinia. Finally, on the "advice" of his physician, Louis Napoleon himself went to the resort of Plombières for a "health cure." By "chance," Cavour, too, found the healing waters of the famous resort necessary to his well-being. Like common conspirators, these two responsible statesmen put their heads together to plot the overthrow of the *status quo* of Europe. In true Carbonari spirit they decided that Austria must be driven from her provinces and her position of influence in Italy. It was Austria that stood as the primary defender of Italian disunity; therefore, Austria must be destroyed. But the pope, the second line of defense of the forces of disunity, could not be treated in so cavalier a fashion by an emperor who drew much of his support from the Catholic clergy. Louis Napoleon well understood that the papal position must be made secure and, if possible, even strengthened, or the Church in France would withdraw its support from his régime.

The new map of Italy which Cavour and Napoleon drew at Plombières was calculated to provide both for the pope and for Italian unity, by the creation of an Italian confederation with His Holiness at its head. They planned to reduce the mosaic of Italian states to four: the kingdoms of Naples, Central Italy, Northern Italy, and the Papal States. The kingdom of Northern Italy would be made up of the state of Piedmont-Sardinia and the Austrian territories of Lombardy and Venetia, which the French armies would free; the kingdom of Central Italy, which would include Tuscany and the smaller central Italian states, was to be governed by Jerome Napoleon and his future bride, the daughter of the king of Sardinia (neither Jerome nor the princess heard of their fate until some time later). The treaty also provided that France should be allowed to annex the French-speaking provinces of Nice and Savoy, as compensation for the work of her armies and the change in the European balance of power.

The plot of Plombières seemed to provide for everything: the pope, Italian unity, the houses of Napoleon and Savoy, and even for France herself. Cavour undertook to make Austria declare war, so that the whole action could be presented to the world as the outcome of a purely defensive war. Ironically enough, this treaty, which was to disturb the peace of Europe and the *status quo,* was signed just at the time when a British minister solemnly assured his queen that the peace of Europe was secure. The negotiations were kept so secret that many of Napoleon's own circle were unaware of their existence until months after the plans for war were well advanced, and Europe only vaguely sensed their import when the emperor startled the Austrian ambassador on New Year's Day, 1859.

The sequel of that speech was not slow in appearing. Cavour and the future king of Italy were anxious to cash Napoleon's check before saner councils could persuade him to stop payment. The feverish activity of the Sardinian army, and the work of Sardinian agents in Lombardy and Venetia rapidly brought Austro-Sardinian relations to a strained state. The powers wished to temporize; perhaps a congress could find a formula which would prevent the war. Great pressure was brought upon Napoleon; he wavered in favor of a European settlement, and, for a moment, men in Sardinia felt that all was lost. But Austria could be depended upon to blunder just when victory was within her grasp There was little doubt that a congress would have left her in secure control of Lombardy and Venetia, but the men around Francis Joseph wanted a decisive diplomatic victory. They dispatched to Sardinia an ultimatum (vaguely suggestive now of the 1914 ultimatum to Serbia), which robbed Austria of her strong moral position by placing upon her the onus of peacebreaker. War followed, with the stupid logic of the contemporary international mind, and within a few days the French army which had been assembled—"to be sent to Algeria"—carried the tricolor and the eagles into Italy. Another Napoleon prepared to make a military reputation on the plains of Lombardy.

The leaders of the French army that invaded Italy in 1859 were well prepared to fight such wars as those of the First Empire. Louis Napoleon himself headed the army, and he obtained an authentically Napoleonic plan of attack from an old soldier of his uncle's day. It did not take into consideration the technological changes of the intervening fifty years, but, with a Napoleon in command, Napoleonic tactics, even if they were obsolete, were inevitable. Such military leadership spelled defeat and disaster eleven years later, when the French eagles stood before Moltke's modern army, but in 1859 the French faced an antagonist whose plans and strategy followed the traditions of the middle eighteenth century. The battles, however, were fought with modern (1859) weapons, and the destruction of life was correspondingly enhanced by the outmoded strategy. The new shells made the battlefields of the Italian war no place for a man with a sensitive stomach, even if his name was Napoleon. The emperor, on more than one occasion, kept his poise only by smoking innumerable cigarettes and looking the other way. The contest, however, went largely in favor of France; the Austrian generals were more stupid than the French, and French guns were better than Austrian. In the end the tricolor won.

The campaign was a quick one; Montebello, Magenta, and, finally, Solferino, added military glory to French arms, and the Austrians were driven out of Lombardy. Upon entering Milan, the emperor announced "to the Italians" that "no obstacle remained in the path of the free manifestation of their legitimate wishes." Such talk and the news of Austria's reverses were infectious. The whole of northern Italy soon moved to realize "aspirations" that revolutionary leaders considered legitimate. In Tuscany, Parma, Modena, and—an omen—the papal provinces of the Romagna, revolutionary movements overthrew their existing governments when the rulers refused to join the crusade for Italian liberty. These revolutionary leaders were "unfamiliar" with the convenient treaty of Plombières. Europe was feeling the birth pains of a new national state!

Europe was, naturally, not entirely pleased. Queen Victoria and her well-meaning ministers exchanged platitudinous notes, which ranged from sympathy for Austria, to fear of Napoleon, to regret that France should be allowed to free Italy by herself. It developed that English statesmen of the 1860's could be depended upon to limit their gifts to good advice, and their intervention to a diplomatic note. From Russia the czar watched the course of events anxiously, while he held a threatening army on Austria's frontier, to remind Francis Joseph of Austria's ungrateful rôle during the Crimean War. But the czar was unwilling to allow the war to result in a general crusade for oppressed nationalities; he solemnly vetoed Louis Napoleon's suggestion that the Hungarians might be used to bring Austria to terms. The wings of Europe—Russia and England—were not willing to intervene, but in the Germanies the war spirit ran high when the news of French victories reached them The German Confederation, by its own constitution, would not be involved in the war until the fighting brought the invader into German Austria, but many publicists and statesmen in the Germanies were anxious to settle the question of Napoleon's place in Europe, without waiting for an invasion of their confederation.

The position of France became precarious when the prince regent of Prussia, William, began to mass the Prussian troops on the Rhine frontier. He had offered the services of the Prussian army in return for an enhanced position for his state within the framework of the Confederation. The Hapsburg officials wished, if possible, to avoid losses in Germany; they temporized with William's suggestions for changes in the constitution of the Germanies. In the meantime, men in Berlin prepared to save Austria in spite of herself, and the Prussian army in the Rhineland made preparations for a trip to Paris. This turn of events was awkward for both Napoleon and Francis Joseph. The main French army was in Italy, and only slender forces stood between Prussia and Paris; urgent telegrams from the regency and the empress made Louis Napoleon see the absolute necessity for liquidating the war before disaster should overtake his state. Francis Joseph, too, was embarrassed. True, it was quite probable that Prussian intervention would crush France and guarantee him peaceful possession of his Italian provinces, but it was also true that the same action would destroy his predominant position in the German Confederation Defeated by Napoleon, Austria would lose out in Italy; saved by Prussia, she would lose out in Germany. It was a difficult dilemma for the Hapsburg court.

Fortunately for Louis Napoleon, the Austrians decided that it would be better to give up something in Italy than to allow Prussia to assume the hegemony of the Germanies. This decision was strengthened by Napoleon's willingness to forego complete conquest of Austria's Italian possessions, in return for an immediate peace which would stave off a Prussian invasion. On July eleventh, 1859, the two emperors met at Villafranca, and arranged the preliminary terms of peace which were later incorporated in the treaties of Zurich. By this agreement, Austria surrendered Lombardy but retained Venetia. The way to Italian unification was opened, but the Austrian power still remained entrenched in northeastern Italy. At the moment, this mattered little to Napoleon; he was fortunate to get out so easily.

The Italians viewed this unexpected turn of events with dismay; they had believed that Austria would be driven out, and the spectacle of a treaty that left Venice in Austrian hands seemed to mean only defeat for their hopes and interests. Within the next few months, however, the rapid course of events changed despair into rejoicing, and it was Louis Napoleon's turn to regard Italy with dismay. The whole problem revolved around the fate of the central Italian provinces that had overthrown their conservative governments to join the war on Austria. At Plombières they were assigned to the new kingdom of Central Italy, but the Plombières treaty was already ancient history, and the revolutionaries were clamoring for annexation to the kingdom of Piedmont-Sardinia. Louis Napoleon still had hopes of an Italian confederation, with the pope as president, but both the pope and the king of Sardinia, for different reasons, sabotaged that idea The emperor wanted to call a congress, but the English would not follow him The Italian Pandora box that was opened in 1859 plagued French policy until the emperor was driven to accept the inevitable solution of annexation of the central provinces by Piedmont-Sardinia "To preserve the balance of power," Sardinia then allowed France to annex Nice and Savoy, after a formal plebiscite in those areas had expressed a desire to join with France. This annexation stripped Louis Napoleon's Italian policy of its moral position, and made the whole campaign "for the liberation of Italy" into a French land-grabbing expedition. Europe poured out its satire upon the "condottieri" emperor, and many of the German princes began to look to their defences against a recrudescence of the policy of "natural frontiers."

The embarrassing consequences of the Italian war did not end with the annexation of northern Italy by Piedmont-Sardinia. One of the provinces involved belonged to the Holy Father, and nothing that the French emperor could do or say could induce him to accept the situation. To indicate his displeasure with Louis Napoleon, Pius IX created an army of his own, and placed it under an exiled Frenchman, General Lamoricière, who was a personal enemy of the emperor The French garrison at Rome found its position extremely awkward, and prepared to withdraw, but before anything could be done, another revolutionary movement threatened to upset the delicate equilibrium of forces in Italy. Garibaldi, an Italian patriot and soldier of fortune, embarked with his thousand "red shirts" on a political freebooting expedition against the kingdom of Naples. The movement swept unopposed through Sicily into Naples, and turned north toward Rome. This gave the Sardinian government a pretext to seize the eastern Papal States and march an army to meet Garibaldi to "protect" the pope. The men around Victor Emmanuel II well understood that France could not allow Rome to fall into the hands of the revolution, but they also knew that Louis Napoleon was too deeply committed to prevent their annexation of the Roman Marches, Umbria, and the kingdom of Naples In Turin, on March seventeenth, the kingdom of Italy was proclaimed, and Europe was asked to accept the *fait accompli*.

THE repercussion of the events in Italy on French politics was immediate. The unification of Italy and the consequent spoliation of the papal domains came to be regarded as Napoleon's own handiwork, by men who resented the alterations in the Italian *status quo*. Opinion, however, was divided. The clergy rallied to the cause of the Holy Father, and condemned the whole adventure as an impious act of plunder. The upper bourgeoisie, angry over the emperor's reversal of the protective system in the treaty with England, and troubled about the terrific expenditure of money for a "useless and dangerous military adventure," tended to join the clergy in criticizing the emperor's rôle in the Italian question. Many of the peasantry, especially after the casualty lists began to come in, listened attentively when their priest or royalist neighbors condemned the imperial policy. On the other hand, the republicans and liberals, who heartily detested the Empire, found much to approve in the rapid development in Italy, and the war was even popular with the radical Parisian proletariat. It was a fateful policy that alienated the friends of the régime and pleased the foes.

The emperor was too deeply involved in the situation to allow the opposition to alter his course. He did all that he could to reconcile Pius IX to the new situation, but the good man refused to listen to Napoleon's honeyed words about compromise. In France, the emperor tried first to convince and then to suppress the opposition. A pamphlet, *Le Pape et le Congrés,* which, while not written by Louis Napoleon, at least was inspired by him, appeared, arguing that the Church would do well to surrender most of its territory and rely for power upon its moral prestige. The pope condemned the doctrine as a heresy, and called upon his bishops to defend him. The problem became serious when *L'Univers,* the leading organ of the clericals, took an active stand in defense of papal rights, and published an encyclical letter in which Pius IX thanked the French bishops for their support of a cause which Louis Napoleon opposed *La Bretagne,* another clerical journal, entered the fray by publishing a letter written by three Catholic deputies whom Napoleon had refused to receive Both journals were suppressed for illegal opposition to the state, but it was impossible to muzzle all of the French clergy.

This breach with the Church was serious Before the Italian war, the Empire had relied upon the clergy as a principal pillar of the régime. The alliance of sentry box and vestry had been every bit as effective as the earlier combination of throne and altar. It had been advantageous to both parties: the Church received favors; the Empire, support. It was, however, too much to ask the clergy to support a policy which had resulted in the pillaging of the Papal States; the clergy could be imperialist as long as the Empire poured benefits in their laps, but not when the emperor joined with the forces of Italian nationalism. In the *Syllabus of Errors,* Pius IX very soon gave the world to know that the Roman Catholic Church could not tolerate the modern heresies. Many of Napoleon's advisers, including the empress herself, counseled against the policy which must deprive the régime of such powerful allies, but the emperor allowed his sympathy for Italy, and his belief in his own "star" and the doctrine of nationalism, to lead him on.

By 1861, it was patent even to Napoleon that the whole idea of Plombières was nothing but a dream The planned confederation of Italy, with a papal president, was still-born in the battlefields of the Italian war, and the new idea of the united kingdom of Italy was well under way When the course of events got out of hand, the emperor was too deeply involved to withdraw. The pope refused to compromise, and the emperor was forced to meet the embarrassing situation by carrying on a war against the Church. *Le Siècle, L'Opinion Nationale* and *La Presse,* republican, anticlerical newspapers, received a freer hand; in return for active support in foreign policy, they were even allowed to criticize mildly the imperial internal policy The churchmen, with their own newspapers muzzled, complained that it was permissible to discuss God and the Holy Father quite freely, but criticism of the Empire remained forbidden.

After the Italian war had begun, the peasants and bourgeoisie, who furnished their gold and their sons to carry on the war, also became more and more distrustful of the imperial foreign policy. To the bourgeoisie the war was pointless in its beginning, and positively dangerous when the Prussians mobilized on the Rhine Although some money was to be made in purveying to the army, it did not compensate for the disturbances of markets and the increase in taxes that inevitably followed war and revolution. The little people, particularly the peasants, resented the waste of their sons, and objected to the release of radicalism and revolution. France distinctly murmured against the policy—particularly the France that had been Napoleon's principal support

To make matters worse, the end of the Italian adventure coincided with the time of the adoption of the liberal tariff reform and the Civil War in America. The treaty that moved toward freedom of trade ran counter to the prevailing economic dogma of the French. Industrialists, merchants, and farmers had stood behind high-tariff barriers for generations, and, although Napoleon and his advisers told them of the advantages of a more liberal tariff policy, they did not approve of it. The measures which the Empire took to alleviate the havoc of the new policy—such as the loans to manufacturers—only partly quieted the complaints. When the Civil War in America began to dry up first the market for French luxury products, and then the source of basic raw materials, it was easy for Frenchmen to blame the government's tariff policy for their troubles. This unpopular tariff reform, moreover, was linked with the Italian war. It was widely believed that Louis Napoleon had bought off British opposition to his Italian policy by betraying French industry.

With the clergy distinctly hostile, and the bourgeoisie and

peasants critical, the Imperial government was faced with a cruel dilemma. Either it must reverse the policies dear to Napoleon's heart, or it must embark on a policy of reform that might well end in the transfer of power into the hands of men who were basically hostile to the principles of the *coup d'état* of the second of December. Naturally, neither choice was acceptable; the Empire stumbled along with half-way measures, and made more blunders that were to alienate other sections of French opinion.

THE men around Napoleon viewed with concern the desertion of the clergy and a section of the bourgeoisie, and it was cold comfort, indeed, to know that the erstwhile radical enemies of the régime gave their support to the imperial foreign policy. That those men would never become real supporters of the Empire was a fact well emphasized when a general amnesty freed all political prisoners, many of the exiles even refused to accept the pardon, and of those who returned, few, indeed, were willing to co-operate with the Empire. It was, however, impossible to change the Italian policy; Louis Napoleon was committed beyond recall after the peace of Villafranca and the annexation of Nice and Savoy. Furthermore, the emperor personally favored the unification of Italy, and the stubborn, recalcitrant attitude of Pius IX did little to alter his opinion. There was nothing for the Empire to do but to fight back at its critics in France, by favoring anticlerical movements, suppressing clerical newspapers, and rapping the bishops whenever an opportunity arose.

This, however, was not sufficient to restore the political balance within the nation Napoleon and a few of his closest advisers decided that a more positive step must be taken Like men in a wrecked ship, they agreed to throw something overboard in the hope of saving their own skins and a part of their cargo On November 24, 1860, the first section of the *coup d'état* of December second went overboard when Napoleon announced that thenceforth the legislative body would be permitted to present an address to the throne in reply to the speech from the throne at the opening of the session. Furthermore, the deputies were thenceforth to be allowed to discuss legislation in secret committees before naming a commission to examine and report, and—most important as far as the public was concerned—the heretofore unreported debates were thenceforth to be published, for all to read To be sure that the government's case would always be well represented, the decree announced that regularly appointed ministers without portfolio would hereafter be present at the sessions of the legislative body to explain and defend the government's policies

Considering that the government did not renounce its policy of controlling elections, and that most of the deputies (all but "the five") were "safe" men who could be depended upon to support whatever measures the government might demand, these concessions did not appear so great. On the other hand, the "half turn to the left," as Proudhon termed it, did break through the strict regulation of the authoritative system to allow criticism of the régime and to end the long political silence. It was de Morny, more than any other of the chiefs around Napoleon, who favored this liberalization of the Empire. He had confidence in the legislative body, and he saw that only by liberalizing the régime could it be saved On the morrow of the concession, he met Ollivier, the leader of "the five" in opposition, with a smile and the remark, "Well, I hope that you are satisfied?" Ollivier's response, "If this is the end, you are lost; if it is the beginning, you are made," gave some indication that the future, if it unfolded properly, would find Ollivier in the ministry.

The new regulations for the legislative body greatly increased interest in politics, even if they did not succeed in endearing the Empire to its enemies. The parliamentary session of 1861 lasted about as long as the sessions of the July monarchy, and politically minded France eagerly followed the debates in the chamber. The emperor's pessimistic councilors to the contrary, the government did not lose control of its majority; like Guizot in an earlier time, Louis Napoleon could always control a large majority of the deputies. The interest came from the amendments and criticisms of the tiny opposition and the clericals Even in the senate the bishops received a chance to express their discontent more effectively than ever before. This new liberty was also accompanied by a slight relaxation of the rigid application of the press laws, especially in the case of "leftist" journals that supported the emperor's foreign policy. The road to a liberal Empire was clearly marked out, but years were needed to complete it.

Late in 1861, the second concession of the government seemed to indicate that Louis Napoleon was really willing to commit himself to the new trend. The public debt of France had mounted rapidly under the Empire; foreign wars and great public works had weighed heavily on the national and departmental budgets; subventions, loans, and grants had proved to be tremendously expensive Early in 1861, *La Revue des Deux Mondes* was reprimanded for calling attention to this growing debt structure, especially since *La Revue* pointed out that it was often increased without the authorization of the legislative body. This grant of power to raise "supplementary credits" without consulting the deputies had long been a sore point with the opponents of the authoritative system. In the fall of 1861, Louis Napoleon called Fould, a representative of French banking interests, to serve as minister of finance. Fould himself had opposed the practice of opening "supplementary credits," and he was expected to do something about it The *senatus consultum* of December thirty-first, 1861, brought about the desired result by altering the Constitution to prohibit the opening of any credits without legislative action Although this ruling was ignored about a year later—when the emperor needed funds—this new statement of the Constitution, re-enforced by the decrees of 1860, went far to change the authoritative character of the régime.

With these changes in the political system, the elections of 1863 took on a new importance. The opposition demanded a free election, with freedom of press and assembly during the time of the campaign. Louis Napoleon and his advisers were not ready to grant any such sweeping changes, indeed, they hoped that, through an election, they could show how slight was the importance of the opposition. To prevent the farce of the elections of 1857 from occurring again—a situation which had allowed the election of men who subsequently refused to take the oath of allegiance to the emperor—the government refused to allow anyone to run who did not take the oath, as a preliminary test of his fitness for candidacy. Only the most ardent supporters of the Bourbon pretender allowed this restriction to deter them from becoming candidates. The republicans, liberals, and Orléanists regarded this oath as a mere form which was in no way incompatible with their opposition to the régime.

Legally, there were no republican, Orléanist, or Bourbon parties, as *Le Temps* explained, there were the party of progress, the party of resistance, and the party of liberty. Only the small group of former republicans had any sort of political organization. In several departments, the opposition groups formed a "liberal alliance" to fight the official candidates, but for the most part the opposition was hopelessly divided and almost completely incohesive. For example, the republicans hated Thiers not much less severely than they did Louis Napoleon himself, until Persigny openly attacked him as an enemy of the Empire Thiers' outspoken objections to universal suffrage had branded him as a reactionary. The good Catholic bishops found it hard to co-operate with anticlericals like Garnier-Pagès, even if they might wish to work against the foreign policy of the Empire. "If you are a writer, write; if you are an orator, speak; if you are a voter, vote!" exclaimed M. Dupanloup, bishop of Orléans, but he wanted support for the Holy Father at Rome, not a more liberal policy in internal affairs. The men of the opposition, in their disunity, resembled the men who had fought Guizot in the 1840's; their opposition was all that they had in common

On the government side, every bit of power available was wheeled into action to assure the election of the official candidates. Jules Ferry's account of the official maneuvers is probably not greatly overdrawn; the government used threats, cajolery, promises, and bribes to obtain support. Men received subventions, political offices, and exemption from military service. Railroads, canals, and public buildings were promised The whole weight of the administrative machine was cast into the balance against the opposition Persigny, for example, even paid close attention to the psychological factor; he threatened opposition newspapers with severe penalties if they persisted in calling the opposition candidates "independents." The very word might suggest to some voters that "official candidates" had no independence By its action, the government gave the impression that the imperial system was the real question at issue; that the votes were for or against the régime

When the ballots were counted, the official lists received 5,308,000; the opposition, 1,954,000 The official list was only 163,000 votes less than it had been in 1857, but the opposition had gained 1,290,000 votes over the election of that year. Out of a total of two hundred and eighty-two deputies, the liberals and republicans elected only seventeen and the clericals only fifteen, the government's huge majority was unimpaired, but it had suffered a moral setback. The most ominous thing about the elections was that the opposition carried Paris, Lyon, Marseille, Bordeaux, Nantes, Toulouse, Le Havre, Brest, Nîmes, Lille, Saint Étienne, Toulon, Metz, Mulhouse, Nancy, and Limoges—in other words, every important city of France showed a majority opposed to the régime. "This is not proof," wrote *Le Siècle,* "that the voters in the country have become imperialists, but only that the government's means of action were more powerful in the country, where each is known and under observation" The politically wise agreed with this statement. The government had won this time, but the returns proved that the régime was losing the nation. Louis Napoleon answered the elections by removing Persigny from office and making him a duke. The man of the second of December, *par excellence,* was thus taken from the political arena.

THE elections undoubtedly signified that the politically minded of the French electorate wanted a larger degree of liberty than had theretofore been given to them. This interpretation greatly strengthened de Morny's case in the inner circles of the emperor's advisers. For several years, he had insisted that only by liberalizing the institutions of the Empire could the throne be saved for the Bonapartes He particularly believed that free discussion of public affairs and some control over the emperor's unlimited power in foreign affairs were imperative. In Prince Jerome Napoleon, the Saint-Simonians, and Victor Duruy, a professor in whom Napoleon III found a kindred soul in his researches on the life of Caesar, de Morny had allies who wished to buttress the Empire with liberal institutions Had he lived beyond 1865, it is not inconceivable that the liberal Empire would have come sooner than it actually did.

There were other advisers in the imperial circle who felt that any concessions must be taken as a sign of weakness that would create further demands, and finally lead to the complete overthrow of the government. The empress, Rouher, the military clique, and most of the men of the *coup d'état* shared this opinion. To grant further liberties would be an invitation to revolution, they feared, and they interpreted the elections to mean that a potentially traitorous minority wished to deprive the majority of the orderly government that the Empire had given to France.

When the new legislative body convened, the opposition skillfully expressed its demands. Thiers, in a classic oration, expanded upon the "five liberties" which France must have before she could accept the Empire (at a time when the Empire was twelve years old!). Individual liberty that could not be encroached upon by special tribunals and laws of security; liberty of the press, unhampered by regulations and suppressions; liberty of free elections, at which the government would remain impartial and allow the people to choose their own chamber, and, finally, liberty of the majority to direct the policy of state—these were the demands of the opposition Thiers did not point out that these "liberties" had not existed under Louis Philippe!

The emperor was not yet ready for the plunge into a parliamentary régime, and the majority of the deputies were ready to follow their master's wishes. The way to liberalization was shown, but at the moment the route was still too difficult to follow. In two important reforms, however, the advocates of liberty found new hope for a more liberal régime, and several of them, including Ollivier himself, prepared themselves for the act of rallying to the new Empire The one was a reform in education made by Professor Duruy; the other a liberalization of the regulations affecting the worker's right to collective action. Professor Duruy won the confidence of Louis Napoleon by assisting him with his life of Caesar, and finally accepted the position of minister of education and governor of the Université. He first attacked minor problems of curriculum, and then introduced new chairs, and finally whole faculties, in the study of political economy in the School of Law. He utilized the existing laws to force many communities to establish schools for both children and adults, and, to the horror of the churchmen and the joy of the liberals, crowned his work by opening public schools for girls. Theretofore, the daughters of France were educated in convents, or not at all; the new laws allowed them the same advantages that their brothers received. The good professor wished to go further; he insisted that primary education ought to be free and obligatory for all. When this suggestion was printed in the official journal, a veritable hornet's nest of protest descended upon the government; the Catholics feared their Falloux laws might be repealed, and dreaded the idea of free lay education, and the bourgeoisie resented the idea that their tax schedules might be raised to provide education for the poor and the socially unwashed. Louis Napoleon stopped short of sustaining this radical proposal, but he did support Duruy's liberalization and extension of French education.

The alterations in the laws regulating the workers' right to strike convinced Ollivier and a number of his friends that there was a real possibility of the Empire's becoming liberal. As early as 1861, Prince Jerome Napoleon had started a movement that was aimed at making imperialists out of the proletariat. The workers had supported the Italian adventure; Bonapartism, as Louis Napoleon interpreted it, could be turned into a democratic, popular doctrine, and education might teach the laborers that the Empire could satisfy their interests. The proletarian movement from the Palais Royal was the first organized attempt to win the workers. Shortly after this movement got under way, a delegation of French workers, with the permission and protection of Louis Napoleon, attended the international workingmen's congress in London, where they listened to Karl Marx and saw with their own eyes that English workers enjoyed better working conditions than they did. But it was hard to keep the workers within the frame of the Empire; they had a tradition for republicanism and Jacobinism that was deeply rooted. Greater favors would be necessary to make the proletariat into full-fledged imperialists.

In 1861–1862 there was considerable discussion of the workers' right to organize, and utilize collective action to better their conditions. Under the existing laws, all combinations, except mutual-benefit societies, were illegal, but even these laws did not prevent combinations which often resulted in bitter labor warfare. De Morny proposed to alter the laws so that the workers would have a legal right to organize, and strike to redress their grievances. Naturally, conservatives of every hue opposed the idea; but de Morny secured the support of the emperor, and Ollivier won the support of a section of the opposition; together they forced the measure through the legislative body. The new law made combinations of both employers and employees legal, and granted to the laborers the right to use the strike as a legitimate measure to secure just treatment. The government, however, reserved the right to intervene to protect property, and freedom of labor, and to prevent fraudulent actions. Many of the radicals regarded these reservations as a means for rendering illusory the worker's new privileges; most of the conservatives regarded the law as a menace to society, and vigorously condemned its framers as "professors of strikes." The law passed only after the official candidates received a nod from the emperor.

In 1865 the death of de Morny and the withdrawal of Prince Jerome from politics temporarily halted the march toward the liberal parliamentary Empire. In an outspoken discourse at Ajaccio, on the occasion of unveiling a monument to the first Napoleon, Prince Jerome spoke of the imperial Constitution of 1815 (Acte Additionel) as the true ideal of Bonapartism, an attempt to reach liberty but not through the Church. The speech was so strongly liberal and anticlerical that it incensed the empress; she sent a copy to Napoleon, who was visiting Algeria, and obtained from him a severe rebuke for Prince Jerome. The prince was furious, and straightway resigned his offices and retired from politics. Only a few weeks before the incident, de Morny's death removed another powerful advocate of liberalism from the imperial circle. The conservatives held the field for the moment, and the liberals, who were ready to rally to a liberal Empire, were at loss to make contact with the emperor.

HISTORIANS, from their superior position in time, often refer to the last years of the Empire as its period of decline, but historians have seen horizons that were unknown lands in the late eighteen-sixties. In truth, the Empire probably declined—surely the emperor was fast losing his position of authority and power—but the men of the day, who had not yet heard the guns of Sedan or seen the Prussian army at Paris, could not understand how clearly the forces within and without France were working toward the complete destruction of the imperial régime Indeed, in many ways the last brilliance of the Empire sparkled more brightly than the first, it is true that the liberalization of the government was delayed until 1870, but Rouher's system of authority was liberalized at the very moment when the older men of the *coup d'état* clamored for more discipline, and, in the end, Ollivier, the champion of the liberal parliamentary Empire, did come into his own. In those last five years, Paris was to witness a spectacular world exposition; she was visited by crowned heads from all over Europe, and a would-be regicide even gave the French the thrill that comes from an attempted assassination by shooting, with rather bad aim, at the czar of Russia. It was true that discontent and revolutionary activity mined the foundations of the state, but it was also true that in 1870 a great plebiscite gave an almost unconditional approval of the Empire.

The fruits of the emperor's labors in the writing of history were a part of the last glow of the Empire When the *Life of Caesar,* by a modern Caesar, began to appear in 1865, it amused and pleased the French to see their master in the rôle of scholar. Naturally, French critics outdid themselves in praise of the work—and, indeed, it was rather better than might have been expected from a ruler, even if he had had learned collaborators. The critics, of course, hardly dared to decry the natural imperial bias toward Caesarism, when the author's position was so learnedly buttressed with the apparatus of scholarship To the scandal of the republican friends of George Sand, the results of the imperial labors were praised as excellent literature even by her. Not only in France did the emperor reap the fullness of praise. In Germany, too, students whose names were usually signed to reviews that bristled with footnotes and scholarship sang of the valuable labors of an amateur. "From the emperor's correspondence," writes Guedalla, "it almost seemed as though Europe, from the Rhine to the Russian frontier, was populated by an impecunious race of scholars, animated by a single ambition to possess (without paying for it) a copy of his book."

This adulation, foreign and domestic, may have helped Louis Napoleon in his personal and public difficulties. The estrangement between him and the empress never healed, and, apparently, there was not much comfort to be derived from mistresses. The unfortunate man suffered horribly from stones and bladder troubles which his physicians seemed unable to relieve In 1866 he was seriously ill, and although he recovered somewhat, the reviews on horseback, the strenuous state occasions, and the very work of office must often have been nearly unbearable torture for him. At the same time, he gradually lost control of the machinery of state—a fact that is amply testified to by the way in which his ministers allowed comparative immunity to newspapers that assaulted the emperor, as long as the ministers themselves were not brought into question Napoleon himself told Ollivier in 1867: "These gentlemen [the ministers] consult me at times, but in general I do not know what they are doing, the newspapers tell me about it." His dislike or fear of "new faces," however, prevented him from reorganizing his cabinet.

Those were also the years when disaster in Mexico brought a weeping woman, the wife of Maximilian von Hapsburg, to his palace, to beg further aid for a lost cause, and when it could not be given, to proclaim that France had betrayed her husband to a firing squad. In Europe, things went as badly as in America. The Austro-Prussian War in 1866, instead of repeating the American Civil War experience, ended quickly on the battlefield of Koniggratz, and Bismarck proved to be a harder bargainer than Victor Emmanuel II in the matter of compensations for the altered balance of power. The border provinces which Napoleon hoped to secure from Germany proved to be compensations that were not to be had Bismarck dangled them tantalizingly before Napoleon's eyes to make it clear that Berlin, not Paris, was to hold the hegemony of Europe These were hard lines for the man who had become "the emperor" so soon after the *coup d'état*

IN 1865, when de Morny and Prince Jerome dropped out of the picture, Rouher, a favorite of the empress and an inflexible advocate of authority, came into power. The fact that Walewski, a natural son of Napoleon I, stepped into de Morny's position in the legislative body, and tried to carry on the work of his predecessor, gave some hope to the men who wished to see a liberal Empire. Louis Napoleon consented to see Ollivier, at Walewski's suggestion, and for some time hesitated between him and Rouher. He would have preferred to combine liberalism and authority by bringing them both into the cabinet, but Ollivier refused to compromise himself so much.

Nonetheless, some decision had to be reached, and Louis Napoleon was inclined toward a more liberal solution In January, 1867, in another *coup de théâtre,* he announced another reform in the Constitution of the Empire. The address to the throne, which had been granted in 1861, was suppressed, but in its place he allowed the deputies the right of interpellation, and also reintroduced the tribune, the favorite framework of French political oratory, into the chamber. The ministers, under the new procedure, were expected to defend their policies in the chamber, but they remained responsible to the emperor alone At the same time, he announced that reforms would be made in the laws governing press and assembly. There was not, however, much reason for rejoicing over these concessions, Rouher had offered to resign in favor of Ollivier, but the empress had persuaded him to remain in office Therefore the cabinet that was expected to introduce liberal reforms was the very cabinet that had no confidence in them

After much discussion, the legislation which Napoleon had promised was written into the statute books. The military law fell somewhere between the provisions for the "people's army" of Prussia and the near-professional army to which the Empire had been accustomed. In 1870, the French army was still based on comparatively long-term recruits, and the reserve was largely untrained. In 1870, the mass army of Moltke, backed up by long-range guns from Krupp, had little trouble in demonstrating its superiority.

Although the new press law of the Empire embodied many of the old restrictions and taxes, the journalists were allowed much more freedom in public questions. The "crimes of the press" were to be punished by a court in which the journalist could defend himself, rather than by mere administrative action. But the fact that a judge, dependent upon the emperor for promotion, rather than a jury, made the decision, did much to vitiate the liberty that the new law seemed to allow. The new law regulating public gatherings removed many of the restrictions, and even allowed for a discussion of politics if permission were properly secured beforehand. Half-hearted in their liberalism as these laws were, they opened for politicians the vistas which had been firmly closed since 1851, and the great game of politics, partly legitimate and partly revolutionary, again became a favorite pastime of many Frenchmen.

The opposition, which had been latent in 1851 and active after 1861, became vigorous after 1868. Catholics, protectionists, nationalists, and partisans of the dethroned royal families joined hands to make a conservative opposition both in and out of the legislative body. Republicans of the Jacobin as well as the more austere bourgeois liberal tradition joined hands to attack the Empire. Even the "social revolution," which had been almost destroyed in June, 1848, again began to gain momentum as Proudhon's "Property is theft!" and Marx's "Workingmen of the world, unite!" assumed new meanings in terms of the increasing industrialization of the nation. Old names and faces, those "beards" of 1848, like Grévy, Blanc, Blanqui, and others, joined with new and as yet unknown names and faces to speak of the new France that must come into being Like the men of 1848, these men of the late 1860's were united in their hopes for the end of the existing régime rather than in plans for replacing it

In 1868, the new laws for press and assembly bore fruit in the creation of three heroes, two more or less authentic, and one absolutely spurious. The pseudo-hero was no less a person than the only legitimate son of Napoleon I (died in 1832) who suddenly became a figure of great importance. Among the new journals that mushroomed into existence after the new law was a red-jacketed sheet, *La Lanterne,* edited by Rochefort, a journalist whose quips had long been thorns in the government's side This new journal bitterly satirized everything connected with the Empire; nothing was sacrosanct to the ubiquitous Rochefort. One of his greatest triumphs was the discovery that he, Rochefort, also was a veritable Bonapartist. He wrote:

> As a Bonapartist I prefer Napoleon II . . . no one will deny that he occupied the throne, since his successor calls himself Napoleon III What a régime! My friends, what a régime! Not a tax; no useless wars with war levies that followed; no expeditions to distant lands in which one spends six hundred million to retrieve fifteen francs; no ravenous civil list; no ministers each holding five or six offices at a hundred thousand francs apiece; there, indeed, is a monarch as I understand him. Oh yes! Napoleon II, I love thee and I admire thee without reserve.

Paris and France smiled, smirked, and guffawed; it was a capital joke, but the barb was too poisoned to be appreciated at the Tuileries. Naturally, *La Lanterne* was suppressed, and Rochefort had to leave Paris hurriedly, but his journal's fame continued *La Lanterne,* published in Belgium, was smuggled into France by every conceivable means. One issue arrived in a bust consigned to an art dealer, another in an antique picture frame. Even if *La Lanterne* became dull at times, it titillated Frenchmen to read a newspaper that came regularly but by amazingly devious routes, and the joke of Napoleon II, model of Bonapartism, never quite lost its zest.

A new taste for history produced another somewhat more authentic hero. The generation of 1868 was quite familiar with the history of Greece and Rome, and even knew something of the great Revolution and the Restoration. Thiers, Blanc, Lamartine, and others had given them several interpretations, and almost any point of view could be satisfied with the offerings at hand. But of the Revolution of 1848, the Republic, and especially of the *coup d'état* of December second, the generation of 1868 knew surprisingly little. The new freedom of the press and the growing daring of the opposition combined to supply them with the missing information. One of the historical studies that appeared in 1868 was an account of Tenot, an editor of *Le Siècle,* entitled *Paris Pendant le Coup d'État.* In his pages, Tenot brought to life one Baudin, a forgotten leftist deputy to the assembly that Napoleon's bayonets suppressed. Baudin had the imprudence to get himself killed under what otherwise might have been regarded as ridiculous and unnecessary conditions. His death had proved nothing more in 1851 than that there was a deputy who would die in defense of his rights, and, to quote what are purported to be his last words, "for twenty-five francs" (the daily salary of a deputy). Poor Baudin had been neglected in his grave for seventeen years, a hero unmourned and unsung

In 1868 he furnished exactly the type of martyr that men had been looking for Had he not died in defense of legality? Had he not been killed to create the régime that the republicans in particular hated most profoundly? A little more careful research into the life and works of their hero might have revealed his presence in the mob that, illegally, had invaded the assembly of 1848; but such embarrassing evidence was unwanted, and the men of the Empire did not stumble upon it. After some exploration, a grave that may or may not have contained the mortal remains of Baudin was found, and a group of the newspapers began a subscription for a monument to the hero of the hour. French taste for political funerals and oratory was to be satisfied at this seventeen-year-old grave. Orléanists like Barrot and legitimists like Berryer joined the more orthodox republicans like Blanc, Hugo, Hébrard, and Delescluze in contributing their money to honor this man who "fell martyred, in defending the law." Someone suggested that Louis Napoleon, had he been wise, would have contributed 500 francs and forgotten the whole affair. Some of his wisest advisers urged that no new martyrs should be made; but the agitation was too patently treasonous to be ignored by the men of the Empire. The ringleaders were haled before the court under the law of security of 1858.

The trial that followed gave the opposition their third hero; Napoleon II and Baudin were dead, this one was very much alive. Among the lawyers for the defense there was a fire-eater from the Midi who was destined to make his name, Léon Gambetta, famous in the politics of his generation. Before the trial, he had enjoyed a local reputation as a vigorous orator and an ardent republican; after the trial Gambetta became a "name" of national importance in French politics. He did not defend his clients; what could have been more useless? Furthermore, a lawyer's reputation can be made even if the client goes to jail! He attacked the Empire at its very roots, the *coup d'état,* shaking his shaggy mane and beard, he roared, he shouted, he quoted the philosophers It was a magnificent display of one of the greatest oratorical talents of his day.

"Listen," he bellowed at the court, "for seventeen years you have been absolute masters of France, the fact which judges you the very best, because it proves your own remorse, is that you have never dared to say: 'We will celebrate, we will place on equality with the solemn occasions of France, the second of December as a national holiday'. . . Ah, well, this anniversary which you have not wished, we will claim it, we will take it for ourselves, we will celebrate it . . . each year it will be the anniversary of our dead until the day when the country . . will impose upon you the great national atonement in the name of liberty, equality, fraternity!"

The *coup d'état,* he insisted, was a heinous crime against society and legality, committed by men with no "talent, or rank, or station," men whom France, up to that hour, "had not known" No amount of sophistry could explain away the fundamental premises of Gambetta's attack, and the newspapers gleefully published the whole proceedings of the court The next day, troops appeared in Paris, and the cemetery of Montmartre, where Baudin supposedly was buried, was guarded by the police.

IN 1868, for the first time in years, the oratorical talent always latent in France found ample opportunity to display itself. The new law governing public gatherings opened vistas of freedom to the talkers, just as the new press law had to the writers. In the fall, when the summer vacations were over, a galaxy of orators met dozens and dozens of audiences to discuss every conceivable topic. Older men recalled the days of 1848, when every available hall housed a "club." Learned economists expounded their doctrines to the socially washed as well as to the underprivileged, in hopes that "reason" would prevail, half-baked philosophers and agitators preached "the word" according to their own dogma Jesuits, Lutherans, atheists, and agnostics confounded each other and their listeners; politicians of all hues finally could get someone to listen to them. The tower of Babel could not have been much more confused; men took to the tribune to discuss "education of children," "women in industry," "heredity," "divorce," "unemployment," "capital and usury," "interest," "the struggle of man against nature," and so forth Utopias were proposed; the *status quo* was almost invariably condemned

De la Gorce, a pious Catholic historian, writes. "In these programs, one searched in vain for a doctrine; there were only hates . . what did one detest the most, God or Caesar? It seemed that God had the privilege of the first rank—after the master above, the master below, the emperor." A few of the meetings were brilliantly conducted, many were somewhat dull, some were stupid, and occasionally one would be funny. One of them, for example, discussed marriage, divorce, and free love; the audience voted against each institution in turn, and hilariously decided to support universal celibacy

The government hesitated to interfere with the "word"; it would be rather inconvenient to explain why privileges once granted should be taken away abruptly. The men around the emperor profoundly hoped that the various "isms" would cancel one another by hopelessly dividing the opposition and frightening "good citizens" who aimlessly had wandered into the radical camp. If this could be achieved, the name Napoleon, as in the fall of 1848, would again appear as the bulwark of order and stability before the sea of threatening chaos

The men in power, of course, directed counterpropaganda against their assailants Officially inspired writers and orators emphasized the positive creations and achievements of the Empire. The great public works—roads, canals, railroads, harbors, docks, boulevards, and buildings—were lauded as benefits from imperialism. The social legislation and the improved economic status of every class in the nation were exhibited to prove that Louis Napoleon had well cared for his subjects. The most telling argument was the contrast between the obvious prosperity of France in 1868 and the economic distress which had prevailed when Louis Napoleon came to power. Needless to say, it lost nothing in the telling when friends of the emperor had "the word." Furthermore, the Empire could point to progressive liberalization since 1861, and its protagonists could assure France that both liberty and order could be achieved under the imperial régime.

THE elections of 1869 assumed considerable importance, in view of the discussions of the preceding year. As the government had foreseen, the opposition parties were greatly divided and mutually hostile. On the left there was a little group of republicans, led by Gambetta, who declared themselves to be "irreconcilable" to the Empire. Next to them were the half-hearted republicans, representatives of the liberal bourgeois tradition, who would be willing to compromise on a parliamentary Empire, Ollivier, whose youthful enthusiasm for opposition had been somewhat calmed by the indifference and the obstacles that he had encountered, was the natural leader of this group of potential *rallieurs*. Another group, the so-called "Tiers Parti," made up of Catholics, protectionists, Orléanists, and even legitimists, held to a doctrine of parliamentarianism, some of them were ready to rally to a liberal Empire, while most of them probably would have preferred a king with a more legitimate background. There were a few die-hard monarchists, some of whom even refused to take the oath prerequisite to becoming a candidate for the chamber. The government, of course, produced its official candidates, the real friends of the Empire who could be depended upon in almost any circumstances because of their loyalty to, or their stake in, the régime.

The campaign was hotly contested, but there were no proper "parties" behind any group of candidates. In the last analysis, each prospective deputy and his local committee made up a tiny political party. In Paris, the government supported the most conservative of the independent tickets, rather than present a candidate sure to be defeated. In the provinces, the lack of an opposition candidate was often made up by importing a public figure from the city to oppose the government machine. As in all former elections, the full power of the administration was wheeled into action to influence the election, but, somehow, it had lost its magic; the elections were not to be influenced so easily as in the past.

When the votes were counted, the "official candidates" had again won a majority in the legislative body, but the Empire had suffered a great defeat! The opposition of all hues had polled 3,355,000 votes; the government, 4,438,000. In 1857, the government's majority had been 4,800,000, in 1863, 3,300,000; in 1869 it was only 1,083,000! The trend was unmistakable; even the blind could see that the Empire was losing ground It is indicative of the trend that Ollivier, one of the original members of the opposition, was defeated in his own district in Paris by one of the "irreconcilable" republicans. (He was subsequently returned from Varr in a run-off election in which he met no opposition from the government.)

The need for radical reorganization of the régime was apparent, not only because of the elections, but also because death and quarrels were rapidly thinning the ranks of the leaders upon whom Napoleon had been accustomed to depend for ministers. Whether he wished it or not, Louis Napoleon must accept "new faces" in the inner circle that ran the state. Two of the outstanding figures of the *coup d'état,* de Maupas and Persigny, publicly called for the change. De Maupas hailed the liberal Empire which would open "a new era," and Persigny, in an open letter to Olliver, explained that the emperor must now follow "the liberal road that he has opened . . . by calling to his service an entirely new generation . . . As for the men of the Second of December, like myself . our rôle is finished." But the empress was afraid, and Rouher was her favorite. Louis Napoleon hesitated; he felt that it might be dangerous to yield before a popular government. For a few months longer, Rouher and the last vestiges of "authority" hung on, while the men of the left and the center prepared for the parliamentary Empire.

THE reign of authority was over; the whole historical process from 1861 had forced Louis Napoleon irrevocably along the path toward a parliamentary Empire, and there was no conceivable way of retracing his steps. The sick man in the Tuileries understood this, too; it was merely a matter of procedure. Ollivier, the first of the opposition to rally to the Empire, provided it would be liberal, was the logical man to assume power. His mandate from the emperor was almost a *carte blanche;* the only restriction that Louis Napoleon insisted upon was that the Orléanists must not preside over the disintegration of the old régime. He had started his career in

1848 somewhat under their tutelage; he did not relish ending it in the same way! On December twenty-seventh, 1869, the emperor, in an open letter to Ollivier, invited him to become prime minister, and added "I request you to designate for me the men who can form with you a homogeneous cabinet faithfully representative of the majority of the legislative corps." Ollivier's task was somewhat simplified, because a solid bloc already had been formed to assume power Its presiding officer had defined its objectives as follows: "We all wish to maintain the Empire, supported by liberal parliamentary institutions Those who wish the Empire without parliamentary institutions, or parliamentary institutions without the Empire, have not the right to be here" Without much difficulty, Ollivier enlarged this group to include a majority in the legislative body, and the liberal parliamentary Empire became a fact.

The Constitution had come a long way since 1852, it seemed to be good tactics to submit the revisions to a plebiscite. This would have two advantages—the emperor would be unable to change the new institutions, and the revolutionaries and anti-imperialists could be shown that France supported the Empire. A *senatus consultum* of April twentieth, 1870, proclaimed the new constitution of France The senate was transformed into a chamber of peers, appointed by the emperor. The council of state prepared projects of laws, but both the senate and the legislative body had the right to propose laws. The whole paraphernalia of parliamentary control was established; the emperor retained the right to declare war and grant amnesties, but the authoritative Empire was definitely at an end. France received the new constitution enthusiastically, a majority of over six million voted in favor of the new régime The republican, Jules Favre, advised a young friend to continue his legal practice, because "there is no longer anything to do in politics," and Louis Napoleon announced, "We ought more than ever to look into the future without fears."

The new régime proved its mettle in the streets of Paris early in the spring of 1870, when a riot was attempted after the funeral of Victor Noir * Loyal troops quickly cleared the streets, proving that a parliamentary government could keep order as well as the authoritative régime had done. As summer approached in 1870, most political forecasters would surely have predicted that Napoleon III would die in the Tuileries, and that his son would ascend a throne almost as stable as the one in London. There seemed to be no obvious reason why a parliamentary régime could not maintain the Empire and assure France of both order and liberty The Empire, however, had only a few more months to exist. A shadow, which had first appeared when the French armies were in Italy, began to darken the sky beyond the Rhine; before 1870 had run itself out, that shadow had enveloped all France, and when light reappeared, the Empire was gone.

THE vicissitudes of Louis Napoleon's foreign policy proved to be the undoing of the Empire. The Italian war and the free-trade treaties aroused an opposition in France that had started the Empire on its course of liberalism when grumbling and even outright opposition forced Napoleon to make concessions. But, even so, the greatest fiascoes of his foreign policy were to follow. To an uncolonially minded generation, which had not yet learned of "the profits and prestige of economic imperialism," the expeditions to Syria and to China seemed a pointless waste of good money and troops. The Polish crisis of 1861–1863 brought new troubles, the czar's brutal repression of a Polish insurrection inflamed French opinion, for the fate of Poland has always captivated French imagination. Napoleon III fell somewhere between retaining the good will of the czar and satisfying the sentiments of his subjects, who made Poland's cause their own. It was humiliating that the great powers refused to listen to the French suggestion of a conference on Polish affairs. In 1864, Austria and Prussia "settled" the Schleswig-Holstein question by a war

* Victor Noir was killed by a relative of the emperor The scandal which followed shocked Parisian society severely

on Denmark Europe was concerned about the fate of the duchies, since their status was regulated by a European treaty, but Bismarck successfully outmaneuvered both France and England. Napoleon's suggestion of a "congress" again was rebuffed, and the German powers "solved" an important European question without benefit of Napoleonic advice. In four years, "the emperor" had proposed four conferences to a Europe indifferent to his suggestions; the much-prized French hegemony appeared to have come to an end

The Roman question, too, made sport of Napoleon's position as arbiter of Europe, and caused him endless embarrassment at home. His Holiness, Pius IX, steadfastly refused to listen to Louis Napoleon's counsel, and the new kingdom of Italy resented Napoleon's position French troops were in and out of Rome, during the decade of the 1860's, to protect a pope whom Louis Napoleon hardly wished to defend. It was expedient to do so in the light of French politics. On one occasion, French soldiers had to shoot down Italian "patriots" who wished a quick solution of the Roman question in the manner of the famous "red shirt" descent upon Naples. The whole affair antagonized the Italy that should have been Napoleon's best friend in Europe, and it never secured the unconditional support of the Church.

One of the greatest fiascoes in foreign policy occurred in Mexico. A French, Spanish, and English expedition descended upon that turbulent Spanish-American republic to collect a bad debt, but Napoleon saw in it an opportunity to extend French influence beyond the sea The moment seemed auspicious; the power of the United States was neutralized by a bitter civil war, and no European state was disposed to interfere The expedition was surrounded by fuzzy thinking in which French commerce, influence, and institutions were mixed up with the desire to do something for the Roman Catholic Church, the family of the Austrian emperor, and, maybe, for the Mexicans. The cost in blood and gold was tremendous; for one reason or another, no inconsiderable number of Mexicans failed to welcome Maximilian von Hapsburg and the French army. The stupid play went on for several years, without showing any of the desired results. Then, at the end of the American Civil War, the French expeditionary force was confronted with the embarrassing alternative of withdrawal from Mexico or conflict with the veterans of the victorious Union armies. It was really no choice at all, Napoleon was confronted with opposition to the Mexican adventure at home, fear of Prussia, and a possible war with the United States, as well as with the Mexican rebels. The French withdrew, and Maximilian, who felt that duty bade him remain, faced a Mexican firing squad.

The French people never understood the Mexican adventure, and there is excellent evidence that, even if they had, they would never have approved of it. It was expensive, and as far as the French could see, not particularly "glorious" One of Napoleon's advisers wrote: "This war will become popular . . . if the government can assure the recovery of the money spent by France." It seemed foolish to the men who felt that the American Civil War had ruined their export and import business, and impoverished themselves and their workers Why embark on an adventure in Mexico when the government could do nothing about the blockade by the Union navy? The New World in the 1860's thus did its share to discredit the imperial foreign policy both at home and abroad.

The hardest blow to imperial prestige came from beyond the Rhine. The unification of the German people had been "in the air" ever since the War of Liberation, but it was not until the 1860's that "the man" whom poets, philosophers, and statesmen had been crying for, made his appearance on the German stage. It must be said that "the man," when he did appear, was not recognized in Germany or the rest of Europe until he had proved to his astonished contemporaries his claim to the title. Count Otto von Bismarck and Emperor Napoleon III took each other's measure early in the Prussian's career; Napoleon thought lightly of the blunt Junker squire, and

Bismarck saw in the emperor "a great, unrecognized incapacity" History was to prove whose judgment was the better In the early 1860's, Bismarck embarked upon his task by tentatively placing his head on the block as a Prussian Strafford. he bullied the king, he defied the Landtag, he ignored the Constitution; he created an army. Under him, Prussia was to become, to quote Sir Robert Morier, a "huge ironclad, from which no sounds are heard but the tramp of men at drill, or the swinging upon their pivots of monster guns."

In 1864, the first indication of the meaning of Bismarck's Prussia should have been apparent when the blunt Junker minister-president extricated himself from an awkward situation by leading Austria and Prussia into a war on Denmark A little fishing in the troubled waters of the Schleswig-Holstein question proved that he was a master of craft; in spite of Europe, Austria, and his own king, Bismarck "solved" the problem in his own way By 1866 he was ready to try for larger fry, and the Deutsche Bund at Frankfort provided him with an excellent pond of muddy water. Austria was to be the next fish on his hook. Napoleon III saw the German civil war in the offing, and, himself a fisherman in troubled waters, prepared to cast his own line into the pond In the end the emperor of the French lost his bait, his hook, his line, and his sinker!

Louis Napoleon completely misjudged the problem of an Austro-Prussian War. With the American Civil War fresh in mind, he confidently expected the two big fish in the German pond to exhaust themselves, and, at the right moment, France could act as mediator. Prussia, which he imagined to be the weaker, he provided with an ally—Italy The Italians were loath to join Prussia, even with Venetia dangling before their eyes; the memories of 1860 were still green in the Italian chancellory. Napoleon reassured them, and acted as sponsor to their union with Bismarck. In a calmer moment, the emperor apparently got cold feet, and himself approached Austria with a treaty by which the Hapsburg court promised to give Venice to Napoleon after they had defeated Prussia; in return, Napoleon agreed to remain neutral and allow a spoliation of Prussia. The treaty was signed, and Napoleon III watched the storm gather in central Europe, confident that, whoever should win, France alone would be the victor

The Austro-Prussian War started and ran according to a schedule—the one prepared by Bismarck and Moltke In a seven-week campaign the Prussian armies overran Germany and defeated the Austrians at Koniggratz (Sadowa). With Germany in her hands, and the road to Vienna open and practically undefended, Prussia was in a position to dictate terms. Europe was slightly dazed at the magnitude of the victory. Bismarck shrewdly seized the first opportunity to consolidate his position, before Europe could decide what ought to be done At the peace of Prague, the Italians received Venetia, after it had been transferred to Napoleon; Prussia reimbursed herself at the expense of Austria's allies in North Germany, and Austria agreed to the dissolution of the Deutsche Bund and her own exclusion from German affairs. By her annexations and the formation of the North German Confederation, Prussia appeared in 1867 as the most powerful state in Europe. The old established balance of power, under Napoleonic hegemony, was rapidly disappearing.

The battle of Koniggratz (Sadowa) placed Napoleon in a quandary. For a moment he thought of persuading Italy to make a separate peace, mobilizing his armies, and menacing Prussia on the Rhine This might re-establish the European balance and pay back the debt of 1859–1860, but it presented difficulties. A large part of the French army was still in Mexico; it might prove embarrassing to ask the Italians to break the very treaty which he had urged them to make, and, not least important, the victorious Prussian army was fully mobilized and in the field. It seemed better to offer French mediation. Even this proved redundant when Bismarck negotiated the peace of Prague before French good offices could be utilized To indicate that he did not consider the matter closed, Louis Napoleon explained to the Prussian ambassador that France would be critical of the changed status in central Europe unless some compensations were granted to her. The ambassador was vague; Bismarck, he thought, might be willing to discuss the problem. France was critical of the emperor's inaction, during the next three years, Louis Napoleon fished about for compensations, and men spoke of Konigratz (Sadowa) as if it had been the French army that Moltke had defeated.

Benedetti, the French ambassador to Prussia, opened the discussion of compensations with Bismarck while the Prussian army was still in the field. He had a list of provinces, including Luxembourg, the Rheinpfalz, and the Saar, that would be acceptable compensation. Prussia, it seemed, was not willing to cede any of her own territory, and Bismarck did not like to give away provinces that did not belong to him. When Benedetti became insistent, the Prussian minister-president informed him that there were 800,000 Prussian veterans in the field, and if France wanted war . . . Prussia would "take Alsace." This gave Napoleon food for thought, but it did not end his hopes of compensations.

In France, his policy evoked criticism, both in and out of the legislative body, that convinced the emperor that he must obtain some results The next move was to offer Bismarck an alliance with France in return for an adjustment of the eastern frontier; Luxembourg, which belonged to the king of Holland, had been garrisoned by Prussian troops since 1815; it would be acceptable. Belgium had large populations, contiguous to France, which were French in culture, that might be annexed to France; the Rheinpfalz or the Saar might also satisfy. Foolishly, Napoleon wrote something on paper that made the British and the South German States more than mildly fearful of French policy. Bismarck listened to this alliance proposal carefully, indicated his interest, and finally consented to discuss ways and means

Luxembourg occupied a large place in the discussions Bismarck indicated that he, personally, would not object if the king of Holland wished to sell, but he feared that William might not be pleased. The wily junker knew his king, and suggested that if French agents were to stir up anti-Prussian press agitation in Luxembourg, King William of Prussia would probably lose all interest in the fate of the Luxembourgers This guess was correct—especially when the Luxembourg press campaign attacked King William as well as Prussia! The king of Holland, at first reluctant, finally consented to sell Luxembourg to France, when he understood that Bismarck would not help him. On March thirtieth, 1867, the treaty was ready for ratification. On April first—an ominous day for an international joke if it was one—a German deputy interpellated Bismarck about Prussia's part in the sale of Luxembourg. Bismarck answered, "I have no reason to believe that the king of Holland will sell" There was a hubbub in the German press. The king of Holland, fortified by German opinion, decided not to ratify the treaty, and the French cabinet thought seriously of a war on Prussia.

Bismarck later maintained that he personally had favored the sale, but the storm in the press forced him to change his mind. The French have insisted that he duped and made a fool of Napoleon to provoke a war. There is excellent documentary evidence to support Bismarck's thesis, but it is not impossible that the Prussian, without leaving documentary evidence, had something to do with the press storm and the interpellations.

"An alliance with Austria," Napoleon announced to the Austrian ambassador, "ought henceforth to be my policy" Austria, so recently humiliated by Prussia, seemed the logical ally for a war of revenge. The fiasco of Luxembourg was not a month old, when Louis Napoleon submitted extensive plans for an alliance to the court at Vienna. In the fall of 1867, he visited the Austrian capital to cement the project. Austria, however, was becoming Austria-Hungary; the Magyars were not interested in a crusade in Germany until they had discussed the East, and maybe not then. Count Beust, the new Austrian foreign minister, lately minister in Saxony, was a small man with big ideas, but even he could not hide the fact that Napoleon had come to secure an ally and found a neutral.

Undaunted, Louis Napoleon pursued his plans; he wished to include Italy in the alliance, stir up ambitions in Austria, and finally encompass the ruin of the terrible Herr Bismarck. The Italians were interested—in the removal of the French garrison from Rome! By 1869, almost two years of hard labor on the problem of an anti-Prussian coalition had produced a friendly letter from Francis Joseph of Austria and a note from Victor Emmanuel II of Italy. The French had the illusion that this was the stuff alliances are made of, and hopefully continued in Vienna, Paris, and Rome an academic discussion of a war on Prussia. It was a little disconcerting to hear of a proposed counteralliance of Prussia, Russia, and England, but this did not daunt those who were hopeful for revenge. At the very time when the Franco-Prussian War prematurely broke out, there was a special Austrian envoy in Paris to continue the discussions.

BETWEEN 1860 and 1870, the imperial policy had received setbacks in Italy, Syria, Mexico, Germany, Poland, and the Far East; in 1870, Spain was to provide an occasion for the last and the catastrophic defeat of the Empire. Spanish politics, habitually revolutionary, had gone through another political gyration; the military clique in control was shopping about in Europe to find a suitable king Several princes turned down the questionable honor of governing the Spaniards, before the good generals listened to German agents, undoubtedly Bismarck's, who had an excellent candidate to suggest. The young man, Leopold von Hohenzollern-Sigmaringen was a Catholic, a brother of the king of Rumania, a relative of the king of Prussia and of Napoleon III, and sufficiently poor in expectations to accept the candidacy of almost any throne.

The king of Prussia and the young man's father raised difficulties; Bismarck suggested to the Spaniards that it would be wise to consult Leopold directly. Since his position in the German army did not look so attractive as the throne, Leopold accepted a renewed invitation. The Spanish generals sent a man post-haste to inform Napoleon; but the newspapers made a "scoop," and the emperor of the French *read* of another European question that was solved without benefit of his advice. It was even more than that; a Hohenzollern on the throne of Spain would tip the balance of power even more sharply against France and in favor of Prussia. Visions of the sorry plight of Francis I in face of Charles V of Spain and Germany danced before Napoleon's eyes, and the press of France became agitated to an extreme degree. It was too much! No amount of explaining by well-intentioned Spanish generals could argue away the conviction that Bismarck (Napoleon intuitively recognized his antagonist) was humiliating France and playing fast and loose with her emperor

Bismarck urged his king to assume an air of injured innocence in case the French should ask questions; it was an air that he, King William, might reasonably assume. The Prussian government had understood that the candidacy had not been accepted; if Prince Leopold had changed his mind, the Prussian king was unaware of it. The empress and his constitutional foreign minister prodded Louis Napoleon into signing a bellicose statement to the effect that France "would not hesitate to do her duty towards a power that upsets the European balance by placing her princes on the throne of Charles V." A diplomatic victory, it was argued, would stabilize the dynasty, and prove that a parliamentary government could be firm in international affairs. Benedetti, the French ambassador to Prussia, was ordered to demand a statement from the Prussian king saying that he did not approve of the candidacy, and that he ordered Leopold to withdraw.

Bismarck in Berlin wanted a crisis; William, at Ems for a rest, did not. Before he learned of the French demand, the Prussian king had written Leopold a fatherly letter urging him to reconsider Queen Victoria and King Leopold of Belgium also sent letters The prince, himself, had no desire to bring down a hornet's nest on Europe, even before he received all this royal advice, he telegraphed his resignation. Bismarck was furious, William said something about a "stone lifted from his heart." Ollivier and Louis Napoleon were satisfied, but the French cabinet decided that it wanted an even more striking diplomatic victory than this In his anger, Bismarck had overlooked the stupidity of the French government. There was no better way to start a war than the course of action upon which the parliamentary cabinet in Paris decided. Benedetti was ordered to request the king of Prussia to state that he would never allow Leopold to accept the Spanish throne.

The request was humiliating enough in itself, and Benedetti did not soften it at all by waylaying the old king in the park at Ems to present it Naturally, William flatly refused. "What shall I tell my government?" Benedetti asked, a bit mournfully. "It seems to me, Monsieur Ambassador," the king replied, "that I have expressed myself clearly, I cannot make such a declaration, and I have nothing further to say"

That night, Bismarck received an account of the proceedings at Ems, with authority to publish it in part or in full, as he saw fit. Bismarck has been unjustly accused of tampering with the meaning of the telegram, he did not. He edited it so that the painful episode in the park at Ems would be clear to everyone who read it The original telegram was wordy and circumlocutionary, Bismarck's edition was to the point; their beloved king had been humiliated! *"Nach Paris! Nach Paris!"* could be heard on Unter den Linden In Paris, men understood that France's ambassador, her emperor, and her honor had been insulted! *"À Berlin! à Berlin!"* could be heard on the boulevards. The war clouds hung heavy over the Rhine; soon the thunder and lightning of the heavy guns would announce another rain of blood. National honor, prestige, and the balance of power had become the mainsprings of political activity. The French government saw in the crisis a way to regain prestige and redress the balance of power, by defeating Bismarck's Prussia, the misfortunes that had dogged the foreign policy of the Empire could be obliterated.

On July fourteenth, 1870, the French cabinet discussed peace and war. Louis Napoleon—a little fearful perhaps—announced that he was a "constitutional sovereign"; the cabinet must decide its position At 10.00 P. M. the cabinet adjourned, with the agreement to temporize. At 11:30 the same evening, in a second meeting, the same cabinet voted to present a declaration of war to the chamber for its approval Two telegrams had arrived in Paris between 10:00 and 11.30 that evening—one from the French chargé in Vienna asking for precise propositions; the other from a French secret agent in Bavaria, saying that Bavaria was hesitant in following Prussia. Strange it is if these telegrams tipped the balance in favor of war, only a few days before, Count Beust had instructed the Austrian ambassador to Paris not to let France believe that Austria would go beyond her promise of neutrality, and Count Vitzthun, the special Austrian envoy, had warned France that Austria could not be counted upon in a military way. Surely, no one believed that Bismarck was afraid of a diplomatic note.

The war spirit appeared to be running high in Paris, and it was amply reflected in the chamber Neither the ministers nor the deputies were impressed by the fact that the great mass of the French had said nothing, and, probably, was largely uninterested in the "prestige" or "honor" of the French ambassador Cheers and boastful, patriotic speeches greeted the proposal to declare war on Prussia Thiers, in a brief moment of lucidity, asked several serious questions about France's preparations for war; his speech was remembered after the war was lost, but at the moment it had little effect. There was much mysterious talk about possible allies, and one responsible official who should have known better announced that France was ready "down to the last soldier's shoestring." Ollivier was destined to write a multivolumed history to explain this light-hearted statement. Needless to say, the declaration of war received the approval of the French chamber and of Bismarck.

The war was one in which the glory accruing to the tricolor was meager, indeed The French army was not prepared to fight, especially not prepared to fight the war that Moltke had in mind. Krupp's new guns allowed the Prussians—they were soon to be Germans—to destroy the French artillery from a distance that rendered themselves immune from retaliation The Prussian infantry was led by men who had studied modern warfare, and took care not to act Napoleonic, and the short-term, mass army soon demonstrated superiority over the semiprofessional battalions. Bavaria, Baden, and Wurtemburg contributed their bits to embarrass the French Austria received a warning from the czar of Russia in which it was intimated that Russia would intervene if Austria entered the war; the Austrians indicated their neutrality, sat back, and begged the French to win a victory The Italians asked questions about the removal of the French garrison from Rome, that produced a French remark about "losing honor on the Tiber while defending it upon the Rhine" Italy declared her neutrality. The British were considerably agitated about the war, but their sympathies were not with the French Empire; Bismarck, very timely, had published the correspondence that showed French designs on Belgium, and the British decided that they, too, were neutral Moltke's armies and Bismarck's diplomacy soon held France in a vise.

When it became obvious that the French armies were not to have a military parade into Prussia, Louis Napoleon joined his troops to assist in repelling the invasion. There was a little flurry in government circles; someone had to be the scapegoat, and the empress expressed her willingness to see her husband get himself killed in action. For his part, the emperor of the French tried desperately to do just that, but fate was against him. Though he exposed himself in battle, only some of his aides were killed. The poor man suffered horribly from his chronic illness and the feeling of impending doom. As the Prussian army closed in around his troops at Sedan, there was nothing to do but to surrender to prevent further bloodshed. France had met her Koniggratz! On September second, 1870, Napoleon III and his army, or that part of it that was at Sedan, surrendered and became prisoners of war. The emperor wrote to Eugénie: "It is impossible to tell you what I have suffered and am suffering . . . the catastrophe . . . is complete, I would have preferred death . . . I am thinking of you, our son, our unhappy country. . . ."

The news of the disaster was a bombshell in the capital. In the legislative body, Jules Favre announced his intention to move the deposition of the emperor and his family. A noisy crowd invaded the Palais Bourbon (it must have appeared to many as a re-enactment of 1848) and Léon Gambetta shouted to the deputies that the dynasty had ceased to reign. While the politicians made plans for a provisional government, crowds on the street shouted *"Vive la république!"* and an American dentist helped Eugénie to escape to England. In Cassel, Napoleon, a prisoner of war, inspected the new breech-loading guns of Krupp, wrote a pamphlet, "On the causes which led to the capitulation of Sedan," and played Santa Claus for German children in the neighborhood! Thus ended the political career of one of the strangest figures ever to govern France. He fatalistically followed his "star," from exile to the pinnacle of fame, and again to exile. He gave France an interlude of Caesarism that failed completely to solve the basic problem of French government.

CHAPTER XI

THE FOUNDING OF THE REPUBLIC

IN THE uprising of September, 1870, the very best French revolutionary traditions asserted themselves. A Parisian movement had overthrown the existing régime, proclaimed a new government from the Hôtel de Ville, and, unembarrassed, had asked France to approve the *fait accompli*. It seemed to be 1830 and 1848 all over again! The imperial eagles had governed France for eighteen years. Seven and a half million Frenchmen had recently approved the imperial constitution, and the war, which gave occasion for the September revolution, had been the work of a government responsible to the representatives of the people. No one, however, came forward to defend either the dynasty or the Empire. The legislative body, elected less than a year before, allowed itself to be overlooked; the senate was declared to be abolished; and the empress fled to England

Everyone knew the part that revolutionary traditions expected him to play. The new provisional government was recruited from the important members of the late opposition After a public acclamation, Favre, Simon, Picard, Gambetta, and Rochefort made their way to the Hôtel de Ville to assume power. General Trochu, who was persuaded to accept the new office of president, is reported to have said, "I'm going down there to play Lamartine." The problems confronting this provisional régime were as urgent as those of February, 1848; the German armies were irresistibly sweeping toward Paris, and the radical, social revolutionary element in the capital was preparing itself for a struggle with the conservatives for the control of the state. The men in the Hôtel de Ville well understood that their rôles would fit into no comic opera, and they hoped to avoid the unenviable possibility of being protagonists in a supreme tragedy.

The first problem was to reach a settlement with Bismarck. As long as the Germans were advancing more deeply into France, no political debate could be conducted satisfactorily. Jules Favre, who became minister of foreign affairs, met with the Prussian chancellor to discuss terms. The latter had hoped to find that Prussia had been fighting Louis Napoleon, but he soon discovered that she was fighting France. Bismarck painfully explained that this war had been forced upon him by the warlike ambitions of France, and that he feared the possibility of another "unprovoked" attack upon his peaceful Germany. To prevent this, he was resolved to insist upon the surrender of Alsace and Lorraine, so that Germany's frontiers could be adequately defended Of course, Prussia also insisted upon an indemnity to pay for the trouble that this war had caused her. Poor Favre was thunderstruck. He wept, he begged, and he entreated; he said something about his unwillingness to surrender an inch of territory or a stone of French fortresses. The conference lasted well into the night, and when Favre returned to Paris, the terms, unaltered, were considered to be completely unacceptable by the provisional government. Paris prepared itself to meet the onslaught of the Germans, and Thiers, who had kept clear of the political activity of the new régime, agreed to make a tour of Europe to see if France might not be able to find an ally—or, at least, a friend.

It was a lost cause. Moltke's troops shut up the army of Bazaine in Metz and held Paris in a ring of fire, while Bismarck's diplomacy successfully staved off any attempt at European intervention, and checkmated Thiers' noble efforts to find a friend With the Prussians besieging Paris, hunger stalked with death in the French capital. The price of rats mounted beyond the reach of most of the inhabitants. The whole city was armed; the men who manned the forts were brave, but bravery could not save Paris from humiliation and defeat. Gambetta dramatically escaped in a balloon, to tour the provinces with an appeal for a mass assault on the invaders, only to learn that Bazaine had surrendered at Metz with his whole army and most of his supplies still intact. The German troops, relieved from the siege of Metz, pressed into the interior, and even a firebrand could not persuade raw recruits to meet those well-armed, trained German veterans. The peace-loving provincials and peasants listened to the orators who shouted about national honor—but there was no help for it; France was defeated. Paris surrendered after a long siege, and a general armistice ended the most humiliating war France had ever had.

Bismarck was anxious to make peace quickly, but he refused to make peace with a provisional government which France could easily repudiate The choice was between Louis Napoleon and an election; wisely, Bismarck chose not to restore the Empire. A national assembly, elected on the issue of the peace, could ratify a treaty which might be considered as binding. There was no other course open; France held elections under the shadow of the German guns, while Bismarck directed arrangements for the proclamation of the German Empire in the Hall of Mirrors at Versailles

The elections, regulated by the electoral law of 1849, were conducted peacefully and in good order. The issue of peace or war was plain. One party, the advanced republicans, demanded a continuation of the war; *la guerre à l'outrance,* urged by Gambetta, made all republicans appear chauvinists and foolhardy patriots. The other party, conservatives and monarchists of all hues, were resolved to accept peace at Bismarck's price. France may have understood vaguely that she was also voting on a form of government—monarchy or republic—but this issue was distinctly subordinate to the burning question of the hour. Although any possibility that a large number of the supporters of the late Empire would be elected was remote, Gambetta attempted to rule them out by declaring that anyone who had been an official candidate of Louis Napoleon was *ipso facto* ineligible for election. When Bismarck intervened to defend their rights as Frenchmen, Gambetta's ruling was repudiated, but the imperialists were immediately branded as "allies of M de Bismarck."

In most electoral districts, "local notables" were returned to the national assembly, giving that body the title "an assembly of rurals." That these provincials had little understanding of, or sympathy for, the problems and interests of Paris, very soon became painfully apparent in the political arena In many districts, however, no plausible "local notable" was available, and a national figure was imported to fill the vacancy. Thiers, for example, was elected in twenty-six departments; Gambetta, in nine; General Trochu, in eight These multiple elections tended to give the assembly an indication of the real notables in its ranks, who could be trusted to carry out the work of rehabilitation.

When all the votes were counted and the deputies presented themselves at Bordeaux to assume their duties, it became clear that the ballots of the electors co-ordinated highly with their personal contacts in the war. Paris and the area in the east occupied by the Germans voted for the republicans, that is, for continuance of the war. They had already suffered about as much as possible, and continued conflict might make their sufferings less futile In the areas untouched by the war, men voted for the conservatives and for peace They could see no use in prolonging a lost struggle, especially since the fighting would be in their own yards Of the six hundred-odd delegates to the assembly, about two hundred were republicans, four hundred were conservative monarchists, and about thirty were imperialists The monarchists were about evenly divided in their allegiance to the Bourbon and the Orléans pretenders. In spite of their majority, the monarchists did not risk an immediate restoration; indeed, they elected M. Grévy, a moderate, conservative republican, to the presidency of the assembly. He was a "safe" man, and the onus of the peace, which must be borne, could more easily be placed on the shoulders of the republican faction.

Obviously, the administrative power of the assembly had to

be concentrated in the hands of a responsible and trusted statesman Thiers, the Cassandra of the Empire and the unsuccessful diplomat of the provisional government, was the logical choice He was an elder statesman, and twenty-six departments had chosen him for their representative. The assembly designated him chief of the executive power, and commissioned him to lead the nation out of the wilderness of defeat. His office, it was clearly understood, was only temporary, and his exercise of power was dependent upon a parliamentary majority. The assembly clearly had no intention of creating anything more than a provisional régime In his initial declaration, Thiers satisfied both royalists and republicans by explaining that it was not his intention to establish a permanent régime; his government would occupy itself with the problems of the hour, and reserve for subsequent consideration the question of a constitution.

The first problem was that of peace In the negotiations, however, Thiers found that he had very little with which to bargain. The whole world knew that the assembly was committed to immediate peace at practically any price, and Bismarck was not a man to surrender an advantage like this. Thiers urged that leniency and reason would pay dividends in future friendly Franco-German relations, but the Prussians refused to believe that France would ever forgive the defeats of 1870. In the course of the negotiations, Thiers managed to save Belfort for France, at the price of allowing King William a triumphal march through Paris, it was, however, only a slight modification of the terms. Alsace and Lorraine were surrendered, France agreed to pay an indemnity of five billion francs, and a Prussian army of occupation remained in France until the indemnity was paid—humiliating terms, which Bismarck might have regretted had he been able to pull aside the curtain of the future to see his beloved Germany in 1919 and 1933.

There was really no alternative for the assembly; sign it must, and sign it did. There was undoubtedly some satisfaction in hearing a deputy from Metz shout: "One man alone would be able to sign; that is Napoleon III, whose name will remain nailed to the pillory of history" Many French historians have labored hard to make this prophecy come true! In ratifying the treaty, the assembly saved its face by adopting the formula: "The assembly, submitting to the consequences of deeds of which it is not the author . . " The vote was 546 to 107 in favor of ratification Deputies from the lost provinces retired from the assembly to join their new fatherland, after pronouncing a ringing denunciation of the instrument that separated them from France. Some time later, Daudet wrote *La Dernière Classe.*

WITH the peace treaty out of the way, the politicians at Bordeaux prepared to clear the decks for action. They assumed the obligation of governing France and stabilizing the constitution To avoid the pressure of the Paris crowds, they chose Versailles as their capital—a clear expression of the monarchical sympathies of the majority in the assembly. Before they left Bordeaux, however, Thiers bound the entire assembly to a temporary political truce. The great problems of the day —rehabilitation and reconstruction of the nation—were to be solved before they approached the question of a final constitution. Thiers, on his part, promised neutrality in the constitutional question, and the assembly agreed to co-operate in the work of reconditioning France. This was the Pact of Bordeaux, which provided a working basis for the governing of the war-torn country. The assembly adjourned on March eleventh, to meet in Versailles on March twentieth, 1871.

Hardly had the assembly established itself at Versailles when it was forced to deal with a terrible civil war. The social radicals, who had been forestalled by the provisional government in September, 1870, and outvoted by the provinces in 1871, did not give up their hopes of creating a social republic. With increasing suspicion, they watched the monarchical, conservative majority of the assembly sign a peace which they considered intolerable, and establish itself in Versailles, the traditional capital of the monarchy. Their suspicions that this assembly had no intention of catering to their ideas were further re-enforced by a series of tactless, ill-considered measures that eventually fanned Paris into open revolt The horrors of civil, class war were to be added to those of the foreign war to make 1870–1871 *l'année terrible* of France.

The choice of Versailles as the seat of the government wounded Parisian pride, and denied to the erstwhile capital an opportunity to influence the work of the new government, but two other measures taken by the assembly struck more deeply by threatening hundreds of thousands of Parisians with bankruptcy and starvation. During the siege, a moratorium on all debts had been proclaimed, in recognition of the irregular economic situation. In spite of numerous petitions by debtors, the assembly revoked this moratorium before regular commerce was re-established, leaving thousands of petty and middle bourgeois in the city to face their creditors and bankruptcy. The other measure concerned the National Guard. When the Prussians surrounded Paris, every male, whether he wished or not, had received arms and had been enrolled in the National Guard The interruption of commerce during the siege soon made the miserable daily stipend that the Guardsmen were paid their sole means of support; and even after the siege was lifted, the slow recovery of commerce created a situation in Paris in which tens of thousands of people depended upon their soldier's pay for bread Naturally, the cost of supporting this army was considerable, and as soon as peace was re-established, the assembly suppressed the payments. If the men at Versailles had set about finding unpopular measures, they would have been hard pressed to discover any more unpopular than these. In Paris it seemed that the assembly wished to defy the city.

The moment was inauspicious to cast down the glove to the radicals In the treaty with Germany, the French army had been disarmed, but the Prussians thought so meanly of the armed citizenry of Paris that the disarmament provisions had not been extended to them. In the spring of 1871, the proletariat of Paris was armed to the teeth and organized in military companies Furthermore, many of their officers were tinged or infected with radical doctrines; hence, it was hardly the time for the conservative assembly to go out of its way to cause trouble. To make matters worse, the months of siege, with the accompanying hardships, had frayed the nerves of the Parisians to a dangerous degree, too much wine, too little food, too many explosions, and too little security had filled the erstwhile gay capital with excitable people The so-called "better element," which presumably should contribute stability to society, had fled from the city either just before or just after the siege, and had not yet returned. Paris, in the spring of 1871, was ripe for the radical propaganda which became insistent when the assembly tactlessly endangered the property and lives of the little people that made up the bulk of the inhabitants. It was a social powderkeg that needed only a spark to blow off the lid.

In due time the spark was struck. The Parisian National Guard had some cannon which, if they belonged to anyone, belonged to the city of Paris. The people had concealed them from the Prussians during the occupation, and they were in little mood to give them up, even to a regularly constituted French government Cannons are dangerous weapons Thiers and his colleagues decided that they ought to be removed to a place of safekeeping A detail of regular troops entered the city with orders to confiscate the guns and carry them out of the city. Through a bit of military ineptitude, the troopers blundered in their mission, became embroiled with a Parisian mob, and lost both the guns and their own commander General Lecomte, who led the troops, ordered them to fire on the crowds, he was captured by a semimilitarized mob, and, with another officer, General Thomas, whose record in June, 1848, counted against him in the eyes of the proletariat, haled before a drumhead court, condemned, and executed. The action amounted to a declaration of war against the assembly A revolutionary government, the Commune of Paris, established itself in the Hôtel de Ville, and issued proclamations to France. The radical leaders of the National Guard and a group of social revolutionaries of all hues were in control.

The government at Versailles took up the challenge As it had been in June, 1848, the radicals of Paris were fighting against bourgeois and peasant France. The precedure of the government, however, differed from the tactics of 1848 Thiers, himself an old revolutionary (1830), a victim of both a revolution (1848) and a *coup d'état* (1851), a historian of both the French and the English revolutions, and a keen student of the whole European movement in 1848, resolved to carry out the plan that he had urged upon Louis Philippe in February, 1848 He reasoned that the regular army could put down a revolt, and, to prove his point, he cited the experiences in Austria of 1849 and Louis Napoleon's tactics in 1851 The army and the provinces would have little sympathy for the radicals, they would gladly assist in the extermination of the Commune at the Hôtel de Ville.

Since the city was armed, this maneuver meant a serious military engagement. Thiers temporized until he was sure of ultimate success. It would be unwise to begin hostilities until the army, in prison in Germany, was released, rearmed, and ready for an assault; he, therefore, withdrew all of his troops from Paris to wait until he was ready to impose capitulation on the revolters Many of his supporters were horrified at this; they did not realize that troopers, if they have nonmilitary contacts with revolution, become easily infected by it. The men of the Commune, strangely enough, regarded the withdrawal of the troops as a sign of weakness, and consented to discuss the situation with mediators, while Thiers gained time to prepare for their destruction.

Karl Marx and the histories of socialist scholars to the contrary, it seems farfetched to associate the Commune of Paris with contemporary communism or socialism. There was great confusion within the movement; in a way, it represented all of the social revolutionary traditions of France. True it is that there were a few Marxist, international socialists in the Commune, but there were also several varieties of anarchists, Jacobin and social republicans, to say nothing of a large number of radicals who were revolutionaries without any clear program. They all feared the assembly with its veiled monarchy; they all had a pattern for liberty, equality, and fraternity that would benefit the little people They called for a decentralized France, a federation of semiautonomous communes, each of which could work out its own problems without benefit of a Napoleonic prefect, but their rule was too short-lived to allow them to crystallize many of their ideas It is evident, however, that the communards in no way presaged the modern communistic state. They did not even molest the gold in the Bank of France which was obviously within their grasp!

When the government forces were ready, Thiers ordered the troops to besiege Paris. Like the revolters of June, 1848, the men of the Commune were predestined to defeat and death. Every day fresh troops arrived from German prisons to fill the government's ranks, and Thiers, in control of the agencies of public opinion, vilified and condemned the communards to their provincial and peasant brothers. This second siege of Paris, like the earlier one conducted by Moltke, was marked by indiscriminate artillery fire to terrify the besieged, but since the Germans occupied some of the forts, it was impossible to reduce the city by starvation. When the loyal troops penetrated the city, it became obvious that Moltke's siege was a mild play compared with Thiers'! Frenchmen fought Frenchmen with more ferocity than Germans and Frenchmen could muster against each other. The troops broke through on May twenty-first; for six days they fought from street to street, barricade to barricade, house to house, until finally the last communards with guns in their hands were executed in Père

Lachaise Cemetery. It was a horrible, bloody affair. The troops gave no quarter to anyone caught in or suspected of a part in the resistance The communards, on their side, executed their hostages, and set fire to the city. The Versailles government was victorious, but Paris was a shambles with the Hôtel de Ville, the Tuileries, and many other buildings in smoking ruins It was an awful climax for *l'année terrible* that started with the declaration of war on Prussia in 1870 and ended with the volleys of firing squads in 1871.

Even the June Days did not create so much bitterness as the Commune, the hatreds aroused in Paris and the provinces in 1871 have not been entirely effaced even to this day. Every trick of propaganda known in 1871 was used to build up an intense hatred and fear of the Parisian radicals in the rest of France. The useless incendiarism, the despairing reprisals, and the inevitable destruction of life and property only served to re-enforce the feeling that the radicals were agents of evil. On the other hand, the ruthlessness of the siege, the brutality of the victorious troops, and the subsequent terror visited on the radicals by the military courts have left a deep scar in the poorer sections of the city. The whole experience was a horrible nightmare, which the French find difficult to forget. Even to this day, it is hard for most French historians to write about the Commune objectively. Their breeding will speak more loudly than their scholarship, and, to escape the necessity of ascribing this horrible experience to their own people, they very often blame Bismarck or foreign agitators for the tragedy of France.

Some French scholars make much of the idea that the vigorous suppression of the Commune made the Republic acceptable to the conservative French. The Commune gave the Republic an opportunity to prove its mettle, they argue, and, without it, the Republic would have followed the pattern of 1848; at the first sign of disturbance, the country would have thrown itself into the arms of a monarchy. This fine rationalization excuses the horrors of 1871 as a necessary evil, a means to the finding of a truly satisfactory solution of the problem of government Though argument by analogy is difficult, it does seem that this interpretation fails to consider that the Second Republic murdered the radicals in June, 1848, quite as effectively as the Third Republic did in 1871, and that, while reprisals may not have been as savage in 1848, no one would consider them very mild. Undoubtedly, the Commune had its part in the creation of the Republic, but many other forces in the evolution of French society undoubtedly played equally important rôles. The responsibility for the Commune cannot be argued away by an easy rationalization; this horrible fratricidal blood-bath was probably an inevitable result of the industrial and political patterns of nineteenth-century France; it was as much an outcome of the forces within French civilization as was any other event of the century.

WHILE tourist bureaus in England and special excursions from New York flooded Paris with foreigners who wished to be thrilled by the "ruins" of the French capital, and while military courts relentlessly continued the grim task of exterminating the communards by execution, exile, and imprisonment, the politicians at Versailles busied themselves with the problems of government. The conservative monarchists, who held a clear majority in the assembly, were anxious to restore the king. But which king would be restored? This was the question that proved to be a stumbling block; the revolution of 1830 had split the monarchist party, and the majority in the assembly was about equally divided between the partisans of the Bourbons and the supporters of the July pretender. The legitimist pretender, Henry, Comte de Chambord, "the child of the miracle," * based his claim on the rights of his grandfather, Charles X, and the Bourbon succession since Henry of Navarre. He was a boy of ten when his family was driven

* He was the posthumous son of the Duc de Berry, *see infra*, Chapter II, p 54

out of France, and at fifty he had all the intellectual furniture of a Bourbon and lifelong exile. He had no understanding of France, and probably less of the question of government. The Orléanist pretender, the Comte de Paris, was the grandson of Louis Philippe; he was younger, more pliable, and the preferred candidate of liberal monarchists, who hoped to re-establish parliamentary institutions in France.

Since the legitimist candidate was without immediate heirs, the way to a compromise stood open. What could be more reasonable than the restoration of the Bourbon monarch, provided that he would recognize the Orléanist pretender as his heir apparent? It was not so easy as it would seem; even if the Comte de Paris could be persuaded to make peace with his relative, the Comte de Chambord was resolved to return to France only upon his own terms. Like Louis XVIII before him, he refused to be bundled into Paris under the wing of the assembly. He would return, but only on condition that the Bourbon traditions, Bourbon principles, and—alas for his cause!—Bourbon flag should accompany him "Frenchmen," he wrote in a manifesto " . Henry V cannot abandon the white flag of Henry IV!" This stubborn, fat man in his fifties, who realized that without the paraphernalia of his ancestors he would be only a fat man, singlehandedly blocked the restoration of his house His friends argued, cajoled, and pleaded to no avail; in the end they had to pin their hopes upon his possible death.

The republican minority in the assembly profited by the embarrassment of their rivals. The *de facto* republic gained prestige and permanence every day that it successfully governed the nation, and there was ever more hope that it might attain a *de jure* status, even if by default. The republicans, too, were divided, but not on the question of the republic. The extremists, led by Gambetta, wished to create a radical, anticlerical, middle-class régime; the more moderate republicans, like Grévy, wanted a conservative, property- and tradition-respecting government Both radical and moderate republicans, however, were convinced that the monarchy must not be re-established In the course of events, the republicans found a powerful ally in the person of Thiers That veteran politician came to the conclusion that the republican sentiment in France was not strong enough to create a republic by itself, but it was strong enough to make any alternative régime unstable. Furthermore, the old gentleman again had tasted power—power, indeed, that he would never have entrusted to a king. A combination of personal ambition and a realization that only under a republic could such power safely be entrusted to a political leader, convinced him that it would be wise to continue the republican régime. His famous definition, "The republic is that form of government which divides us the least," and the assurance from the moderates, "The republic will be conservative," combined to strengthen the impression in France that the republic might well bring political peace

Under Thiers' presidency, the republic gained prestige by the effective solution of many difficult problems. Parliamentary commissions assisted the president in some of the necessary, but unpopular, work that was done, such as the inquiry into the finances and conduct of the late war, the readjustment of military honors and ranks, the problem of pardons and clemency. Effectively, the president and a parliamentary commission handled each of these problems without exploding their potential political dynamite. New laws and decrees reorganizing municipal administration, regulating the army, organizing a press régime, and so forth, followed in fairly rapid succession, to show that the government under a republic could be efficient. The majority in the assembly, however, came to distrust Thiers, as his republican leanings became more and more evident. Somehow they realized that this little old man was necessary to France, but they were ready to be rid of him as soon as it became possible.

Thiers' most significant achievement was the liberation of France through the payment of the indemnity. As long as German troops were camped on French soil at French expense, the vivid memories of the humiliating *année terrible* could not be obliterated Since Bismarck was willing to remove his troops only when the indemnity was paid, the great task of the hour was the reorganization of French finances and credit to pay the ransom. The ease with which Thiers found money to pay the huge indemnity should be a monument to the prosperity that France had enjoyed under Napoleon III, and to the faith of middle-class France in the stability of the country. The war of 1870 had been a short one that did not draw heavily upon the reserves of the nation, and when Thiers opened the government's books for the popular subscription to a loan, a stream of francs poured in from all sides, oversubscribing the issue By 1873, enough money had been transformed into gold and exchange on London to pay off the whole indemnity. Ironically enough, this flow of gold caused a boom and then a panic in Germany, which inspired Bismarck to remark that next time he would insist on paying the indemnity In France, the assembly voted that Thiers "merited well" of his country for his work of freeing the national territory

With the German troops out of France, the political pot in Versailles began to boil over. Thiers may have merited well of the country, but the same majority that expressed this opinion felt that Thiers merited not too well from the monarchists. His persistent leanings toward the republican solution convinced them that he must be supplanted by a more trustworthy man. The problem became acute when by-elections to the assembly provided evidence that the country, too, was swinging away from the monarchical solution The republicans and—shades of the past!—the Bonapartists were winning in these elections Prompt action alone would save the monarchical cause An intrigue was hatched against Thiers, and only a few weeks after the last German troops crossed over the frontier, the little man who had "merited so well" of his country was forced out of office. In his place, General MacMahon, a monarchist with a good military record, was elected president to keep the throne warm for the presumptive king.

Like several other Frenchmen before and after him, General MacMahon was cast for the rôle of a French General Monck. That worthy English officer could not have realized how important his part in the English Restoration would seem to French monarchists in the nineteenth century. Although it had proved impossible to heal the schism in the monarchist ranks, the negotiations in progress seemed to promise an early settlement. General MacMahon was a man who would be willing to step aside as soon as the king could be brought back to France, and, therefore, he was the man to fill the chair of the president of the republic To regularize his position, and to assure themselves that he would not share the fate of Thiers, the majority passed a law, known as the "Law of the Septennate," which declared that the office of president was to be held for a seven-year term The monarchists never worried over the fact that seven years would be too short a time to prepare France for a restoration!

The general's régime repeated the pattern of the early months of Louis Napoleon's presidency in 1848. The "elder statesmen" of the party of "moral order" took over the control of affairs. Indeed, some of the same men who had rallied to the prince-pretender as a possible General Monck of 1848 plotted to make MacMahon fill the part. There was, however, an essential difference between the moral orders of 1848 and 1873; these men, many of them liberals of the eighteenth-century pattern, had learned a lesson in the *coup d'état* of 1851. They had no desire to return to Caesarism, even if they had to accept a parliamentary republic to avoid it Furthermore, MacMahon was no pretender to the throne, nor did he entertain ambitions of becoming a dictator, he may have preferred to re-establish the monarchy, but only if it could be done legally. He was not the man for a *coup d'état*.

The problem of the restoration drifted another year. A compromise between the two royal families came when the Comte de Paris made peace with his Bourbon cousin and recognized his prior claim to the throne. There were comings and goings, plots and counterplots, in the salons and cloakrooms, and heated discussions in the assembly. If by-elections be taken as evidence of the opinion of France, the country was disapprovingly suspicious of the whole procedure, for each new election increased the republican and the Bonapartist factions at the expense of the monarchists Was the choice between a republic and a Caesar? The monarchists disliked both They could work with the imperialists as long as the Bonapartes were in exile, but they could not accept the Empire. They could work under the Republic as long as they held a majority, but they could not accept the republicans. It was a paradox and a dilemma.

This became embarrassing to a high degree when, in spite of the compromise between the two pretenders, it became increasingly apparent that no restoration could be accomplished in the near future The Comte de Chambord and his principles balked the royalist cause. The old gentleman stubbornly refused to adjust himself to the needs of his supporters. In an open letter, he reasserted that he would never return to France without his flag and his principles Principles can be confused and covered up, but not the emblem of the nation France, every realist knew, would not accept the white flag, and the Bourbon would not accept the tricolor. There was a suggestion of a *coup d'état,* but the parliamentary leaders and MacMahon refused to listen. There was nothing for the monarchists to do but make a republican constitution that could easily be changed into a monarchical one when the situation should become ripe for it

The continuous undertone of criticism from the nation emphasized the necessity for some action Many influential Frenchmen were beginning to ask what sort of future the assembly wished to prepare for France The assembly held its mandate from the people, but the people had voted four years before under conditions that no longer existed. The suggestion was often made that it was high time for the assembly to finish its task, and allow for another election. Thus, the assembly, controlled by monarchists, had the uncongenial task of framing a constitution without the possibility of providing a king.

There were many constitutions written in France between 1789 and 1875 that might have served as models for the assembly. Most of them proclaimed the rights of men and Frenchmen, many lectured on the duties of citizens, and all of them provided in elaborate fashion for governmental organization and operation. It was notorious that even their framers had failed to understand the implications of most of these documents The assembly produced no such state paper No one believed that the constitution written in 1875 could possibly be permanent, and there seemed no good reason for producing an elaborate document to meet a temporary emergency. Ironically enough, it is this constitution, unloved by its framers, which has given France the most stable government that she has known since 1789.

The assembly contented itself with passing a series of constitutional laws that provided for the component parts of the new government. The Law of the Septennate (1873) remained intact as the definition of the presidency. Elected by the national assembly (the senate and chamber in joint session) for a seven-year term, the president was clothed with the powers of a constitutional monarch; he chose the ministry, acted on state occasions, and was not answerable for his actions except in case of high treason. The relationship between his actual powers and those of the two houses was not clearly defined, tradition, rather than constitutional laws, has given France a figurehead president. The bicameral legislature was created by two laws that defined the senate and the chamber of deputies. The chamber—the popular, democratic branch of the legislature—was to be elected by direct, universal manhood suffrage for four-year terms. It could be dissolved by the president with the consent of the senate The senate, incorrectly envisaged as the more important branch of the legislature, was to be chosen by indirect election, for nine-year terms. One-third of the elected senators were to retire every three years, so that the senate could keep in close contact with the people but at the same time retain its conservative character. To assure a continuation of its policy, the assembly appointed from its own ranks for life terms seventy-five of the three hundred senators. Another law provided for a ministry appointed by the president but responsible to the legislature. To the premier, or president of the council, was given a preeminent place in the cabinet; the whole ministry must stand or fall together under his leadership In only one place did these laws recognize that the government which they created would be a republic. Wallon proposed an amendment which said "The president of the republic . . .", this amendment carried by only one vote.

The Constitution satisfied no one completely; it was a compromise between a republic and a constitutional monarchy that failed, in the minds of the men of 1875, to meet the requirements of either From both the left and the right, men looked hopefully to a revision of these documents that they had drawn up They had, however, builded better than they knew; they had preserved the only pattern of self-government that the French had ever learned to operate The vagueness of the provisions allowed tradition and experience to mold the form more exactly, and left ample play for the conservative and liberal elements of French society. France may never come to revere her constitution as the people of the United States do theirs, but she has come to recognize that it is a fortunate solution of the problem of government

EARLY in 1876, France held general elections, the first since *l'année terrible* The conservatives were not a little surprised, when the senate met, to find 149 republicans to 151 monarchists; they were shocked and astonished when the chamber of deputies met with 340 republicans to a mere 153 monarchists (of whom 75 were imperialists) France had moved greatly to the left since 1871 There were many reasons for this swing A large number of Frenchmen will support any government that respects their property and persons—rather than risk an adventure into the politically unknown. Thiers, by demonstrating that the republic could keep order and would respect property, had led a large section of the bourgeois Orléanists into the conservative republican camp Another important factor stemmed out of the international situation. In 1871, the republicans were the "war party" and the monarchists stood for peace. In 1876, the rôles were reversed. The Roman question in Italy and the *Kulturkampf* in Germany had changed the Catholic monarchists into a party which might easily embroil France with either Germany or Italy, while the anticlerical republicans insisted that France must leave the pope to work out his own salvation in Rome and must remain neutral in Germany's fight with the Church The French undoubtedly wanted peace, and, as in 1871, they said as much with their ballots

A closer examination of the chamber showed that the problem of government in 1876 was not so simple as the two parties would make it seem There were at least four groups of republicans: the center, hardly distinguishable from the liberal monarchists, and made up of recent converts to the republic, the center-left, composed of the old-line conservative bourgeois republicans; the "irreconcilables," Gambetta's party, the radical republicans of the last years of the Empire; and beyond, on the extreme left, a small group, the "intransigeants," who were even more radically lower middle-class republican than Gambetta. If a ministry were formed from the conservative republicans, as it was, its tenure would be insecure as long as it failed to satisfy the last-named two groups The monarchists, too, were divided between supporters of the houses of Orléans, Bourbon, and Bonaparte. Their conservatism was their only bond of unity. The multiparty system, so characteristic of the Third Republic, was very much in evidence as early as 1876

President MacMahon hoped to combine the center republicans and the center monarchists into a government that would give France stability and order. Dufaure, a conservative republican, undertook to form the first cabinet. Almost immediately, all manner of difficulties arose, and Dufaure's cabinet lasted only about nine months. A second republican premier, Jules Simon, was forced out of office even more quickly. Disputes developed over financial policy, amnesty for the communards, foreign policy, and the question of dismissing officials To make matters worse, President MacMahon really called two cabinets—the one official, controlled by republicans, the other unofficial—a sort of "kitchen cabinet" to advise the president—and composed of the monarchists. Naturally, the chamber resented this second cabinet, over which it had no control. When the marshal attempted to exercise the power that he and his personal advisers believed to be inherent in his office, a conflict between the chamber and the president was inevitable All through 1876 and early 1877, the politicians were preparing for the conflict that should settle finally the relative spheres of influence of the presidency and the chamber.

Marshal MacMahon threw down the challenge to the republican majority in the chamber on May sixteenth, 1877, by dismissing Simon's republican cabinet, and summoning the Duc de Broglie to form a ministry of the right. The new ministry stood squarely upon MacMahon's right to call a ministry that, in his opinion, would save the fundamental institutions of France. The republican ministries had failed; therefore he called men who "thought as he did" to organize a government. Without giving the chamber an opportunity to answer this argument, de Broglie adjourned the session until June sixteenth. This brief respite gave the "government of May sixteenth" an opportunity to clean house in the administrative corps, and prepare itself to fight "radicalism" in the traditional French manner.

The session of June sixteenth was a stormy one. One climax in the debates has become the subject of a great saga of the Republic, and celebrated in verse and on canvas De Fourtou, in speaking of the work of the late assembly, attributed to it the honor of delivering France from the army of occupation. A republican deputy jumped to his feet, pointed to Thiers, sitting with the republicans, and shouted. *"Le libérateur du territoire, le voilà!"* The whole left sprang to its feet and gave Thiers a long ovation—a bit of drama not lost on the France that remembered Thiers as the conservative who favored the Republic. The debates brought out the arguments of both sides, but oratory was not to affect the vote. The men of the left listened unmoved to the ministers' assurance that they were there to save France from radicalism and internal disorder. They were equally unwilling to accept the idea that the president had, by the constitutional laws, the power to call any ministry that he wished. The vote was 363 to 158 against the ministry. The senate promptly authorized (149 to 130) the dissolution of the chamber.

Wild talk of a *coup d'état* circulated in all sections of French society, and the republicans began to look about for measures of defense. There was, however, no danger of a coup from MacMahon and de Broglie; they well understood that it might result in civil war, and, if successful, probably would benefit only the imperialists. Their plan was not a *coup de main,* but a stroke at the elections. With the administrative machine firmly in their hands, the men of "moral order" set about to assure a majority in the next chamber by traditional methods. The monarchies and the Empire had perfected techniques for influencing elections. Every department of the government knew just what was expected of it. Republican newspapers were harassed, their sale was forbidden on the streets, and a number of them were suppressed on trumped-up charges Over three thousand persons were haled before police courts, and many of them sentenced to prison Gambetta himself was condemned to three months in jail for saying, "After the nation has spoken, it will be necessary [for President Mac-

Mahon] to submit or to resign." Over six thousand functionaries were dismissed or moved, and the voters were threatened, promised, propagandized, and cajoled by every means known to an ingenious administrative corps It was a tremendous effort of the right to force France into the mold of "moral order."

The republicans forgot petty differences for the moment to make common cause against the enemies of the Republic. The untimely death of Thiers prevented him from making a tour of the provinces to counteract MacMahon's speaking program, but the funeral of Thiers became a gigantic public demonstration for the republican cause Grévy, a man as conservative as Thiers, was pushed into the limelight as the republican candidate for president in the next election to counteract the royalist claim that Gambetta, the radical, was the leader of the republican faction. The men of the left made much of the absolutist and clerical character of their opponents, which, they insisted, would lead France into war with Italy to restore the pope, and probably with Germany to intervene in the *Kulturkampf*. "It is for France to decide," ran the appeal of the republican committee, "whether her government shall henceforth be a personal power directed by clericals and absolutists, or whether the nation intends to continue to rule itself . . . One speaks of radicalism and demagoguery; the sole revolutionists are those men who seek to return to the impossible past!" Hampered by police and prefects, the republicans succeeded none the less in pointing the lesson that France could not turn the clock back.

The elections proved to be a republican victory; of 543 seats in the new chamber, the republicans controlled 326. De Broglie and his cabinet resigned, but MacMahon, rather than appoint a republican ministry, called General de Rochebouet, a man unknown in the political arena, to form a ministry of national concentration. It looked very much as if the long-heralded *coup d'état* might be at hand. If the marshal was not planning a *coup d'état,* at least it was obvious that he was trying to introduce a new tradition into the Constitution, for not one of Rochebouet's cabinet was a parliamentarian. The new chamber flatly refused to have anything to do with the new ministry, and prepared to resist any illegal attack on its prerogatives. There was, however, no occasion for alarm; when MacMahon discovered that the senate would not consent to another dissolution of the chamber, he repudiated Rochebouet, and called Dufaure to head a republican government that the chamber would support.

The new government's first act was to take revenge upon the officials whose activity in the recent election had been unendurable to the republicans. Even while the purge of the civil service was under way, the ministry turned to the army, where some of the highest officers had compromised themselves by urging a *coup d'état.* The old Marshal MacMahon fought hard to save his erstwhile comrades in arms, whose continued service, in his opinion, was necessary to the safety of France. Even if the ministry had wished to listen to his appeal, it would have been impossible, for the men on the left were demanding action. The senatorial elections of January, 1879, decided the whole question; the republicans won a clear majority of the seats in the senate, and, as they had control of both chambers, further resistance was manifestly out of the question. On January thirtieth, 1879, MacMahon tendered his resignation as president of France, and withdrew from public life. "The only government whose fall I have not regretted," he remarked, "has been my own." He had served his country as he believed to be proper; his struggle for power was a deciding factor in making the president of the French republic a ceremonial figurehead of minor political importance

Upon the resignation of the marshal, the senate and chamber of deputies met together to elect a new president. The conservative republican, Grévy, was chosen by a large majority. Ironically enough, it was the same Grévy who had fought hard to prevent the establishment of a presidency, for fear of the power a president might come to exercise He had before him the fiasco of MacMahon's attempt to influence policy, and he had within himself a deep conviction that the office of president might some day become a danger to his beloved republic. These two factors made Grévy the first president of France who consciously attempted to minimize the power of his office. He resolved to remain absolutely neutral in politics; to keep his office as a ceremonial symbol of French sovereignty which was to influence in no way the course or formation of policy. His successors have not all held true to his interpretation of the duties of the president, but enough of them have done so to make valid the tradition which he started Presidents of France who have not been content with their empty rôle have inevitably run into the uncomfortable position of Marshal MacMahon.

IN CONTROL of the legislature and the presidency, the republicans set themselves to the task of remaking France a little closer to their hearts' desire. The régime of the assembly and the marshal had been, in effect, a continuation of the Empire system, indeed, it was somewhat less liberal than the promise of the parliamentary Empire of 1870 had been. The authoritarian régime was systematically supplanted through more liberal and democratic laws and regulations passed by the republicans as soon as they gained control. As a sign of their intentions, the seat of the government was moved from Versailles to Paris; the senate installed itself in the Palais Luxembourg, the chamber took over the Palais Bourbon, and the president remained at the Elysée. The inscriptions "Liberté, Égalité, Fraternité," again appeared on all public buildings, and the *Marseillaise,* the song of the Revolution and the barricades, became the national anthem. July fourteenth, Bastille Day, became a national festival anniversary, celebrated for the first time in 1880 with fireworks, banquets, oratory, and dancing Just as in 1852 the symbols of the Empire heralded its establishment, so in 1879–80 the classic symbols of the Republic announced the intentions of the men who had come to power

The shaping of a republican legislative program was characterized by fierce political battles These early years of the Republic, like the later ones, were marked by keen political and personal rivalries The clashes of personalities and party factions have made the political history of the Republic a stormy story Only the patient delver into history can trace the conflicts which accounted for the rise and fall of ministries and men—and, even then, one must have a taste for the story of political fights if he is to keep his interest in the problem Behind and above these factional fights, however, there has usually been a more or less well defined program which a majority of the deputies wished to carry out There were many parties in the chamber, but usually they could be reduced to two groups: the parties of the right and the parties of the left The interplay of these two groups has made the political history of the Third Republic Political, social, or economic questions which demand solution are bitterly fought out in the chamber, but in the end they are solved in a manner satisfactory to a majority of Frenchmen It is interesting to watch a political program, usually sponsored by a group on the left, being fought through the chamber and finally embodied in the legal system of the nation Its sponsors, with a new appreciation of the *status quo,* will then usually become conservative, and find that their interests gradually shift from the left to the right Thus, the men who in 1830 were the party of the left were the party of the right in 1879, and the party of the left in 1879 was to become a party of the right in the postwar era. The system may not be efficient, but it does satisfy legitimate demands as they arise, and today millions of Frenchmen would fight to preserve the right to solve their own problems in their own, if inefficient, way.

After 1879, the republicans set about to give France a liberal democratic régime. After years of "authority," the liberals were ready to pass laws that would assure the basic liberties that eighteenth-century nationalistic philosophers and nineteenth-century liberal bourgeois politicians considered indispensable for good government. It was easy to unite the republican ranks, from the extreme left to the center, upon a program to break the régime of repression. Once the basic liberal laws were passed, however, disagreement within the republican ranks was almost inevitable The representatives of the petty bourgeoisie and the proletariat had ideas about "equality" to which the upper bougeoisie could not subscribe It was in the first few years of republican control that a sheaf of laws fundamental to any liberal régime were passed without great difficulty; after that the problem became much more complex

Basic to the establishment of a liberal democracy were those laws passed between 1879 and 1882 guaranteeing the political liberties of the French Under the Empire, both the Orléanists and the republicans demanded political liberties that were about to be granted when the Empire collapsed. While the assembly and MacMahon's government of "moral order" ruled France, there seemed to be no time to consider the problem, but after 1879, when the republicans controlled the machinery of government, the régime of political liberties could no longer be postponed Naturally, freedom of press and assembly bulked large in this program A law of June, 1881, granted to Frenchmen the right to hold a public meeting without the necessity of securing permission; open-air meetings and political clubs remained under control, but the right of assembly was essentially granted. The press law of July, 1881, gave to France the freest press in Europe, it became practically impossible to introduce any curb on daily and periodical journals which refrained from treason and provocation of crime. This law is probably responsible for the license of the French press; "yellow journalism" in the rest of the world has much to learn from the French Concomitant with freedom of press and assembly were laws that removed restrictions on the public sale of newspapers, books, and pamphlets on the streets, and laws that allowed more freedom in the establishment of cafés and wine shops. These basic civil liberties were deemed necessary for the free evolution of a liberal, democratic régime.

Another measure forced upon the chamber by the extreme left was the amnesty granted to the men implicated in the Commune. The republicans well understood that the parties of the left could not hope to maintain the Republic if the memory of the Commune remained an open sore to embitter the proletariat against the government. There was considerable agitation after 1875 for a general amnesty; on several occasions, imprisoned or exiled men were elected to political offices, and by 1880 the republicans were faced with the problem of either granting the amnesty or splitting their ranks into two opposing camps As the political problem developed, the proletariat, with their increasing dislike for "the sinister trinity, Caesar, Shylock, and Loyola, with the saber, the vault, and the aspersorium," were the natural allies of the anticlerical republicans in their fight against the Church, the army, and high finance. Accordingly, it was good political tactics to grant an amnesty in July, 1880.

It was only natural that the republicans should run afoul of the Church in the first years of their régime. The clergy had been the backbone of the party of "moral order," and in both foreign and internal affairs the clergy disapproved of the republican concept of policy. Had not the reigning pope, only a few years before, roundly condemned practically everything for which the republicans stood? Gambetta had translated this natural animosity between the two into a ringing republican war cry: *"Le cléricalisme, voilà l'ennemi!"*—a challenge which the clergy were not slow to take up The question of education first brought this conflict out in the open. The victory of the Prussian schoolmaster at Sedan—a nice rationalization for the French military men—had become axiomatic in France after 1871. The literate German troops defeated the unschooled French. The moral was clear; France must educate her sons. But education in France always introduced the Church into politics; churchmen feared the rationalistic, godless education of the state, and liberals feared the conservative, clerical education of the Church. The republicans were resolved to educate the young in republican traditions, and the churchmen, with equal zeal, had no intention of surrendering the rights that they had won.

The republican program called for lay, gratuitous, obligatory education; but the whole program involved so many problems that it could not possibly be enforced at once. The difficulty of finding school buildings and teachers to replace the Catholic schools was in itself insurmountable in 1880—not to mention the problem of finding schools and teachers for the masses that did not yet go near the schools. An immediate program called for the enforcement of Guizot's law concerning normal schools to train teachers, the departments were required to attack the problem seriously, for the first time, after the republicans came into control. Another regulation generalized Duruy's public secondary schools for girls, and created a normal school at Sèvres to train secondary-school teachers. It was impossible to consider either obligatory or lay education at the moment, but a law of June, 1881, did abolish tuition in the state primary schools, and placed full responsibility for their support upon the budget of the communes France was still a long way behind the advanced countries in education, but she had made considerable progress since 1815

In all this discussion of education, the left and the right joined issue largely on the basis of the prerogatives of the Church. The biggest fight in these first years raged around the question of unauthorized Congregations. The Empire had been generous in authorizing the establishment of religious orders, and particularly lax in enforcing the law that prohibited unlicensed orders from teaching In 1880, there were eighty-two religious houses, with almost two thousand teachers not authorized by the state. In addition to the teaching orders, there were many other nonauthorized Congregations operating monasteries and charitable institutions Under the practice before 1850, these Congregations (they included twenty-seven Jesuit schools with over eight hundred teachers) were liable to expulsion An attempt to close down these nonauthorized Congregations, in particular the Society of Jesus, led to a bitter fight, in both the senate and the chamber, which the republicans lost. They did, however, succeed in excluding all nonprofessionals from the councils of instruction. In place of clergymen and army officers, the elected delegates of the teaching profession and the appointees of the minister of education filled the councils.

By 1884, the moderate republicans rounded off much of their program. The law that allowed the government to suspend judges gave them a weapon against their old enemies on the bench whose life tenure had seemed adequate protection for their antirepublican actions The *rentes* were converted from five to four and a half per cent, and a new set of agreements, in many ways humiliating to a sovereign state, were concluded with the railroad companies. New regulations affecting labor unions also were passed by the republican majority, on the insistence of the extreme left, under these regulations the French labor syndicates received an independence that greatly extended their power, and allowed for the development of a vital labor movement. The law reintroducing divorce, banned since 1816, was another measure in the liberal program that was also successfully pushed through the legislature This social and economic program was the initial work of the republicans when they came to power—a program that they considered essential for the creation of a liberal democracy.

IN 1875, when the constitutional laws were passed, republicans and monarchists alike promised themselves and their constituents that the revision of this Constitution would be a major part of their program. In August, 1884, the two chambers met together as the national assembly, to consider the question of revision, but nine years of political experience had given to the republicans a considerable respect for the constitutional laws. A four-point program of revision that left the

Constitution essentially unchanged satisfied the majority: first, the public prayers which opened the sessions were suppressed, secondly, the ministry, in case of a dissolution of the chamber, was to be obliged to call for elections within two months, and to summon the chamber to meet ten days after the election; third, the "republican form of government" was declared to be open no longer to question or revision, and members of former ruling houses were made ineligible for the office of president, and, fourth, the method of electing senators became a problem for simple legislative action This revision was satisfactory to the republicans, who a few years before had roundly condemned the "constitutional monarchy without a king"

With this crowning act of constitution making, the Third Republic appeared to be firmly established and acclimated in French soil. For the first time in almost a hundred years, a true majority of Frenchmen appeared behind the constitutional settlement. On the morrow of these additional laws, the Republic again came under fire, but the political history of the next thirty years was to prove that—for the time, at least—France had found a government which could satisfy the needs of a significant majority of her citizens

CHAPTER VII

THE THIRD FRENCH REPUBLIC, 1880–1914

THE political history of the third French Republic has been so filled with storm and fury that the casual observer might easily conclude that anarchy would provide a more orderly system. Major political crises have frequently brought the whole régime into question, and ministerial instability has been so common that it almost seems to be inherent in French politics With alarming regularity, the chamber of deputies has repudiated one cabinet after another; if a government has lasted two years it has seemed almost miraculous; the average one has maintained itself for about nine months To one accustomed to British or American politics, these violent fluctuations of governments and the concomitant clashes of personalities have no significance, no rhyme or reason It is easy to attribute the apparent chaos to French emotional immaturity and political indecision; nothing, however, could be more false. Foreigners do the French a great injustice by regarding their rapid turnover of cabinets as a sign of political incapacity. French democracy, as it functions under the Third Republic, is a complex pattern not understandable unless the observer is willing to forego the easy generalization that the French are "a people that do not know their own mind" or "a race that substitutes the barricades for political wisdom" One who wishes to probe into the problems of French politics must leave behind his preconceptions based upon Anglo-Saxon practices

Unlike the Anglo-Saxon democracies, French democracy has never been able to compress all political interests and aspirations within the bounds of two great, disciplined party organizations This fact arises partly out of French traditions, partly out of the French electoral practices, and partly out of French temperament. As the history of previous régimes has shown, there have always been multiple divisions in French political opinion. If this was true under the system of limited suffrage, when one might reasonably expect a great degree of political homogeneity, it was even more true after 1848 when universal suffrage allowed a freer expression of the interests of all classes The French system of elections has largely contributed to and preserved these wide, possible variations in political belief, and, at the same time, has discouraged the development of disciplined political opinion. Elections for the chamber of deputies are much more like those for the town council or board of aldermen in an American city than those for the United States Senate or House of Representatives. The deputies are chosen by their friends and neighbors, who attach more importance to their personal knowledge of the individual candidate's possible performance in Paris than they do to any party flag that he happens to fly; and the deputies realize that their own record, rather than solidarity with this or that political group, will constitute their best recommendation for re-election. This has tended to make political parties in France more a matter of postelection alliances than pre-election organizations or platforms It has been difficult to create disciplined party organizations in a country where the electors have a possibility of knowing a great deal about the candidates for whom they vote.

No generalization about the characteristics of a nation is quite true; nevertheless, it is not far wide of the mark to say that the French are highly individualistic. It is no idle joke that any French politician would consider an ideal political party one which was made up of himself and enough voters to elect him to the chamber of deputies For practical purposes, this ideal has to be foregone, but the resulting political institutions have some resemblance to the ideal. The blocs or parties that are formed, some of which have developed into proper political parties, are often the results of postelection agreements between men whose opinions are similar. Party discipline is exceedingly difficult when the deputies group themselves in small cells within a so-called party under this or that leader, and refuse to consider themselves bound to the party by any but the loosest ties This type of organization has allowed free play for the personal jealousies and conflicts that have been the bane of French political life

These parties or blocs—some with over a hundred members, others with less than a dozen—range themselves in the chamber of deputies like a fan The radicals find their seats to the speaker's left; the conservatives, to his right. On the border lines between the parties there is always considerable migration; the debate or the issues of the day might drive a "leftist" radical socialist into the camp of the socialists, or a "rightist" radical socialist into co-operation with the center groups During the entire history of the Third Republic, no one of these loosely united parties has been able to obtain an absolute majority in the chamber Since the cabinet must enjoy the confidence of a clear majority, it has always been necessary to form coalitions or cartels of parties to support the ministry One writer has convincingly explained the matter by saying that the organization of these coalitions goes to prove that France really has a two-party system, for there are roughly only two possible coalitions or cartels—the one of the right, the other of the left. There is much in French political practice to support this idea, but just as the parties find it almost impossible to discipline their own members, the coalitions are usually unable to discipline the parties.

Personal feuds, political differences—often very minute—and divergences of opinion within the parties of the left or the right confuse the issues and becloud the two-party idea in France. It is hardly true that France is governed by either the right or by the left; the coalitions so often overlap in the center that it is easier to build up a case to prove that the center, where compromise is possible, really has ruled the Third French Republic. On the border lines between the right and the left there has usually been a group of men willing to work with either side of the chamber, these men very often have played the decisive rôle in political life.

A closer examination of the actual mechanics of the political life will reveal the fact that the frequent ministerial crises do not necessarily mean instability. *Ministries* in France change often, *ministers* change slowly. Rare is the cabinet reshuffling that does not produce a new cabinet composed of old cabinet members Ministers may go, but the politicians who form the ministries have a tendency to remain Whenever a cabinet is defeated on any one issue, the premier and all his colleagues must resign, but the political situation in the chamber that made his cabinet possible in the first place still continues, and the new cabinet will probably contain many of the same men who made up the old one Furthermore, defeat on one issue does not mean that the chamber has lost confidence in the program of all the ministers. The defeat of a cabinet may have very little to do with the making of political policy, petty jealousy, revenge, or desire for spoils of office has been ample cause for the upsetting of a ministry.

If we regard cabinet alterations in this light, we can see that, in spite of its apparent fickleness, French political life is essentially stable. The multiparty coalition system forces the government to be sensitive to changes in public opinion and alterations in the political barometer, so it does not go far from the line of the nation's wishes. Such great changes as those which take place in England and the United States when liberals or laborites supplant conservatives, or republicans replace democrats, are rare in France The pendulum of French politics moves often, but its oscillations are seldom violent or far-reaching.

In addition to the element which we now recognize as stability, there is another factor which may have even greater influence in the maintenance of continuity of French policy. Even before, and certainly since, the time of the great Napoleon, France has been a nation governed by functionaries. One writer hostile to the system has said that the functionaries have made France into a nation whose body is in chains. The administrative corps is a well-organized, disciplined, trained body of officials, who carry the burden of government regardless of cabinet alterations. Their work and organization are well defined, and regulated by an extensive body of administrative laws and a system of administrative courts that are the product of more than a century of political evolution. These men, secure in their positions irrespective of political changes, exert tremendous influence upon the course of government. The minister—a college professor, a small town doctor, a lawyer, or whatever his profession may have been—is often incompetent for the task that politics has given him, and usually is ignorant of the complexities and the routine of his office His tenure is dependent upon the cabinet's satisfying the chamber, and his energies must be divided between politics and the business of government. He must rely upon the highly trained functionaries in his ministry to supply him with the necessary information, often (if not usually) to draft his proposed legislation, and always to carry out the policies that have been decided upon. Ministers go, but the functionary remains. These men have had experience in handling politicians of all varieties, right or left, and they have built up machinery to control the politicians so that the functionaries, in the last analysis, control the bureaus. Their permanence, their careerist mentality, and their *esprit de corps* act as a stabilizing balance wheel in the government of the Third Republic

Their balance and stability, however, do not necessarily contribute to democratic government. While the chamber is sensitive to the barometer of public opinion, the functionaries can afford to be quite indifferent to it. Recruited as they are by examination, and enjoying, as they do, practically life tenure, the functionaries represent an aristocratic influence in French government. It is, perhaps, an aristocracy of brains rather than of blood, but it is an aristocracy, none the less. The functionaries, many Frenchmen complain, rule the nation for the ends of the bureaus, and the politicians are often powerless to check their régime. Dismissals are rare and usually a cause of violent conflict, this leaves the withholding of promotion or new honors as the only effective weapons against a stubborn official. Several ministers have attempted to fight the cool assumption of official superiority, but rarely has a politician succeeded in leaving a real impress upon his bureau The minister is almost helpless against the technical knowledge of his permanent subordinates; the routine of office, unless the functionaries point the way, will suppress even an able politician.

Thus, in spite of the apparent instability of the Third Republic, there have been powerful political forces within the organization of the legislature and the government that have worked to achieve stability. A minute study of the rise and fall of cabinets, of the amorphous, chameleonlike changes in political alliances, and of the issues that separate the parties and men is interesting and highly instructive, but it is entirely too complicated to be encompassed in a short history of France. It is enough to note here that there are both rhyme and reason in these political battles, and that the instability of French political life is much more apparent than real.

NO SMALL part of the confusion in French political life finds its origin in the two points of cleavage in contemporary French political thinking. The first is largely political, born of the great Revolution and most easily expressed in terms of the French conceptions of equality and popular sovereignty The second is largely economic, nurtured by the new industrial and commercial institutions that the machine age has produced, and most easily explained in terms of class conflict and the struggle for social democracy These two points of division have created the paradox of the French statesman whose "heart is on the left while his pocketbook is on the right," and at the same time they go far to solve many of the problems that have confronted republican France since about 1880.

The great Revolution has left in French thinking the legacy

of political equality—a mystic doctrine found in primitive Christianity and Rousseau—which the French have attempted to translate into political action. It does not have the communistic implications that one finds in Marxist thinking, but rather expresses a firm belief that one man is as good as another, and that, although there may be differences in wealth, education, and so forth, every man has a right to an equal voice in the affairs of state. It is not enough merely to support the Republic, the whole conception of popular sovereignty must be included and freely granted, to satisfy the protagonists of equality. That is to say, a fundamental test between right and left rests in the conviction that the nation is to be ruled from below rather than from above; that the democracy actually must control the destinies of the nation The men who hold true to this mystic doctrine range themselves against all those who believe that wealth, blood, breeding, and brains are prerequisites for a ruling class. This does not mean that brains, breeding, or blood should exclude a man from politics, but rather that the leaders must recognize—or, at least, act as if they recognized—that the final authority in government arises from the popular will.

This doctrine is deeply rooted in French political life, the motives behind it, however, are often less idealistic than Rousseau would have believed possible. For example, Mauriac tells us that it is the mortal sin of envy that ranges the peasant on the side of popular sovereignty He "shuts his eyes and casts his vote for the left, certain that he can make no mistake if he votes against those who wash and go to mass; he loathes any distinction in dress, occupation, or ideas" The proletarians discovered early in the century their hatred for authoritarianism; before the peasants understood that there was a "left" or a "right," the proletariat had come to hate the "ruling class" They were the first converts to republicanism as a weapon against the "elector" or the "official candidate" of earlier régimes who failed to recognize political equality. It was the bourgeoisie, however, that first adopted the mystic conception of popular sovereignty as a weapon with which to break down the walls of the old régime. As early as 1789 they shouted "Equality!" at the men with blue blood in their veins, and with that doctrine they won their right to exercise power. Many of them, however, never really believed in it, with Guizot, they saw government as the prerogative of the able, the wealthy, and the well born. Others of them have passionately defended the ideal, even though they feared its consequences

The Church, the army, the administrative corps, and, of course, the society of the wealthy nobles and bourgeoisie are honeycombed with people who may be rallied to the Republic but refuse to believe in its mystic dogma The Roman Catholic Church is fundamentally committed to the belief that all authority must come from above, and the French Church has always firmly held to the conception of social hierarchies The *Syllabus of Errors* specifically condemns the modern political philosophies as doctrines in which Roman Catholics cannot believe In spite of its loss in prestige, the Church even to this day wields great influence among all classes of French society, especially among the women who, even if their husbands are outspoken anticlericals, very often hold true to the consolations of religion The administrative corps and the army, by the very nature of their functions in French society, train their members either in disbelief or cynical acceptance of the popular conception Men who are used to command, and who gain scant respect for the representatives of the people through their contacts with them, find it difficult to believe in political equality. This was especially true in the first thirty years of the Republic, when both the administration and the army were filled with men who had grown up under the authoritarian régime.

The upper bourgeoisie and the nobility, from years of contact with the poor, have, quite naturally, acquired a deep distrust of their judgments and their motives, and at the same time have developed the desire to bring them under their tutelage One keen observer of contemporary France expresses the opinion that there is probably not a single salon in France in which the hostess unquestioningly accepts the doctrine of popular sovereignty It is difficult for people of wealth and power to admit that their authority comes from the dumb masses; they may pay lip service to the idea, but at heart they do not believe.

The industrial revolution, which defined more clearly the distinction between bourgeoisie and proletariat, is responsible for the second point of cleavage in French political opinion As early as 1848, a social radicalism as dangerous to the wealth of the bourgeoisie as the earlier political radicalism had been to the privileges of the old nobility, made its appearance in French politics, when the socialist philosophers condemned the exploitation of men by men, and demanded social justice. In the Commune of 1871 further evidence of a social democratic political opinion was manifest, and after 1880 this socialistic viewpoint, a curious blend of native and imported doctrine, became a fixture in the French political constellations The socialists have accepted the Revolution without question, and, in addition, have demanded an extension of the doctrine of political equality to the field of economic life. Social democracy, they have insisted, is necessary to give political democracy any meaning.

Socialism, in any of the several political forms that it has taken in France, will find it difficult to assume large proportions in the life of the nation until France becomes more highly industrialized than she is even today The proletariat does not bulk large in the French social structure The socialist left grew rapidly after 1890, and today the several socialist parties form a large minority in the chamber of deputies, but this does not mean that a large percentage of the French is committed to a social democratic solution of the problems of government. Indeed, it is almost a commonplace in French politics to say that many of the voters who support the several socialist parties would greatly disapprove of a socialist régime.

Many little people—peasants and petty bourgeois—vote for the socialists merely to express their generalized leftist opinion. They are voting against privilege and place, rather than for radical political experiments The true socialists are the laborers who, acutely conscious of the class struggle, wish to use the state to overturn the advantages that wealth gives to their bourgeois employers

The confusion in French politics that these two points of cleavage have created is enhanced by the political psychology of the French The mass of the people—peasants, bourgeoisie, and proletariat—like to think of themselves as men of the left This is partly the result of the great Revolution, but largely the result of their political experience between 1815 and 1870 The constitutional monarchies and the Empire were essentially authoritarian in their outlook; the interests, hopes, and fears of the majority were neglected in favor of those of wealth and breeding Thus, anyone who was mildly liberal before 1848 could reasonably be found on the "left" It was possible for a conservative like Thiers or Barrot to claim to be a "man of the left" in 1845, even Guizot belonged to the "left" in 1829! Is it any wonder that most of France feels that it is leftist? But what is "the left"? In the Bourbon régime, Laffitte, Guizot, Casimir Périer, and Molé represented the left; under the July monarchy, Thiers, Barrot, de Tocqueville, and Lamartine were on the left, under the Empire there were Ollivier, Grévy, and Gambetta; under the Republic, Gambetta, Floquet, Clemenceau, Jaurès! But Jaurès made Clemenceau appear to be almost conservative, Clemenceau was too radical for Gambetta; Grévy could not tolerate Gambetta's radicalism; Thiers was a conservative compared with Grévy or Ollivier—and so on back to Barrot, Guizot, and Casimir Périer In other words, the left of yesterday became the center, and yesterday's center became the right! But every group wishes to be on the left; the right is too reactionary.

This popularity of the "left" is reflected in the nomenclature of the political parties. In the United States there should be no trouble in understanding that party flags mean very little, when we see a Senator Norris or a Senator Nye belonging to the party of President Hoover, and a President Roosevelt in the same party with a Senator Glass In the United States, politicians of all shades group under the same banner In France, the problem has worked out a little differently, politicians with similar ideologies group together under a common banner, but the name of their party has little to do with their ideas Most of the parties attempt to convey the impression that they are much more "leftist" than they really are "Radical republicans" and "republicans of the left" may be the party name for a conservative rightist or center party, the radical socialists are neither particularly radical nor in any way socialistic, and republican democrats are quite conservative. The parties, like many of the voters, can almost be summed up in the amusing war cry of a politician who shouted· "To the left, to the left, but not one bit further!"

The situation is not, however, so chaotic as it seems on first examination. In French politics, problems arise that demand solution They are usually championed by the parties on the left and contested by the right, but the tendency is to the left, and eventually solutions are written into the laws When their program is completed, the men who championed it inevitably become respecters of the *status quo*—but, as elsewhere, in France the *status quo* cannot be of any long duration New problems bring new men to the left—men more radical than their colleagues who have just won a victory—and the cycle begins all over again With this in mind, it will be seen that, although the nomenclature of the parties may seem chaotic to an American, their political action is not Under the Third Republic, the swing toward the left has given to each social or economic group in the nation the possibility of achieving its political aims within the framework of the Constitution—a factor that has obviated the necessity of returning to the barricades to obtain political redress by force

THE THIRD FRENCH REPUBLIC, 1880–1914

THE mere fact that the presidency and the control of both the chamber and the senate were in the hands of the republicans after 1880 did not augur permanence for the Republic Since 1789, Frenchmen had seen the rise and fall of many régimes, and since none of them had lasted two full decades, there was no reason to assume that the Republic would prove an exception. Indeed, the stormy debates and the rapid changes in cabinets that characterized political life after 1875 often pointed to the early demise of the régime. The great questions of the day revolved around the authority and influence of the army and the bureaucracy, the rôles of Church and state in society and education, and the larger issues of high politics and economic imperialism. To these political problems the economic demands of the bourgeoisie, the peasants, and the proletariat added sheaves of important questions, while corruption in high places gave the zest of scandal to prevent ennui in the chamber of deputies.

The French electorate had given to the republicans the control over the state, but the conservatives were far from displaced from positions of power. Call them what you will—the party of resistance, the party of "moral order," or merely the party of the right—men of the kind that had ruled France for almost a hundred years were not to be dislodged by an election or two The army, the administrative corps, and the judiciary were staffed by men with technical knowledge that made them indispensable They never really accepted the Republic as final, and they held in contempt the little men representing French democracy. The upper brackets of French society—the men who owned the ships, the shops, the factories, and the banks, the women who presided over the fashionable salons and set the tone for polite society; in short, the class with wealth, influence, and education—were filled with people who looked confidently to the establishment of an authoritarian régime in the place of the liberal, democratic Republic. The Church, with its schools, charities, and immense public prestige, also considered the Republic as temporary, and worked with all of its resources to undermine the existing order. This solid opposition seemed in itself enough to assure the early collapse of the Republic.

It should not be imagined that the republicans of the 1880's were wild-eyed radicals anxious to upset all of the traditions of their country. Indeed, the contrary was the case. The fall of MacMahon left France in the hands of the moderates, bourgeois republicans who could be counted upon to protect property and traditions. Gambetta, the hero of the war of 1870, the darling of the "irreconcilable" republicans, the spearhead of the opposition to MacMahon and "moral order," was far too radical to suit the republican majority, and his radicalism was mild compared with that of the men of the extreme left, the radical socialists,* who spoke of income and inheritance taxes, separation of Church and state, equal military service, and even the election of judges. But even Gambetta, whose radicalism was merely violent republicanism, was blocked from the avenues of power by his conservative colleagues. Only once did he form a cabinet, and its life was pitifully short. It was the Ferrys, the Freycinets, and the Waddingtons, "safe" men who respected all the household gods of the middle and upper bourgeoisie, that held firmly the wheel of government from cabinet crisis to cabinet crisis. These men were eighteenth-century liberals who felt that under the Republic France could achieve the most secure political liberty.

As we have seen, when MacMahon and the party of "moral order" were finally defeated, the republicans lost no time in developing their political régime. Liberty of press, assembly, speech, and so forth, for which Frenchmen had fought ever since 1789, was speedily granted Pushed by the extremists, the moderates also agreed to an amnesty for the communards, more liberty for labor organizations, and a consideration of the question of the rôle of the Church in education. In the conflict over schools, however, the moderates refused to go the

* This term does not mean socialist in any Marxian sense These men represented the petty bourgeoisie

whole way with the radicals Free, compulsory, lay education was out of the question in 1880, because of both the opposition of the Church and the financial impossibility of creating an educational plant capable of servicing the needs of the nation As we have seen, the republican government did succeed in closing the Jesuit schools, extending state education for girls, creating state-supported normal schools, and legalizing obligatory primary education. The bulk of the program of the extreme left, however, was not considered as long as the moderates kept control of the policy of the Republic

In searching in French society for allies against their enemies, the republicans turned to two groups that, shortly before, had been the chief props of the Empire—the peasants and the businessmen. These two groups were willing to support any régime that gave them order and some consideration and assistance in their economic affairs. Neither of them was unquestionably allied with the monarchists or the clericals, and their support could be purchased by the sort of legislation that most appealed to the moderate republicans, who were themselves largely recruited from the bourgeois classes and were only a step removed from the peasantry.

The peasants were sorely in need of governmental assistance. French agriculture, traditionally backward when compared with that of the more progressive nations, suffered a severe blow from the diseases that struck at the wheat and the vines. To add to the discomfort, these disasters came at precisely the moment when cheap ocean transportation and the railroad system of the New World opened the world market to agricultural products of the Americas, and when rejuvenated Italy began to pour its wine into the marts of Europe. The government acted vigorously to bring relief to the wine growers, by relieving them of taxation and assisting them to rehabilitate their vineyards This direct aid, however, was not enough; before French agriculture could really recover, the standards of culture had to be raised through education The whole agricultural population benefited from the educational measures by which the government sought to improve the soil culture in every section of the country. Model farms, government-paid professors of agriculture, agricultural colleges, and governmentally subsidized research in agricultural problems went far to show the peasant that the Republic could look after his interests. The tariff schedules of 1881 did not help the peasant so much, but there was a promise that protection would be extended to him as soon as possible.

The republicans courted the businessmen even more assiduously Clemenceau, Gambetta, and the men of the left whose petty bourgeois outlook might have frightened the businessmen into the arms of the royalists were held in safe check until they appreciated that the state "must help business." The tax schedules, which eschewed radical departures from the traditional French indirect taxation, and the tariff of 1881, which held out greater promise to business as soon as the Napoleonic treaties should expire, were definite peace offers to the commercial and industrial interests. Grévy, Ferry, Say, and the other high priests of the moderate republican party, took an attitude toward business very much like that adopted by the Republican politicians in power in Washington after the Civil War, and by the staunch defenders of expanding capitalism who ruled Victorian England. Defense of the interests of business was the order of the day; even if they did amnesty the offenders of the Commune and allow the workers to form labor unions, the moderate republicans were primarily solicitous of the interests of the well to do.

IN LENDING aid and assistance to the foreign enterprises of French bankers and businessmen, the men of the 1880's sorely endangered the Republic itself Napoleon III had shown French financiers and exporters that overseas interests would yield handsome profits; and, in the fourth quarter of the nineteenth century, France, in company with the rest of Europe, accepted the doctrine that the state must protect, defend, and extend the interests of the citizens in the so-called backward areas of the globe. A new age of imperialism was opening about 1875; Asia, Africa, and the islands of the Pacific and Indian oceans were about to be divided among the civilized nations. There were men in France who were anxious that their country should join England and Germany in bringing the blessings of European civilizations to these backward lands. Ambitious French bankers had already staked out claims in Egypt, Tunis, Turkey, and Morocco by lending, at usurious rates, large sums of money to the financially naive rulers of those states. French adventurers, merchants, administrators, and manufacturers cast covetous eyes in the direction of Africa, China, and the islands. The demands of these neo-imperialists could not be overlooked by the men who were ruling France, especially when other European states were also preparing to inherit the earth.

Colonialism, however, had a bad reputation with many people in France. The little folks—peasants and petty bourgeoisie—could not see why the wealth and energies of the state should be squandered in strange and distant lands. Frenchmen would never colonize them, and all experience had taught that they were an expensive liability. Those men who remembered Alsace-Lorraine—a surprisingly large number of the articulate population—felt that the energies of the nation should be stored for the coming war of "revenge" rather than wasted on colonial adventures that threatened to repeat the experience in Mexico.

The grumbling and warning of the opponents of the new economic imperialism were disregarded, and France plunged into the mad scramble for colonial possessions. Egypt, Tunis, Madagascar, Central Africa, and Indo-China began to loom large in the press and to absorb the interest of the foreign office. The people could ask "Why?" but the government, under the prodding of Jules Ferry, pushed ahead. Even the "traditional enemy" was temporarily forgotten when France made a working *entente* with Bismarck to force England to recognize the ambitions of the continental powers. But things seemed to turn out badly. The protectorate over Tunis drove Italy into the arms of Germany and Austria, the Egyptian affair started with Anglo-French co-operation and ended with British control.* Madagascar and Central Africa appeared in the press to be "rat holes" which no amount of troops or gold could fill, and premature news of a great defeat in Indo-China convinced the anticolonials that Ferry's imperialism would end in the same fiasco that had followed Napoleon's Mexican adventure two decades before.

In the elections of 1885, the whole question of economic imperialism came up for serious consideration The republican party was split wide open. The moderates insisted that their policy was fundamentally sound The extreme left, suspicious, on principle, of colonialism, insisted that this new imperialism was wasting the energies of the nation on fruitless adventure overseas while the real interest of the nation—"revenge" and the recovery of Alsace-Lorraine—was neglected. The monarchists—anxious to utilize any issue that might prove politically profitable, joined hands with the extreme left to drive the moderates out of office. The first ballot showed that the agitation had had a definite reaction in France, a reaction that frightened the whole republican party. The monarchist parties made a sensational recovery from their defeated status in 1878–80, and, if the moderate republicans had not supported the radicals in the second round of voting, it would have been possible for the right to gain control of the chamber. The republican majority was reduced from 340 to 163, and the split between the moderate and radical republican parties made even this majority a matter of questionable importance

Cynical observers of French political life pointed out that the Third Republic was fifteen years old, and, if the experience of past régimes amounted to anything, the republic's early demise could be expected. No régime since 1789 had lasted a full twenty years. The clamors from both the right and the

* It was not British duplicity but French indecision that gave to England the control over Egypt See below, Chapter XIV

left for a rigorous revision of the Constitution, and the sharp divisions within the chamber, gave every reason to believe that the next few years would witness a crisis that would give France a new political system. On both the right and the left, the heirs-apparent to the bourgeois liberal-democratic republic were grooming themselves for their rôles.

THE royalist right was greatly strengthened by the deaths of the son of Napoleon III and the Bourbon Comte de Chambord. The Orléanist Comte de Paris remained as the principal contender for the throne The Church, harassed by the education laws of the Republic, rallied closer to the monarchists, and many of the bourgeoisie, fearful of the nascent beginnings of socialism as well as the rise of labor unions, looked to a monarchy as a possibility. The anticolonialists, who distrusted Ferry's policy and who could not work with the radicals of the left, also prepared to join with the royalists France, many people felt, needed to be governed, and the republicans, it seemed, were incapable of governing. It became obvious that the monarchists were at hand to assist in the rebirth of a monarchy when the rightist press reported the marriage of the daughter of the Comte de Paris to the son of the king of Portugal as if the comte were already ruler of France rather than pretender to a nonexistent throne.*

Not so dangerous to the Republic as the monarchist movement, but almost equally incompatible with the political *status quo,* were the demands of the radicals. They were republicans, but they wished to alter the Republic to satisfy the petty bourgeoisie and the proletariat Their program called for abolition of the presidency and the senate; election of judges, separation of Church and state; graduated income and inheritance taxes, equal, obligatory military service; free, compulsory lay education; regulation of labor contracts and conditions;

* A law was passed after this marriage, prohibiting pretenders from living in France The vote in the chamber was 315 against 232, in the senate, 137 against 122

social legislation, revision of railroad, mining, canal, and other public franchises; administrative decentralization; and a frank recognition of the sovereignty of the people Marxian socialists were unimportant in the 1880's, but these extreme leftists, who wished to reorient their France to conform with the political and economic preconceptions of the petty bourgeoisie, were radical enough to scare conservative Frenchmen

There was another tradition, in the left, even more dangerous to the Republic than this politico-economic program of the radicals. Traditionally, the left had harbored chauvinistic patriotism and Jacobin expansionism It was the left that had urged war on the tyrants to liberate the Poles and destroy the Metternich system; the left had supported Louis Napoleon's Italian policy when most of France opposed it; the left had urged war to the end in 1870–71 when Moltke's legions occupied France. A war of "revenge" in face of Bismarck's diplomatic system was not only impractical, but also impossible to realize; nevertheless, the left was overcrowded with men who saw such war as the sole aim of French high politics. Reasonable statesmen demurred from throwing down the glove under impossible conditions; even Gambetta at one time planned to visit Bismarck to show that the recovery of the lost provinces was to be postponed. But the Rocheforts, the Déroulèdes, and even the Clemenceaus never forgave or forgot the humiliation of 1871. Writers of stories like *The Last Lesson,* inflammatory orators, and revisionist publicists labored to keep alive the hope that the statues of Metz and Strasbourg in Paris could again shine resplendent without the wreath of mourning

One writer has called this warlike tradition the "original sin" of the left Be that as it may, after 1885 the agitation for *la revanche* stirred up a movement that threatened to undermine the Republic because many republicans could not bide their time and wait for favorable conditions to work out their revenge. In 1882 a society was founded—the League of Patriots—with the express purpose of keeping alive the tradition of *la revanche*. In 1885 it fell under the presidency of Déroulède, a popular, patriotic poet, whose rabble-rousing genius was to make him a national figure. His plans were simple; he advocated an alliance with Russia, and a war of extermination against Germany. If the Republic refused to listen to the plans of these patriots, they were willing to turn to any "strong man" who would. A popular hero was all that was needed to make *la revanche* a grave danger to the régime.*

Ironically enough, when the popular hero did appear, he was able to appeal to both the royalist right and the chauvinist left—a fact that probably contributed to his failure to fulfil the dreams of either. In 1886, upon the recommendation of Clemenceau, Premier Freycinet included General Boulanger in his cabinet as minister of war. The general was theretofore unknown and unnoticed by the politicians, but it was generally assumed that he was a republican, and his first official acts confirmed this assumption. In the political arena, General Boulanger cut a sorry figure; unaccustomed to public speaking and probably slow-witted as well as inarticulate, he confined himself to a few laconic remarks and much posing that gave him the reputation of a strong, silent man. Outside of the chamber, however, he played a more dashing rôle. He appeared solicitous for the welfare of the troops, made a brave show at reviews, and, whenever possible, placed himself in the public eye. The French have always loved military heroes, and Boulanger, mounted on a spirited black charger, was a sight to swell the breasts of the patriotic. It was not long before he was the darling of the crowds, and "Général Revanche" to the League of Patriots. Here was the man who would lead France back to honor and glory!

After 1887, several incidents occurred that brought Boulanger to the front, and created Boulangism as a political movement fraught with danger for the Republic. A French official named Schnaebelé was enticed into Germany on the

* Cf Chapter XIV, p 473

pretext of a conference with a German official, and then arrested. The Schnaebelé incident caused feeling to run high in France; protagonists of a war of revenge were convinced that Bismarck was insulting French honor, and that only blood could wash out the stain. The cabinet, realistically appraising France's powers, remained calm, and in due time Schnaebelé was released with proper apologies. Patriots, however, saw the whole affair as an example of the government's pusillanimity Further disgrace was in store for the Republic. Grévy had been re-elected to the presidency on the expiration of his first term,* but the old gentleman's second term ended badly, through no fault of his own It was discovered that his son-in-law, M Wilson, had been trafficking in the awards of the Legion of Honor. The highest distinction that France had to offer to her illustrious sons had been sold in the marketplace. It was a scandal of the very worst kind, and even Grévy's resignation was not enough to satisfy many of the people. Was not this all, they argued, that could be expected from men who knew not how to defend French honor abroad? The new president, Sadi-Carnot—in spite of his name, which recalled the very best traditions of the First Republic—could not erase the dishonor that the scandal involved. Dishonor at home and abroad brought the stock of the Republic to a new low. Moreover, 1887 was a year of crisis, when war was in the air; Russia and England, Russia and Austria, France and Germany, all seemed about to spring at each other's throats. In this uncertain international situation, General Boulanger appeared as the man who could lead France most effectively.

Even before the virtues of the brave general were proclaimed in contrast to the corruption of the Republic, the rising popularity of "Général Revanche" made the republicans look with suspicion upon the "Eaglet" in their midst It seemed impossible to form a cabinet without him, but the politicians

* Ferry was the most plausible candidate, but his record as an enthusiast for colonial expansion blocked his chances

were anxious to be rid of this popular idol. After the Schnaebelé incident, Boulanger was dropped from his post to avoid giving unnecessary provocation to Germany. When he was assigned to a command in the provinces, his followers on the boulevards saw this "exile" as another indication of the cowardice of the Republic. On the day that he left for his new post, a huge crowd gathered at the Gare de Lyon to see him off. It was with difficulty that the general mounted his train to escape from the necessity of leading the mob in a *coup de force* against the régime.

Boulanger in "exile" did not mean Boulanger forgotten A committee was formed to capitalize upon his popularity. He was press-agented in France much as Hollywood builds up a new movie star. Pictures, news stories, pamphlets, and handbills were showered upon France to announce the virtues and the promise of "the man on horseback" Royalists and chauvinists joined hands in extolling the hero of the hour. Money poured into his campaign from the war chests of men who wished to overturn the régime. The scandal of the Legion of Honor sales boomed the stock of the "man of honor" so much that the republicans came to realize that his very presence was a danger to their Republic. It was not difficult to find a charge against him, and a committee of inquiry removed Boulanger from his command and put him on half pay.

Free from the restraints of army discipline, the man who was now expected by some to be the "Général Revanche" and by others to be the long-awaited General Monck could enter the political arena without compromising his army career His friends laid out an effective program of action. the general would appeal to France for popular support A plebiscite was impossible under the Constitution, but he could test his popularity by running for the chamber of deputies in every by-election, no matter where it occurred (In France a candidate may stand for election in any and as many districts as he wishes) Time and again Boulanger was elected by huge majorities in many sections of the country, only to resign and run in another constituency His popularity was apparently invincible. In the chamber, he explained plans for revising the Constitution that would suppress both the senate and ministerial responsibility and enhance the powers of the president, so that France could have the strong, authoritative régime that alone could bring order and honor. His motion led him to a duel with a leftist republican, in which the general was wounded; strangely enough, this wound from a civilian did not impair his popularity

The climax of Boulangism came when the brave general ran for office in Paris itself; he had won victories in the provinces, but Paris was the real test. The republicans, fully aroused to their perilous position, made the election almost tantamount to a test of the régime, and, to their horror, it was found that even radical Paris had been seduced by the man on the black horse. On the evening of the election, a great crowd assembled outside of the general's hotel; it is probable that he could have led his supporters to the Élysée and captured the helm of the state, but Boulanger was not a Napoleon III or a Hitler! He lacked the courage to follow up his advantage. His royalist followers wanted him to pave the way for a restoration; his chauvinist supporters wanted a dictatorship. But Boulanger slipped out of the back door while his supporters were begging for a leader, and spent the night with his mistress "Caesar," said one of his disgruntled followers, "was only a garrison Romeo." March, 1889, was a critical month for the Republic, but Boulangism failed to be the movement to take advantage of the crisis.

The denouement was soon to come The ministry decided to bring the troublesome general and his patriots before the senate on charges of treason. In the meantime, the police frightened Boulanger's mistress into leaving France, and the "brave general," fearful of arrest, followed her into exile The whole affair collapsed with the retreat of its principal, and a year or two later, when the impoverished Boulanger committed suicide over the grave of his mistress, France paid scant attention to the report.

The fiasco of Boulangism was immediately reflected in French politics The radicals, thoroughly frightened by the apparition of a Caesar, had renounced their campaign to revise the Constitution, even before the "brave general" fled from France, and French democracy, in the elections of 1889, repudiated both the chauvinists and the royalists, by giving staunch moderate republicans a strong majority in the chamber of deputies In France, and in Europe, the politically wise realized that the Republic had successfully passed a severe test, and that talk of its early demise had become "wishful thinking" For the moment, the republicans of all hues closed ranks to present a united front, but before the decade of 1890–1900 was well under way, the chasm between the moderates and the radicals opened again to expose the régime to another shock that would threaten its existence.

ONE of the first fruits of the victory over the "man on horseback" was the acceptance of the Republic by the Roman Catholic Church Leo XIII, one of the most skillful diplomats to occupy the chair of Peter in our times, realized that the Church could not remain indefinitely on bad terms with Catholic France. Furthermore, the formation of Catholic parties in Germany, Belgium, and elsewhere had shown the way for effective Catholic political action under universal suffrage The obvious defeat of the monarchists made papal recognition of the Republic the politically expedient and—in the pope's opinion—the wise course of action. The Cardinal Archbishop Lavigérie, of Algiers, dramatically announced the new orientation of the Church, in a toast given, in the episcopal palace, at a reception to the officers of the Mediterranean squadron. The announcement that the Church wished to recognize the Republic was badly received by the archbishop's guests (the navy was filled with Orléanists) and even more ungraciously by the high clergy of France Apparently, neither the pope nor the cardinal realized how repugnant the Republic was to the French Catholic conservative leaders The pronouncement scandalized all those that detested the atheistic Republic On the other hand, it quickly converted many of the more liberal Catholics who realized that the Republic was not to be overthrown, and therefore could not be ignored There was a verbal battle at Rome when the royalists protested the betrayal of their cause, but His Holiness remained firm in his decision, and a Catholic republican party made its appearance in French politics

The papal encyclical letter of February, 1892, expressed the fundamental point of view of the Church. It pointed out that the Republic was as legitimate a form of government as any other, and that good Catholics ought to accept the legitimately constituted authority. The pope, however, distinguished sharply between the acceptance of the Republic and the acceptance of its laws. If the laws did not conform with Christian teaching, he argued, they must be changed The formula was a simple one—the Church would accept the Republic in order to change its laws. This radical departure horrified the Catholic monarchists; Leo's political opportunism ended their hopes for an immediate restoration. Many of them refused to consider themselves bound by this papal political heresy, but a large enough number of them did join to form a Catholic republican party which further split the conservative right.

Almost simultaneously with this break in the conservative party, another movement began to gain momentum, a movement that was destined to split the radical left. The amnesty granted to the communards of 1871, the political liberties of press and assembly, and, lastly, the legalization of labor unions, opened the way for the formation of a proper socialist party. Socialism in France had had a stormy and varied history long before the Republic came into being, but its followers were never united under a single banner. In 1848 and in 1871, only the brutal pressure of its opponents succeeded in giving a temporary unity to the socialist doctrines, and the fiascos of the June Days and the Commune further disunited socialist thinking After 1880, three new currents were introduced into French proletarian thought. Many of the communards in exile came in contact with Marxian socialism, and when they returned to France, they brought with them the "true faith." The formation of the labor unions, after 1884, introduced another trend, which found roots in indigenous French proletarian thought, and was to develop in full in the doctrine of syndicalism, with its political pluralism, and its great "myth" of the general strike. Lastly, Leo XIII encouraged the formation of Catholic working men's associations, that were to develop into Christian socialism. The formation of the Second International in Paris (1889), and the vigor of the Marxist leaders, gave the "true" socialists a slight advantage in the struggle for the allegiance of the French proletariat

No matter which flags they carried, the immediate aims of the socialists were about the same. They wished to alleviate conditions of labor, shorten working hours, and raise wages. It was a social program that they sought to annex to the political program of the leftist radicals in the chamber, but without much success In the 1890's the weakness of their numbers and the division in their leadership prevented the proletariat from exerting any great influence on political life. They were able to capture control of municipal councils in several of the industrial cities, and Jaurès, the great socialist leader, proclaimed the foundation of a parliamentary socialist party in the chamber of deputies Later, the socialists were to pile up considerable strength in the parliament, but it is questionable whether all of their supporters truly sympathized with socialist principles—in France, as we have said, to vote "to the left" is often an indication of displeasure with the right, rather than a desire to reorganize society. This socialist movement, however, was destined to split the radical left into two groups, since many of the petty bourgeoisie could never accept the socialists' "additions" to the radicals' program

IT WAS neither the right nor the left that supplied France with the political *affaire célèbre* of the early 1890's. The Panama Canal scandal, which "retired" a host of republican politicians, was essentially an affair of the parties that supported the *status quo*. One of the great difficulties in French political life has grown out of the fact that so many of the staunch republican leaders who have become deputies have been men of limited means, and, too often, of very elastic conscience. Their salaries as deputies have not conformed very realistically with their expenses, and the temptations that inevitably follow political power have opened ways to balance personal budgets. The Republic has been plagued with petty corruption, but only occasionally with a major scandal to show how great a problem is created by the election of impecunious politicians to important offices. Such an affair was the scandal of the Panama Canal. The financial irregularity of the Panama question was complicated by another factor. De Lesseps, the builder of the Suez Canal and the chief engineer of the Panama, was something of a national hero, and the promoters of the Panama Canal capitalized on his reputation to make the venture appear to be a great national undertaking. When the fiasco of the whole affair became obvious, the government hesitated to expose the promoters, since many politicians as well as the "national hero" apparently were deeply implicated.

Basically, the affair grew out of the difficulties that the French contractors encountered in Panama. The link between the Pacific and Atlantic oceans was a much more difficult engineering task than the Suez had been, and, to complicate the problem, disease proved to be an insurmountable obstacle. When the canal was finally built, sanitation was a task as formidable as the actual digging itself. The French canal was a sink that absorbed quantities of capital, with no end in sight. Of all this the French investors knew nothing. The politicians authorized further security issues; the little people bought them Money disappeared in Panama, and even before it got to Panama. In 1893, the lid finally blew off, and the public was treated to an extensive airing of a first-rate scandal in the court room, in the press, and in a parliamentary investigation. There were charges and countercharges in the chamber, the finger of accusation was pointed at more than a hundred theretofore respectable politicians. The investigations were blocked by the mysterious death of one of the principals and the flight of another, but the public learned enough to see that their trust had been grossly betrayed. Of all the accused, only one deputy—who had not been able to "forget"—was definitely connected with the affair, and in the end, he, with the rest of them, was cleared by the Statute of Limitations Cleared or not, dozens of politicians—the redoubtable Clemenceau among them—found their reputations so shattered that retirement seemed expedient

The conservatives were too weak to take advantage of the embarrassment of the republicans; one of their number summed up the situation nicely by remarking that Boulanger had been a fool to kill himself. No other Boulanger was available at the moment, and without a popular leader the royalist cause had no chance of success The chief political consequence of the Panama scandal was the retirement of many of the republican leaders, their places were taken by younger politicians who, not having fought against the party of "moral order," hardly realized the terrific battles that had been necessary to establish the Republic. These new men, especially the moderate bourgeois politicians, had less trouble working with the conservatives on the right than their predecessors had had; the Catholic republicans and the heirs of the moderate republicans were often able to work quite harmoniously together Both of them were willing to forget the conflicts of 1876–79 because both of them were afraid of the rising tide of radicalism on the extreme left.

NEW faces in the political arena did not mean political peace for France. The Panama scandal had hardly ceased to make good newspaper copy, when a definite and apparently unbridgeable gap opened within the ranks of the republican parties The political maturation of the petty bourgeoisie and the beginnings of a truly proletarian party were primarily responsible for the split. The little people of France had theretofore accepted more or less willingly the leadership of their more wealthy republican colleagues who were fighting for liberal democracy against the politics of authority Although there was a "radical left" before 1890, the moderate republicans could usually obtain its support The petty bourgeoisie and the proletariat, as a rule, merely considered themselves to be "republicans," and as long as the moderates were fighting for the existing Republic or for an extension of political liberties, they could count on the support of these little people. After 1890, however, when the liberal, democratic Republic was apparently firmly established, the little people came to realize that they wished a more extensive program of political action than the moderates were willing to sponsor. With the ballot as a tool for exerting influence and with the gradual acquisition of political experience, the little people prepared to force their opinions upon the councils of the nation.

Their program was the "'radical republican" program of the 1880's, with a few additions grafted upon it by the socialists. It ranged from a demand for graduated income and inheritance taxes, through proposals for state intervention to regulate hours, wages, and conditions of labor, to socialist projects for the nationalization of all railroads, mines, and utilities The questions of separation of Church and state, the disestablishment of religious Congregations, and the elimination of the clergy from education also bulked large in the program They further demanded a series of lesser reforms in the army, the administration, the judiciary, and local government which, presumably, would assure greater political equality In the light of the experience of the twentieth century, their program does not seem very radical, but in the decade of the 1890's Briand, Millerand, Viviani, and Jaurès—leaders of the left—were considered "reds" who were splitting the republican party.

Naturally, men of wealth and substance rejected a program which suggested an income tax, to say nothing of the more radical economic measures that the left advocated Furthermore, after the Church rallied to the Republic, many of the moderates, like their predecessors under the July monarchy, were coming to see that the Church could be an able ally in a struggle against socialism. This impression was deepened in the early years of the 1890's by a series of outrages perpetrated by anarchists Sadi-Carnot, the president of France, was murdered, a bomb was exploded in the chamber of deputies; and other acts of terrorism startled French society. Many who could not distinguish clearly between anarchism and socialism linked this political radicalism with the strikes that broke out simultaneously in the industrial districts, in several cases causing considerable bloodshed. Moderate and conservative republicans, fearful of the excesses of the left, turned to make common cause with the Catholics and monarchists on the right. And since there were many in France—peasants and petty bourgeoisie, as well as wealthy capitalists and friends of the Church—whose misunderstanding of politics made them susceptible to being stampeded to the right by a "red" scare, the possibility of a clerical Republic loomed large on the horizon in the middle of the 1890's.

THE end of the decade provided France with a new issue that was destined to break the power of the right and open the way for leftist republican solutions of many of France's most troublesome problems. It was the Dreyfus case that became the great *cause célèbre* at the end of the century. From a mere question of miscarriage of justice in a military court, this case became a paramount issue in French political life. Before it had worked itself out, the trial of Captain Dreyfus divided French society into two opposing camps, and touched practically every phase of French political life No one who could read was able to avoid taking a side in the case.

The case itself seems of no great moment. Captain Dreyfus, a rich Alsatian Jew, was accused before a military court of selling army secrets to Germany. In spite of his declarations of innocence, the flimsiness of the evidence against him, and the obvious lack of motive, Dreyfus was publicly condemned, drummed out of the army, and sent to Devil's Island for life The news that a traitor had been apprehended and punished was received with satisfaction; the fact that he was a Jew confirmed the anti-Semitic opinion that had been growing in France for many years. The satisfaction, however, was to be rudely shattered. The Dreyfus family continued in their belief of the captain's innocence, and started an investigation to track down the real culprit. At about the same time, a brilliant Alsatian officer, Colonel Picquart, who became head of the army intelligence department, re-examined the Dreyfus *dossier,* and reached the conclusion that an error had been made. He stated that Esterhazy, a penniless Hungarian adventurer—rather than Dreyfus—was the real author of the *bordereau* that had sent Dreyfus to Devil's Island. Colonel Picquart's superiors transferred him to Tunis for his trouble, but not before he had informed Senator Scheurer-Kestner of the secret

In no time, the Dreyfus case became a political issue The ministry, the war department, and the army refused to consider it as anything but a closed case, but the leftist press and a daily increasing band of intellectuals and politicians insisted upon making it an issue. Scheurer-Kestner demanded a retrial; the brother of Dreyfus publicly accused Esterhazy of guilt. To silence this rising chorus of criticism, Esterhazy was haled before a military court, and acquitted of all connection with the case. The army felt that no one, surely, would question the honor and integrity of the defenders of the nation The growing band of Dreyfusards, however, were not impressed by this military hocus-pocus Émile Zola, the foremost literary light of his generation, after a conversation with the German ambassador assembled the data in favor of Dreyfus, and boldly wrote the famous letter "J'accuse," which was published in *L'Aurore*. It was a challenge for a public trial that could not be ignored.

The trial that followed was a farce The court was decidedly against Zola, information was withheld, witnesses refused to testify, and in the end everyone that would see understood that Zola's condemnation to a year's imprisonment was another case of the miscarriage of French justice. Events moved rapidly after the trial. In quick succession war minister followed war minister, when the high officers in the army refused to consider any reopening of the trial. Then, like a bomb, a new furore opened in the case. One bit of evidence that sent Dreyfus to Devil's Island was a note alleged to have been written by a foreign military attaché. It transpired that the note had been forged by a certain Colonel Henry, who committed suicide in prison when apprehended for the offense. Esterhazy fled to London, and admitted that he was the author of the *bordereau,* but said that Dreyfus was the real factor behind his action. The cat was out of the bag, and there was no alternative to a new trial

The stupidity of the military clique led them to another blunder. In the re-trial at Rennes, Dreyfus was found guilty "under extenuating circumstances," and sentenced to ten years. It was too much for anyone to take President Loubet pardoned the condemned man, and a reorganization of the army followed. Even so, it was seven years before a military court completely exonerated Dreyfus and restored both him and Colonel Picquart to their ranks in the army

No brief statement of the case can make clear the great social and political forces that played around it. The Dreyfus affair aroused political passions in France that even the World War (1914–1918) failed to still entirely. It was a perfect political case, it involved religious and race prejudice, social and military justice, clericalism in politics, popular sovereignty and authority These were the issues that rallied men for and against Dreyfus; his cause came to mean "liberty, equality, and fraternity" to the men of the left.

The line-up was just what was to be expected. The monarchists, clericals, and authoritarians of all varieties wrapped themselves in the mantle of patriotism to repel a base assault upon the military honor of the nation They rallied to their side the prejudices against the Jews, against spies, and against Germany to lure the support of the masses The League of Patriots and kindred associations took up the cry against the "defamers of national honor." Practically the entire weight of the Church was thrown against any reconsideration of Dreyfus's case; a Jesuit paper in Rome set the tone by attacking the condemned man as both a traitor and as a Jew. The army, almost to a man, resisted the notion that a group of "wild-eyed intellectuals" and "professional agitators" could be right and the *sacra sacrorum* of the general staff wrong!

On the other side, the first to rally to the cause of Dreyfus were a group of college professors and writers derisively dubbed "intellectuals," and the socialists led by Jaurès. Before the fight had gone far, however, the republican parties of the left realized full well that they were confronted with Boulangism under a new flag—that of ardent patriotism Clemenceau, who had been out of politics since the Panama scandal, returned with Dreyfus as his chief cause. Others followed, until the whole left, with different shades of intensity, joined in the campaign The fact that the old enemies of the Republic were lined up solidly in the anti-Dreyfus camp finally forced even the moderate republicans to return to the republican front against authoritarianism

The story of the *affaire* is filled with tragi-comic dramatic incidents Duhamel, in *The Pasquier Chronicles,* ably describes the dilemma in which thousands of families found themselves when it became impossible to mention politics at the dinner table, because even within the families the division of opinion had formed a deep chasm. In the streets the anti-

Dreyfus cohorts clamored for a military *coup de force;* Déroulède even tried to force a general officer to lead his troops against the Élysée, and Marchand, after the Fashoda incident, was embarrassed by the popularity which his supposed willingness to lead a *coup d'état* gave to him. One of Dreyfus's most effective lawyers, the fiery Labori, was shot by a radical anti-Dreyfusard, and there was even an attempt upon the life of President Loubet.

The Dreyfus case proved to be a new cement for the republicans. At first, most of the politicians attempted to suppress the issue, to avoid detonating the political dynamite inherent in it. Unwise handling of the *affaire,* it was feared, might easily lead to trouble with Germany, at the very moment when France and England faced each other in the Nile basin with war in their hearts. Furthermore, it was as dangerous to break down popular confidence in the army as it was to antagonize the military men by political interference in what appeared to be a routine army affair. The cause of Dreyfus seemed to be sponsored by professional agitators and a few intellectuals with whom the politicians, at first, feared to ally themselves. As the story unfolded toward the startling exposure of the Henry forgery, Esterhazy's admission of guilt, and, finally, the blundering second trial, the picture began to clear up Obviously, this was no mere question of military injustice; the liberties of France as well as of Dreyfus were at stake. Republicans of all shades saw that a new "sixteenth of May," or a new "Boulangist movement," was concealed behind the hue and cry of the anti-Dreyfusards. "Patriotism" was an old mantle for the enemies of the Republic, and its reappearance in the Dreyfus affair did not blind the men of the left to the dangers involved in the case.

The issue was joined after the sudden death of President Félix Faure, whose anti-Dreyfusard leanings were well known. The republicans banded together to elect Loubet, whose leftist leanings were unquestionable, and to defeat Méline, who was suspected of dealings with the reactionaries Loubet called Waldeck-Rousseau, a one-time protégé of Gambetta and a colleague of Ferry, to form a ministry to attack the problems posited by the Dreyfus case Waldeck-Rousseau brought together a ministry that included men from all parties on the left, even Millerand, a socialist, joined the cabinet This rallying of the parties of the left was to give a stable government for several years, and to allow the parties of the left to work out part of the program of the radical republicans.

The new ministry, with the experience of the Dreyfus case and the thirty-year-old struggle with the right as a background, turned its attention to the problem of liquidating its enemies Many years before, Gambetta had isolated the clericals and branded them as supporters of the reaction, when he gave the left the war-cry, *"Le cléricalisme, voilà l'ennemi!"* Political experience, from the beginning of the Republic, gave ample credence to this momentous pronouncement. The Church had refused to recognize the Republic until after the complete fiasco of the Boulangist movement had proved that the régime could not easily be overthrown, and, even then, recognition, apparently, was granted on the assumption that a Catholic party would be able to dominate the policy of the state. In the Dreyfus case, the Church lined up solidly behind the opponents of Dreyfus, and placed its immense influence in the scale against a cause that eventually proved to have justice on its side. The debacle of the anti-Dreyfus movement left the churchmen in an exposed position, hence it is not surprising that a ministry composed of anticlericals should take advantage of the Church's embarrassment to consolidate the republican program.

One of the first acts of the new ministry was to institute an investigation of the anti-Dreyfus agitation This eventually led to the trial of a number of the agitators and an inquiry into the activities of the several "leagues" that had borne the brunt of the opposition to the reconsideration of the case. Among others, the Congregation of the Assumptionist Fathers, which edited a clerical paper, *La Croix,* was brought to trial, with a spectacular exposé of the political machinations of the monks. The immediate result of the trials was the imprisonment and exile of several of the leaders of the anti-Dreyfus movement, but more far-reaching was the anticlerical legislation that eventually ended in complete separation of Church and state.

In 1901, the chambers passed a law that ordered the dissolution and expulsion of all unauthorized religious Congregations in France This law affected hundreds of religious houses, and thousands of monks and nuns, and struck a rude blow at the influence of the Roman Catholic Church in France. The law was laxly enforced until 1902, when Waldeck-Rousseau resigned because of ill health, and Combes, a stubborn anticlerical, became premier He at once announced his intention of carrying out the letter of the law. A terrific storm of protest broke out from the Catholics; a "League of Women" petitioned Madame Loubet, peasants offered to barricade the monasteries, and monks and nuns pretended that authorization was unnecessary, or besieged the ministry for authorization before the ax could fall. In the end, authorization was granted to very few. The execution of the order affected over 19,000 monks and nuns, and closed about 1,500 religious houses. Protests there were in abundance, but since the radicals could depend upon a majority in both the chamber and the senate, they did not alter their course.

In 1904, a further blow was struck at the influence of the Church by a partial repeal of the Falloux laws and the closing of the schools of the rest of the Congregations. There was some opposition to this measure, since it would necessitate the construction of about 336 schools for boys and 1,920 schools for girls. Furthermore, it would require the employment of 7,500 lay instructors, and would extend the education costs of the state by about nine million francs a year. The law was modified to allow the process of closing some 3,000 schools to be spread over ten years, but the Catholic schools and the teaching orders of monks and nuns were doomed to extinction. The republicans felt that only thus could they be assured that the younger generation would be instructed in the republican tradition The result has been that the teacher and the priest in many French communities have come to represent diametrically opposite schools of thought.

This vigorous attack upon the Church coincided with the first years of Pius X on the throne of St. Peter. The pope was a holy man, somewhat of a mystic, and undoubtedly sincere in his interest in the spiritual welfare of his subjects, but he lacked the insight, the judgment, and the adroitness that had made his predecessor, Leo XIII, one of the great statesmen of the century. The pope naturally objected to the attacks upon the Congregations, but he failed completely to understand that the French clergy had invited trouble. He placed the blame on the shoulders of the Freemasonry and agnosticism which, in his opinion, could dominate Catholic France only temporarily From his point of view, it was inconceivable that the Roman Catholics in France would long support a government that attacked their Church. Lulled by this delusion, Pius X allowed a series of incidents to develop into a crisis that ended in the complete separation of Church and state.

The pope, of course, did not have to go out of his way to find trouble with the French government; Combes was more than willing to meet him half way! A dispute arose over the appointment of a bishop—a time-honored excuse for friction between "pope" and "emperor" Combes ignored the usual custom of consulting the pope about a candidate, and the pope refused to invest the candidate presented. A troublesome debate followed; it was hardly settled by a halfhearted compromise, when President Loubet's visit to Rome created a more serious problem. Before the French president went to Italy, Combes attempted to arrange for his reception by the pope as well as by the king of Italy, but Pius X took the attitude that a visit to the king was an insulting recognition of the stroke of force that had deprived him of the city of Rome.

The pope not only refused to receive President Loubet when he visited Rome, but also protested against the visit in terms that gave Combes an excuse for withdrawing the French minister from the Vatican The breach might have been closed, but a new crisis followed close on the heels of this strain in Franco-papal relations Without consulting the French government, the pope ordered two French bishops to hand in their resignations, the papal nuncio had clearly gone beyond his rights under the concordat, and Combes broke off diplomatic relations with the pope The fat was in the fire, there was to be a contest between the radical left and the pope for control in France

The basis of the dispute, of course, was the hundred-year-old Napoleonic concordat The republicans felt that this document placed them in an equivocal position; the clergymen were paid servants of the state, but, at the same time, they worked untiringly to undermine the republican régime. On the other hand, the clergymen were not entirely satisfied to see their Church under the ministry of cults, when, often enough, an agnostic or a freethinker was the minister. Separation of Church and state—or, at least, alteration of the concordat—had long been discussed by all groups concerned, but no one believed that any alteration of the status was possible until the remote future. It was a difficult problem to handle. The proponents of separation had always to point out carefully that they did not intend to interfere with the spiritual labors of the Church; that their only desire was to eradicate clericalism and ultramontanism in politics. The opponents of separation were never slow to point out that the existing concordat was not entirely satisfactory, but they feared that any alteration in the *status quo* would expose their beloved Church to difficulties.

There was, however, no hope for it. The trend turned toward separation of Church and state as the only solution. When the Combes ministry resigned, Rouvier took over the premiership, and Combes in the senate and Briand in the chamber pushed through the legislation that resulted in separation. Rouvier was unwilling to work for the project, but there was a substantial majority in both houses to pass the bill that guaranteed religious liberty to all, but at the same time withdrew the support of the state from all churches With this law, France departed from the European tradition of concordats, and adopted the American tradition that guarantees free exercise of religious worship, but leaves the matter of religious organizations to private initiative

Naturally, Pius X was not willing to take this blow without a struggle. In the encyclical letter, *Vehementer,* of February, 1905, he condemned the law and the principle of separation as contrary to the constitution of the Church. Furthermore, he insisted that the French government had no legal right to take unilateral action on the concordat; it could be changed legally only by negotiation. He instructed French Catholics to ignore the law, and to resist any invasion of their churches. This amounted to an invitation to civil war, for the government had decided to take an inventory of the church property prior to transmitting it to the church associations that, henceforth, were to be responsible for it.

There was some trouble, a few riots; several lives were even lost. It would, in all probability, have been much more serious if Briand had not administered the liquidation so tactfully The problem was a delicate one, and any false step might easily have led to serious consequences. For several years following the separation, the government labored arduously to complete the transfer of church property. The Church, of course, gave no official assistance, but the firmness and tactfulness of the government finally succeeded in completing the work without allowing the question to develop into the civil war that churchmen at Rome hoped to see As long, however, as the Church refused to be satisfied with the new arrangement, the Republic was in danger from a clerical reaction, and it was not until the postwar era that Rome officially made peace with the Republic.

THE last ten years before the Great War were marked by a growing interest in and apprehension about problems of foreign affairs on the one side, and the agitation of the proletariat on the other The growing international tension and the repeated crises, especially after 1905, forced France to enlarge considerably her annual military credits, at the expense of a balanced budget The costs of armament were such that the mounting national debt had assumed menacing proportions by 1914 On the other hand, the preoccupation with the demands of the laborers led to an open conflict within the ranks of the leftist parties, and effectively blocked the program of reforms that Clemenceau's radical left hoped to introduce after 1906. The World War was to engulf both budget and reform program, and present France with a whole series of new and difficult problems.

Before 1905, the proletariat had realized some of their ambitions under the Republic, but not so completely as the bourgeoisie had achieved theirs. The crux of the matter was found simply in the fact that the bourgeois ambitions fitted nicely into the traditional customs of French government. The Republic gladly continued Louis Napoleon's policy of backing the interests of French commerce, industry, and banking, both at home and abroad, by subsidies and direct aid. Furthermore, the Republic willingly altered the unpopular tariff policy of the Empire, to return France to her traditional system of protection.* Such policy was congenial to the traditions of the nation, but the proletariat asked the state to intervene in the relations between labor and capital. This demand was quite contrary to the traditional French political practice. In France, the employers of labor had traditionally resisted the inroads of the state into their private affairs. Universal manhood suffrage and the growth of class-conscious labor movements, however, were to impose upon the Republic a more solicitous consideration of the interests of the prole-

* Cf Chapter XIII

tariat. They received the right to organize labor unions (1884); a series of laws regulated hours and conditions of labor (1890–1905), the *livret* was abolished; and old-age relief and optional social insurance came into being But France embarked upon no such wide-sweeping social program as did Germany under Bismarck or England under Lloyd George

The French proletarian leaders, however, organized, and prepared themselves for the "struggle" with the bourgeoisie Educated in the revolutionary philosophy of Marx, Sorel, and others, they demanded a larger share in the emerging civilization of the twentieth century. Had not their grandfathers shown the efficacy of direct action in the revolutionary struggles of the past? They, too, were ardent believers in a new type of direct action—sabotage and the "general strike" From 1890 on, strikes became more and more common, and since they were often accompanied by bloodshed, each new outbreak seemed dangerous to the state After 1900, it became more common for the government to utilize force to protect property, and, incidentally, to suppress strikes. This practice, in a series of serious disturbances between 1905 and 1910, led to the rupture of the parties of the left. The socialists, whose political power was augmented with each election, protested more and more vehemently against the use of troops. It finally came to a showdown between Jaurès and Clemenceau, and a cessation of the program of the radical party.

One of the greatest problems arose over the question of the right of governmental employees and workers in public utilities to organize and strike. The interruption of the services of the government or of railroads, telegraphs, and so forth, was considered by many as an act of rebellion against society. In 1910, a railroad strike whose ramifications involved telegraph and postal services was broken by the use of troops and by mobilizing the strikers into the army and forcing them to return to their work under military discipline Briand, who engineered the government's answer to the strikes, was roundly condemned as a turncoat. Only a few years before, he, as a socialist orator, had urged the efficacy and the legality of the strike as a labor weapon The demands of the proletariat for shorter hours and more pay continued unabated until the Great War broke out in 1914. The government proved itself unable to solve the problems that these demands posited for French society. In the postwar era, with a larger representation in the chambers, the laborers again took up the problem of securing a larger share of the national income for themselves and their families

The other great question that troubled France was her relations with foreign countries.* Here French democracy seemed quite incapable of exercising very much control. The issues of world politics revolved around larger centers of gravity, and were manifold in their complexity. Politicians in the chamber of deputies or the senate might make speeches that were conciliatory or chauvinistic, but over the sweep of events that were leading Europe to a huge bonfire they were able to exercise but little control. From the time of Thiers on, the army's needs had been carefully nurtured, so that the military power of the nation would never again be in the deplorable condition of 1870, but the great problem of inequality in population, wealth, and industry between France and Germany always demanded increasing sacrifices from the French taxpayer and the French youth To maintain an army at all comparable to that of their powerful eastern neighbor, the French were forced to pay an inordinately large percentage of their national budget for military expenses, and an increasingly larger percentage of their population had to shoulder arms to prepare for the defense of the fatherland. Just before the war started, the chamber raised the term of military service from two to three years, in the fond hope that an additional show of force might mean greater security for the nation.

---

* See Chapter XIV

The political instability created by the ever-increasing demands of French labor and the ominous outlook in international affairs prevented any effective work on the constructive ideas of the majority in the chamber While the internal peace and the external safety of the Republic were in jeopardy, it proved impossible to develop any policy There were projects for reform demanding attention, proportional representation, income taxes, nationalization of railroads, administrative decentralization, and social legislation were in the forefront of the leftist program. The war engulfed the whole of French society, and, for the time, forced indefinite postponement of all reforms. When peace returned, the problems of the prewar decade were only a small fraction of the work that faced the victorious French nation

CHAPTER XIII

REPUBLICAN FRANCE BEFORE 1914

THE tone of official and polite society changed very little between 1815 and 1880 The Bourbon régime may have been more aristocratic, the July monarchy more plutocratic, and the Empire more military, but, in general, the men who counted in politics, as in society and affairs, were almost exclusively recruited from the upper section of the social structure They were men of wealth and breeding, whose blood and gold furnished the keys to political and social preference. Occasionally, an adventurer or an intellectual intruded into their select group, but, for the most part, little people of all kinds were excluded. In the first years of the Republic, this pattern continued almost unrelaxed; life under the assembly and during the presidency of MacMahon was ordered much as it had been under Napoleon III. After 1880, things began to change. Polite society and the world of big business continued to be the domain of the wealthy, but in politics humbler people came into power The middle bourgeoisie and the professional classes, wealthy peasants, petty bourgeoisie, and even an occasional proletarian found that democracy opened the way to political position. As a result, France, just before the war (1914–18), was governed by men who often would not have fitted into Guizot's famous definition of the ruling class.

This change can most easily be seen by a glance at the deputies, the senators, and the ministers; in the early years of the Republic the whole machine of government was heavily loaded with men of noble blood and considerable wealth. After 1890, and particularly after 1900, it became increasingly difficult for the country gentleman, bourgeois or noble, and the wealthy industrialist, banker, or merchant to be elected to office; and if elected, the very wealthy and the well born found it almost impossible to become ministers In their places were men who became professional politicians—well-to-do peasants, shopkeepers, professors, lawyers, doctors, teachers, and even more humble folk who were willing to serve time as councilor, *maire,* deputy, and finally, senator As a rule, the cost of a political campaign, which each candidate had to take care of himself, prohibited the very poor from running for office, just as prejudice and envy precluded the wealthy and well born from being elected In local government, the exclusion of the rich was even more marked than it was in the national government, for poorer peasants and even workers could aspire to become councilors, while they often realized that professional people could better represent them in Paris The "separation between the possession of public power and wealth or social prestige," writes a distinguished French historian, "this divorce between authority and influence, became a new characteristic of French society."

While the advent of democracy entailed an alteration in the political balance of power, the Republic did not produce a social revolution. France, at the opening of the World War (1914–18), was still a nation with great social and economic inequalities. The lack of income-tax statistics makes impossible an accurate analysis of the relative distribution of wealth, but the evidence available does show that great wealth was really concentrated in very few hands In 1908, the land of France, for example, was divided into more than five and a half million plots, but under thirty thousand (.005 per cent) of them were larger than two hundred and fifty acres Of one hundred thousand inheritances, 98.1 per cent were worth less than $20,000, and only .0012 per cent were worth more than two hundred thousand dollars. Professor Seignobos concludes that "comfort is less general, and individual fortunes more concentrated, in France than one had believed" In 1914, the French social structure resembled a pyramid with a very broad base of poor people and a very small apex of very wealthy; it had not changed greatly in the hundred years of the nineteenth century.

The families, bourgeois and noble, on the top of this pyramid still enjoyed the greatest social prestige, and continued to consume a disproportionate share of the goods and services of the land. A country château as well as a town house, membership in the exclusive clubs, and the ability to waste conspicuously, were indispensable for inclusion in their select society In the latter half of the nineteenth century and the beginning of the twentieth, their social contacts broadened to include the upper circles of the cosmopolitan society of London, New York, Rome, Madrid, and even Berlin. Their world outlook and interests became increasingly international rather than French, and their wealth extended its influence far beyond the frontiers of their native country Many of the older nobility, by tradition and taste well suited for this select company, found it increasingly difficult to keep the pace set by sons of bankers, merchants, and manufacturers. Their alternatives were, often, either to retire to the country and live a life of rural elegance, or to marry the daughter of an American or Jewish capitalist who could afford the luxury of supporting a title for the prestige involved.

Those on top, with their international orientation and their immense wealth, did not surrender all of their influence over French life when the rise of democracy robbed them of their traditional seats of power. They still exercised a large measure of control over the ships, factories, railroads, and banks. The Bank of France, a fortress of entrenched wealth, gave these people a powerful stronghold from which to guide the destinies of the nation. They learned to use their wealth to control public opinion by the purchase of newspapers, newspaper men, and publicists. They could hire lawyers of talent, who showed them the way around inconvenient legislation, and they even found that impecunious deputies, senators, and ministers were often purchasable at a very reasonable figure Bureaucrats would yield to pressure politics, and the flag of "national interests" often covered their economic ventures in foreign lands. Thus, the ballot box alone was not enough to exclude the wealthy and the well born from power in the democracy of the Republic

The gay and superficial life of this upper society was well known to all who could read Their comings and goings, their pleasures at the Opéra, the races, the gaming tables, the exclusive clubs, and at the fashionable beaches, had long been recorded as important events in the pictorial magazines, and even in the democratic press Pictures of their mode of living, their clothes, their dogs, their horses, and their automobiles were available for everyone. Not infrequently, their emotional crises and their family lives had been made public property, when a scandal or a "society divorce" made a journalistic holiday for the masses Their children were educated by tutors or in exclusive, fashionable schools The gay round of parties, balls, trips, and sporting events which made up their lives were, for the men, occasionally interrupted by the more serious duties of business meetings and conferences; but many of these people learned that it was easier and safer to hire the brains of professional people to look after their affairs Of the commonplace, daily lives of the extremely wealthy, the masses knew little; but they did grasp the idea that there were people whose existence was so fabulously different from their own that it might have been translated from a fairy tale.

Just below this upper crust stood the middle bourgeoisie and the country gentry, probably the most substantial group in the entire society They formed the bulk of the professional classes—lawyers, doctors, professors, higher government functionaries, army officers, highly placed journalists, and the like. They were the well-to-do businessmen, landlords, and *rentiers*. These people were purely French in their interests and orientation; the foreigner had to wait long before he was accepted in the bosom of their families. Although foreign bonds—Russian, Turkish, or American—might be found in their portfolios, the vital interests of most of these people were largely bounded by the frontiers of their own country. It is questionable if more than six to eight per cent of the entire population could reasonably be classified as within this group, but they, with the plutocrats, dominated the important economic life of France.

The political and social inclinations of the middle bourgeoisie and the country gentry were by no means uniform In their ranks were ardent Catholics, whose fathers had been converted by the "reds" in the forties or whose grandfathers had turned from freethinking during the Revolution. Others of them were confirmed agnostics, freethinkers, anticlericals, or Freemasons who would make neither peace with nor concessions to the Church. The novelists have often described family conflicts that arose when father and son adopted opposite points of view. Some of them were republicans, some royalists, and some imperialists; occasionally (Léon Blum, for example), one of them would make common cause with the laboring people, in a socialist program. The latter type, however, was a distinct mutation; by and large, these men wished to see a conservative, property-respecting government in power. With the exception of a few intellectuals and idealists, they opposed any concessions to the proletariat, the income tax, or any other political credo that might affect their economic position Even those men whose family traditions and personal inclinations made them friendly to the Revolution, looked askance at the petty bourgeois and proletarian radicalism of the democratic left. Their hearts might be on the left, but their pocketbooks were securely anchored to the right.

Naturally, these men played a large rôle in the political life of the nation The vast majority of the ministers were recruited from their ranks; they staffed the bureaucracy, the army, and the navy. These were the men with both the intelligence and the educational opportunities to make themselves the leaders of society, and since many of them were neither tarred with the brush of reaction nor wealthy enough to excite too great passions of envy, they were often able to capture and keep the confidence of the French democracy Lawyers, doctors, notaries, and small or medium-sized businessmen, were in fairly close contact with the everyday life and interests of their poorer neighbors, and often able to become their leaders. Their realization of the power and the prejudices of the masses often led to amusing political situations; it was not uncommon to find that the son of the country gentleman, even of noble birth, tried to obtain the votes of his peasant neighbors by announcing himself for candidacy under the banner of the left

It was these middle-bourgeois and country-gentry families that supported much of the culture of the Republic Their sons and daughters frequented its schools for advanced learning They bought the books, subscribed to the reviews and magazines, purchased the concert, opera, and theater tickets, visited the art galleries, and patronized the painters before they became too famous. These people were able to afford commodious living quarters, fine furniture, and the details of elegant living They, of course, did not live on the scale of the plutocrats—indeed, their hardheaded care of their wealth often laid them open to the charge of stinginess—but they lived in the comfort and ease which made for gracious living The foreigner who has been fortunate enough to visit their homes, and the reader of French novels that picture their lives, can hardly fail to be impressed with the civilization that made their cultured existence possible. On the other hand, as Georges Duhamel so eloquently describes, not all of this class were capable of gracious living. The expansion of economic horizons allowed many people from the lower classes, whose traditions were somewhat crude, to push into this élite society With all of the marks of parvenus and social climbers, these newcomers were excellent targets for the satire of both the stage and the novel.

These people, like most of their compatriots, did not open their lives for public gaze. "The French," writes a distinguished man of letters, "have always been known as builders of enclosures, lovers of walls . . . [they have a] zealous sense of privacy, a hankering after locks and keys, and a desire for security, this characteristic which people in other countries sometimes deride" This desire for privacy, combined with the unsavory reputation of the city streets, which is probably well deserved, has led to all sorts of malicious tales about the morals of the French It is true that the French, with their keen appreciation of economic realities, often regard marriage as a financial agreement, and strictly separate it from love and sentiment; it is also probably true that "affairs" are not uncommon; but it should not be overlooked that the typical Frenchman of the substantial middle class is sober, industrious, and well behaved. The night life of Paris is and was largely a business highly unrelated to the French. There is no greater libel against any people than the foreigner's conception of the immoral, riotously living French.

Below this group of landlords, businessmen, and professional men, whose wealth allowed considerable freedom, was the petty bourgeoisie. The highly skilled artisans, the wealthier peasants, shopkeepers, schoolteachers, petty functionaries, and white-collared workers of one kind or another fell into this class. All of these people had some little invested wealth, but not enough to live on too comfortably, even with the additional income not resulting from their labors They were always forced to practice strict economy to maintain their position in society. Under previous régimes, these little people were rigorously excluded from the councils of the nation, and their aims, interests, and ambitions received only cursory attention from the powers that controlled the country. Democracy, however, armed them with the ballot, and their numbers gave them strength; under the Republic, it was impossible to prevent them from exercising considerable influence over affairs They elected men from their own ranks to the councils, the chamber, and the senate, or they chose lawyers, doctors, professors, or others, who sympathized with their outlook, to represent them in Paris. In the years just before the war, well over a third of the deputies held their seats in the chamber because they satisfied these men.

The memory of years of association between the Church and authority under previous régimes, as well as the fact that the *curé* and the château or mansion were often in obvious alliance, had ingrained anticlericalism deeply in these men. In many of the villages and small towns—the real France—the views of the *curé* and those of the schoolmaster or the town agnostic split society. The one stood for traditions; the other, for "progress", and the vocal struggles in the provincial cafés and wine shops, as well as the contests in the ballot box, gave these humble folk the illusion that they were fighting in the front trenches of humanity. It does not follow that these people broke formal relations with the Church; they were much too conservative for that. The *curé* baptized, married, and buried them, and often firmly held the loyalty of their wives and daughters, but he had difficulty directing their life while their health was good and "progress" was at stake. They unhesitatingly gave their support to the men who rallied around Gambetta's famous slogan, "Clericalism—there is the enemy!" a program that finally expelled the Church from education, and separated it from the state.

Closely associated with their anticlericalism was their passion for equality. These little people all seem to have been infected with the sin of envy. They recognized the inevitability of economic inequality, but they wished always to protect the small against the great, the poor against the rich, the weak against the strong. "We are always ready," writes Siegfried, "to protect the small and the weak, the little landowners, the little employers, the little pensioners, and even the little cheats." To these people the little man, with a little house, a little garden, and a little income, is the ideal citizen. Their penchant for the "little" has made *Le Petit Parisien* France's largest newspaper! This passion for equality, which they interpret largely to mean that everyone should be cut down to their level, led these little people to support the radicals' program for graduated income and inheritance taxes, and equal military service, as well as anticlericalism.

As the twentieth century approached, however, the petty bourgeois and the wealthier peasants discovered that there was a radicalism more radical than their own The socialist doctrine, which would not stop short of real economic equality, came to appear as dangerous to them as it earlier had appeared to the upper bourgeoisie. With the rise of a Marxian party and the development of syndicalism, these little people realized that they really were moderates. In the years immediately preceding the war, and especially in the postwar era, these people with a little money invested in land, a shop, stocks, or bonds came to drop much of their earlier economic radicalism. They had no desire to see their own little holdings endangered by an attack from the left. In parliamentary parlance, they still were voting for the left, but in actual fact, many of their representatives, even in the radical socialist party itself, were men of the center, interested primarily in maintaining the *status quo*.

These little people sent their children to the free schools, and, occasionally, to a normal or technical college, but only rarely to the university. Their reading material was largely confined to the newspaper—often enough read at the café to avoid purchasing it. At the opening of the century, books and periodical magazines were still quite expensive. Their search of pleasure rarely took them beyond the café or wine shop, or, if they lived in the cities, the public park, until the bicycle opened new vistas of amusement. The bicycle did more to popularize and democratize "sport" than any other one thing. Frenchmen largely imitated the English in "le sport," even to the extent of using the English word. Golf and tennis were known before the time of the Republic, but only as games of the very wealthy. When the bicycle came, the world was suddenly opened even to the little people. This new toy allowed explorations and activities theretofore impossible, and in its wake came a broad, democratic interest in swimming, hiking, and, later, the various ball games. Of course, this was largely true only for the young; the elders saw in the bicycle a means of cheap, efficient transportation.

The twentieth century also saw the gradual disappearance of the traditional costumes. With cheap transportation came wider adoption of a common mode. Theretofore, style was something of interest to the wealthy only; the little people dressed in their traditional manner. In the twentieth century, the colorful clothes were not entirely discarded; they were still worn on festival days and for the benefit of tourists seeking the quaint. The idea of the mode, however, had made a great impression, and the gradual appearance of cheap, ready-made clothing popularized the tendency to ape the dress of the well to do. But clothes were still chosen with as much of an eye to their durability as to their style, and often enough they were still made at home. The necessity for economy prevented too much foolish copying of the dress of one's social betters.

Under the Republic, there was a general betterment in diet of all Frenchmen, but, probably, these little people made greater comparative progress than either the very poor or the comfortably well to do. The traditional emphasis upon bread was lightened by the introduction of more vegetables, meat, cheese, and other dairy products. In addition, many commodities like coffee, tea, cocoa, and oranges, which had to be imported, became much more common on the tables of the humble people. The peasants, who formerly had to send most of their produce to the market, were able to keep more for themselves, and, even in the country, white bread began to replace the coarser breads formerly so common. It was also under the Republic that the petty bourgeoisie began to patronize the restaurants and cafés as an occasional relief from eating at home. The French, especially in the cities, find in an occasional meal at a sidewalk café an entertainment much to their taste.

There is not much doubt that these humble people—rather

than the very poorest, practically landless, peasantry and the proletariat—made up the bulk of the population. In the country, about one-half of the peasants were their own masters, *chefs d'exploitation,* either by virtue of owning their own land, or renting it as tenant farmers or *métayers.* And in the cities and towns, the artisan who was his own employer, the petty shopkeeper, and the petty functionary, teacher, or clerk, formed a sizable proportion of the inhabitants. All of these people, peasant or townsman, were close to the soil. The well tended little garden plots of the town dwellers gave a clear indication of the attachment that the land had for them All of them had something of the peasant's outlook upon life. On the other hand, as Siegfried ably points out, all of them, peasant or townsman, had something of the attitude of the bourgeoisie, especially after rail transportation and free schools linked the nation into a single, homogeneous block. The canniness and thrift of the peasant, the caution and carefulness of the bourgeoisie, seem to be basic to the make-up of the majority of Frenchmen

On the very lowest levels of French society were found the urban proletariat and the day laborers in the country. Too much emphasis can hardly be placed upon the fact that an American, an Englishman, or a German must not think of the French proletariat in terms of his own experience; this was particularly true before the war of 1914–1918. They were just as miserable as their brothers in the more industrialized countries, perhaps more so, but they did not make up so considerable a proportion of the population, nor were they concentrated in great industry to the degree found elsewhere. And in the country, while the landless peasant laborer was not uncommon, a great number of the day laborers owned little scraps of land, so that they were really not entirely dependent upon their daily earnings.

The country laborer and his plight attracted considerable attention from the class-conscious socialist agitators. "Socialists," writes Professor Clapham, "tried to stir up within them a noble discontent in the alcoholic atmosphere of country town . . . days, but generally retired in disgust The servant had his drink, made his bargain, and went to live in his master's house, where he usually slept on straw in the stable; and the socialist went away to tell his comrades at a congress, not without truth, that a detestable social system had reduced these men to the level of the beasts." The rural workers were too scattered, and too incapable of defending their interests, to make a stand against their more prosperous employers Here and there—in the forests and the vinelands, particularly—these wretched people were able to combine and strike for better standards. In many cases, the complaints were directed as much against the long working hours as against the low salaries, since the laborers wished a little time to work on their own little fields.

Not too much may be said about these rural laborers and servants. Their living quarters were bad, their diet was poor, and their wages were low. But the fact that they were unaccustomed to higher standards made them not too dissatisfied with their lot. It was the army that gave them their only touch with the great world. The village recruit, conscripted into the army, usually put on weight, learned to walk like a man, and found that there were standards of cleanliness and diet with which he had never been familiar. Very often, the more ambitious of them never returned to the land, since, in the army, they learned of the possibilities for employment, at magnificent salaries *(sic!)*, in the factories of the towns. In the forty years before the war, the country lost some three million of its inhabitants to the cities, and most of them came from this very lowest class.

The Republic took more interest in the lot of the city worker than did any of the previous governments. There was a gradual extension of governmental regulation over hours of labor, hygienic conditions in factories, safety devices for moving parts, and insurance against loss of life or limb. The onerous requirement of the *livret* was discontinued, and the worker received much greater freedom to work for better conditions of life. But no widespread social code, such as Bismarck introduced into Germany or Lloyd George in England, was adopted in France until after the war.

The city and town proletariat, skilled and unskilled, were under considerable handicap during the first years of the Republic, since bourgeois and peasant France blamed them for the horrors of the Commune. In the reaction after 1871, the proletarian movement was decapitated by the execution, exile, or imprisonment of most of its natural leaders, and by the strict supervision that every labor movement was forced to undergo To this handicap must be added the fact that nineteenth-century France provided stony soil for any workers' program. There was less "practical socialism" in the form of aggressive taxation or public ownership of utilities in France than in any other of the industrial nations. Furthermore, the endless array of small farms, small shops, and small industrial establishments scattered the proletarians widely and acted as a brake on labor organization

French labor, under the Republic, started its organization under the leadership of a republican journalist named Barberet, who held that strikes were acts of treason against democracy. It was not until the end of the decade of the 1870's, when the exiles of the Commune began to drift back into France, that the labor movement assumed socialistic forms. Jules Guesde, who left France as a communard and returned a Marxist, led the movement away from milk-mild co-operation and moderation, to form a fighting labor organization. In the early 1880's, the movement received legal status, and the workers began to learn the first principles of labor cooperation. But it was difficult work, even in 1914, the typical French syndicate (labor union) was weak, poor, and badly organized The statistics on the size of the labor union movement are probably not complete, but those available are not far off. In 1890, there were only 140,000 members; in 1895, 420,000; in 1901, 589,000; in 1906, 836,000; and in 1911,

1,029,000. "Even allowing for France's much smaller industrial population," writes Professor Clapham, "this 1,000,000 compares badly with the United Kingdom's 3,018,903 for the same year." Not more than one of five potential members of the French syndicates had joined by 1914

In 1892, the first federal organization of the French labor movement came with the Federation of Labor Exchanges; three years later, another, the *Confédération général du travail* (C. G T.), which was to achieve fame beyond France's frontiers, came into existence. In 1902, the two were merged, and the C. G. T. became the official spokesman for French labor. Guided by Sorel, a brilliant intellectual, the C G T developed the doctrine of syndicalism with fighting tactics As political pluralists, they had no faith in, or use for, the monistic state, with its claims to omnicompetence They insisted that direct action, violence, sabotage, and, as a final stroke, the "general strike," were methods more congenial to proletarians than was the bourgeois parliamentarianism of the orthodox Marxist socialist party. The strikes, particularly in 1906, were often violent and bloody, but they never were able to achieve the proportions of the expected "general strike," and even erstwhile socialists conspired to bring them to naught.

The proletariat shared with the other classes in French society in the general increase of comfort. Using the year 1900 as a base for both average of salaries and the average cost of living, the following table shows an approximation of the gradual rise in living conditions for the workers.

Year	*Salaries*	*Cost of Living*
1850	51	85 5
1870	71	103
1880	82	110
1890	92	103
1900	100	100
1910	110	104

The enormous increase in the consumption of sugar, tobacco, and coffee gives some indication that these luxury articles must have become more widely used even by the proletariat

In 1850, France consumed about 3.2 kilograms of sugar per capita; in 1913, she consumed 18 kilograms per capita. The consumption of coffee rose from one-half kilogram to three kilograms in the same years, and the total consumption of tobacco rose from 19,000 kilograms in 1850 to 43,000 kilograms in 1913. Since a reduction in the number of hours per week of labor accompanied the rise in wages and the expansion in luxury consumption, it can fairly be said that in the quarter century before the war the laboring classes enjoyed more comfort than they had at any preceding time.

A comparable betterment in lodgings did not come before the war. The industrial population in the cities continued to live in badly lighted, unsanitary houses. The building of the boulevards did something to destroy some of the worst rookeries, and, in certain manufacturing towns, the employers provided somewhat better houses than most of the proletariat enjoyed. The French people, however, were largely indifferent, and the workers were accustomed to the unsanitary, wretched living conditions. Disease, particularly tuberculosis, typhoid, and syphilis, ravaged the lower classes, for the French, in spite of Pasteur's work, refused to become really alarmed about the germ-infected, unsanitary living conditions of the poor.

BY THE end of the nineteenth century, the population of France had almost ceased to grow. The first half of the century had seen an increase of eight millions; the second half, of only four millions. In the early years of the twentieth century, statisticians warned the nation, ominously, that the natural increase from legitimate births was not enough to maintain the population; it was only by the immigration of Poles, Spaniards, Italians, and Belgians, and by illegitimate births, that a slight increase in population could be insured. Studies of the problem pointed conclusively to the fact that the decline was due to comfort rather than to misery. "The most numerous births," one reporter discovered, "are produced in the most backward areas, the poorest regions, the most destitute families, the workers of the country or the city." In other words, the sensational decline in the birth rate was probably the result of the volition of the people rather than of a lack of fertility. Men with only a small inheritance and only a small income found that it was advisable to limit their families, so that the financial strain of child care would not be too heavy, and the patrimonies would not be divided too much.

A decline in the birth rate became a common phenomenon in all of the advanced countries of Europe during the latter half of the nineteenth century, but France led the others by a wide margin Undoubtedly, one of the explanations—probably the principal one—can be found in the fact that the bulk of Frenchmen were petty bourgeois or peasants. Additional children would have been a great strain on their parents, and, as required under the French law, the division of the inheritance among several children would have resulted in dissipating both the petty savings of the little bourgeoisie and the land of the peasants, into ever smaller and smaller parts. When methods of limiting population became fairly well known, the French—who were Malthusians without having read Malthus—unhesitatingly limited the number of their offspring. In the years before the war, the threat of an absolute decline in population began to cause considerable consternation, France, once the most populous nation in Europe, was slipping into fifth place, with the probability of an even greater relative decline. The fear that reduced man power would be a handicap in war and economic competition led to the formation of leagues and alliances to encourage an increase in population, as well as the passing of laws favoring fathers of large families. But the decline in the birth rate went on unabated.

As important as the decline in the birth rate was the shift from the country to the city. In 1861, about 71 per cent of the population was rural; in 1881, about 65 per cent; and in

1911, about 55 per cent. It is difficult to evaluate these statistics, since so much depends upon the distinction between a rural and an urban town; more convincing of the real shift that was taking place was the growth of the large cities. Between 1887 and 1913, there was an increase from 4,163,000 to 5,396,000 in the population of cities over 100,000. In 1913, fourteen French cities had more than 100,000 inhabitants each; sixty-five cities, between 30,000 and 100,000; and fifty-five, between 20,000 and 30,000. The French urbanization movement was neither as rapid nor as extensive as it had been in England or Germany, but it definitely pointed to the fact that France was losing her predominantly rural character.

With urbanization came shifts in occupational and social classifications. Unfortunately, reliable statistical data for the whole nineteenth century are not available, and even those of the Third Republic are open to some question. Nevertheless, it seems clear that between 1896 and 1906 the percentage of the population employed in agriculture, fishing, and forestry dropped from about 47.9 to 44.8 per cent, while the percentage employed in commerce and industry rose from 44.6 to 47 per cent. The professional and retired groups remained constant at 8.3 to 8.2 per cent of the population.

DURING the first ten years of the Republic, the economic life of France continued much as it had been under the Empire. In spite of the terrible year 1870–71, and the indemnity which had to be paid to Germany, the prosperity of France seemed unimpaired. The government continued to follow the program of public works that the Empire had started; the Opéra was built, the boulevards of Paris were completed, the program of railway, canal, and road construction was enlarged. The severe economic crises in Germany, England, and the United States in the 1870's barely affected French development. To many, it seemed that the prosperity that had appeared under the Empire must inevitably continue unabated—that a new era of well-being for all was opening for France At the end of the decade, a great program of public works—the Freycinet plan—was adopted to complete the railroad, highway, and canal system Billions of francs were to be poured into the national economy, by the will of the state. This tremendous outlay gave rise to speculation of all kinds· values on the Bourse skyrocketed out of sight, new companies mushroomed up to supply materials and engage in various kinds of production. Credit expanded to the utmost. Inevitably, the boom was followed by a crash Several important banks closed their doors, the whole inflated structure collapsed, and France found herself in the midst of a depression that was to last almost twenty years Like all "eras of continued prosperity," the boom of the 1870's came to an abrupt end, and left men looking for an explanation of their troubles.

There have been many explanations for the fall in prices and the subsequent deflation of French economy. The irrational expansion of values, and the subsequent collapse, can hardly explain the fact that it was not until almost the beginning of the twentieth century that the crisis really began to let up. Many people have attacked the problem by pointing out that the world adopted the gold standard just about the time when the gold production of the world began to decrease This led to an appreciation in the value of gold and a necessary decline in prices, so that the economy of the world was crippled. Since it was French agriculture that suffered most from the crisis, this explanation is obviously only part of the answer, for there are other very good reasons for the difficulties of the French peasants. It was just about 1880 that the railroads of the United States were completed, and opened up the great grain-producing area of mid-west America to the world market. At the same time, steam-powered ocean freighters made the cost of transporting bulky commodities such as wheat, hides, and cotton practically negligible. After 1885, the introduction of effective refrigeration allowed even meat, butter, and fruit to cross the seas without spoiling This meant that the produce of the Americas, Australia, the Danube basin, and Russia began to invade the agricultural markets of Europe. French farmers with their small plots and expensive methods of cultivation found it difficult to compete with the mechanized agriculture and the rich grazing lands beyond the seas. To make matters worse, this competition came contemporaneously with a great disaster. The phylloxera invaded the French vinelands, destroying thousands of vineyards and cutting the harvest of French wine to the lowest point in the nineteenth century. The grape growers, moreover, were unable to take advantage of scarcity to raise the prices, for cheap Italian and Spanish wines flooded the market to take the place of the local product. Faced with impossible competition from abroad, and struck by a disaster at home, it is small wonder that French agriculture languished for more than a decade.

The long depression also weighed heavily upon French industry. Falling prices and a contracting market in France made it increasingly difficult for them to sell their commodities at the very moment that they were forced to meet new and more vigorous competition from abroad. After about 1880, machine technique and large-scale production became more firmly established in the United States and Germany as well as in England; these three countries, provided with an abundance of iron and coal, utilized the new production system far more effectively than did France. The small French factories found themselves faced with a competition which they, with their resources and organization, met only with great difficulty. The industrialists and merchants solved some of their problems by retrenchments and by the adoption of more efficient techniques, but in a land where so much of the production was carried on in small shops or petty factories, even these expedients were insufficient. It almost seemed as though French industry was doomed, in face of the overwhelming economic depression.

Both peasant and industrialist turned to the state for assistance; in the crisis, no theory of laissez-faire economics could be allowed to destroy the prosperity of the nation The traditional French method of relief had been found in tariff protection. In 1860, Louis Napoleon had broken with the past to introduce a more liberal system; after 1880, the demand for a return to the high protective tariff, supported by both the right and the left, became more and more imperative. The imperial treaties prevented an abrupt change in policy, but throughout the decade of the 1880's the rates were boosted whenever possible When the government was unable to exclude foreign goods by tariff, it often found other means of guaranteeing the monopoly of the local market to French producers. American meat, for example, was excluded from France on hygienic grounds! In 1892, with the advent of the Méline tariff, the last of the Empire tariff system was overthrown, and France took a front place in the ranks of the protectionist states. When French industry and agriculture received a virtual monopoly of the home market, prices in France began to rise above the world price. The crisis was gradually alleviated, and, although advocates of free trade insist that the French had to pay dearly in terms of lessened consumption and high prices, the return of comparative prosperity convinced many people of the wisdom of the policy

Whether or not it was the tariff that ended the long period of depression is a question not to be settled easily. Those men who explain prices in terms of gold find a ready answer in the great increase in the quantity of the precious metal that resulted from the opening of new mines in Africa and America at the end of the century. Surely, there is evidence that France was not alone in the enjoyment of "good times"; as soon as the crisis of 1893 was liquidated, England, Germany, and the other industrial nations of Europe enjoyed a prosperity as vigorous as France's Furthermore, by 1900 Europe had achieved a position in world economy that made her almost a universal creditor; her banks, factories, and brains dominated and dictated the policies of world economic life.

In return, Europe harvested a golden crop of "tribute," in the form of interest and profits paid to her by creditors in all corners of the globe This rôle of world creditor undoubtedly contributed greatly to Europe's prosperity And, lastly, although the tempo of the new economy continued to accelerate unchecked, the men of the twentieth century had more experience with, and were better adjusted to, the machine age than were the men in the previous period. In any case, the fifteen years before the war, with two minor exceptions, were years of rising prices and expanding economic possibilities, and advocates of high tariff will find it difficult to attribute French prosperity to the tariff alone.

UNLIKE the other great western powers, even in 1914 France remained preponderantly rural. During the whole of the nineteenth century, the countryside was losing its population to the cities, but in 1913, approximately fifty-five per cent of the French people lived in the rural villages. The national wealth followed about the same ratio; it was not until the last decade in the century that industrial and commercial investments about equaled those in agriculture The developments of the nineteenth century, however, had made a great impression on the economy of the peasants The railroad, highway, and canal systems had quickened the tempo of life and opened even remote villages to some contact with world economy. The introduction of new crops, better breeds of animals, and new methods of soil cultivation had greatly increased agricultural production, and contributed to the rise in the standards of living of the peasants. Rural France, it is true, remained backward and old-fashioned when compared with the rural areas of the more progressive states, but the nineteenth century had wrought considerable alteration in the life on the countryside.

There had been, however, in the nineteenth century, no radical change in the basic pattern of land ownership The large estates, which had survived the great Revolution, continued to play an important rôle, in spite of the tendency toward splitting them up for sale to the smaller peasants. The average holding continued to be small, but the middle-sized holdings did increase in number, while the very smallest showed a decline. As at the beginning of the century, about one-third of the rural population owned most of the land, the remaining two-thirds owned practically nothing, or at least too little to enable them to make a living without working the soil of their wealthier neighbors About one-half of the peasants, however, were classed as *chefs d'exploitation*—that is, either owners of their own soil, or renters, or *métayers*. But since many of the remaining half owned some little scraps of land, and might hope—not too seriously, to be sure—to become *chefs d'exploitation* themselves, there was not a large class of proper rural proletarians in France. Indeed, it was usually necessary to import seasonal agricultural laborers fom Italy, Spain, and even Poland, to harvest the crops.

To one accustomed to the American countryside, the most difficult thing to understand about French rural economy is the smallness of the holdings. A plot of 100 to 250 acres is considered large; indeed, in 1908, in all France, there were only 29,000 plots over 250 acres. The vast majority of the plots—87 per cent—were of less than twenty-five acres, and out of a total of five and a half million holdings, two million were less than two and a half acres in extent Further to complicate the pattern was the fact that many of the individual holdings were scattered about the village in several small plots, rather than consolidated in one piece of ground. The land was cut up in a crazy, crisscross patchwork pattern to a degree almost incomprehensible to one who is used to thinking in terms of American quarter-sections

The Republic—particularly in the years after 1895—saw important changes in the methods of cultivation of the soil. The practice of letting fields lie fallow, universal in 1815, had practically disappeared by 1900. In its place, crop rotation and artificial fertilizers maintained the fertility of the soil, and even greatly increased the annual yield. New crops, useful for industry, came to take their place alongside the traditional wheat, rye, and oats, the cultivation of potatoes and other vegetables that were unknown, or only slightly used, in 1815, occupied much of the land The numbers of the livestock, with the sole exception of sheep, greatly increased, and the quality was improved. The fat hogs of 1900 bore as little resemblance to the lean, long-legged "razorbacks" of the preceding century as the fine dairy and meat cattle did to their predecessors of the time of Napoleon I. The meat-eating, vegetable-demanding cities provided a ready market for these commodities, and the peasant himself, with new standards for his table, was able to consume more of the fruits of his labor.

The introduction of agricultural machinery was an extremely slow process It was not until 1895 that there was any spectacular progress The great difficulty lay in two obstacles that, especially during the period of depression, were almost insurmountable On the one hand, most of the peasant holdings were too small and too scattered to make the use of much machinery practicable; on the other, the peasants were too poor to obtain the money necessary for the purchase of expensive equipment. After 1900, however, when agricultural prices began to rise, there was a boom in the farm-implement business. A large number of agricultural machines were imported from the United States, and a substantial farm-implement industry was established in France. According to the incomplete statistics available, there were more agricultural machines in one province in 1913 than in the whole of France some twenty years earlier. Even so, at the time when France entered the war, a surprising amount of the work was done by hand, and an astonishing number (one would not expect to find any) of the plows were merely curved sticks with an iron point.

In spite of the increased yield from the soil which followed the more scientific agricultural methods, the peasants of France suffered severely from the depression after 1882. With the sole exception of dairy products, the prices of all agricultural commodities fell from ten to fifty per cent. Land values give an important clew to the problem of the peasants. In 1852, just after the depression of the "hungry forties," the agricultural land of France was estimated at about 61 billion francs; by 1880, under the influence of the Napoleonic prosperity, it had risen to over 90 billions; and by 1895 it had fallen back to 60 billions. The peasants, burdened with mortgages, saw their equity in the land dwindle, and they were powerless to stop the process. It was this that made them into protectionists. They felt that their government could save them by guaranteeing to them control over the French market.

It is no wonder that the French peasants regard protectionism favorably The Méline tariff of 1892 raised French agricultural prices appreciably above the world prices, and assured the farmers not only of a profitable market for their produce but also of an opportunity to dispose of a greater annual yield at a profit. With foreign produce practically excluded from the market, French farmers were able to increase their agricultural production to meet the food requirements of the nation. This involved the utilization of considerable marginal land, as well as more efficient culture of the good land. In 1914, France, alone of the great European nations, was not only able to feed herself, but even had an exportable surplus of certain luxury vegetables and fruits. After the vineyards were replanted with stock that could withstand the phylloxera, cheap Italian and Spanish wines were excluded from the French market. The French crop proved to be sufficient for domestic needs and, in addition, provided a surplus of liquors, and fancy and sparkling wines, for export. This balance of economy probably cost France dearly in terms of higher living costs, but it gave her an independence of world economic conditions not enjoyed by either England or Germany.

It was during the long depression that many of the French peasants learned the value of co-operation. In certain areas, co-operative enterprises—in the manufacture of cheese, for example—were well established long before 1870, but—by chance, almost—the law authorizing the establishment of labor syndicates opened great possibilities for agricultural co-operatives. After 1882, and particularly after 1895, the co-operative societies, *comices* or syndicates, engaged in all manner of business. They were the focal points for the dissemination of agricultural information. They purchased, at wholesale prices, chemical fertilizers, paints, machinery, and the like, and organized co-operative marketing and processing. They even operated land banks. On the eve of the World War (1914–1918) the movement was one of the most progressive forces in the French countryside. The evolution of federations of co-operative societies even made it seem possible that the most individualistic peasantry in Europe was in the act of creating one of the really co-operative organizations of our times.

LIKE French agriculture, French industry entered the twentieth century with the small unit typical of the economy. While England, the United States, and Germany were developing enormous industrial plants and combining them in pools, trusts, and cartels, France continued to be the home of the small factory and the petty industrialist. Naturally, France also developed some large-scale industry, and the existence of the *Comité des Forges* is a clear indication of industrial combination, but these were the harbingers of modern industrialism. It was the small industry, however, employing fewer than ten workers, that dominated the production of the nation. Compared with the highly industrialized nations, French industry on the eve of the war was unimpressive, but when it is more justly compared with the industrial development of mid-century France, it becomes obvious that France had made steady progress.

The French were severely handicapped by a lack of raw materials. They had no extensive coal fields comparable with those of England, Germany, or the United States and the coal that was available to them was poor for coking. Furthermore, inefficient French mining practices, possibly as much as the poverty of the mines, made coal at the pit heads much more expensive than it was in England or Germany, and the pit heads were not located strategically for cheap transportation. Like French coal, French iron was limited in quantity, mediocre in quality, and at an unsatisfactory distance from the coal fields. Without an adequate supply of either iron or coal, French industry could not be expected to compete with its more fortunately endowed neighbors.

The introduction of scientific research as a basis for modern industrial production also laid a heavy handicap upon the French The huge German and American industries could amply afford to create and subsidize laboratories for further research in industry. These laboratories yielded generous dividends by introducing new ways of processing and utilizing all the materials, much of which heretofore had been wasted, and by developing new and useful commodities. The French, with their small units, could afford no such expenditure, and without laboratories it was difficult for them to keep up with their aggressive competitors The state and several semipublic institutions attempted to provide well-equipped laboratories, which were available to any manufacturer for solution of his problems, but it was often impractical for the small industrialists to take advantage of the opportunities thus offered to them Shielded behind the protective tariff wall, they were largely able to control the French market, and, through lack of vision, initiative, or ambition, they were willing to allow English, German, and American industry to grapple for the world market.

As we have already seen, the Second Empire ushered in a new era in which steam power set the pace for industrial development. After 1880, the expansion of the uses for the steam engine continued apace. In 1880, France generated about a half million horsepower, in 1893–95, about a million; by 1903, the figure was two millions; and on the eve of the war, almost four millions. In addition to steam power, the twentieth century witnessed the development of internal-combustion engines and electric motors Electricity opened great possibilities to French industry. The numerous mountain streams of France provided a potential source of cheap power capable of relieving some of the pressure for coal The prewar era, however, saw only the beginnings of the development of this hydroelectric power potential.

Under the Republic, the metallurgical industries showed steady progress The increasingly mounting demands for iron, steel, and other metals gave active stimulus to the development of this heavy industry Steel and steel alloys began to replace iron as the principal metal, after the processes developed by Thomas, Gilchrist, Bessemer, and the Frenchman, Martin, made large-scale production of steel both cheap and easy. France did not develop a Pittsburgh or an Essen, but she did make great strides. In the first decade of the twentieth century, aluminum became available for industrial use In 1880, it had cost one hundred francs a kilogram; by 1890, nineteen francs a kilogram; and in 1900, only one franc seventy centimes a kilogram. Its manifold uses, however, were not widely exploited until after the World War.

These metals were worked into useful commodities by a host of industries, of which one of the most interesting was cutlery manufacture. French cutlery has enjoyed, for many years, a justifiable reputation for excellence and good craftsmanship. The industry, traditionally, was organized on the domestic system—that is to say, much of the work was done by the workers in their own homes. The introduction of the small electric motor made it possible for the cutlery workers to keep their traditional system; in 1906 there were 18,500 workers employed in some 3,400 separate workshops, and only 130 of these shops employed more than ten workers. As a handicraft industry, the making of French cutlery was able to maintain itself in the markets of the world, as well as to keep a near-monopoly of the French market.

Of course, the cutlery workers used only a small part of

the metals produced by the French foundries The rolling mills, wire-pulling machines, boiler factories, machine and implement workers, and armament manufacturers utilized most of the product After 1880, the railroads replaced their iron tracks with steel, and the new roadbed construction, which practically doubled the French rail system, uniformly used steel rails The making of locomotives, cars, spikes, angle bars, and steel rails kept many of the forges busy. The architects and bridge builders, too, discovered new uses for structural iron and steel. The building of the Eiffel Tower, for example, showed the wide possibilities of new uses for the products of the forges. The wider use of agricultural implements also gave an important outlet for the machine and implement factories, while industrial machines, hardware, and gun factories and shipyards increasingly consumed more metals of all kinds.

The loss of Alsace was a severe blow to the textile industry, since by far the most important cotton factories were in that province. After 1870, however, an extensive cotton industry developed in the eastern provinces remaining to France. In the twenty years before the World War (1914–1918), France's raw-cotton importations almost tripled in volume. The Méline tariff, by excluding English textiles, greatly helped the French manufacturers. The woolen industry, too, made spectacular progress. French weavers specialized in making light woolen cloth suitable for women's clothing, and succeeded in building up a considerable export business in novelties. The absolute decline of the French flocks in the last half of the century forced the woolen manufacturers to look abroad for a large part of their raw materials. Hand labor, in the woolen industry, persisted longer than it did in cotton, but by the twentieth century the machine, powered by steam or electricity, was almost everywhere triumphant Only a few hand weavers kept their looms, producing expensive novelties to be worked into final form by the exclusive dressmakers of Paris.

The silk industry, long acclimated to French soil, retained, in spite of the competition from cheaper textiles, much of the prominence that it had acquired earlier in the century. The makers also accepted mechanized techniques, except in the case of the manufacture of the beautiful luxury cloths for which French hand weavers were justly famous. In spite of all competitors, the finest French silks were easily sold in the world markets. The most serious threat to silk manufacture came from a French invention, the rayon process. It was not long before French rayon manufacturers were faced with English and German competition, but in the prewar period they ably held their own Rayons, before the war, were not yet perfected, and so their inroads on the silk market were not so great as they have been since 1920 Both rayon and silk production well suited French industrial genius, and easily found markets in the France that had become the arbiter of the feminine mode throughout the world.

While the cotton, woolen, silk, and rayon textile industries made substantial progress, linen manufacture fell into an absolute decline Between 1883 and 1913, the French flax crop dropped from 300,000 metric tons to 114,000. Imperfectly mechanized technique in the manufacture of this traditionally popular textile made it difficult for linen to compete with cotton. Linen increasingly came to find its market restricted because of the relatively high cost of the cloth.

After 1880, the production of ready-made clothing, especially for women, became an important French industry. Machine technique and factory organization combined with the ever-increasing importance of the "mode" to make many consumers wish to purchase their clothing ready-made. The growth of department stores and specialized shops firmly established this industry, both as a luxury traffic and a utility industry. The industrial revolution had taken another rampart of the domestic economy. In 1913, the goods produced by French garment workers were valued at about four hundred million francs.

The chemical and the electrical industries in France lagged

painfully behind their competitors in other countries. One great difficulty was in technical education in France. Although the nation has a long and justly famous record for technical schooling, in the latter part of the century her schools did not turn out the streams of technicians that were necessary to develop these industries properly. Unlike prewar Germany and postwar United States, the engineering schools of France did not flood the labor market with young men—intellectual proletarians—prepared to solve the scientific problems involved in chemistry and electricity The chemical industry was further handicapped by France's poverty in raw materials, and inefficient exploitation of the resources available. The lag in the electrical industry is less easily explained, since, as we have already noted, France is handsomely endowed with potential hydroelectric power Both industries probably suffered from French conservatism They were new and untried, and the French often have shown a dislike for experimenting with their capital.

Other industries followed the same pattern The French excelled only in those commodities that required the skill of the artisan craftsman In the mechanized, large-scale production fields, they fell behind competitors in the United States, England, and Germany. The adoption of the high-tariff policy, however, saved the French market for French industry, in spite of the fact that many French commodities often were much more expensive than those of foreign origin. This tariff policy allowed France to keep her self-sufficiency, and, in a measure, to protect herself from the vicissitudes of the international market. When the Great War came in 1914, however, the French discovered that their "self-sufficiency" cost them dearly. The German armies overran much of the efficient large industry that the nation owned, and the inefficient, small-scale factories that remained were unable to cope with the need for supplying the materials of war. It was only through extensive importations from the United

States and England that France and the French armies were able to keep in the war until victory could be assured.

AS WE have seen, the social, economic, and political framework of France was affected but not altered by *l'année terrible* of 1870–1871 In much the same way, the intellectual and artistic vogues of the Empire continued to dominate French development for years after Louis Napoleon had ceased to be emperor of the French The impetus that the mid-century generation had given to the cultural growth of the nation continued to play an important rôle for full twenty years after 1870. Indeed, it was not until the 1880's that the men whose careers were to dominate the cultural life of the Republic came to take their places on the French scene.

During the Empire, many brilliant figures had entered the literary field under the banner of realism These men had discarded the escape mechanism of the romanticists that had led to the vivid portrayal of the distant in space and time, and, finding material for their art in their own society, they had created a literature that rang true to the life around them. Often they were brutal in their portrayal of their contemporaries, but, always, they tried to capture the realities. Many of these literary realists spanned both the Empire and the Republic with their careers Lemaître, de Lisle, de Bainville, Coppée, and others, continued to write long after Louis Napoleon's régime was all but forgotten The greatest of their number, Émile Zola, began his career in the last days of the Empire, and continued to dominate the literary scene for thirty years after 1870. He developed naturalism—an extension of realism—as a literary vogue His vivid, often brutal, portrayals of the motives and actions of his contemporaries were magnificent social histories of the times.

Victor Hugo was another carry-over from the earlier period. Indeed, he was almost the personification of the whole century. He began his career when the restored Bourbons ruled

France, and continued to produce—unevenly, to be sure—until his death in 1885 Because of his untiring opposition to Louis Napoleon as much as because of his established reputation, the venerable old man had acquired a halo in the eyes of many of the men who had overthrown Napoleon. Hugo, with the younger men of the mid-century, set the literary tone of the first years of the Republic

The period after 1880 was in many ways extremely favorable for the men of letters. The liberal, democratic Republic, by guaranteeing freedom of press and by combating illiteracy, opened new opportunities to literature. The concomitant economic development greatly increased the number of people with the means to purchase books. No generation of writers before had had so large an audience of readers who could afford to pay the creative artist so well With the disappearance of illiteracy, however, the demands of a new audience began to make themselves felt The masses, whose lack of interest and intellectual immaturity precluded their reading the subtle or philosophical works of the masters, also wished to be entertained. To appeal to the many-sided interests of the enlarged reading public, the literature of the Republic took many forms—some of which seemed addressed to the simple and adventure-seeking, others to interest the cultured and the philosophical.

For one reason or another, poetry failed to appeal to the democratic public as strongly as the novel, the short story, or the drama As a result, many of the poets under the Republic were either literary dilettantes who did not pretend to make a living with their pens, or writers who depended upon their novels, plays, or essays for their principal literary expression. To list the names of the writers of the Republic would be a meaningless activity, there are a large number of men, unmentioned in these pages, whose works were valid and important to the cultural pattern of the day, but in a short history it is possible to mention only a few whose importance now seems beyond question. Any Anglo-Saxon reader will be familiar with the work of Guy de Maupassant; carrying forward the traditions of realism, he developed the short story into an almost perfect vehicle for literary expression. Less known to Americans are the works of the psychological novelists—Bourget, Huysmans, Proust, and others. These men, even before Freud had uncovered the subconscious to the inquisitive world, began to explore the psychological factors that are responsible for human behavior Where Zola interpreted men's actions in terms of their heredity and their environment, these men sought to show that the mainsprings of human action are to be found in the inner workings of the human mind. In the postwar world, the psychological novel and drama were to become common; these early practitioners of the art of writing were pointing the way to a valid field for artistic exploitation.

Perhaps the most brilliant light of the Republic's literary galaxy was Anatole France In him, urbane intelligence and great learning were combined with delicacy of expression A satirist and a mocker, he allowed his imagination to range from the revolt of the angels against God, through the sufferings of the early Christians, to the conditions of his own days. No matter what he undertook, he always brought to his subject a subtle wit and a penetrating insight In his explorations of the psychological as well as environmental factors that motivated his characters, France was always careful to keep himself aloof and objective—an attitude of mind not possible for most of his contemporaries. He and Émile Zola (died in 1902) were undoubtedly the most distinguished representatives of the prewar literary scene in republican France.

The drama, under the Republic, continued to present the comedy of manners that had been so popular under the Empire. The influence of Ibsen, however, introduced a more serious note, in the form of the problem play that treated of social questions One of the most popular playwriters of the day, Brieux, mildly shocked Paris by discussing marriage and venereal disease, in his play, *Damaged Goods* (1901). Rostand, another very able playwright, turned from the sternness of Ibsen to produce charming, imaginative dramas that met with the enthusiastic approval of his countrymen One of his best known, *Cyrano de Bergerac,* has had a wide audience even in foreign lands

The fine arts, too, were not greatly disturbed by the transition from Empire to Republic The fierce dispute between the painters and the critics continued much as it had throughout the century. In 1850, Courbet's *Funeral at Ornans* introduced realism in art as a new style. By the end of the Empire, he and the Barbizon painters had achieved recognition But the debate between realism on the one side, and classicism and romanticism on the other, was only a prelude to the artistic conflicts that were to be fought in the salons, galleries, and newspapers of republican France New schools—impressionists, post-impressionists, and others—were to knock at the doors of respectable galleries, and finally to attain admission after an almost interminable debate. In the thirty or so years before the war, French artistic thought undoubtedly led the world, and French artists produced some of the masterpieces of all times

Like the writers, the painters found in the period after 1880 opportunities to exploit their talents commercially that were undreamed of by their predecessors. When American millionaires competed with the plutocrats of Europe for the works of painters who had "arrived," amazing things happened to the values of canvases Some of the men were able to live to see their own works valued almost equally with those of the old masters Unfortunately, too many of the men now regarded as the greatest painters of the time did not "arrive" during their lifetimes. The bourgeois buyers were more impressed by the sentimental, classic paintings of Gérôme and the huge, historical pictures of Meissonier than by the works of Manet, van Gogh, or Monet. Several of the truly great artists were hopelessly exploited by unscrupulous dealers, while second-rate painters attracted the attention of the public.

Nevertheless, many artists were well paid for their labors. The fact that van Gogh almost starved to death while his contemporaries handsomely rewarded the efforts of a painter now recognized as second-rate, only emphasizes the poor judgment of the picture buyers, not their unwillingness or inability to support the muse of painting As in the case of men of letters, there were many highly talented painters, during the years of the prewar Republic, that are not mentioned in these pages, because a general history cannot go into too great detail. In the early years of the Republic, the "new" schools of painters were derisively dubbed "impressionists." It is a name almost meaningless when all of the practitioners so labeled are assembled, but a name that has been used to describe their works ever since their time. These men were experimenters and scientists. They built upon the works of earlier, realist painters, by utilizing new techniques and varied subject matters, they opened up great artistic possibilities Pissarro and Monet, two of the foremost of their number, in the 1870's turned from the studio-posed techniques to paint in the open air Sunlight and atmosphere were really their subjects; the informal compositions clearly reflect a lack of interest in the formal relationships that had theretofore been so important. In the 1880's, Dégas—and, above all, Toulouse-Lautrec—began to introduce sociological problems to canvas. Later in the century, Cézanne and Renoir, dissatisfied with the informalities of impressionism, took a greater interest in composition and organization. In many ways they harvested the fruits of the whole movement. A trip to any art museum that pretends to include the works of the masters of the late nineteenth and early twentieth centuries cannot fail to impress the visitor with the vigor and the brilliance of prewar French art

Even the architects and the sculptors of the Empire were allowed to continue their work after their principal patron was in exile. The public-works program of the first years of the Republic continued the improvements started by Louis Napoleon. The Opéra, completed in 1878, was probably the highest expression of the artistic taste of the mid-century. It will always be considered a superb monument erected by a generation that worked out its artistic pattern without consideration for any but the very wealthiest classes of society. Toward the end of the century, the new architecture made its first bid for recognition Modernism in architecture, closely related to the development of structural steel and glass for building purposes, had first appeared in the bridges that the engineers made from structural steel and cables. In 1889, at the Paris fair, the Eiffel Tower showed that this new architectural material could be used for more diverse purposes The modern architecture—in that it allowed greater spans and more secure heights than any earlier forms—was well suited to the needs of the society created by the industrial revolution and the emerging liberal democracy. The demands for large railway stations, great department stores, and well-lighted factories were best met by the new architectural forms.

Under the previous régimes, French musical taste had been without distinction. Musical education was reserved for only a very few; the vast majority of the people, even those who could well afford it, had little or no instruction in music. Furthermore, there was a widespread idea that appreciation of fine music was something for snobs and eccentrics rather than for ordinary citizens. The serious works of Berlioz, which had achieved great popularity elsewhere, made hardly an impression on the French. The great symphonic works of the Germans, and even the music dramas of Wagner, were largely ignored in Paris. It was the sidewalk-café orchestra with a popular singer, rather than the grand opera or the symphonic concert, that attracted attention. Under the Empire there was a gradual education of French taste. Gounod, Thomas, and Offenbach succeeded in attracting a following for lighter operas, and occasionally one of Wagner's or Verdi's works would not be too unfavorably received—but even so, it was difficult for a serious musical performance to get a hearing in France.

After 1880, serious attempts were made to educate the French. Leagues and societies for the development of musical appreciation were formed, new orchestras and choral societies were organized, and a number of important music schools came into existence These efforts were rewarded By the end of the century, it was possible to offer a program composed entirely of music by Bach, or to present a series of operas like Wagner's *Ring,* without fearing a completely unsympathetic reception The introduction of the Russian ballet, a most satisfactory combination of music and stage, was also well received The continued popularity, however, of Gounod's *Faust,* Bizet's *Carmen,* and Thomas's *Mignon,* performed by the second-rate stars that walked the boards in Paris, is a clear indication of the extent of French musical appreciation.

In this same period, however, there were French composers and teachers of considerable merit Paradoxically enough, French instruction in the piano and particularly in the wood winds was excellent, and the symphonic orchestras of Paris were staffed with first-rate musicians whose technique was well appreciated by those who knew. César Franck and his disciples formed a school of symphonic and chamber-music composers; they were, perhaps, unrecognized by those who saw Gounod's operas as the highest manifestation of music, but later generations of music lovers have paid them due honor. Saint-Saens and Debussy, with great understanding of orchestration and tonal shadings, opened new ways for musical expression These men, however, were creating an art that was little understood by their fellow countrymen; the democracy of France was yet to be educated to love and enjoy good music.

In the realm of philosophy and learning, Renan and Taine overshadowed the last third of the nineteenth century. Both of these scholars were historians, men of letters, and philosophers. They were representatives of the older school of savants whose literary style was every bit as important as the philosophical content of their writings; the men who followed them were researchers and scientists primarily interested in the content of the monographs that they were producing rather than in the way in which the material was written Unlike the novelists and the artists, both Renan and Taine were deeply impressed by the events of 1870–1871 Both of them were in debt, intellectually, to German scholarship; they knew and admired the Germany of the universities, and they were profoundly shocked to discover that they had overlooked the Germany of Bismarck and Moltke The Commune of 1871 had an even more important effect upon Taine. After 1871, he turned his whole attention to an analysis of the traditions and forces that were molding French culture, and, in his great history, he produced the most striking defense of the conservative point of view that appeared up to his time Just as he was profoundly distrustful of France's revolutionary past, he was naively sure that the British traditions were infinitely superior. French democracy had no strong appeal for Renan, either; he would much have preferred a society governed by the intellectual élite rather than by universal manhood suffrage. It is interesting to note that no republican theorist of the intellectual caliber of either of these men appeared to defend the revolution and liberal democracy.

Much of the philosophical and social thought of the last years of the nineteenth and the first years of the twentieth century was the work of specialized research scholars in one or another field of the social sciences. The monograph and the short article in a learned *revue* provided the most significant outlet for their efforts. The positivism of Comte came into its own under the Republic, when the professorial chairs were filled with men who took seriously the scientific side of the social sciences. Most of these men were interested primarily in method or in uncovering facts, they regarded the enlarging of the sum of "positively" established information as their principal mission. It was a fertile period of study, even though no great philosopher was able to synthesize into a complete picture the mass of evidence that was assembled.

In the first years of the new century, Bergson provided his contemporaries with a new philosophical point of view. Hegel had dominated the second half of the nineteenth century, but his ponderous march of ideas was ill suited to French genius. Bergson introduced pragmatism, which he had learned from the Americans. In no time, pragmatism became the philosophical mode, Bergson was quoted in the classroom, the salon, and even the socialist meetings. It was a complete success. Freed from the doctrines of thesis, antithesis, synthesis, from the idea of the identity of opposites—indeed, from the whole philosophical thought of the nineteenth century—the French intellectuals were happy to follow their new leader, who gave them a pragmatic, anti-intellectual interpretation of human experience. Intuition rather than intellect became the key to understanding.

The most spectacular achievements of the human mind in the period before the World War (1914–1918) came in the field of science. The scientists lived in an age regulated by bankers, businessmen, and politicians, but it is not improbable that Pasteur, who worked in the era of Bismarck, will be remembered long after the Iron Chancellor's alliance systems have lost much of their significance, and it is possible that Lister and the Curies will be recalled when both Foch and Moltke have been forgotten. In their laboratories, the scientists were unlocking many of the secrets of the universe and opening the way for a profound alteration in the environment of man. Their labors transcended national frontiers, French, German, or English science as such existed only in the minds of the chauvinists who wished to inflate their own egos The works of the scientists may have brought renown to the civilization that supported them, but they were the property of civilized man all over the world.

Probably the most significant scientific achievements of the period—not only in France, but also in the whole world—were those of the bacteriologists Pasteur and his disciples at the Pasteur Institute contributed greatly to the work that led to the germ theory of disease Pasteur's research was begun under the Empire, and it came to fruition under the Republic. His isolation of bacteria as a cause of disease and his significant achievements in the field of immunization have earned for him a special place in the ranks of the immortals. The Pasteur Institute, founded in the 1880's by popular subscription, has carried on his work and has become a world-famous center for scientific research

While the bacteriologists held the center of the scientific stage, they were by no means the only ones to merit attention. In astronomy, a French invention led to the use of photography in plotting and exploring the skies. Jules Henri Poincaré, the cousin of Raymond Poincaré, the famous statesman, led a school of mathematicians that ably carried forward the work started under the Empire. In the fields of physics, chemistry —and, particularly, radioactivity—French scientists made significant contributions. The work of Becquerel and the Curies in the problems of radioactive matter greatly expanded men's understanding of physical chemistry, and provided a new weapon in the war upon disease. In the biological sciences, the botanists, zoologists, and physical anthropologists found in the theory of evolution a new weapon for attack upon their problems Their findings modified the theory as Darwin stated it, and at the same time provided material for an endless debate. Engineers and industrial chemists, also, used the laboratory in their work that has so greatly altered the life of man. Everywhere one turned at the end of the century, the scientist was at work devising new tools for controlling or understanding the world. Neither the war of 1914-1918 nor the twenty-year truce that followed it was able to check the progress that was made in the laboratory—and, unfortunately for men in Europe, the laboratories were equally unable to check the forces of war.

It would be difficult to generalize on the artistic and intellectual life of the prewar Republic. The creative writers and the painters were excelled by none of their generation anywhere in the world; French musical appreciation showed considerable progress, and French composers showed both originality and a keen understanding of orchestration; and French scientists fully contributed their share to the scientific knowledge of the age The social scientists and the philosophers were probably not so prolific or so profound as those of the German schools, but their work led to no obtuse doctrines In many ways, the artistic and intellectual civilization that was developing under the liberal democracy was the most brilliant of the entire century.

CHAPTER XIV

THE REPUBLIC IN INTERNATIONAL POLITICS AND WAR

THE years following the crushing defeat at the hands of Prussia were difficult ones for the directors of French foreign policy. Two hundred years of political and cultural hegemony in Europe had adapted French reactions and habits of thought to patterns quite out of line with France's prestige and power in the world after 1871. Defeated, forced to surrender two of her provinces, burdened with an indemnity, and obliged to support an army of occupation, France found her unaccustomed position extremely humiliating; modern times had not yet witnessed so disastrous a defeat as she had been forced to accept The proclamation of the new German Empire at Versailles and the obvious contempt with which Bismarck treated France were insults added to injury, but the crowning indignity came when the assembly was forced to make war on the city of Paris under the very eyes of the German army of occupation. It is small wonder that millions of Frenchmen, seeing Germany alone as the author of their misfortunes, hoped to witness the day when France would have her revenge.

Bismarck's diplomacy, however, was far too subtle to allow that day any prospect of immediate realization. The League of the Three Emperors (Austria, Russia, and Germany) and the chancellor's obvious friendship with England left France so isolated in Europe that sober-minded statesmen well realized that revenge was not for their time. "You may witness Bismarck's death," Thiers told a chauvinistic friend, "but you will never see his humiliation." It was so obviously impossible for France to hope for an early revision of the treaty of Frankfort that even Gambetta counseled his friends not to talk about revenge—but never to forget about it! Indeed, the vast majority of the French people—peasants, artisans, and bourgeoisie—at the moment ardently hoped only for peace They would willingly take advantage of any troubled waters in Europe to fish for the return of the lost provinces, but only a fire-eating minority would approve any policy that might bring Herr Krupp's guns and the spiked helmets back on French soil Thiers' policy of reconstruction and rehabilitation was immensely popular By paying off the indemnity, and thereby ridding France of the German army, and by rebuilding the frontier fortifications and reorganizing the French army, he regained for the nation part of its lost self-respect, without jeopardizing the future. Hot-heads called for revenge, but saner counsels urged moderation, and the mass of the people wanted most an opportunity to live in peace.

The fall of Thiers and the presidency of MacMahon brought new counsels and new policies to the fore The monarchists and clericals were probably as sincere desirers of peace as the rest of France, but circumstances contrived to make them appear dangerous to the continued peace of Europe. When the French garrison left Rome to help to defend France against the Germans, the Italian army marched into the Eternal City and proclaimed it the capital of united Italy. Pius IX, refusing to recognize this *fait accompli* that deprived the Roman Catholic Church of its temporal power, called upon Catholic Europe to restore him to his throne. This Roman question naturally became a focal point in Franco-Italian relations as soon as the clericals came to power in France Almost at the same time, Bismarck became involved in a struggle with the Roman Catholic Church in Germany, the *Kulturkampf,* that made him extremely sensitive to clericalism in politics anywhere. There is excellent evidence to show that the men who were responsible for French foreign policy had no intention of becoming involved in either of these questions, but, at the time, the clerical-monarchist government made Europe fear that France might re-establish her old-time position as "eldest daughter of the Church," and embark upon a policy that would lead to war with Italy or Germany or both.

The pronouncements of French bishops, the unauthorized speeches of clerical politicians, and the rabid tone of the Catholic press created tension between France and her neighbors At the same time, the rapid recovery of the French army and the increased expenditure for military affairs under MacMahon made men in Germany pay undue attention to the revenge sentiment that was becoming linked with Catholic France's sympathy for the Catholics in Germany. In Italy there was a widespread fear that Catholic France might attempt to re-establish her military prestige by a quick war to return Rome to the Church. The clerical explanation for the defeat of 1871 did not do much to weaken these fears: France, they argued, had been punished by God, Prussia was only the tool in God's hand. It followed that if Prussia abused her victory—which, of course, she did—God would not hesitate to punish her for her arrogance, and France might well be God's instrument to accomplish Prussia's humiliation. As for Italy, there could be little doubt that the Italians had sinned grievously in robbing the Church of its lands! It is no wonder that French military rehabilitation was regarded suspiciously by France's neighbors.

In 1875, the tension that "revenge" and clerical propaganda had maintained in Franco-German relations was increased greatly by a pseudo-war scare. It was largely made up of newspaper articles that might have passed without an incident, but the situation became serious when the French foreign office attempted to use the excitement created by the press to secure friends in Europe and humiliate Bismarck It is highly questionable that Decazes really feared that a preventive war was being planned in Germany, but he succeeded in convincing Europe that Bismarck was going to attack France without provocation. There were flurries in the European chancellories, and the czar's minister even spoke to Bismarck personally about the inadvisability of disturbing the peace The whole matter blew over quickly when Europe discovered that French fears were groundless Much of French opinion kept its head, and refused to believe in the danger even when the drums were beating loudest. The royalist and clerical politicians, who had cried "Wolf! Wolf!" so loudly, were branded as warmongers, and in the elections that followed on the heels of the "crisis" the republicans, posing as men of peace, won substantial victories

AFTER 1879, when the republicans came into their own, the danger of war subsided, and even the propaganda for revenge died down to a mere whisper No responsible statesman would have dared to recognize the loss of Alsace-Lorraine as final, but for practical purposes the moderate republicans were content to let things go on as they were. The wounds of 1871 had healed sufficiently for an occasional journal or newspaper to suggest that it would be best for France to forget the lost provinces entirely and to give up the romantic dreams for revenge that actually hindered the realization of important French ambitions. Men on the right and on the extreme left repudiated such sentiments, but it found wide acceptance among the moderates who were governing France. Bismarck, on his part, also became more accommodating; he favored the republicans, for he believed that a French Republic would never be able to find an ally in Europe. Time and again he reassured the French that his alliance systems were built up to maintain peace rather than to harm France. There was some satisfaction in these assurances, even though the peace of Frankfort was a vital part of Bismarck's *status quo.*

The relaxation of tension between France and Germany assumed more significance when the French discovered that Bismarck was willing to lend a sympathetic hand to almost any French aspiration—with the exception, of course, of the recovery of Alsace-Lorraine. At the Congress of Berlin, the chancellor paid marked attention to the French envoy, and even persuaded the British to recognize France's pre-eminent rights and interests in Tunis Later in the 1880's, when French diplomacy conflicted with British imperial policy, this friendly attitude almost developed into a Franco-German entente As an indication of the changed relationship between the two countries, Gambetta, who had taken the trouble to learn German and inform himself about conditions in Germany, even planned a visit to Berlin to interview Bismarck There were, of course, good reasons for the change France, isolated in Europe, was no match for the German Empire, and France, like Germany and England, was embarking on a program of colonial expansion Furthermore, England, rather than Germany, opposed the French colonial ambitions, indeed, only with Germany's help were they realizable

The last quarter of the nineteenth century witnessed a great era of colonial expansion Africa was partitioned, the islands of the Pacific were divided up, and preparations were made for eventual European control of all China France was somewhat handicapped in the colonial race, she lacked the continuous colonial traditions of England as well as the lusty economic exuberance of Germany France had no surplus population and comparatively few industrial commodities suitable for colonial markets, and her people had little imagination for the glory of a colonial empire Earlier French colonial activity had ended in a fiasco when France lost out to England in both India and America French historians never tired of asserting that colonialism was a fruitless policy, since, as in the cases of the thirteen English colonies and the Spanish and Portuguese colonies in the Americas, colonialism would end in independence for the colony before its value to the mother country became important Furthermore, the recent experience of the Second Empire in Mexico had left a bad impression on the French mind; overseas ventures were costly in blood and gold, and there were no advantages to be reaped from them. To many it seemed that the limited commitments in Algeria were more than enough for France to assume, especially as long as Alsace-Lorraine remained in the hands of Germany

On the other hand, there were men whose vision for glory,

prestige, and profits transcended the anticolonial arguments Businessmen and bankers, who saw in colonies an opportunity for economic advantages, soldiers and explorers, who relished glory and adventure in foreign lands, publicists and statesmen, who undertook to link profits and glory with national prestige and the recovery of French self-respect—these were the men who wished their country to join the other powers in the partition of the world. Their arguments were similar to those of "imperialists" elsewhere. "France's civilizing mission," "opportunities for profitable investment of French gold," "new sources of raw materials and new markets for French industry" loomed large in their propaganda for colonial expansion. French explorers, missionaries, and merchants had bravely opened backward areas of the globe to European civilization, they argued, and it became the duty of the nation to continue their work. Bankers and explorers, in particular, had gone far in forcing their government's hand; the former had loaned huge sums of money at exorbitant interest to rulers of backward states, so that the government was forced to intervene to protect French investors, and the latter had discovered vast tracts of land and had claimed them in the name of the French people.

In the early 1880's, the new economic imperialists had their way. Jules Ferry, a dominant figure in the moderate republican camp, was a sincere advocate of colonialism, both as a way of assuring economic advantages for the future and as a means of regaining French prestige. Tunis, Madagascar, Equatorial Africa, the southern Sahara, Indo-China, and a number of islands in the Pacific dramatically passed under the flag of France. Each move was presented to the chamber as an unavoidable adventure, and requests for credit were parceled out a little at a time, so that the costs did not appear so very great. As each new territory came under French control, the French people were systematically taught that France had gained a valuable prize that would assure her position as a great power.

The opponents of Ferry soon found a weak place in his armor. England was attempting to block the colonial expansion of all the continental states, and Ferry, as well as Bismarck, realized that only if the continental states presented a united front could they hope for success Co-operation between France and Germany, in the minds of the Germanophobes, was tantamount to a renunciation of the lost provinces The men on the right and the extreme left—roughly, the same people who later supported Boulanger—had no particular affection for England, but they also refused to believe that the German chancellor would do anything for France that might be to French advantage The German gift horses, they insisted, must be looked in the eyes and the teeth, and returned to the donor

This hue and cry against colonialism and the German entente began to appear plausible and appealed to the basic anti-colonial ideas of millions of Frenchmen as soon as some concrete disadvantages of the new imperialism began to manifest themselves Tunis was brought under French protection in 1881, and even the opponents of colonialism who first called Tunis "another Mexico" had to admit that the protectorate was a rich prize But it soon developed that Italy, in wrath over France's action, had made her peace with Austria and joined the Triple Alliance. Thus, an obvious result of the protectorate was the further isolation of France in Europe. The British occupation of Egypt was also, but unjustly, laid at the economic imperialists' doorstep France had had a traditional interest in the Nile valley ever since the time of Napoleon I. She had supported Mehemet Ali in 1840 against all Europe, and French bankers had lent to his successors large sums of money. In the 1870's, France and England jointly intervened in Egypt to protect their "investments"; but in 1882, when a nationalist uprising in Egypt further endangered these interests, France, because of opposition in the chamber, did not send her navy to assist the British in bombardment of

Egyptian cities and the military occupation of the country. When the British showed no haste in removing their troops from Egypt, French imperialists were forced to listen to bitter complaints at home.

It was the news of a disaster in French Indo-China, however, that proved to be the last straw Ferry had pictured as a mere expedition the war that was developing in the Orient, and, in obtaining credits, he had carefully scattered them out and minimized them, so that the conflict appeared to be a simple military promenade The news of an unexpected defeat at the hands of the Chinese—news that the government sought to cover up—almost ended in a revolution in Paris In the crisis in the chamber, Ferry's government fell, and Ferry himself, the founder of the French colonial empire, was practically exiled from public life. The antagonists of the new imperialism did not give up the gains of their predecessors, but they called upon their followers never to forget that Germany was the enemy.

This defeat of colonialism in 1885 brought continental affairs more urgently to the fore. The men who had overthrown the economic imperialists largely enjoyed the support of the peace-loving, adventure-fearing mass of the French people, but these men were, in addition to being anticolonials, the leaders of the idea of revenge. Undoubtedly the mass of the people, while they might have hoped for the eventual return of Alsace-Lorraine, would not have approved of any policy that might precipitate a war, but within the very heart of the anti-imperialist camp were the men whose chauvinism almost gave France a revolution and Europe a war. Déroulède and his League of Patriots, and Boulanger with the odd assortment of radicals, monarchists, Bonapartists, and emotional chauvinists who followed or pushed him, gave France and Europe a crisis in 1887–1888 The uncertain international weather of 1887, filled as it was with thunderstorms in Anglo-Russian and Austro-Russian relations, and disturbed by Bismarck's uncertainty about the wisest policy for him to adopt in face of Boulangism and the crisis in his alliance system, made that year a most tense one for all Europe.

GAMBETTA had advised Frenchmen to stop talking, but not to stop thinking, about revenge. In the early 1880's, it almost seemed that they had even stopped thinking about it; after 1885, they obviously disregarded his advice about silence From 1871 to 1914, there was a persistent minority, now fairly quiet, now extremely raucous, that demanded a war for revenge. After about 1885 this group had an eloquent leader in Paul Déroulède, an intensely patriotic poet, ex-soldier, and ex-lawyer, who devoted his life to the recovery of France's lost provinces and lost prestige. Dissatisfied with the selections of textbooks used in the schools (books which surely were not exactly pale in their patriotism!), Déroulède decided that French youth needed another source of patriotic inspiration and instruction. To supply this need, he took a leading part in the formation of the League of Patriots in 1882 The league closely associated itself with existing sport clubs of one kind or another, and opened a vigorous campaign to spread patriotic propaganda

It was in 1886 that the league announced its primary aim to be the revision of the treaty of Frankfort and the return of Alsace-Lorraine. The methods of propaganda included street demonstrations, boycotts on German goods, and an almost endless array of books, articles, poems, and lectures. *Le Drapeau,* the official newspaper of the league, ably expressed the league's philosophy of education when it said: "Would not the pitiless recital of our unprecedented disasters be a certain means of planting, in those hearts of sixteen and eighteen, the desire, the passion, the rage for vengeance? We wish to make this exposition as cruel, as complete as possible." The league never was important from a numerical point of view, but by its noise it made up for its lack of numbers. Brutal attacks upon German citizens who happened to be in Paris, turbulent demonstrations, and a voluminous literature made the league appear much more important than, probably, it really was. Naturally, the Germans eyed with suspicion this society, which never lost a chance to talk about "Frenchmen in chains" just beyond the frontier

It was the Boulanger movement that gave the league a sinister importance in both internal and international politics After 1886, Boulanger appeared on the French political scene as the "man on horseback" who would restore French honor. The enthusiasm of his supporters and the "brave general's" obvious ambitions soon made Boulangism a danger to European peace as well as to the continued existence of the Republic. Bismarck utilized the existence of the League of Patriots and the popularity of the general to obtain larger credits for his army, and, although he disclaimed any intention of making war on France, his speech before the Reichstag left Europe on edge The press, in both France and Germany, was discussing the question in a way reminiscent of the war-scare year of 1875, when an incident threatened to let loose the dogs of war Schnaebelé, a French frontier official, was enticed into Germany, and then arrested on a charge of espionage. In Paris, this seemed to be a brutal answer to the furor raised by the league, an invitation to declare war if France dared.

President Grévy received the prime minister with the words, "My friend, I receive many people; no one desires war, neither in the chamber nor the country!" Goblet, however, decided upon a strong stand—not strong enough for Boulanger, but certainly sufficient to defend French honor. It turned out that Bismarck was not behind the Schnaebelé affair and that he did not want war, so the crisis was quietly settled, and French honor suffered no disgrace.

The incident, however, served to heighten the internal crisis created by Boulangism, since, shortly after it, the republicans found the courage to drop the "brave general" from the war office. Patriots professed to believe that their hero was sacrificed to placate Bismarck, and Boulangism began to be a dangerous factor in French politics. Its fiasco was, it will be remembered, more the fault of the general than attributable to lack of enthusiasm of his followers. Since all Europe understood that the triumph of Boulangism might well mean war, Europe followed the crisis to its rather humorous end with great interest.

The year 1887 passed without any disturbance of the European peace. Bismarck's skillful diplomacy created a new set of ententes and alliances that successfully tied all the hands in Europe, and imposed peace. For twenty years, the "Iron Chancellor" spun alliances, agreements, and understandings for the maintenance of a *Pax Germannica,* for twenty years, France had been isolated, and excluded from an important rôle in European affairs, except in so far as Bismarck wished to grant her place and favors. As long as Bismarck ruled in the Wilhelmstrasse, German hegemony on the continent was assured, and in France, reasonable men well understood that revenge was a thing for dreams alone. But in 1890, Bismarck left the Wilhelmstrasse in the hands of men less capable of directing either Germany's or Europe's destinies. The young emperor, William II, dropped the pilot who for twenty years had charted a safe course for the empire, and, himself at the wheel, struck out on the high seas to find a "new course." The first casualty was the very keystone of the Bismarck system, the Russian alliance, which acted as a check in the Balkans and held off the danger of a war on two fronts. The men in the Berlin of William II could not believe that "holy," autocratic Russia would make common cause with red, republican France, and, disregarding all of Bismarck's teaching, they cut Russia loose on the sea of high politics.

IN THE ten years following the resignation of MacMahon, an alliance between "holy Russia" and republican France would have been almost unthinkable, even from the French point of view. Unlike the monarchists, who had started the

Republic on its career, the real republicans had no use for the autocratic Russia that oppressed Poland, exiled and executed liberals and radicals, and appeared in Europe as the champion of authority. By 1890, however, a number of factors had altered the official opinion of France sufficiently to make the Russian alliance not only acceptable but welcome In the first place, twenty years of isolation were beginning to tell on French morale; the French were finding it harder and harder to reconcile their own opinion of their importance with the limited rôle that circumstances allowed them to play in high politics. An attempt to separate Italy from the Triple Alliance had ended in a fiasco; an understanding with Germany was impossible; and England, almost as much as Germany, was the *bête noire* of French international aspirations. Russia, in the east, was in a position to threaten Germany, and she was the apparently implacable enemy of England. France and Russia had already learned to co-operate against England in Egyptian affairs, and, if the Pan-Slavic faction, which regarded Germany as Russia's enemy in the Balkans, could ever come to power, France and Russia might even learn to co-operate against Germany The "patriots" in France and the Pan-Slavists in Russia had clamored for an alliance in 1887; the defeat of Boulangism did not destroy the idea that a Russian alliance might solve many of France's problems

If French republicans had hesitated to consider an alliance with Russia, what could have been the attitude of Russian conservatives toward an alliance with "red" France? There were always a number of "policies" in Saint Petersburg, but it is safe to assume that even in 1890 no one of any considerable influence wished to ally Russia with France. Czar Alexander III and his ministers desired to maintain the close association with Bismarck's empire that had been the traditional policy of Russia But, with Bismarck gone, this connection was no longer possible. In spite of Russian begging, the Re-insurance Treaty was allowed to lapse, and the new German chancellor steadfastly refused to commit himself in writing on any of Russia's Near Eastern interests. To make matters worse—from the Russian point of view—this refusal almost coincided with the signature of the Anglo-German Heligoland Treaty and a noisy renewal of the Triple Alliance There was also much talk in the press about England's joining the Triple Alliance; this rumor appeared to be quite well founded when a series of friendly visits and naval demonstrations pointed to a possible quadruple alliance of England, Italy, Germany, and Austria-Hungary.

The young Kaiser William seemed to be going out of his way to alarm Russia. Giers, Russia's minister of foreign affairs, was distraught; the czar was discouraged and angry. The friendship with Prussia-Germany, which had been basic to Russian policy almost uninterruptedly since the days of Catherine II, seemed about to end. Russian statesmen, seeing themselves isolated—indeed, in danger of having a hostile coalition formed against them—found it a little easier to drop some of their repugnance for "red" France, especially since "red" France was in the process of changing its color somewhat.

Among the many factors that made a French alliance palatable in Russia, the rôle of Leo XIII cannot be overlooked The pope, irritated by Germany and Italy, did all in his power to bring France and Russia together His recognition of the Republic and the formation of a Catholic, conservative republican party did much to make France respectable in Russian eyes If the head of the Roman Catholic Church could reconcile the Republic with his conservatism, even Russia must recognize that France was not so radical There were also economic considerations involved in Russia's attitude. Russia needed capital, for railroads and other enterprises, that she herself did not possess, and the Germans, in an effort to force Russia to sign a commercial treaty very favorable to Germany, had closed their markets to Russian bonds. Paris was willing to loan money, but there were considerations The mistreatment of the Jews, the purchase of war materials, and, finally, some sort of political understanding had to become topics of discussion before the French money market could be opened to provide funds for the trans-Siberian railroad.

The formation of an alliance between Russia and France was no easy task; almost five years elapsed between the first feelers and the final signature Many times the Russians wished to drop the whole affair; and, had William's Germany been more accommodating, they probably would have done so. To the French, the flirtation period often appeared dangerous, popular demonstrations and newspaper discussions went far beyond the actual status of the negotiations, to make France's position extremely delicate. Nonetheless, the negotiations proceeded; a general, vague understanding was succeeded by a military agreement, and finally, in 1895, by a military alliance. When the treaty of alliance was signed, Bismarck's Europe had come to an end, and France came out of her isolation.

The alliance was immensely popular in France. To the little people it meant the end of isolation and a step along the way to the recovery of Alsace-Lorraine. In the popular mind, the great Russian bear became the subject of many illusions, and the Russian army, the "steam roller," became an invincible force to strike terror in the hearts of the adversaries of France. Officials, both in Paris and in Saint Petersburg, knew that the Russians had no intention of recovering Alsace-Lorraine for France, and that the alliance was primarily a defensive agreement, but the people could not help allowing their dreams to soar beyond the treaty terms—which were secret, anyway.

THE Russian alliance, however, did not solve all of France's problems, nor did it remove the danger of war. In the last years of the century, the consolidation and rounding out of the colonial empires occupied much of the attention of Europe. To the irritation of many, France found herself, along with Germany and Russia, intervening in the Far East to save Russia's ambitions from incipient Japanese imperialism. Several times, Anglo-French opposition in Siam, Madagascar, and elsewhere troubled the international scene. It was in the Nile valley, however, that there appeared the most serious problem that France had faced since 1871 For thee decades, France and England had been moderately bitter enemies; in 1898, their friction almost led to war. The economic imperialists' taste for alliteration, that had created the German dream of Berlin-Byzantium-Bagdad, was also responsible for England's ambitions for Cape-to-Cairo and French aspirations for Senegal-to-Somaliland The British and French schemes were mutually exclusive. It was at Fashoda that the two paths of empire met, and France was forced to back down.

The great difficulty in the way of the realization of French ambitions in the Sudan was that the French did not adequately prepare the Marchand expedition diplomatically. They assumed that the British would accept their thesis, that the Sudan was open to colonization as a result of the Anglo-Egyptian withdrawal in face of the Mahdi in the 1880's. It was an assumption that they had no right to make, in the face of every British public pronouncement opposing it. Since this was England's known attitude, France was foolhardy in sending an expedition to the upper Nile without first obtaining the support of the entire European continent. The French public was badly informed about the expedition until the whole story broke in the press, just about the time that Paris began to be excited about the Dreyfus case France's thesis was simple: Marchand and his men had braved the way from the Congo to the Nile, and had arrived at Fashoda before the Anglo-Egyptian expedition; this priority gave France a "claim" on the whole Sudan But the English insisted that the French were interlopers, and must move on. Delcassé, the foreign minister, was willing to consider evacuation "for a price," but the British, not interested in saving French face, brutally insisted that France must get out! In the end, the French had to retreat ignominiously; they were in no position, single-handed, to fight England, and there was no power in Europe, including Russia, that wanted to break a lance in behalf of the French. It was the most severe blow to French prestige since the Treaty of Frankfort.

The immediate reaction to the Fashoda incident was a demand for revenge on England. The "patriots" now shouted, "England is the eternal enemy!" and many of them began to discuss the possibility of a German alliance. Kaiser William however, wanted to go slowly, the French seemed about to throw themselves into his arms, but behind him was his own experience of an attempt to better Franco-German relations. He had sent his mother to Paris, only to have her visit almost cause a riot. He had attempted to obtain intellectual and artistic co-operation, only to have the press raise a hue and cry against him. The approach to Germany by some of the very men who had preached revenge was treated cautiously. The press discussions soon showed the difficulty that stood in the way of a Franco-German agreement; the French started by talking about an understanding, and ended with schemes for the return of Alsace-Lorraine as basic to the understanding. Under such conditions, nothing could come of the whole affair; Germany would not risk offending England by listening to French proposals of an alliance, any more than she would offend Russia by listening to British proposals.

WITH the opening of the new century came new developments and new diplomatic constellations. Great Britain emerged victorious in the Fashoda crisis, but almost immediately she encountered major difficulties in South Africa. The Boer War sorely tried England's strength, and at the same time demonstrated the fact that England's isolation was not nearly so "glorious" as it had seemed several years before. As did the Italians in our own time, the British succeeded in drawing down the hatred and criticism of the civilized world by their suppression of the independence of an African state. When British statesmen tried to come out of isolation, however, it was not easy to do so. Germany, the most prized potential ally, rebuffed British advances, and not until 1902, when the alliance with Japan was signed, was any alliance possible The Japanese alliance, however, did not solve the European problem, for Britain needed friends on the continent as well as in Asia.

England's need and desire to reduce her commitments and to relieve the tension between herself and her neighbors came almost contemporaneously with the realization in France that the French nation would not be a match for England without the aid of Germany Since German aid was predicated upon French recognition of the loss of Alsace-Lorraine, it was impossible. Therefore, the opinion that France must make her peace with England rapidly gained ground. Both Delcassé and Lansdowne, who respectively directed the foreign affairs of the two countries, came to see that an entente on colonial affairs would remove causes of friction between France and England, and at the same time satisfy the needs of both nations. Thus, in spite of the logical reasoning to the contrary, upon which the German foreign office relied, England and France found an entente over colonial questions comparatively easy.

Since the imperial ambitions of the two nations had been the source of conflict, these very ambitions were resolved in the understanding. The center of the discussion revolved around British interests in Egypt, and French interests in Morocco. Egypt, on Britain's life line to the east, had long been a vulnerable spot in the British armor; France for twenty years had made Britain's position in Egypt somewhat difficult. Morocco, on the other hand, was of special geographic, economic, and political importance to France, and England had always opposed French interests and ambitions in that area. By recognizing French interests in Morocco and British interests in Egypt, the accord greatly relieved the friction between the two countries. Other minor causes of friction, scattered in Asia and Africa, were also quietly removed, and, by 1904, when the entente was signed, there was a firm basis for Anglo-French friendship This agreement, after it was strikingly strengthened by Germany's attempt to break it, and re-enforced by naval and military conversations, became one of the chief props of the famed Triple Entente

Not slow to take advantage of British generosity, Foreign Minister Delcassé also succeeded in making agreements with both Italy and Spain to assure their recognition of French interests in Morocco, and then suggested to the sultan that Morocco should follow Tunis by passing under the protection of the French flag Unfortunately for the tranquillity of Europe, he had neglected to approach Germany for an agreement. There is no reason to assume that Germany had any more respect for the rights of backward nations, or for the Treaty of Madrid,* than had any of the other states, but Chancellor Bulow wanted "something" in return for Germany's acquiescence in French absorption of Morocco, and nothing had been offered to him. The Germans, believing that they could break up the Anglo-French understanding, proceeded to make a crisis. Kaiser William visited the sultan of Morocco, Bulow insisted on a conference, and Delcassé was dropped from the French cabinet. The French were in no situation to insist upon the maintenance of their position, since Russia, their ally, was at the moment engaged in a war with Japan, and British support was contingent upon German aggression. The conference of Algeciras temporarily solved the problem, by giving France the substance of victory, while Germany got the appearance of winning. No one could have believed that Morocco would long remain independent.

The first response in France to Germany's interference in the Morocco affair and even to the dismissal of Delcassé seems not to have been extremely hostile to Germany In the last years of the nineteenth and the first of the twentieth century, "revenge" was rapidly becoming a theme suitable for historians, vaudeville artists, and a few fire-eaters; the younger gen-

* Signed in 1880, guaranteeing Morocco's independence and the "Open door."

eration remembered little of *"l'année terrible,"* and many of them yawned at the idea of revenge. The first reaction of French public opinion held that Delcassé had tried to play Richelieu, but without Richelieu's finesse France would not follow him into war, to make good his mistakes. When, however, it appeared that Bulow had decided to try to get more than "something" in return for Morocco, that Germany's real aim was to break up the Anglo-French entente, and, especially after Björko, to force France into a German-Russian-French agreement in which France would play only a limited rôle, French opinion changed violently. The war scare of 1875, the Schnaebelé incident, and the Morocco "blackmail" were linked together as examples of Germany's brutal diplomacy which Frenchmen, young and old, were urged to resist

The fiasco of Germany's program at Algeciras, which was accentuated by the fact that only Austria-Hungary stood firmly beside her, brought satisfaction in France, but in the ensuing years, when Russia and England patched up their difficulties to complete the Triple Entente, the French were more than exultant. French publicists joyfully proclaimed the end of Bismarck's *Pax Germannica,* and talked about "the new Europe" in terms that showed that French hegemony through the Triple Entente was the cornerstone of their system. International relations in Europe were becoming more and more tense, and each new indication that France, England, Russia, and possibly Italy were facing Germany and Austria-Hungary provided stimulus for chauvinistic journalists and politicians.

In 1908, when the Casablanca affair * broke out, it seemed to many observers that the whole French nation was solidly united in its determination no longer to tolerate any concessions to Germany. Just as the lull in the "revenge" sentiment between 1879 and 1885 was followed by an intensive wave of anti-German feeling, so the lull of 1899–1905 was followed by a more intense nationalistic attitude. The names of Poincaré,

* This "second Morocco crisis" flared up over the question of deserters from the French Foreign Legion who were aided by the German consul at Casablanca

Clemenceau, Tardieu, and others which the war was to make famous, became associated with this new anti-German agitation. Clemenceau ably presented the attitude of this group of men toward a war of revenge, when he explained to Georges Louis that a war in Europe was inevitable. "I have even written as much," he said, "which is perhaps unnecessary. We will do nothing, we must do nothing to provoke it, but we must be ready to wage it . ."

The Casablanca crisis of 1908 was settled in 1909, apparently to the satisfaction of both France and Germany, but Morocco was still to trouble the relations between the two countries. French interests there seem inevitably to have led to the next crisis. France was deeply involved in the country, and the French government could not resist the pressure for a further extension of its power. In 1911, new troubles led to the sending of a French army into Morocco, and there was no immediate prospect of its withdrawal. The German government, anxious to have the whole affair settled, hinted its willingness to trade Morocco for "something," and, when the hints were ignored, a German battleship turned up at Agadir (1911) "to protect German interests." Another prolonged crisis followed, but since neither country was willing to let it go into a war, it was not so dangerous as was currently believed. In the end, the French surrendered a large slice of Equatorial African jungle to Germany, in return for a recognition of French "rights" in Morocco. Even though Morocco became a French protectorate, the chauvinists saw the German demand for a slice of the Congo as a reiteration of the annexation of 1871. "After the Agadir crisis," writes Professor Carroll, ". . . some of the men then in power, and others who were about to acquire it, co-operated in the effort to arouse a nationalist spirit. They were determined that France should not suffer another Agadir."

The establishment of the Moroccan protectorate released forces in high politics that pushed Europe headlong into the crisis of July, 1914. The Italian government, ambitious to obtain the share of North Africa that had been allotted to her by the French, declared war on Turkey, and invaded Tripoli. This diversion excited the hopes of the Balkan states, under the wing of Russian diplomacy, the neighbors of the sultan prepared to take advantage of Turkey's involvement with Italy The Balkan Wars that followed stimulated South Slav nationalism greatly, and paved the way for the crisis of July, 1914 An Austro-Serbian problem became an Austro-Russian crisis, and finally a world war, when Slavic and Austrian aims in the Danubian area came into open conflict.

Ironically enough, just at the time that Austria and Russia were moving toward war in the Near East, the western powers, England, Germany, and France, were finding that it was possible to solve many of their problems by diplomatic methods. The Anglo-German and the Franco-German agreements over the Bagdad railroad, and the Anglo-German colonial accord were reached in 1914 Indeed, if the World War had not come in August, the Germans and the English would have formally signed the treaties, which would have removed important causes of friction between the two states, on about the same day that Germany declared war on Russia. The chain of events started when France proclaimed the Moroccan protectorate that led to the crisis of 1914 engulfed and destroyed this constructive work for world peace

FRANCE'S part in the crisis of 1914 was largely a passive one. President Poincaré, in Saint Petersburg just before the crisis broke, gravely assured his ally that France was willing and able to honor her signature to the Franco-Russian alliance This "blank check," like the one given by Germany to Austria a few days before, allowed the more irresponsible—or, at least, the more reckless—members of both alliances a comparatively free hand in the crisis The French grimly watched the storm gather and break in the late summer of 1914, without doing anything to help it along. They had not willed the crisis, but when it came, the governors of France calmly watched the armies of Europe mobilize and fall upon one another. To the chauvinists, the war, in which France would be supported by the Russian "steam roller" and the British navy, was the war of revenge of which they had dreamed for over forty years. To the majority of Frenchmen, it was an unavoidable trial placed upon their shoulders; they had not sought the war, but they would fight it for all that they were worth.

There were those that exulted in the opportunity that the war offered to settle an old score with Germany, but the vast majority of the French people regarded it as a serious calamity, unavoidable but undesired. The elections early in 1914 had definitely shown the pacifistic sentiment of the nation; the socialist left, the party that had urged an understanding with Germany, had made sensational gains, and a clear majority of the chamber ardently desired to check the wild armament race that weighed so heavily upon the French budget. These men would never have favored an aggressive policy that might lead to war against Germany, but the war came in spite of them. The French government did not feel that it could risk the isolation that might follow if it attempted to check Russia's policy; it did not even dare to interfere with its ally's ambitions as much as Chancellor Bethmann-Hollweg of Germany had done in the case of Austria. The Austro-Russian conflict over Serbia, whether they wished it or not, pulled both France and Germany into the maelstrom. It is small wonder that indignant scholars in the postwar era have condemned the prewar "defensive-alliance systems" as the most terrible inventions of our age.

The news of the crisis began to occupy the attention of France in the third week of July, but men who had seen the Moroccan crisis, the Bosnian crisis, and the Balkan Wars settled by diplomacy could not believe that this Austro-Serb-Russian dispute would end in slaughter. Surely, some arrangement could be found—or, even if the diplomats should stumble, there were those who believed that the Socialist International would prevent the governments from taking the fatal step The French foreign and war offices, however, could not afford the luxury of such optimism: France's premobilization military precautions kept pace with and even exceeded those of Germany, while French diplomats, particularly in London and Rome, worked overtime to be sure that France would not have to face the German army alone. The German ultimatum and Ambassador von Schoen's lame excuse for the declaration of war came as no surprise to the Quai d'Orsay The French had had little to do with the crisis, but they grimly awaited its outcome

THE declaration of war presented a number of pressing problems. For some time, there had been fearful questioning whether mobilization could be ordered without having the labor leaders and pacifist radicals create serious disturbances. As a precaution, a list of over two thousand names had been prepared, so that the police could arrest potential disturbers before they had an opportunity to interfere with the general mobilization of the armed forces At the last moment, however, the government decided not to take these men into custody It was argued that the workers would resent the arrest of their leaders at the moment when they were mobilized to fight for the fatherland. This confidence was rewarded; the French mobilization proceeded even more smoothly than the general staff had hoped. The arrests were not made, but the years of propaganda by the rightist press bore some fruit anyway The *bête noire* of the conservatives was Jaurès, leader of the socialists. His outspoken attacks upon the conservative classes and his demands for an understanding with Germany had earned for him a primary place in the hatred of the right. On the eve of the war, he was brutally murdered when he returned from the last prewar meeting of the Socialist International.

The death of Jaurès did not, however, act as a signal for a workers' revolt against conscription. Indeed, the dead man almost became a symbol around which the "sacred union" of French parties was formed. He was mourned by his followers, and even those papers that, morally at least, shared in the guilt for his death spoke respectfully about him. On the fourth of August, a great popular demonstration was held in his honor, and Premier Viviani, Jouhaux who represented organized labor, and many other speakers, eulogized the dead man and urged Frenchmen to stand together in the hour of crisis

Later in the same day, the chamber of deputies met to consider the war. Deschanel, its president, opened the meeting with a eulogy of Jaurès, and then Viviani read President Poincaré's famous war message exonerating France from the responsibility for the war, and urging the politicians to form a "sacred union" for the defense of the fatherland. When Viviani left the chamber to go to the senate, the deputies voted the emergency war bills by a show of hands The chamber was feverish in its patriotism, and the session closed with cries, "Vive la France!" "Vive la République!" and "Vive Alsace!"

In war, however, cheering and voting of credits are not enough; action must necessarily take the place of words. By 1914, military science had developed to a degree where nearly every major nation was amply prepared to fight the war of 1871. All over Europe, large armies of conscripts, provided with heavy guns and great trains of supplies, were poised to be thrown at the enemy shortly after mobilization was ordered. The Germans were operating on a plan that von Schlieffen had worked out years before, on the general basis of Hannibal's great battle of Cannae. The main army was to march through Belgium, pivot on Luxembourg, swing around Paris, and drive the French army into Germany, so that France would be crushed before the Russians had time to engage the German army of the east. But von Schlieffen was not there to execute his masterpiece, and his successor, Moltke, had tinkered with the plan enough to endanger its chances for success. The French plan called for an assault upon Alsace-

Lorraine, as von Schlieffen had calculated, and depended for its success largely upon the *élan* of the French soldier and the celebrated efficiency of the French "seventy-fives." Neither plan won the "eight-weeks' war" that war colleges had been discussing for a generation.

In the first days of the war, the French army invaded the "lost provinces," routed a frontier guard, and sent home a German war flag to hang in the Invalides Museum Rumor had it that the Cossacks would soon be in Berlin, and Paris, at least, was sanguine over the prospects of an early peace. The French press ignored the German army's rapid advance through Belgium until crowds of refugees began to pour into Paris with stories of German atrocities. The German advance seemed irresistible. The field-gray army, equipped with heavy mobile guns never before seen outside of a fortress or a battleship, literally pounded its way through Belgium, shattered the British and Belgian armies, and drove the French before it. All northern France seemed doomed to fall into German hands. To add to the disaster, the French army that invaded Alsace-Lorraine ran into difficulties. French soldiers were brave, and their *élan* was excellent, but their blue coats and red trousers made perfect targets for machine guns! The French losses in these first days were enormous, and retreat was the only alternative. In Paris, all seemed lost, and the government hastily decamped to Bordeaux to avoid capture

The Germans, however, did not have the strength to deliver the fatal blow. There have been many excuses for the failure of the Schlieffen plan: Moltke had tampered with it; the French, foolishly, had been driven out of Alsace-Lorraine; the supply trains had not kept pace with the invading army; and so forth. For the purposes of this history, however, it is enough to note that the French army, re-enforced by troops rushed in taxicabs from Paris and by some of the men who Schlieffen had hoped would be in Alsace, rallied and stopped the German drive at the Marne. At the end of this first exchange of blows, both armies dug in, and Europe began that awful war of the trenches that was to last for four more years.

THE war proved to be a severe test of the Constitution of 1875 For a long time, friends of the Republic had feared that it could never survive the strain of war. "Make a king, or make peace," was the advice of an eminent socialist shortly before the war broke out. He argued that the shock would be too much for the republican régime. Even so thoughtful a scholar as Hanotaux had written of the Republic: "It will probably adapt itself badly to a crisis where the fate of the fatherland is in question" In Germany, as well as in France, there was a widespread belief that the first news of French defeat would bring on a revolution in Paris, and the news of the assassination of Jaurès was followed up in the German press by wild stories about "social revolution in Paris" A modern war requires stable leadership, and observers who had seen the rise and fall of French cabinets could not believe that the French system, accustomed as it was to ministerial crises, could ever adjust itself to the necessities of war Revolution or military dictatorship, or both, many people thought, might well be the natural outcome of the war.

Obviously, the war did not bring an end to cabinet problems, but it did show that the French Republic was tougher and more stable than observers had believed The first shifts came in the cabinet, when Viviani broadened the political representation of his ministry, to make the "sacred union" a reality. Viviani's leadership gave way in 1915 to that of Briand, who formed a cabinet of "all the talents," and in 1917, when Briand resigned, first Ribot and then Painlevé attempted to keep up the pretext of united political action. Late in 1917, Clemenceau formed a partisan cabinet that governed France until 1920. In none of these changes was the Third Republic in any danger; when things looked blackest, in 1917, the French general staff was never allowed to play any rôle comparable to the one that Ludendorff and Hindenburg assumed in Germany. Even Generalissimo Foch, at the height of his power, was excluded from politics. At several times, there were suggestions for an alteration in the Constitution of 1875, but the peace finally came with the republican régime intact, and, indeed, strengthened by the experience of war.

The war, naturally, necessitated a great concentration of power in the hands of the executive. During the first year, the chamber of deputies practically abdicated its rights to the cabinet, but, between the fall of 1915 and 1917, the chamber worked hard to regain its rightful position Through secret commissions and committees, the deputies found ways of criticizing and, in part, controlling the action of the ministers. This, however, was not satisfactory; parliamentary control enfeebled the government just when it was most necessary to have a strong executive Briand resigned when the chamber refused to delegate legislative power to the council of ministers, and his immediate successors were equally unable to form the strong government necessary for the war situation, because of opposition from the left In November, 1917, when Painlevé resigned after a formal vote, Clemenceau formed a new government. The "sacred union" was broken, and Clemenceau summarily dealt with the opposition by literally dominating both the parliament and his cabinet It was his government that won the war and made the peace, and although this government ruthlessly controlled all France, it held its authority from the parliament by the traditional means of republican control. The most extraordinary demand that he made on the parliament was the right to rule over the whole domain of the country's economic life.

As in the rest of Europe, the war brought in its train a great expansion of the authority of the French state over the individual. The first act of the government was to declare a state of siege, which gave the military authorities almost complete power over all France. By a stroke of the pen, the liberties of the people were curtailed, and the means at the government's disposal to enforce its will were greatly expanded. New courts-martial, with practically unlimited authority, appeared to maintain military discipline and to check treason or espionage. The censorship was established to control the press, and rights of assembly and freedom of speech disappeared There was much that was distasteful about the régime, but the great mass of the people docilely accepted the restrictions and regulations as an inevitable consequence of war. However, tales of injustices committed by the courts-martial at the front and foolish acts of tyranny incidental to the exercise of the government's unusual power were relayed to the chamber of deputies, where protests against the system could be registered. The journalists, Clemenceau at their head, protested bitterly against the stupidity of the censorship, and began the practice of sending censored articles to friends in the chamber.

In the autumn of 1915, the clamor for readjustment yielded some results, when there was a slight relaxation of the state of siege far behind the lines, and the police and judicial functions in a large area were restored to the civil authorities. The courts-martial, too, were deprived of some of their power by providing the possibility of an appeal from their judgment. The censorship, however, continued, and even under Clemenceau, who had so rigorously insisted that "the right of insulting members of the government must be inviolable," the strictest press control was maintained. During the last year and a half of the war, when defeatism began to sap civilian morale and espionage became more persistent, the system of regulation became almost as severe as it had been in 1914

The economic life of the nation also came under greater and greater state control. When the war began, the French military authorities assumed that it would be a short one. It was generally believed that the economic life of the nation must slow down while the workers went to war, and that the army would live upon its accumulated supplies until the war was over. The war, however, did not follow the plans of the staff colleges, and, reluctantly, the military authorities were forced to the conclusion that it would last for at least a year, and that the supplies in their bins were inadequate for the needs at the front Even so, the French government did not organize a "plan" for the mobilization of France's economic resources, but, by force of circumstance, the government was gradually obliged to assume more or less control over the whole economic structure. It regulated prices, wages, and hours of labor It prevented strikes by threatening to send striking workers to the front. It controlled industrial production by bringing the plans under direct government supervision Without a plan, however, this "statism" became a thing of great confusion. Each ministry, each bureau, had its own organization, and there was little or no collaboration The parliamentary committees only added confusion to the near-chaos, and although both Briand and Clemenceau tried to bring some order into the system, the end of the war found French "totalitarian economics" in almost hopeless anarchy.

The fact that the German invasion overran the most industrialized section of France inflicted grave losses upon French war-time economy Almost from the very beginning, France was forced to depend upon importation to maintain her armies in the field and to keep her people fed and supplied with commodities Furthermore, since approximately 20 per cent of her population was mobilized to fight the war, the economy of the area under French control was seriously crippled. It was necessary in 1915 to demobilize thousands of skilled workers in order to keep the industrial machine running at all. This occasioned considerable bitterness, since it meant that the brunt of the fighting had to be borne by the peasants, even though they, too, could demonstrate a severe labor shortage In 1914, French economy was ill prepared to fight a long war, and only large assistance from the factories and fields of England and the Americas made it possible for France to hold out until the victory was assured

AFTER the war settled down to trench fighting and the government returned to Paris, the French adjusted themselves to war living Women, children, and old men had to carry on the multiple tasks in the fields, the factories, and the commercial houses, while the able-bodied males fought for their country. Even the traditionally sheltered Frenchwomen were to learn that they could drive the trams, oil the locomotives, and work in munitions factories The big cities, especially Paris, were soon overrun by soldiers of the allied powers, and both the soldiers and the civilians, keyed up by the war to a new tempo, demanded entertainment and excitement such as France had never seen before. The governmental ban upon cafés, wine shops, and theaters was lifted to satisfy this increased pressure for entertainment. It was this excited, war-crazed France, filled with men who might reasonably expect to be killed within a month and with women who were taking the place of men in industry and agriculture, that gave the Americans a mass impression of "gay and wicked Paris!"

The front, of course, occupied the minds of everyone. There was hardly a family in France—in all Europe, for that matter—without one member or more engaged in the trenches. Husbands, sons, fathers, uncles, nephews, and cousins made up the armies standing in the mud of eastern France. These men, almost daily exposed to violent death, were defending their homes and their country with their lives, while their relatives at home prayed and worked to help them to win the victory

Victory, however, was a puzzling problem. The military strategists of Europe could not seem to find the key that would open the door. None of their textbooks had warned them that the two armies would dig themselves in, and, when the trenches appeared, it caused them no little consternation. Unable to discover a plan, the soldiers settled down to a war of attrition. When the people wanted to hear of a military victory, their generals told them how many Germans they were killing each day Somehow, the people were expected to believe that this war of attrition would eventually reduce the German male population to a point where victory would be assured

There were, of course, great battles. In 1915, the Germans had driven the Russian army out of Poland by launching a gigantic drive at one point in the Russian lines, so that the whole Russian army was forced to abandon the trenches The tactics apparently won a great victory, even though the Russian army still remained in the field But the same strategy, when transported to the western front, proved to be disastrous to both armies The trenches in the west were more tightly held than in the east, and the transportation problem behind the lines was more easily solved. The preliminary bombardment merely notified the enemy of the approaching attack, so he could prepare a counterattack For three years, the big guns churned up the mud of eastern France, and men killed each other with bayonets, shovels, grenades, but only a few feet of ground ever changed hands!

The Germans, too, were unable to find the "knock-out blow" necessary for victory, and so they turned to the matter of "reducing" the French male population. They chose the great fortress of Verdun as a point which the French would certainly sacrifice millions of lives to defend, and ringed it with great guns. Verdun was to be a gigantic meat chopper in which to destroy the French army. The French bravely responded to the challenge *"Ils ne passeront pas!"* became the war cry of the Republic. But the Germans lacked the courage of their convictions. The plan had been to reduce Verdun, and kill all of its defenders, with long-range heavy guns The military mind, however, was obsessed with the idea that men fought with cold steel rather than with machines, and, finally, before the French *were* destroyed, an attack was launched Verdun today is a shrine for both France and Germany; hundreds of thousands of their best men died there without bringing either army any nearer to final victory. Verdun merely proved that the French could and would defend themselves, but the world knew that already.

The greatest crisis came in the winter of 1916–1917. After a mild autumn, Europe suffered a most rigorous winter. The suffering in the trenches, naturally, was acute, but even far behind the lines in France the civilian population faced dire need. There was a real shortage of both coal and food, and the cost of living, which had gradually gone up, fairly skyrocketed out of sight. Defeatism grew in alarming proportion, and several serious mutinies on the front even brought the integrity of the French army into question. The government's difficulties, too, were multiplying. Three years of war had reduced the supply of gold and foreign exchange, and even the possibility of securing credit, to a dangerous point, and both France and England were having serious trouble in finding the wherewithal to pay for the increasingly large flow of war materials that had to be purchased in the United States and elsewhere. The military situation looked even less hopeful. Rumania had entered the war, only to be crushed by the German army; the long-awaited Russian offensive had been repulsed; and the war of the trenches in France offered no solution. When the Germans ordered unrestricted submarine warfare, and revolution broke out in Russia, the prospects of the allies had reached their lowest point. Defeat—or, at best, a stalemate that would mean mutiny and perhaps revolution—faced France squarely in the face.

In this dark hour, the intervention of the United States afforded a great source of hope. The American armies were, as yet, nonexistent, but there were American gold and war material, and the American navy to help to break the submarine blockade. The very idea that the United States was joining them in their hour of need raised the morale of men who had seen three years of war. With America in the war, victory, it seemed, would be assured. In the postwar era, when questions of war debts and their payment embittered French public opinion against "Uncle Shylock," the material and psychological aid that the United States brought to the allied cause was played down or forgotten. But in 1917 the politicians in Paris, the poor devils in the trenches, and the man on the street well knew that the United States would turn defeat or stalemate into victory.

The war was not to end for another year and a half. The French watched their own army fail to break the German lines, and saw the complete debacle of Russia in the early summer of 1917; in the fall, the Germans fell upon Italy, and, for a moment, it appeared that Italy would follow Belgium, Serbia, Poland, and Rumania under the German yoke. But the allies were growing stronger every day. Millions of fresh men, whose aid in the war might be more psychological than military, and tons and tons of provisions and supplies were pouring into France It was just a matter of time until the war must be over. The Germans, however, had enough energy left for one last fling at victory. In the spring of 1918 they repeated the invasion of 1914 by making a terrific lunge at the junction point of the French and the English armies Long-range guns shelled Paris from seventy-five miles away, and the advance guard of the German attack must have been close enough to see the city with their own eyes. Again on the Marne River the decisive engagement was fought, and again the German army had to give way.

When this famed "peace offensive" of Ludendorff broke down, the German army was doomed The allies, finally under a united command with Generalissimo Foch at the head, began the offensive which drove the Germans back to the Hindenburg Line, broke through it, and finally forced the German general staff to ask for an armistice It took more than four years of most awful slaughter before the "civilized nations" of Europe were ready to try to settle their problems at a peace conference.

PEACE came to eastern France and the world on November eleventh, 1918, on terms that left no doubt about the allied victory. The invaders were defeated, the shame of 1870–71 was erased, and the awful carnage had come to an end. It is no wonder that France was jubilant. The celebrations in Paris, in which men from more than two dozen nations joyfully participated, were spectacular to a high degree The victorious allied armies filed down the same Champs Élysées that, only forty-seven years before, had been the parade ground for the Prussians. The crowds on the street went wild with excitement Amid cheers from the inhabitants, the tricolor reappeared in Strasbourg and Metz, and, all over France, men and women gave thanks for peace and victory The armistice, however, ended only the fighting; the pressing problem was to write a peace treaty that would end the war In January, 1919, the representatives of the allied and associated powers gathered in Paris to discuss and formulate plans for the new world, and to draw a new map of Europe

Liberals throughout the world, before 1933, held one opinion in common with the Nazis· they both agreed that the treaties that followed the war were bad. The Nazis reached their conclusion from German self-interest; the liberals reached theirs from hindsight and a little political wisdom. It would be decidedly unfair to expect either of these deductions from the men who wrote the treaties of peace. Indeed, if one will consider the passion and propaganda of the war period, and the extreme complexity of the problem that the conflicting political tensions of 1919 presented to the peacemakers, it is probably unfair to expect them to have done more than they did. The men who wrote the treaties, were, after all, merely human beings, more or less subject to all of the frailties to which flesh is heir. They could not be expected to tear aside the curtain of the future, nor could they remain insensitive to the passions and political tensions of their time.

The problems confronting the conference were enormous.

Even the Congress at Westphalia and the Congress of Vienna were not asked to solve so many complex questions. It was soon discovered that little or nothing could be done around the conference table when all of the victorious powers sat down together, and, in spite of President Wilson's statement about "open covenants, openly arrived at," it became imperative to do the real work of peacemaking by means of smaller committees. First, the council of ten, then the council of four, and finally, when Italy walked out, the council of three, became the brain and will of the peace conference Wilson, Lloyd George, and Clemenceau wrote most of the treaty in secret session, and presented it to their allies and associates—and to the vanquished—for signature.

The French case at the conference was ably represented by Clemenceau, a veteran republican politician whose career extended back to 1870. He was an ardent nationalist, a fighter, and an advocate of severe terms for Germany. His adamant refusal to believe that the Germans would understand any language but force, and his firm conviction that France must take full advantage of her opportunity to adjust her relationship with Germany to France's profit, made him the very incarnation of the war spirit of his country He well understood that French opinion demanded two things from the conference: security and reparations. France had suffered much from the war, and she wanted assurance that she would never suffer again from invasion, as well as a promise of a complete restoration of her devastated lands and treasury. Clemenceau was the man to get both, if it were humanly possible to achieve them by the methods available to France in 1919. He was an able negotiator, and he had taken the measure of his colleagues. He, more than either the American or the Englishman, was the architect of the treaty of Versailles.

France's problem was, indeed, a difficult one. There were eighty-odd million Germans in central Europe, and, if the population statistics proved anything, the future would see at least a hundred million of them. These Germans, moreover, had developed a powerful economic structure, and four years of warfare against great odds had proved their fighting stamina. On the other hand, there were only some forty million Frenchmen in Europe, and, unless the birth rate changed radically, there would never be many more The French had not created a great industrial economy, and there was little prospect that this nation of peasants, artisans, and bourgeois would ever build a state as powerful as that which the capitalists, junkers, proletariat, peasants, and bourgeoisie had created in Germany. France in 1919, with the aid of half the world, emerged victorious over Germany, but no one familiar with the history of Europe could have any confidence in the future It was too easy to recall that less than fifty years before Bismarck had dictated the terms of peace

Security against a recurrence of the invasion from Germany was a natural desire of France, and, with the ideology of 1919, it was just as plausible that this wish should be expressed by determination on destruction of German military power. No French statesman could have allowed Wilson's idealistic statements about national self-determination to influence his opinion on the German question. It would have been considered treason, or even worse, if the French representative had allowed the German Republic to come out of the war stronger and more populous than the Kaiser's empire had been in 1914. Security for France, it was believed, could only be achieved by dismembering and disarming Germany and loading her with debt. Her military and economic power were to be crippled, so that she could not recover for years. Wilson and Lloyd George succeeded in obtaining somewhat milder terms than France wished to prescribe, but only after they had agreed to an Anglo-American-French alliance to assure France against the enemy.

Almost equally as imperative as the demand for security was the French cry for reparations Four years of war had devastated large areas of eastern France. Whole villages had disappeared, towns were shambles. Factories, mines, churches, and private homes were in ruins The Germans had used systematic destruction as an instrument of war with a thoroughness not even excelled in the famed "march to the sea" in another great struggle, and before there could be even thought of life going on in many sections of France, complete reconstruction was absolutely necessary Furthermore, the war had enfeebled both French credit and the French treasury, the nation was smothered in debt, and the franc was losing its value. There were two alternatives. France could devaluate her currency and bleed herself white with taxation, or she could try to force Germany to pay for the war With these possibilities, it is small wonder that the nation demanded that the latter course should be explored.

The treaty, as it was finally written, disarmed Germany, fixed upon her the moral responsibility for the war, deprived her of her colonies and a considerable part of her territory in Europe, and loaded her with a debt that was too great even to calculate. It prevented the Germans of the old Hapsburg Empire from joining with the rest of their people, and created in central eastern Europe a tier of states whose vested interest in the peace settlement would, presumably, make them pro-French. It was a formidable document for any state to accept, but to the Germans was given the alternative of signing or facing an invasion. The treaty received some criticism in France because it was *too mild,* and when the United States Senate refused to ratify either the treaty of alliance or the League of Nations, this criticism became quite articulate There were people in France who felt that Lloyd George and Wilson had forgiven Germany at France's expense, and had tricked Clemenceau into accepting it by the promise of the alliance that was never ratified.

In the Hall of the Mirrors at Versailles, just forty-eight years after Bismarck had proclaimed the united German Empire in the same room, the treaty of peace with Germany was signed. The German delegation, whose only function at Paris had been to sign the treaty, affixed their signatures to the document that was supposed to bring peace to Europe. It was a great day for France Her lost provinces were returned, the shame of 1870 was erased, and she stood at the head of a great coalition of nations to dictate the peace To many who saw this ceremony, it seemed that, after years of defeat and disgrace, France had finally received justice To others, more cynical, it was just another turn in the wheel of Franco-German relations—a more spectacular treaty, perhaps, but no more permanent than its predecessors had been.

The Republic's foreign relations had gone through many phases since 1870 After years of isolation, republican France had found an ally in Russia, and later a friend in England; she had managed to accumulate an overseas empire, and to maintain her dignity as well as monarchical or imperial France had done. In the Great War (1914–1918), republican France emerged with undisputed hegemony on the continent of Europe. But the postwar world, filled with shocks and setbacks for French society, was destined to be merely one of a twenty-year truce, not a new world made safe for French or any other kind of democracy.

SELECTED BIBLIOGRAPHY

(Revised, 1962)

THERE is a wealth of monographic and source material dealing with French history since 1815, but it does not seem necessary to list an extensive bibliography in a general study like this one. Any student wishing to probe deeper into the subject should, in addition to the usual bibliographical guides, consult the excellent bibliographical articles by Robert Schnerb (J. M. H., Vol. VIII, pp. 338–355), and R. A. Winnacker (J. M. H., Vol. X, pp. 372–409), and, of course, "*Clio*", *Introduction aux études historiques,* vol. IX by Renouvin, Préclin, and Hardy.

Allison, J. M. S., *Thiers and the French Monarchy, 1797–1848.* London, 1926.

Anderson, F. M., *Constitutions and Other Select Documents Illustrative of the History of France, 1789–1901.* Minneapolis, 1908, 2nd ed.

Arnaud, René, *La Deuxième République et le Second Empire.* Paris, 1929.

Artz, F. B., *France under the Bourbon Restoration, 1814–1830.* Cambridge, 1931.

Bertaut, Jules, *L'Opinion et les Moeurs.* Paris, Éditions de France, 1931.

Blanc, Louis, *The History of Ten Years, 1830–1840.* Tr. by W. K. Kelly, Philadelphia, 1848.

Bourgeois, Émile, *History of Modern France, 1815–1913.* Cambridge, England, 1919.

Brogan, D. W., *The French Nation, 1815–1940.* New York, 1958

Bruun, Geoffrey, *Clemenceau.* Cambridge, Mass., 1943.

Castenet, Jacques, *Histoire de la troisième république.* Five volumes. Paris, 1952–1960.

Challener, Richard D., *The French Theory of the Nation in Arms*. New York, 1955.

Charlety, S., *La Monarchie de Juillet*. Paris, 1921

———, *La Restauration*. Paris, 1921.

Clapham, J. H., *Economic Development of France and Germany, 1814–1914*. Cambridge, England, 1921.

Clough, S. B., *France, A History of National Economics, 1789–1939*. New York, 1939.

Dautry, Jean, *1848 et la IIe République*. Paris, 1948. (Communist view.)

Debidour, Antonin, *Histoire des rapports de l'Église et de l'État en France de 1789 à 1870*. Paris, 1898.

———, *L'Église catholique et l'État sous la Troisième République, 1870–1906*. Paris, 1906–1909.

Dunham, A. L., *The Anglo-French Treaty of Commerce of 1860*. Ann Arbor, 1930.

———, *The Industrial Revolution in France, 1815–1848*. New York, 1955.

Elton, Godfrey, *The Revolutionary Idea in France, 1789–1871*. New York, 1923.

Fournière, E., *Le Régime de Louis Philippe*. Paris, 1906.

de la Gorce, Pierre, *Histoire de la Second République Français*. Paris, 1887.

———, *Histoire du Second Empire*. Paris, 1894–1905.

———, *La Restauration, Louis XVIII*. Paris, 1926.

Gouault, Jacques, *Comment la France est devenue républicaine* Paris, 1954.

Guedalla, Philip, *The Second Empire*. London, 1922.

Guerard, A. L., *French Civilization in the Nineteenth Century, a historical introduction*. London and New York, 1914.

———, *Napoleon III*. Cambridge, Mass., 1943.

Hanotaux, Gabriel, *Contemporary France*. Westminster, 1903–1909.

Hudson, N. E., *Ultra Royalism and the French Restoration*. Cambridge, England, 1936.

Jackson, J. H., *Clemenceau and the Third Republic*. New York, 1948.

Joughin, Jean T., *The Paris Commune in French Politics, 1871–1880*. Baltimore, 1955

Lamartine, A M L, *Histoire de la Restauration* Paris, 1856–1858.

Lefranc, George, *Histoire du travail et des travailleurs* Paris, 1957

Levasseur, E., *Histoire des Classes Ouvrières en France de 1789 à 1870*. Paris, 1903–1904

———, *Questions Ouvrières et Industrielles en France sous la IIIe République*.

Louis, Paul, *Histoire du Parti Socialiste en France, 1871–1914*. Paris, 1922

Lucas-Dubreton, Jean, *La Restauration et la Monarchie de Juillet*. Paris, 1937.

Mason, E. S, *The Paris Commune*. New York, 1930.

McKay, D. C., *The National Workshops*. Cambridge, Harvard University Press, 1933.

Miquel, Pierre, *L'Affaire Dreyfus* Paris, 1959

Morazé, Charles, *Les bourgeois conquérants XIX Siècle*. Paris, 1957.

Muret, C. T, *French Royalist Doctrines since the Revolution*. New York, 1930

Pinkney, David, *Napoleon III and the Rebuilding of Paris*. Princeton, 1958.

Plamenatz, John, *Revolutionary Movement in France, 1815–1871*. London, 1952

Pouthas, C.-H., *La population française dedans la première moitié du XIX Siècle*. Paris, 1956.

Recouly, Raymond, *The Third Republic*. London, 1928.

Remond, Rene, *La Droite en France en 1815 à nos jours*. Paris, 1954.

Penard, G. F., *La Révolution de 1848*. Paris, 1907.

Renouvin, Pierre, *Histoire des relations internationales*. Volume V: *Le XIX Siècle de 1815 à 1871*. Paris, 1954. Volume VI· *Le XIX Siècle de 1871 à 1914* Paris, 1955.

Robertson, Priscilla, *Revolutions of 1848. A Social History* Princeton, 1952; Harper Torchbook edition, 1960.

de Roux, M , *La Restauration* Paris, 1930
de Sauvigny, Bertier, *La Restauration.* Paris, 1955.
Sée, Henri, *La Vie Économique de la France sous la Monarchie Censitaire, 1815–48* Paris, 1927
Seignobos, Ch., *La Révolution de 1848—Le Second Empire* Paris, 1921.
———, *Le Déclin de l'Empire et l'Établissement de la 3e République.* Paris, 1921.
———, *L'Évolution de la 3e République* Paris, 1921
Simpson, F A , *Louis Napoleon and the Recovery of France.* London, 1923.
———, *The Rise of Louis Napoleon.* London, 1925
Thompson, David, *Democracy in France.* London, 1946
Viallate, A , *L'Activité économique en France de la fin du XVIIe Siècle à nos jours.* Paris, 1937
Weber, Eugene, *Nationalist Revival in France, 1905–1914.* Berkeley, California, 1959
Weill, G., *La France sous la Monarchie Constitutionelle.* Paris, 1912.
———, *Histoire du Movement Social en France, 1852–1924* Paris, 1924.
———, *Histoire du Parti Républicain en France, 1814–1870.* Paris, 1900.
Woodward, E. L., *French Revolutions.* Oxford, 1934.

INDEX

D

N

O

INDEX

S

T

SAMUEL NOAH KRAMER Sumerian Mythology TB/1055

FERDINAND LOT The End of the Ancient World and the Beginnings of the Middle Ages Intro by Glanville Downey TB 1044

J M WALLACE-HADRILL The Barbarian West *The Early Middle Ages, A D 400–1000* TB/1061

History Renaissance & Reformation

JACOB BURCKHARDT The Civilization of the Renaissance in Italy *Intro by Benjamin Nelson and Charles Trinkaus Illus* Vol I TB 40 Vol II TB/41

EDWARD P CHEYNEY The Dawn of a New Era 1250–1453 *50 illus* TB/3002

WALLACE K FERGUSON et al The Renaissance Six *Essays* TB/1084

MYRON P GILMORE The World of Humanism 1453–1517 *64 illus* TB/3003

JOHAN HUIZINGA Erasmus and the Age of Reformation *32 illus* TB/19

PAUL O KRISTELLER Renaissance Thought *The Classic, Scholastic, and Humanist Strains* TB/1048

NICCOLÒ MACHIAVELLI History of Florence and of the Affairs of Italy *from the earliest times to the death of Lorenzo the Magnificent Intro by Felix Gilbert* TB/1027

J E NEALE The Age of Catherine de Medici TB/1085

ERWIN PANOFSKY Studies in Iconology *Humanistic Themes in the Art of the Renaissance 180 illus* TB/1077

J H PARRY The Establishment of the European Hegemony 1415–1715 *Trade and Exploration in the Age of the Renaissance* TB/1045

FERDINAND SCHEVILL The Medici *20 pp illus* TB/1010

FERDINAND SCHEVILL Medieval and Renaissance Florence *Vol I Medieval Florence Illus* TB/1090

FERDINAND SCHEVILL Medieval and Renaissance Florence *Vol II The Coming of Humanism and the Age of the Medici Illus* TB/1091

History Modern European

MAX BELOFF The Age of Absolutism, 1660–1815 TB/1062

CRANE BRINTON A Decade of Revolution 1789–1799 *Illus* TB/3018

J BRONOWSKI and BRUCE MAZLISH The Western Intellectual Tradition *From Leonardo to Hegel* TB/3001

CARL J FRIEDRICH The Age of the Baroque 1610–1660 *49 illus* TB/3004

LEO GERSHOY From Despotism to Revolution 1763–1789 *Illus* TB/3017

ALBERT GOODWIN The French Revolution TB/1064

DAN N JACOBS Ed The New Communist Manifesto *and Related Documents* TB/1078

HANS KOHN, Ed The Mind of Modern Russia *Historical and Political Thought of Russia's Great Age* TB/1065

SIR LEWIS NAMIER Vanished Supremacies *Essays on European History, 1812–1918* TB/1088

JOHN U NEF Cultural Foundations of Industrial Civilization TB/1024

FREDERICK L NUSSBAUM The Triumph of Science and Reason 1660–1685 *49 illus* TB/3009

RAYMOND W POSTGATE, Ed Revolution from 1789 to 1906 *Selected Documents* TB/1063

PENFIELD ROBERTS The Quest for Security 1715–1740 *Illus* TB/3016

PRISCILLA ROBERTSON Revolutions of 1848 *A Social History* TB/1025

N N SUKHANOV The Russian Revolution, 1917 *Eyewitness Account* Ed by Joel Carmichael Vol I TB/1066 Vol II TB/1067

JOHN B WOLF The Emergence of the Great Powers 1685–1715 *47 illus* TB/3010

JOHN B WOLF France 1814–1919 *The Rise of a Liberal-Democratic Society* TB 3019

Intellectual History

HERSCHEL BAKER The Image of Man *A Study of the Idea of Human Dignity in Classical Antiquity, the Middle Ages, and the Renaissance* TB/1047

J BRONOWSKI and BRUCE MAZLISH The Western Intellectual Tradition *From Leonardo to Hegel* TB/3001

NORMAN COHN The Pursuit of the Millennium *Revolutionary Messianism in medieval and Reformation Europe and its bearing on modern totalitarian movements* TB/1037

ARTHUR O LOVEJOY The Great Chain of Being *A Study of the History of an Idea* TB/1009

ROBERT PAYNE Hubris *A Study of Pride Foreword by Sir Herbert Read* TB/1031

BRUNO SNELL The Discovery of the Mind *The Greek Origins of European Thought* TB/1018

Literature, Poetry, The Novel & Criticism

JAMES BAIRD Ishmael *The Art of Melville in the Contexts of International Primitivism* TB/1023

JACQUES BARZUN The House of Intellect TB/1051

W J BATE From Classic to Romantic *Premises of Taste in Eighteenth Century England* TB/1036

RACHEL BESPALOFF On the Iliad TB/2006

ABRAHAM CAHAN The Rise of David Levinsky *a novel Intro by John Higham* TB/1028

ELLIOTT COLEMAN, Ed, Lectures in Criticism by *R P Blackmur, B Croce, Henri Peyre, John Crowe Ransom, Herbert Read, and Allen Tate Intro by H Cairns* TB/2003

ERNST R CURTIUS European Literature and the Latin Middle Ages TB/2015

GEORGE ELIOT Daniel Deronda *a novel Intro by F R Leavis* TB/1039

ETIENNE GILSON Dante and Philosophy TB/1089

ALFRED HARBAGE As They Liked It *A Study of Shakespeare's Moral Artistry* TB/1035

STANLEY R HOPPER, Ed Spiritual Problems in Contemporary Literature TB/21

HENRY JAMES The Princess Casamassima *a novel Intro by Clinton F Oliver* TB/1005

HENRY JAMES Roderick Hudson *a novel Intro by Leon Edel* TB/1016

HENRY JAMES The Tragic Muse *a novel Intro by Leon Edel* TB/1017

ARNOLD KETTLE An Introduction to the English Novel *Vol I Defoe to George Eliot* TB/1011

ARNOLD KETTLE An Introduction to the English Novel *Vol II Henry James to the Present* TB/1012

JOHN STUART MILL On Bentham and Coleridge *Intro by F R Leavis* TB/1070

PERRY MILLER & T H JOHNSON Editors The Puritans *A Sourcebook of Their Writings* Vol I TB/1093 Vol II TB/1094

KENNETH B MURDOCK Literature and Theology in Colonial New England TB/99

SAMUEL PEPYS The Diary of Samuel Pepys *Ed by O F Morshead 60 illus by Ernest Shepard* TB/1007

ST.-JOHN PERSE Seamarks TB/2002

GEORGE SANTAYANA Interpretations of Poetry and Religion TB/9

C. P. SNOW Time of Hope *a novel* TB/1040

DOROTHY VAN GHENT The English Novel *Form and Function* TB/1050

MORTON DAUWEN ZABEL, Editor Literary Opinion in America Vol. I TB/3013; Vol. II TB/3014

Myth, Symbol & Folklore

JOSEPH CAMPBELL, Editor Pagan and Christian Mysteries TB/2013

MIRCEA ELIADE Cosmos and History *The Myth of the Eternal Return* TB/50

C. G. JUNG & C. KERÉNYI Essays on a Science of Mythology *The Myths of the Divine Child and the Divine Maiden* TB/2014

ERWIN PANOFSKY Studies in Iconology *Humanistic Themes in the Art of the Renaissance. 180 illus.* TB/1077

JEAN SEZNEC The Survival of the Pagan Gods *The Mythological Tradition and its Place in Renaissance Humanism and Art. 108 illus.* TB/2004

HEINRICH ZIMMER Myths and Symbols in Indian Art and Civilization. *70 illus.* TB/2005

Philosophy

HENRI BERGSON Time and Free Will *An Essay on the Immediate Data of Consciousness* TB/1021

H. J. BLACKHAM Six Existentialist Thinkers *Kierkegaard, Nietzsche, Jaspers, Marcel, Heidegger, Sartre* TB/1002

ERNST CASSIRER Rousseau, Kant and Goethe. *Intro. by Peter Gay* TB/1092

FREDERICK COPLESTON Medieval Philosophy TB/76

F. M. CORNFORD From Religion to Philosophy *A Study in the Origins of Western Speculation* TB/20

WILFRID DESAN The Tragic Finale *An Essay on the Philosophy of Jean-Paul Sartre* TB/1030

ETIENNE GILSON Dante and Philosophy TB/1089

W. K. C. GUTHRIE The Greek Philosophers *From Thales to Aristotle* TB/1008

F. H. HEINEMANN Existentialism and the Modern Predicament TB/28

IMMANUEL KANT Lectures on Ethics. *Intro. by L. W. Beck* TB/105

BERTRAND RUSSELL et al. The Philosophy of Bertrand Russell. *Edited by Paul Arthur Schilpp* Vol. I TB/1095; Vol. II TB/1096

GEORGE SANTAYANA Winds of Doctrine *and* Platonism and the Spiritual Life TB/24

L. S. STEBBING A Modern Introduction to Logic TB/538

ALFRED NORTH WHITEHEAD Process and Reality *An Essay in Cosmology* TB/1033

WILHELM WINDELBAND A History of Philosophy I: *Greek, Roman, Medieval* TB/38

WILHELM WINDELBAND A History of Philosophy II: *Renaissance, Enlightenment, Modern* TB/39

Philosophy of History

NICOLAS BERDYAEV The Beginning and the End TB/14

NICOLAS BERDYAEV The Destiny of Man TB/61

WILHELM DILTHEY Pattern and Meaning in History: *Thoughts on History and Society. Ed. with an Intro. by H. P. Rickman* TB/1075

JOSE ORTEGA Y GASSET The Modern Theme. *Intro. by Jose Ferrater Mora* TB/1038

W. H. WALSH Philosophy of History *An Introduction* TB/1020

Political Science & Government

JEREMY BENTHAM The Handbook of Political Fallacies. *Intro. by Crane Brinton* TB/1069

KENNETH E. BOULDING Conflict and Defense *A General Theory* TB/3024

CRANE BRINTON English Political Thought in the Nineteenth Century TB/1071

JOHN NEVILLE FIGGIS Political Thought from Gerson to Grotius: 1414-1625 *Seven Studies. Introduction by Garrett Mattingly* TB/1032

F. L. GANSHOF Feudalism TB/1058

G. P. GOOCH English Democratic Ideas in the Seventeenth Century TB/1006

J. P. MAYER Alexis de Tocqueville *A Biographical Study in Political Science* TB/1014

JOHN STUART MILL On Bentham and Coleridge. *Intro. by F. R. Leavis* TB/1070

JOHN B. MORRALL Political Thought in Medieval Times TB/1076

JOSEPH A. SCHUMPETER Capitalism, Socialism and Democracy TB/3008

Psychology

ANTON T. BOISEN The Exploration of the Inner World *A Study of Mental Disorder and Religious Experience* TB/87

WALTER BROMBERG The Mind of Man *A History of Psychotherapy and Psychoanalysis* TB/1003

SIGMUND FREUD On Creativity and the Unconscious: *Papers on the Psychology of Art, Literature, Love, Religion. Intro. by Benjamin Nelson* TB/45

C. JUDSON HERRICK The Evolution of Human Nature TB/545

ALDOUS HUXLEY The Devils of Loudun *A Study in the Psychology of Power Politics and Mystical Religion in the France of Cardinal Richelieu* TB/60

WILLIAM JAMES Psychology: *The Briefer Course. Edited with an Intro. by Gordon Allport* TB/1034

C. G. JUNG Psychological Reflections. *Ed. by J. Jacobi* TB/2001

C. G. JUNG Symbols of Transformation *An Analysis of the Prelude to a Case of Schizophrenia* Vol. I TB/2009; Vol. II TB/2010

C. G. JUNG & C. KERÉNYI Essays on a Science of Mythology *The Myths of the Divine Child and the Divine Maiden* TB/2014

ERICH NEUMANN Amor and Psyche *The Psychic Development of the Feminine* TB/2012

ERICH NEUMANN The Origins and History of Consciousness *Illus.* Vol. I TB/2007; Vol. II TB/2008

RELIGION

Ancient & Classical

HENRI FRANKFORT Ancient Egyptian Religion *An Interpretation* TB/77

G. RACHEL LEVY Religious Conceptions of the Stone Age *and their Influence upon European Thought. Illus. Intro. by H. Frankfort* TB/106

MARTIN P. NILSSON Greek Folk Religion. *Foreword by Arthur Darby Nock* TB/78

ALEXANDRE PIANKOFF The Shrines of Tut-Ankh-Amon *Ed by N Piankoff 117 illus* TB/2011

H J ROSE Religion in Greece and Rome TB/55

Biblical Thought & Literature

W F ALBRIGHT The Biblical Period from Abraham to Ezra TB/102

C K BARRETT, Ed The New Testament Background *Selected Documents* TB/86

C H DODD The Authority of the Bible TB/43

M S ENSLIN Christian Beginnings TB/5

M S ENSLIN The Literature of the Christian Movement TB/6

H E FOSDICK A Guide to Understanding the Bible TB/2

D WINTON THOMAS, Ed Documents from Old Testament Times TB/85

Christianity Origins & Early Development

EDWARD GIBBON The Triumph of Christendom in the Roman Empire *(Chaps XV–XX of "Decline and Fall," J B Bury edition), illus* TB/46

MAURICE GOGUEL Jesus and the Origins of Christianity *Vol I Prolegomena to the Life of Jesus Intro by C Leslie Mitton* TB/65

MAURICE GOGUEL Jesus and the Origins of Christianity *Vol II The Life of Jesus* TB/66

EDGAR J GOODSPEED A Life of Jesus TB/1

ADOLF HARNACK The Mission and Expansion of Christianity *in the First Three Centuries Intro by J Pelikan* TB/92

R K HARRISON The Dead Sea Scrolls *An Introduction* TB/84

EDWIN HATCH The Influence of Greek Ideas on Christianity *Intro and Bibliography by Frederick C Grant* TB/18

JOHANNES WEISS Earliest Christianity *A History of the Period A D 30–150 Intro and biblio by Frederick C Grant* Vol I TB/53 Vol II TB/54

Christianity The Middle Ages and After

G P FEDOTOV The Russian Religious Mind *Kievan Christianity, the tenth to the thirteenth centuries* TB/70

ETIENNE GILSON Dante and Philosophy TB/1089

WILLIAM HALLER The Rise of Puritanism TB/22

A C McGIFFERT Protestant Thought Before Kant *Preface by J Pelikan* TB/93

KENNETH B MURDOCK Literature and Theology in Colonial New England TB/99

H O TAYLOR The Emergence of Christian Culture in the West *The Classical Heritage of the Middle Ages Intro and biblio by Kenneth M Setton* TB/48

Judaic Thought & Literature

MARTIN BUBER Eclipse of God *Studies in the Relation Between Religion and Philosophy* TB/12

MARTIN BUBER Moses *The Revelation and the Covenant* TB/27

MARTIN BUBER Pointing the Way *Intro by Maurice S Friedman* TB/103

MARTIN BUBER The Prophetic Faith TB/73

MARTIN BUBER Two Types of Faith *the interpenetration of Judaism and Christianity* TB/75

FLAVIUS JOSEPHUS The Great Roman-Jewish War *with* The Life of Josephus *Intro by William R Farmer* * TB/74

T J MEEK Hebrew Origins TB/69

Oriental Religions Far Eastern, Near Eastern

TOR ANDRAE Mohammed *The Man and His Faith* TB/62

EDWARD CONZE Buddhism *Its Essence and Development Foreword by Arthur Waley* TB/58

H G CREEL Confucius and the Chinese Way TB/63

Philosophy of Religion

RUDOLF BULTMANN History and Eschatology *The Presence of Eternity* TB/91

RUDOLF BULTMANN AND FIVE CRITICS Kerygma and Myth *A Theological Debate* TB/80

RUDOLF BULTMANN and KARL KUNDSIN Form Criticism *Two Essays on New Testament Research Trans by F C Grant* TB/96

MIRCEA ELIADE The Sacred and the Profane TB/81

LUDWIG FEUERBACH The Essence of Christianity *Intro by Karl Barth Foreword by H Richard Niebuhr* TB/11

ADOLF HARNACK What is Christianity? *Intro by Rudolf Bultmann* TB/17

FRIEDRICH HEGEL On Christianity *Early Theological Writings Ed by Richard Kroner and T M Knox* TB/79

KARL HEIM Christian Faith and Natural Science TB/16

IMMANUEL KANT Religion Within the Limits of Reason Alone *Intro by Theodore M Greene and John Silber* TB/67

PIERRE TEILHARD DE CHARDIN The Phenomenon of Man TB/83

Religion, Culture & Society

C C GILLISPIE Genesis and Geology *The Decades before Darwin* TB/51

H RICHARD NIEBUHR Christ and Culture TB/3

H RICHARD NIEBUHR The Kingdom of God in America TB/49

ERNST TROELTSCH The Social Teaching of the Christian Churches *Intro by H Richard Niebuhr* Vol I TB/71 Vol II TB/72

Religious Thinkers & Traditions

AUGUSTINE An Augustine Synthesis *Ed by E Przywara* TB/35

KARL BARTH Church Dogmatics *A Selection Intro by H Gollwitzer, Ed by G W Bromiley* TB/95

KARL BARTH Dogmatics in Outline TB/56

KARL BARTH The Word of God and the Word of Man TB/13

ADOLF DEISSMANN Paul *A Study in Social and Religious History* TB/15

JOHANNES ECKHART Meister Eckhart *A Modern Translation by R Blakney* TB/8

MAURICE S FRIEDMAN Martin Buber *The Life of Dialogue* TB/64

WINTHROP HUDSON The Great Tradition of the American Churches TB/98

SOREN KIERKEGAARD Edifying Discourses *Edited with an Intro by Paul Holmer* TB/32

SOREN KIERKEGAARD The Journals of Kierkegaard *Edited with an Intro by Alexander Dru* TB/52

SOREN KIERKEGAARD The Point of View for My Work as an Author *A Report to History Preface by Benjamin Nelson* TB/88

SOREN KIERKEGAARD The Present Age *Trans and edited by Alexander Dru Intro by W Kaufmann* TB/94

SOREN KIERKEGAARD Purity of Heart *Trans by Douglas Steere* TB/4

WALTER LOWRIE Kierkegaard Vol I TB/89 Vol II TB 90

GABRIEL MARCEL Homo Viator *Introduction to a Metaphysic of Hope* TB/97

PERRY MILLER & T H JOHNSON, Editors The Puritans *A Sourcebook of Their Writings* Vol I TB/1093 Vol II TB/1094

A D NOCK St Paul TB 104

PAUL PFUETZE Self Society Existence *Human Nature and Dialogue in the Thought of George Herbert Mead and Martin Buber* TB/1059

F SCHLEIERMACHER On Religion *Speeches to Its Cultured Despisers Intro by Rudolf Otto* TB/36

PAUL TILLICH Dynamics of Faith TB/42

EVELYN UNDERHILL Worship TB/10

G VAN DER LEEUW Religion in Essence and Manifestation *A Study in Phenomenology Appendices by Hans H Penner* Vol I TB 100 Vol II TB/101

NATURAL SCIENCES AND MATHEMATICS

Biological Sciences

A BELLAIRS Reptiles *Life History, Evolution, and Structure Illus* TB/520

LUDWIG VON BERTALANFFY Modern Theories of Development *An Introduction to Theoretical Biology* TB/554

LUDWIG VON BERTALANFFY Problems of Life *An Evaluation of Modern Biological and Scientific Thought* TB/521

HAROLD F BLUM Time's Arrow and Evolution TB/555

A J CAIN Animal Species and their Evolution *Illus* TB/519

WALTER B CANNON Bodily Changes in Pain, Hunger, Fear and Rage TB/562

W E LE GROS CLARK The Antecedents of Man *An Introduction to the Evolution of the Primates Illus* TB/559

W H DOWDESWELL Animal Ecology 61 *illus* TB/543

W H DOWDESWELL The Mechanism of Evolution *Illus* TB/527

R W GERARD Unresting Cells 173 *illus* TB/541

DAVID LACK Darwin's Finches *Illus* TB/544

J E MORTON Molluscs *An Introduction to their Form and Functions Illus* TB/529

O W RICHARDS The Social Insects 51 *illus* TB/542

P M SHEPPARD Natural Selection and Heredity *Illus* TB/528

EDMUND W SINNOTT Cell and Psyche *The Biology of Purpose* TB/546

C H WADDINGTON How Animals Develop *Illus* TB/553

Chemistry

A FINDLAY Chemistry in the Service of Man *Illus* TB/524

J R PARTINGTON A Short History of Chemistry 127 *illus* TB/522

J READ A Direct Entry to Organic Chemistry *Illus* TB/523

J READ Through Alchemy to Chemistry TB 561

Geography

R E COKER This Great and Wide Sea *An Introduction to Oceanography and Marine Biology Illus* TB/551

F K HARE The Restless Atmosphere TB/560

History of Science

W DAMPIER, Ed Readings in the Literature of Science *Illus* TB/512

ALEXANDRE KOYRÉ From the Closed World to the Infinite Universe *Copernicus, Kepler, Galileo, Newton, etc* TB/31

A G VAN MELSEN From Atomos to Atom *A History of the Concept* Atom TB/517

O NEUGEBAUER The Exact Sciences in Antiquity TB/552

H T PLEDGE Science Since 1500 *A Short History of Mathematics, Physics, Chemistry and Biology Illus* TB/506

GEORGE SARTON Ancient Science and Modern Civilization TB/501

HANS THIRRING Energy for Man *From Windmills to Nuclear Power* TB/556

A WOLF A History of Science Technology and Philosophy in the 16th and 17th Centuries *Illus* Vol I TB 508 Vol II TB/509

A WOLF A History of Science, Technology, and Philosophy in the Eighteenth Century *Illus* Vol I TB 539 Vol II TB/540

Mathematics

H DAVENPORT The Higher Arithmetic *An Introduction to the Theory of Numbers* TB/526

H G FORDER Geometry *An Introduction* TB/548

GOTTLOB FREGE The Foundations of Arithmetic *A Logico-Mathematical Enquiry into the Concept of Number* TB/534

S KÖRNER The Philosophy of Mathematics *An Introduction* TB/547

D E LITTLEWOOD Skeleton Key of Mathematics *A Simple Account of Complex Algebraic Problems* TB/525

WILLARD VAN ORMAN QUINE Mathematical Logic TB/558

O G SUTTON Mathematics in Action *Foreword by James R Newman Illus* TB/518

FREDERICK WAISMANN Introduction to Mathematical Thinking *Foreword by Karl Menger* TB/511

Philosophy of Science

R B BRAITHWAITE Scientific Explanation TB/515

J BRONOWSKI Science and Human Values *Illus* TB/505

ALBERT EINSTEIN Philosopher-Scientist *Edited by Paul A Schilpp* Vol I TB/502 Vol II TB/503

WERNER HEISENBERG Physics and Philosophy *The Revolution in Modern Science Intro by F S C Northrop* TB/549

JOHN MAYNARD KEYNES A Treatise on Probability *Introduction by N R Hanson* TB/557

Lightning Source UK Ltd.
Milton Keynes UK
UKHW030933100219
337061UK00005B/37/P

9 781178 694918